STEALING FROM THE SARACENS

T0322484

DIANA DARKE

STEALING

FROM THE

SARACENS

*How Islamic Architecture
Shaped Europe*

HURST & COMPANY, LONDON

First published in the United Kingdom in 2020 by
C. Hurst & Co. (Publishers) Ltd.,
41 Great Russell Street, London, WC1B 3PL

This paperback edition published in 2024 by
C. Hurst & Co. (Publishers) Ltd.,
New Wing, Somerset House, Strand, London WC2R 1LA

Distributed in the United States, Canada and Latin America by
Oxford University Press, 198 Madison Avenue, New York, NY 10016,
United States of America.

A Cataloguing-in-Publication data record for this book
is available from the British Library.

ISBN: 9781911723479

This book is printed using paper from registered sustainable
and managed sources.

www.hurstpublishers.com

Printed in Great Britain by Bell & Bain Ltd, Glasgow

CONTENTS

PREFACE

This book is dedicated to Notre-Dame. The catastrophic fire of 15 April 2019 was also the spark that ignited this book, once I saw how little the cathedral's architectural backstory was understood. I want to acknowledge the genius of Notre-Dame's medieval architects and masons, whose painstaking and devoted labours over the course of two centuries produced a prodigious organic structure which lived and breathed the history of France, its revolution, the coronation of Napoleon I, and the funerals of many presidents. It became an eternal resident of the city, a spiritual core, a comforting presence—its immortality, perhaps, taken for granted.

As today's engineers struggle to stabilise the structure, the magnitude of the task ahead is becoming clear. The French parliament has passed a law requiring the cathedral to be rebuilt exactly as it was, but therein lies the challenge. President Macron's vow to reconstruct in five years is way off the mark. Ten is more realistic, probably longer. An estimated 1,300 oaks were felled to build the cathedral, but France no longer has trees of the same size and maturity. Even beyond the issues inherent in replicating the ancient materials, there is another, infinitely more complex problem. How can we re-create, in our computer-driven age of precision planning, the building's original energy and force? Guided by instincts honed through generations of experience and passed down from master to apprentice, the builders left no records. Nothing was written down beyond a few unscaled drawings.

PREFACE

The danger is that, in our rush to reconstruct Notre-Dame 'exactly as it was' with the aid of our digital devices, we may end up losing the building's very soul, unwittingly expunging the subtle imperfections that are integral to its essence and identity.

These are the mysteries which lie at the heart of medieval Gothic or 'Saracenic' architecture, the origins of which this book seeks to unravel. As the dark shadow of the 2020 Coronavirus pandemic forces us to confront new uncertainties, one likely outcome—even in those who profess no faith—is the rediscovery of religious architecture and its power to calm and heal. May the future Notre-Dame remain forever true to the spirit of those mysteries.

INTRODUCTION

This book has risen from the ashes of the 15 April 2019 fire at Notre-Dame de Paris.

On that fateful night the world was gripped by images of the cathedral engulfed in flames. No one imagined that a building on fire could spark such interest and mesmerise global audiences for days on end. The French nation went into mass mourning on a scale that took everyone by surprise.

Why? What did this building represent to the French and to the world? In due course, statements by international leaders, not least French president Emmanuel Macron himself, would suggest that the cathedral somehow encapsulated French nationhood. All of France was burning in sympathy. In a country where statistics show that before the fire only 5 per cent of the population was church-going and 47 per cent described themselves as non-practising Catholics, what could explain such an outpouring?

Part of it, without doubt, was a reaction. France has a long tradition of *laïcité*, secularism, that began with its revolution in 1789, and its constitution today guarantees that 'all citizens regardless of their origin, race or religion are treated as equals before the law.' But the twenty-first century brought unforeseen challenges. During Europe's migration crisis in 2015, France found itself overwhelmed with Arab and African refugees, most of whom were Muslim. Later that year, the streets of Paris were convulsed by a series of terrorist attacks, inspired by the extremism of Islamic State. In response to these upheavals and the perceived threat of Islam, many sought to revive a Christian national identity.

Now the French were in danger of losing this magnificent treasure at the heart of their capital city, the very symbol of their Catholic faith. The non-church-going mayor of Paris said she was convinced the cathedral had been saved from collapse by the power of prayer. After the fire, church attendance soared and the number of pilgrims walking between Notre-Dame and Chartres, especially the young, reached new heights. France, that most secular of countries where even wearing a crucifix to work is not allowed, is having a religious renaissance, a spiritual awakening.

But what if that very building itself, that intricate Gothic style so deeply associated with Catholicism in Europe, was in fact inspired by Islamic architecture brought into Europe centuries earlier? How would people feel about that?

The answer soon became clear after I put out a tweet the morning after the fire:

> Notre-Dame's architectural design, like all Gothic cathedrals in Europe, comes directly from #Syria's Qalb Lozeh 5th century church—Crusaders brought the 'twin tower flanking the rose window' concept back to Europe in the 12th century. It's in #Idlib province, still standing…[1]

The reaction within a matter of minutes was staggering. Realising the tweet had struck a nerve, I decided to explain more in a blog on my website that same morning. I called it: 'The heritage of Notre Dame—less European than people think'.[2]

It created a storm of interest. By lunchtime I had been contacted by *Middle East Eye* and by *Asharq al-Awsat* asking if they could reblog the piece on their websites. Within the next few days the blog was published by AFP Beirut and ended up being translated into Arabic, French, German, Chinese, Japanese and Hindi for most international media outlets. For whatever reason, this kind of information no longer seems to be mainstream and has somehow dropped off people's radar.

Are we ready, in the current climate of Islamophobia, to acknowledge that a style so closely identified with our European Christian identity owes its origins to Islamic architecture? I wonder. In October 2019 I visited the British

Museum's 'Inspired by the East' exhibition, not expecting to find anything of relevance to this book since the focus was on portable objects, like Orientalist paintings, ceramics, glass, jewellery and clothing. But one exhibit caught my eye—the widely reprinted and influential fifteenth-century pictorial map of Jerusalem showing all the Christian pilgrimage sites carefully labelled in Latin. It was a Christian vision of Jerusalem, with any evidence of the contemporary Mamluk Muslim rule quite literally airbrushed out of the picture—or so the map-maker thought. I laughed out loud, for the central building of the map, dominating all else, was an enlarged representation of the Dome of the Rock, carefully mislabelled as King Solomon's biblical temple. The unwitting Bernhard, canon of Mainz Cathedral, in documenting his pilgrimage of 1483, had perpetuated the mistake of the twelfth-century Crusaders, who did not realise the structure was a Muslim shrine built in 691 by the ruler of Islam's first empire. As a result, well into the eighteenth century when the error was finally realised, many European churches were modelled on a Muslim shrine.

A profound Islamic influence can be seen in many of Europe's most iconic buildings. This may be an uncomfortable and startling thought, when some still struggle even with the concept of 'Arabic numerals'. A 2019 survey in the US asked Americans if they would ever use Arabic numerals—'Certainly not!' came the resounding response.[3]

Yet while we in the West may not be ready to acknowledge our debt to Islamic architectural influence, Sir Christopher Wren, regarded as Britain's greatest architect, was. He saw it clearly over three centuries ago, when he wrote, after extensive study and research: 'The Gothic style should more rightly be called the Saracen style.'[4]

How could our great European Gothic cathedrals, the very incarnation of our national and Christian identities, have any connection with the Saracens, or, as Wren says, 'what is the same thing, the Arabians and the Moors'? What could he possibly have meant by that and what was the evidence for such a bold statement?

The title of this book, *Stealing from the Saracens*, builds on his assertion but still requires some more explanation, for it was chosen with care and can be read in several ways. The word 'Saracen' has dropped out of everyday language these days, but in Wren's time it was commonly used as a pejorative term to describe the Arab Muslims against whom the Crusaders fought for some 200 years, from 1095 onwards, in their 'Holy War' to regain Jerusalem. Scholars give several derivations, but the most common etymology is from the Arabic root 'saraqa', meaning 'to steal'. The clear connotation was that 'Saracens', seen from the Eurocentric point of view, were looters and thieves—never mind the fact that the Crusaders looted their way across Europe, Jerusalem and later Constantinople. The title is therefore meant to convey the double irony that we in the West are 'stealing' from those we think of as thieves.

While recognising the Saracen origins of Gothic, Wren himself was no fan of the Gothic style, dismissing its weak roofing, its poor construction, and its fiddly decor and ornamentation. In his writings he is consistently rude about its shortcomings. It is another irony that his avowed dislike of the Gothic led him to reject it as the style for the new St Paul's Cathedral after the old one was destroyed in the Great Fire of London in 1666, despite coming up against strong resistance from the church authorities of the time, who clung to the Gothic architecture of the old St Paul's as a symbol of their national identity, just as tenaciously as the French cling to Notre-Dame. Church architecture all across Europe was closely associated with the Gothic style, much loved and treasured. Gothic cathedrals are seen as representing the pinnacle of Christian spirituality.

If Wren's theory is right, that the origins of Gothic are Islamic, it would mean that Muslims provided the inspiration for what Christianity regards as its own unique architectural formula—a most inconvenient truth.

Wren far preferred the classicism of 'the Ancients', as he called them, with its true sense of perspective, clean lines and symmetry. Yet he too 'stole' from the Saracens, not their style but their method, specifically their more advanced vaulting techniques, all of which were based on their mastery of geometry. Wren clearly states in his Tract on Architecture that he has used the superior 'Saracen' method of vaulting at St Paul's to support the colossal weight of the dome, even providing a diagram to show why it is the best way—successful vaulting is all about highly complex geometry.[5] That is why the front cover of this book shows the inside of the St Paul's dome.

After attending a mass beneath the dome at St Paul's in June 2019, I mentioned Wren's theory to the priest who had been officiating. He visibly blanched. This is what we have come to in Europe. We have arrived at the point where the Middle East and Islam are associated only with negative images of violence, extremism and terrorism. Few Westerners have had the chance to go and experience the region for themselves since the Arab Spring of 2011 and its resultant civil wars. But even if we cannot go—as indeed Christopher Wren himself never went beyond France—maybe we can still, like him, keep an open mind about the knowledge and cultural influences that had their origins in that part of the world. No society exists in isolation and everything is interconnected. As John Donne, poet, priest and onetime Dean of St Paul's, now buried in its crypt, expressed it: 'No man is an island.'

***

The current European inward-looking mindset, in addition to the prevailing strong hostility to Muslim immigrants arriving in Europe after fleeing war in their own countries, makes this book a necessary and important corrective. I've long been fascinated by architecture, by the force that pushes people to design buildings in certain ways in specific locations and for specific purposes. It was an interest in early human civilisation and the world's first buildings and communities that led me to study Arabic at the University of Oxford back in the 1970s in the first place.

In architecture there are always reasons behind the facade—nothing is accidental. Wren was a hands-on 'surveyor'—the profession of 'architect' did not exist in his day—who worked on site with his masons and craftsmen most days for the thirty-six years that it took to build St Paul's. The three years I spent restoring my house in Damascus with local craftsmen—including stonemasons, carpenters, tilers, painters, plumbers and electricians—gave me many insights into building design that I could never have acquired solely through research, although my subsequent MA in Islamic Art and Architecture at SOAS helped deepen my knowledge. Even before the Damascus experience, I'd spent a year supervising and collaborating with a similarly wide range of workmen during the complex renovation of my nineteenth-century home in Kent.

Starting in my early twenties, I'd spent decades travelling round the Middle East, absorbing the archaeology and architecture of the region, writing about it, touching the stones. Maybe I was always an architect manquée.

***

Christopher Wren was a highly rational man of science, not of whim, a reasonable man with restraint and self-discipline, not given to making wild unfounded claims. Such a man could not possibly have arrived at so bold a conclusion, that Gothic architecture should more rightly be called Saracen architecture, without having first satisfied himself of the evidence.

To understand his thinking we must first look closely at the man himself, at the influences he was exposed to throughout his own ninety-year life. And we also have to know what he meant by the 'Saracen' style.

What was the architectural legacy of the Crusades in both the religious and the military arenas? What did Europe learn from its first mass venture into the Holy Lands of the Middle East, the lands where Christianity itself was born? What about earlier borrowings of architectural styles from Andalusia—Muslim Spain—Sicily and Italy centuries before the Crusades, and from cross-cultural trading hubs like Venice, Malta, Rhodes and Cyprus in the years that followed the Crusades? And what about the Ottomans, the superpower on Europe's doorstep for 400 years, with whom Wren was contemporary—what did he know of them and their architecture?

When embarking on the construction of St Paul's, Wren dug right down through the London clay to the shingle riverbed of the Thames, far deeper than the previous foundations of the old Gothic St Paul's. Likewise, the footings of this book—the opening two chapters—dig down into the man himself and give an exploration of the Gothic = Saracen concept. Then, foundations laid, the story unfolds chapter by chapter, starting from the pre-Islamic architectural inheritance of the region which forms today's Syria, Iraq, Iran, Lebanon, Jordan, Palestine, Israel and Turkey. The aim is to track these visible influences as they entered Europe. Far from being a simple linear process, it is more like a giant circular jigsaw.

It is essential to see the picture in the round and to acknowledge that many characteristics of Islamic architecture grew out of the earlier Byzantine heritage already extant. The Byzantine, Arab Christian heritage in turn had grown out of the Hellenistic-Roman legacy of the eastern Mediterranean region, but it is important to recognise that this does not make it 'Western'. The architectural influences on the Near East have their roots in ancient Mesopotamian traditions which, as will be explained later, were incorporated into the subsequent development of church architecture.[6] Before the Greek and Roman conquests imposed an east–west political division on the Near East, the whole area was far more culturally unified than the brief, superficial appearance of a few Graeco-Roman art forms might imply.[7] Everything builds on and is influenced by what came before, and although academic historians like to focus on one period or another, as if they are distinct and separate, the reality of history is that everything is a continuum—nothing just appears out of a vacuum.

Wren freely acknowledged the European debt to Saracen architecture in his writings, mentioning it no fewer than twelve times, even as the Ottoman armies pressed at the gates of Vienna in 1683, when he was in the thick of building St Paul's. He was a man of science, not of politics, whose mind was open to all knowledge, no matter where it came from. From his extensive experience after a lifetime of research and study, he devised his own views on the origins and early development of architecture. Starting 'from the most remote Antiquity', he examined universal 'principles' or 'grounds of architecture' and concluded that these are 'not only Roman and Greek, but Phoenician, Hebrew and Assyrian… founded upon the experience of all ages.'[8] Such an approach speaks volumes of Wren's openness to foreign influences, wherever they came from, even if from the enemy. It is precisely this openness that enabled him to produce in St Paul's such a harmonised blend of styles, which did not simply follow the earlier models but built on them, improving on them. No society exists in isolation. If it does and closes in on itself, it will soon die, for lack of stimulation and original thought.

On some primordial instinctive level, it is this that we respond to in St Paul's. We recognise that it transcends the norms to achieve something higher. That's what makes it an icon.

Sir Christopher Wren (1632–1723) , painted in 1711 aged seventy-nine, after St Paul's was completed in 1708.

1

CHRISTOPHER WREN

The Arch-Synthesiser

Almost every school child in Britain is probably familiar with the name of one architect—Christopher Wren (20 October 1632–25 February 1723), subject of over a hundred biographies. Rarely do architects become household names, so what made this one so remarkable?

Christopher Wren was a visionary, a 'big picture' scientist and philosopher who will always be remembered for St Paul's, England's first Protestant cathedral, the masterpiece he spent thirty-six years building in the heart of the City of London. Most projects of such duration and scale have multiple architects, but Wren was the single mastermind throughout the construction. He was also a practical man, attending the site himself most days, collaborating with the master craftsmen as each problem presented itself and as the building evolved. There were no precedents to follow—it was the first time anyone had ever attempted to build such a large dome in Britain.

How different when compared to today's techniques, where computer-aided design means that architects sit in offices fiddling with images that can be changed, enlarged or reduced in an instant at the mere tap of a key. Complicated engineering questions are digitally calculated in a flash. Ready-made plans are then sent out to developers who simply follow the instructions—like assembling a piece of IKEA furniture.

Wren was an instinctive synthesiser of ideas and techniques. In order to understand his way of thinking and how he was able to come up with his

'Saracen theory', it is necessary to take a close look at his early life and the ideas that would have influenced him. Born in 1632, ten years before the outbreak of the English Civil War between Royalists and Parliamentarians, Wren was the only boy in a large family, surrounded by sisters, three older and three younger. He was pronounced a sickly child, thought unlikely to survive into manhood, which may account for why he was privately tutored at home with his family in Royalist-occupied Wiltshire, attending Westminster School only briefly, probably in 1645–6 after the Parliamentary occupation of Wiltshire and his father's five-month imprisonment. Wren's father, Christopher Wren the Elder, was a Royalist and fell out of favour when the king was executed in 1649, leaving his son in financially straitened circumstances. Wren held his father and his brother-in-law, William Holder, as major intellectual influences.

Wren's father was the dean of Windsor and was closely involved in his son's education, wanting it to be as all-embracing as possible. He exposed him to natural phenomena of all sorts. His extensive library, which passed down to Wren after his death, was filled with heavily annotated volumes by philosopher Francis Bacon and polymath Thomas Browne, as well as travel literature and works on fields ranging from agriculture, horticulture, animal behaviour and botany to climatology. Other interests included universal chronology, and the reconciliation of biblical and profane history. In these beginnings, under the influence of his father, the seeds of Wren's later development were sown.

Wren's son, also called Christopher, tells us in the family memoirs that as a father himself, Wren had firm views on child-rearing and education. He forbade breastfeeding at night and held that too much mother's milk was harmful. 'Sitting at school' was something he considered 'the greatest mischief' for children, 'hindering their growth and dulling their spirits'. 'The best rule is to let them have as much liberty as may be, and to give account of their day's talk every morning.'[1] That said, Wren sent his own son to Eton, 'not much caring what Latin he learned' but so that he would 'learn how to shift and live in the world.'[2]

When Wren arrived as a young man at Wadham College at the University of Oxford, his prodigious talent was quickly recognised. The political climate of the time was very much part of his education, coinciding as it did with the nine-year Civil War (1642–51) and the execution of Charles I in 1649, leaving

Charles II in exile till his Restoration in 1660. Oxford became the Royalist stronghold and seat of the besieged Court, creating a challenging environment for academic activity. This chaotic, unstable milieu formed the essential backdrop to Wren's teenage years and early adulthood.

At Wadham, Wren became part of a very special community of open-minded free-thinkers. The group deliberately distanced themselves from 'matters of theology and state affairs', forming the nucleus of what was later to become the prestigious Royal Society. This nascent gentlemen's 'philosophical club' had members with both Parliamentary and Royalist affiliations. Though he was the son of an ardent Royalist, Wren's diplomatic skills, even at a young age, were such that he maintained good relations with all, experience that would stand him in good stead throughout his career, as he had to contend with vacillating political circumstances and the reign of six monarchs. In Wren's time the word 'club' had different overtones to today. Members of the club, generally clerics and intellectuals, professed neutrality and consciously suppressed their political differences in order to focus on common pursuits of the mind. They often pooled their financial resources since they were not on the whole wealthy.

The appointment of John Wilkins, a Parliamentarian, in 1648 as Wadham's warden turned the college into arguably the most enlightened in the university at that time. In an age dominated by sectarian intolerance on both sides, Wilkins, aged only thirty-four, emerged as a unique figure, able 'to combine his intellectual interests in science and invention with the practical business of ascending the Caroline, and later Parliamentary, ladders of preferment.'[3] An Anglican clergyman and shrewd politician, he married Oliver Cromwell's sister, yet still managed to become bishop of Chester in 1668. He walked the Aristotelian 'middle way', detesting extremes, and willing to serve any balanced *de facto* government. 'He saw God as a reasonable Creator of nature rather than the upholder of sacred kings or popular covenants.'[4]

Wilkins's range of learning and unprecedented intellectual energy undoubtedly had a huge influence on the young Wren. During his twelve-year tenure, Wadham became one of the scientific focal points of Europe, the regular meeting place for researchers keen to push the boundaries of knowledge. None of their activities were on the curriculum—far from it, as their experimental interests were considered fringe at best in the university world of

1650. Wilkins himself had already published his *Mathematical Magick* in 1648, filled with designs for submarines, flying machines and perpetual motion devices. In his earlier works, he had argued for travel to the moon, defended Copernican astronomy, and devised secret codes and a universal language. Nothing followed a traditional pattern. From Wilkins's informal club of astronomers, anatomists and chemists would emerge England's first real body that pursued systematic experimental research.[5] Their original ideas were deeply challenging to the traditional philosophy of ancient classical learning.

At the time Wadham was considered a relatively 'new' college, having been founded only a few decades earlier by Dorothy Wadham in 1610, in compliance with her husband Nicholas Wadham's will. A devout Catholic by persuasion at a time when England had just reverted to Protestantism, the redoubtable Dorothy also had to battle against corruption in the city council, not to mention the greed of church and government authorities. Wadham archivists have uncovered how bribes had to be widely distributed, including £50 each to the serving lord treasurer, lord privy seal and lord chamberlain.[6]

Under the university statutes of the early seventeenth century, students earned their bachelor's degree by studying two terms of grammar, four of rhetoric, five of logic, three of arithmetic and two of music. To continue their studies with a master's degree, they then spent three further years on geometry, astronomy, natural philosophy (what is today called 'science'), moral philosophy and metaphysics. As a 'fellow commoner', Wren was neither wealthy nor poor, and the college accounts show that different rates applied to different students according to their means. So-called 'battellars', for example, could reduce their charges by looking after themselves and fetching their own food from the kitchen. In Hall, strict hierarchy was observed, with fellows, scholars and commoners at separate tables. Hair styles were also strictly controlled through an approved barber, 'for I do not permit any poor student in my college to grow his beard, or let his hair fall on his shoulders, nor crop it too close,' said Dorothy.[7] The scholars and fellows used Latin, while the commoners and battellars used English, 'all that was expected of them'.

Wren took on his first architectural creation, a collection of 'transparent apiaries' for the warden's garden, at the age of twenty-two while at Wadham. Each apiary had three storeys, decorated with miniature sundials—a childhood time-keeping fascination Wren shared with his father. The idea was to permit study of the internal organisation of the bee community while also allowing honey to be collected, all without having to destroy the bees. It displayed that perfect combination of scientific experiment and practical environmental awareness that was Wren's peculiar gift. He called the invention 'The Reformed Commonwealth of Bees'.[8] So successful was the design that famous diarist and antiquarian John Evelyn, a friend of the warden, requested one for his own garden. Archival material shows that Evelyn and the warden, the 'universally Curious Dr Wilkins',[9] went on to correspond about the virtues of their respective beehives for the next two years.

In 1652, a new Latin edition of William Oughtred's *Key to Mathematics* appeared, exactly as Wren was deep in collaborative scientific work with those who would become his future Royal Society colleagues. It even included Wren's own translation into Latin of a treatise on sundials. In his preface to the 1652 *Key to Mathematics*, Oughtred gives special mention to Wren, the mathematical prodigy: 'A youth generally admired for his talents, who, when not yet sixteen years old, enriched astronomy, gnomics, statics and mechanics, with brilliant inventions, and from that time has continued to enrich them, and in truth is one from whom I can, not vainly, look for great things.'[10] It was thanks to the high profile of this seminal text that Wren, despite his family's strong Royalist connections, was appointed by the university commissioners, Parliamentarians, to a fellowship at All Souls College at the unusually young age of twenty-one in 1653.

Even after leaving Wadham for All Souls, Wren continued to attend the Wadham meetings, experimenting with flying machines in the college garden. He was made professor of astronomy at Gresham College, London, in 1657 at the age of twenty-five, but still continued to rent a room in the Wadham tower gatehouse till 1663. Wren was elected Savilian professor of astronomy at Oxford in 1661, and, based on his qualifications as an astronomer, was asked to design the new observatory at Greenwich in 1675—an unusual example of a professional astronomer designing his own perfect workplace based on his special combination of expertise.

On top of all his scientific and mathematical skills, throughout his career Wren was also a practical man, a skilled carpenter and draftsman. He understood money, budgets, the logistics of obtaining materials and how to administer three separate architectural offices, together with employing and then managing large teams of skilled and unskilled workers on a number of simultaneous complex building projects. The architectural theories of such a

The Sheldonian Theatre, Oxford, one of Wren's first commissions.

man, reached towards the end of his life and based on a wealth of practical experience, could not possibly have been arrived at lightly.

Wren only turned to architecture aged thirty, after more than a decade of scientific study. In Oxford today we can see one of his earliest commissions, the Sheldonian Theatre, built in 1664–9 and named after its chief benefactor, Gilbert Sheldon, warden of All Souls, a powerful cleric in the High Anglican tradition after the Restoration.

The building was multi-functional, being first and foremost a grand space in which all university graduation ceremonies would take place, but also a venue for lectures and musical performances, while the basement was to house the university printing presses. What Wren produced to fulfil this complicated commission is a distinctive D-shaped building of perfect proportions next to the Bodleian Library. Today the Sheldonian stands as a Grade I Listed Building and continues to perform the same functions, except for the basement. Modelled on the first-century BCE Theatre of Marcellus in Rome, its exterior is of the same local golden-coloured stone as many of Oxford's buildings, yet it stands out as a blend of classical features with several modern innovations. Wren had never been to Rome but had seen a sixteenth-century engraving of the theatre drawn by Serlio, which was enough for him to be able to recreate the design.

The main challenge was the roof, since there was no design precedent, exactly the kind of challenge Wren found stimulating. The Theatre of Marcellus, like all Mediterranean theatres, was open-air and had no roof—clearly not an option in Oxford. Wren's whole building was a clean break from the city's Gothic past, and accordingly he rejected the option of a Gothic roof with supporting pillars from the outset. The D-shaped roof space measured over 70 feet (21 metres) across, far too long for any timbers to span. Wren began to experiment with a geometrical design for a self-supporting structure, based on a weave of flat wooden timbers on which he had worked with fellow mathematician John Wallis years earlier. Through complex geometry it was held up by its own weight, so strong that the university press was able to store books on top of it in the loft space. Surveyors summoned to inspect it after Wren's death pronounced, 'the whole fabrick of the said theatre is, in our opinion, like[ly] to remain and continue in such repair and condition, for one hundred or two hundred years yet to come.'[11] It was for many years the largest such roof in existence, and has only needed one repair in 300 years, due to decaying timbers, not faulty design.

From the inside of the Sheldonian Theatre, the complexity of Wren's spanned geometric wooden ceiling was concealed from the audience by elaborate scenes painted on the ceiling. The structural elements were hidden, something he strove to achieve in all his architectural creations and which he had learnt from the mosques of Istanbul, as will be explored in Chapter 8. All who attended performances in the Sheldonian were also struck by the perfect acoustics. The galleried open space produced no unwanted echoes, and this was no accident either, as Wren, together with his contemporaries in the Royal Society, was constantly striving to achieve the ideal space for sound to travel in the best way possible. A round space, ideally with a domed rather than a flat or vaulted ceiling, was Wren's idea of perfection. When he put forward his proposals for the renovation of the old St Paul's before the Great Fire of London in 1666, the designs contained what he called a 'spacious dome' instead of the old spire at the centre of the cross-shape, so that the middle of the church would become a 'very proper place for a vast auditory.' His main concern was that:

> in our reformed religion, it should seem vain to make a parish church larger than that all who are present can both hear and see. The Romanists, indeed, may build larger churches; it is enough if they hear the murmur of the mass, and see the elevation of the host, but ours are to be fitted for auditories.[12]

The big open space at St Paul's, as at the Sheldonian, is also a more egalitarian space, unrestricted by conventions of hierarchy where status is reflected in seating position. It was Wren's choice to abandon the long, thin Gothic nave with its hierarchical space in favour of a church centred on a dome, a clear preference in both early Christian and Islamic architecture.

Until now, the standard university approach had been Aristotelianism, a rigid body of ideas that defined the boundaries of human thought. 'Twas held,' John Aubrey wrote about the universities in 1649, 'a strange presumption for a man to attempt an innovation in learning.' The scientific revolution challenged this view, based on the discoveries of the Renaissance. Galileo's

The Roof of the Theatre at Oxford.
Fig. 1.

Fig. 2.

Wren came up with an ingenious geometrical design so the Sheldonian roof could support itself, as illustrated here in his own drawing.

17

telescopic discoveries after 1610 had seriously challenged the classical earth-centred cosmology, just as William Harvey's circulatory physiology of 1628 did for Galenic medicine. However, Wren and his experimental philosopher friends knew that this knowledge, lost to them in Europe's Dark Ages, had been pioneered centuries earlier by the Arabs in around the year 1000, and that it had been developed to extremely high levels. Writing much later as an architect whilst working on St Paul's, Wren made his appreciation of this knowledge clear: 'the Arabians wanted not geometricians in that age, nor the Moors, who translated most of the useful old Greek books.'[13]

As chancellor of the university from 1629 to 1641, the formidable William Laud, academic and archbishop of Canterbury from 1633 to 1645, was aware of this treasure trove of lost knowledge, so much so that he ordered each English ship setting sail to the eastern Mediterranean to return with at least one Arabic manuscript. His collection of Arabic manuscripts swelled and can be found to this day in the library of the Royal Society and in the Bodleian Library in Oxford, covering subjects such as astronomy, language, law, medicine, poetry, proverbs, the occult, and several historical texts. He endowed the first chair of Arabic, known today as the Laudian professor of Arabic. The chair and the manuscripts transformed Oxford into one of the principal centres for Arabic studies in Europe. Laud even established a 'learned press' capable of printing in Arabic.[14]

John Wallis, with whom Wren had experimented on the Sheldonian's wooden flooring, was made Savilian professor of geometry at Oxford in 1649, at a time when interest peaked in the study of Arabic at Oxford and Cambridge, especially for the purpose of reading and understanding new scientific and geometric documents. Before that he had served as cryptographer and code-breaker to the Parliamentarians during the civil war, where he would have been a beneficiary of the Arabic manuscripts recently translated into Latin, since Arab scientists were the first to devise codes—our English word 'cipher' comes from the Arabic *sifr*. In his *Opera Mathematica*, Wallis cites Al-Tusi's 'proof' of Euclid's parallel postulate, crediting his friend Edward Pococke with the translation from Arabic. Pococke (1604–91), the West's greatest Arabic scholar of his day, had graduated from Corpus Christi College, Oxford, where teaching of the 'three languages'—Greek, Latin and Hebrew—was traditional, as at most colleges. Pococke had recently returned from six years in Aleppo, where he had been chaplain to the merchants of the Levant Company till 1636, when Oxford's chancellor, William Laud, had ordered him to return to take up the newly created Laudian Arabic professorship.[15]

Aleppo was not just a major commercial centre at the time, but also a centre for learning and scholarship. As well as having ample opportunity to learn Arabic to a very high level from local scholars, Pococke also collected, on Laud's instructions, many magnificent Arabic manuscripts. Among them was the famous text by Apollonius of Perga, *The Conics*,[16] written in around 200 BCE in eight books, of which only four survived in the original Greek while seven were still extant in Arabic. The geometric theories explained in *The Conics* were vital in geometrical constructions, such as in the design of mirrors for focusing light and the theory of sundials. Wren's use of this conic theory can be seen in the design of the Sheldonian roof, and later in all his dome constructions.

Pococke sent all of the manuscripts that he collected to the Bodleian. The library acquisition dates show a big influx in 1633–5 while Pococke was in Aleppo, and again in 1638 during his three years in Constantinople. It is inconceivable that Wren was ignorant of or had not seen these translations, since all the scientific experimenters of the day clearly shared their knowledge and discussed new ideas constantly. There are many accounts of scientists, Wren and Pococke among them, drinking coffee together in Oxford's first coffee houses. Pococke had learnt to drink coffee while in Aleppo to such an extent that he developed a 'palsy in the hand' in later life, which was attributed to his addiction. In 1659 Pococke had even published a sixteenth-century text in Arabic, along with its English translation, describing the nature of coffee as a drink that 'allayes the ebullition of the blood, is good against the small poxe and measles, and bloudy pimples; yet causeth vertiginous headheach, and maketh lean much, occasioneth waking, and the Emirods, and asswages lust, and sometimes breeds melancholly.'[17]

Another scholar and contemporary close friend of Pococke was John Greaves (1602–52) from Merton College, Oxford. Greaves developed a deep interest in mathematics and astronomy as well as in Arabic, to such an extent that even after becoming Savilian professor of geometry at Oxford in around 1631, he travelled abroad so extensively that he was away from his post for six years out of ten. Greaves and Pococke later travelled to Constantinople together, as described in Chapter 8 on the Ottomans. Greaves's stated purpose was three-fold: to collect Arabic manuscripts, to improve his knowledge of Arabic and other languages, and to make astronomical observations. In a letter written from Constantinople to Laud back in Oxford, Greaves promised to have: 'most of the Greeke mathematicians, translated into Arabicke, brought home and, it may be, some of those, that are lost in the Greeke, stil extant in the Arabick.'[18] This network of men was closely interlinked at Oxford, publishing many writings including 'A Description of the Grand Signor's Seraglio, or the Turkish Emperor's Court' (London, 1650), which Wren is bound to have read, given the date and his appetite for knowledge from beyond the shores of Europe.

Greaves also spent six months in Alexandria to make clandestine astronomical observations. He smuggled his instruments into Egypt by bribing customs officials and lost a 'fair manuscript of Euclid, in Arabic, with vowels' to robbers when travelling between Rosetta and Alexandria. On the whole he was very disappointed with what he found in Egypt by way of Arabic manuscripts.

When Greaves died in 1652, the Arabic manuscript collection passed to his three brothers, but it was then acquired by John Selden for the Bodleian: 'you know he was owner of some Arabic books which (I believe) are not to be found in Europe again; unless you think fit to buy them yourself, I would willingly put in for this University.'[19] Among Greaves's manuscripts was the Arabic version of Apollonius's *On the Division of a Ratio*, which astronomer Edmond Halley later translated. In correspondence, Greaves also said he had 'extracted observations of the Indians and Persians' from a manuscript of his by Al-Hashimi, 'an Arabian author' who must be Ilal al-Zijaat, 'a work of great interest for the early history of Islamic astronomy'. He also collected Al-Farghani's *Elements of Astronomy*.[20] Only Pococke and Robert Huntingdon collected more than Greaves of the great collection of Arabic manuscripts in the Bodleian today.

Wren Starts Building St Paul's

When Wren was given the job of rebuilding St Paul's—along with fifty-one other parish churches—after the destruction inflicted on London by the

Great Fire of 1666, it was thanks to his unique combination of skills as a mathematician, inventor, designer, astronomer and geometrician. He was appointed royal surveyor by King Charles II, known as the 'Merry Monarch', in 1669, a position he held under the next five monarchs—James II, William and Mary, Queen Anne and George I—a feat suggesting that 'diplomat' ought to be added to his list of qualifications.

St Paul's had been destroyed and rebuilt many times before—the first church on the site dated to 604—and when Wren had first surveyed it, even before the fire, he was astonished to find how negligent the builders of the previous structure had been: 'they seem'd Normans, and to have used the Norman foot; but they valued not exactness. … Nor were they true in their levels. … the work was both ill design'd and ill built from the beginning. … the roof was too heavy for its butment.' In summary he criticised the 'deformity of the tower itself', adding that 'the tower from top to bottom, and the next adjacent parts, are such a heap of deformities, that no judicious architect will think it corrigible.'[21]

> I cannot propose a better remedy, than by cutting off the inner corners of the cross, to reduce this middle part into a spacious dome or rotundo, with a cupola, or hemispherical roof, (which may be a very proper place for a vast auditory) and upon the cupola, (for the outward ornament) a lantern with a spiring top, to rise proportionably. … the outward appearance of the church will seem to swell in the middle by degrees, from a large basis, rising into a rotundo bearing a cupola, & then ending in a lantern: and this with incomparable more grace in the remoter aspect, than it is possible for the lean shaft of a steeple to afford.[22]

> [T]o begin with the dome may probably prove the best advice, being an absolute piece of itself, and what will most likely be finished in our time; will make by far the most splendid appearance; may be of present use for the auditory, will make all the outward repairs perfect; and become an ornament to His Majesty's most excellent reign, to the Church of England, & to this great city, which it is pity, in the opinion of our neighbours, should longer continue the most unadorn'd of her bigness in the world.[23]

Writing in the family memoirs, Wren's son explains how his father used St Peter's and the Pantheon as models for the look of the dome from the outside. St Peter's, the largest church in the world, was conceived from the outset as the biggest and most imposing church in Christendom, and is built on the supposed tomb of Peter, 'the Rock of the Church' who became the first bishop of Rome. Like all ancient shrines, it has been rebuilt many times over the centuries. The current St Peter's was started in 1506 and took 120 years to complete. Its financing was so controversial, via blatantly marketed indulgences, that the resultant backlash against the Church of Rome led directly to Luther and the Reformation. Over twelve architects were involved during the period of its construction, including Michelangelo. It was quite a contrast to St Paul's, the work of just one architect over thirty-six years and funded by a tax imposed on sea-coal. Prior to 1675, voluntary contributions 'of pious and charitable people' had come in so slowly 'in proportion to the greatness of the work' that it had only enabled Wren 'to execute a third part of what was necessary.'[24]

The St Paul's site was constrained by surrounding buildings and could not expand for a structure the size of St Peter's in Rome to be replicated. Thus Wren always knew how challenging it would be to achieve an imposing building, but his son tells us 'his endeavours were to build for eternity.'[25] He began by investigating the foundations in the northeast corner and found a pit where the previous Temple of Diana had been, with urns, pots, stag horns and boar tusks. Wren dug down for 40 feet, 'through firm sea-beach to the original clay, which confirmed what was before asserted, that the sea had been in ages past, where now St Paul's is.'[26] To stabilise that corner and make certain of sound foundations, he then began to build a square pier of masonry, 10 square feet, to support the crypt.

The foundations were obviously critically important, but for Wren, as at the Sheldonian, the challenge was the roof, in this case the dome. How could such a vast stone structure be supported? He knew that the answer lay in the geometry, to get the weight to be taken by the design itself. He explains how he considered the various options:

The different forms of vaultings are necessary to be considered, either as they were used by the Ancients, or the Moderns, whether Free-masons, or Saracens. Another way, (which I cannot find used by the Ancients, but in the later Eastern Empire, as appears at St Sophia, and by that example, in all the mosques & cloysters of the Dervises, and every where at present in the East) and of all the others the most geometrical, is composed of hemispheres, and their sections only: and whereas a sphere may be cut in all manner of ways, & that still into circles, it may be accommodated to lie upon all positions of the pillars. …

Now because I have for just reasons followed this way in the vaulting of the Church of St Paul's, I think it proper to shew, that it is the lightest manner, and requires less butment than the cross-vaulting, as well as that it is of an agreeable view. …

Being evidently the least and the lightest, and the center of gravity nearest to D, I have therefore followed in the vaultings of St Paul's, and, with good reason, preferred it above any other way used by architects.[27]

Thus Wren clearly concludes that the 'Saracen' method of vaulting using hemispheres is the most efficient and the lightest, based on their advanced understanding of the geometry involved. Not only that, but he also copies their double dome technique, whereby the outer dome that provides the height for the skyline is supported via a cone constructed of bricks, which distributes the weight of the 850-tonne lantern of St Paul's. These inner workings are concealed from view by the lower dome, and only when a repair was conducted in 1928 was the elaborately complex methodology exposed. It is recorded for posterity thanks to an isometric projection by Mervyn Edmund Macartney.

When Michelangelo, then in his seventies, was asked in 1547 to complete St Peter's and its dome, he is known to have studied the domes of the Pantheon in Rome, Florence Cathedral and Hagia (St) Sophia in Istanbul. The job was forced on him by Pope Paul III, and he did not take it on with relish. In fact, to escape from the task he even considered taking up an offer from the Ottoman court to go and work in Istanbul instead.[28] He eventually took the

St Peter's commission on condition he had free rein to complete the building in whatever way he saw fit.

Given the Ottoman job offer, Michelangelo is likely also to have had knowledge of the method of dome construction used in the contemporary Ottoman mosques of Sinan, master architect to three sultans. The great Süleymaniye Mosque in particular, built for Süleyman the Magnificent, was under construction around that time (1548–57); Michelangelo's dome base was finished in 1552, and the cupola itself in 1564 twelve years later, the year of his death. The two men, Sinan (1490–1588) and Michelangelo (1475–1564), were contemporaries, both living well into old age. In his final design, Michelangelo used a double shell technique very similar to that used in the contemporary mosques of Sinan, with spur-like buttresses fronted by pairs of columns alternating with the windows in the drum.[29] Sinan also openly acknowledged that he himself learnt from the dome construction of the Hagia Sophia cathedral. He was even asked to rebuild it after one of its many collapses, so knew it intimately. Architects like Sinan worked intuitively, from experience, and though he is known to have drawn plans of his buildings for the benefit of his patron, none of these survive. It was the same throughout the Middle Ages in Europe, where most Gothic-era building was anonymous. Brunelleschi too left no drawings of how he constructed the Florence dome, though that seems to have been deliberate, to keep his methods secret.

St Peter's was initially intended to resemble Hagia Sophia, under Michelangelo's design, with twin towers and subsidiary semi-domes, the same look that Wren chose for St Paul's, though he kept the semi-domes internally, for structural and aesthetic reasons, but not on view externally. But after Michelangelo's death in 1564, the St Peter's twin towers were dropped and the subsidiary domes simplified. The outer shape of the dome itself was also changed by a subsequent architect between 1588 and 1593 to give it a steeper profile like that at Florence Cathedral; the architect decided that it would be 'more beautiful as well as stronger.'[30] Even so, the St Peter's dome today has no fewer than ten strengthening iron chains hooped round its base, compared with two at St Paul's. Michelangelo's centralised plan was also changed through the addition of a nave in 1607, but even after all those alterations, the learned Pietro della Valle, a traveller from Rome who visited Istanbul in 1614,

To WILLIAM DUNN, *FRIBA*
who first suggested the idea of shewing the construction of St. Paul's Cathedral by Isometric Projection
this drawing is inscribed by MERVYN EDMUND MACARTNEY *FSA.* Surveyor to the Fabric
Measured and drawn by R.B. BROOK-GREAVES in collaboration with W. GODFREY ALLEN
Valuable assistance has been rendered by Matthew Dawson *FRIBA* & E J Bolwell

This 1928 isometric projection of St Paul's Cathedral shows the 'Saracen' method
of vaulting used by Wren, based on advanced geometry. It also reveals the Islamic
dome-layering technique, which enabled the outermost dome to project a great height.

was still struck by the similarity between the mosques of the city and St Peter's of Rome, writing:

> That which is noteworthy are the mosques, in particular four or five of them built by the Turkish emperors, all of them situated on the highest hilltops in such a way that they almost form a row, visible from one end of the sea to the other and equally distributed along the whole length of the city. They are well built in marble and differ little in architecture from one another, being in the form of a temple composed of a domed square, like the design of St Peter's in Rome by Michelangelo; and I believe they have taken as their model Hagia Sophia which they encountered there.[31]

Wren was equally concerned with the importance of vista and visibility. St Paul's, he writes in *Parentalia*, 'is lofty enough to be discerned at sea eastward, and at Windsor westward', with other viewing points like Richmond Park along the way. The dome of St Paul's can still be seen from King Henry's Mound in Richmond Park today.

Della Valle promised to bring back paintings so that modern Italian architects could also find inspiration from the Istanbul monuments. The great scholar of Ottoman architecture, Harvard-based Gülru Necipoğlu, tells us that at least one Italian architect, Borromini, made drawings of Hagia Sophia while designing the church of S. Ivo alla Sapienza in 1642.[32] Measured hand-drawn diagrams thought to be of Hagia Sophia (though possibly of one of Sinan's mosques) were also discovered in the 1980s among some papers associated with Wren and found at St Paul's Cathedral. Experts consider them to have been based on two sources: an illustrated travelogue by French artist Guillaume-Joseph Grelot published in 1683, under the title *A Late Voyage to Constantinople*, and unpublished drawings brought from Istanbul to London by Grelot's patron, the wealthy Huguenot merchant John Chardin, with whom Wren became friends after Chardin settled in London at the end of his life.[33] One of the three diagrams shows a cross-section in freehand pencil, not a mere replica of Grelot's drawings, but clearly derived from them and perhaps from further conversations with Chardin, showing the construction methods used and revealing features that would have been unknown in England at that point. The other two show details from a corner ground plan, complete with internal staircases, which are very similar to the St Paul's equivalent corner constructions. These two drawings, in a hand asserted by art historian Kerry Downes to be that of Wren himself (though disputed by others), make clear that Wren took ideas from mosques in Istanbul, then synthesised them into his own unique solution.

Grelot had managed to get permission from the Ottoman authorities to take detailed measurements inside Hagia Sophia, by then a mosque, and was able to produce fourteen engraved plates based on those visits, during which he recorded both interior and exterior detail. The timing of this publication, just two years before Wren started work on St Paul's, was perfect, causing quite a stir and much interest. John Chardin himself gave a presentation in 1680 to the Royal Society, straight after arriving in London from his eastern travels. Wren was among the event's attendees.[34]

Wren is also known to have consulted English merchants and businessmen who had travelled extensively in Asia Minor (modern Turkey) about contemporary dome construction techniques in use in Smyrna (modern Izmir) and in Constantinople, and was specifically curious to know how the Ottomans covered their domes in lead and got it to stay in place.[35] Having established their method, he decided it was too insecure and too risky to try at St Paul's, devising his own solution instead. He wished to achieve the desired soaring high dome profile through balancing lightness with exactly the right supporting strength, a formula he arrived at through his grasp of the geometric solutions required, together with a knowledge of the necessary modifications that arose from unexpected problems during construction. Wren's biographer Lisa Jardine tells us that 'the final resolution of the problem of the dome as a whole was largely as a result of the mathematical advances in understanding stresses in arches.'[36] The virtues and complexities of Islamic double domes are discussed and explored further in Chapter 8, in connection with Sinan, court architect to the Ottoman sultans, and the question of the early dome and its evolution will also be explored in greater depth in Chapter 3 on the pre-Islamic legacy.

Wren was on site for hours at a time, consulting with master masons and master carpenters. The construction was a collaborative effort, guided by Wren himself. The final stone of St Paul's was placed on the summit of the dome in 1708 by Wren's son, also called Christopher, together with the son of the master mason with whom Wren had worked throughout. They had worked closely and talked together on site, in the true English medieval tradition, whereby buildings were constructed to the needs of the patron in accordance with the suggestions of building professionals, such as master carpenters or master bricklayers.

The two fathers were present, watching, but too elderly to balance precariously in the required positions. Wren was by this stage nearly seventy-six years old, 'his limbs enfeebled, but his mind sharp as a razor', as his son tells us in the *Parentalia*.

When completed, St Paul's with its iconic dome did not meet universal approval. The clergy, with their backward-looking traditions, had wanted something closer to the original Gothic-style St Paul's with its spire. They contrived to get Wren sacked. At the time of Wren's death, his masterpiece was unappreciated and unacknowledged, yet the reputation of St Paul's has grown with the years, and that of its architect alongside it.

Wren's son Christopher evidently felt the injustice of this state of affairs, which must be why he and his own son, Stephen, chose to make public his father's notes as published in the *Parentalia*. They reveal the original thinking of a brain capable of synthesising many disciplines simultaneously, the realisation of which stands before us in St Paul's Cathedral. Wren understood how to combine the best of all worlds. He understood instinctively how to draw on innovative ideas and techniques from all over the globe, and even though the only foreign trip he ever made himself was to Paris, where he stayed for six months in 1665 to escape the dangerously infected air of the Plague— over 100,000 died in London in those six months—he made thorough studies of the books of travellers to the New World and the Near and Far East, carefully analysing the illustrations of far-away buildings. As a child he had his father's library to browse through and be inspired by, and auction records show his own library included such works as du Perier's *Voyages and Travels— Voyage to Constantinople* (1699) and Jacob Spon's *Voyage d'Italie, de Dalmatie, de Grèce et du Levant* (1679).

Apart from the Fire and the Plague that had preceded it, Wren's great longevity meant that he lived through civil wars, foreign wars against the

St Paul's Cathedral interior, showing the choir, apse, baldachin, stained glass and 'Saracen' roof vaulting, all elements which originated in the early Christian and early Islamic Middle East.

French and the Dutch, and bloody conflicts between Catholics and Protestants. All this he survived till he died aged ninety of a chill while sitting quietly in his chair after dinner.

At the bicentennial of his death on 26 February 1923 at the Wren Banquet, Sir Reginald Blomfield said of him: 'He had received no systematic training in architecture at all. He possessed inexhaustible invention and resource. His mind, of great natural acuteness, was trained to a fine razor-edge and went straight to the heart of matters.'

On the same occasion, Stanley C. Ramsay concluded: 'We live in an age of specialists, but Wren belonged to a broader and more generous time. He was a universalist, imagining the whole rather than fancying the parts. He is the great national architect.'

Today St Paul's, London's cathedral, is probably the most familiar, most celebrated, most talked-about building in the British Isles—because of its distinctive dome. But its repute also spread across Europe and beyond. Even as far afield as Persia in the nineteenth century, an annotated map of London read in Farsi: 'with the exception of St Peter's Basilica, St Paul's Cathedral has no equivalent in any other country.'[37] With a capacity of 2,500, St Paul's is the largest church in London and has been used historically for great state events, like the funerals of famous people from Nelson and Wellington to John Donne and Henry Moore, and more recently Margaret Thatcher. Many of them are buried in its crypt. The marble coffin of Nelson's tomb had to be specially lowered down from the floor of the dome. Only rarely has the church been used for weddings, like that of Princess Diana and Prince Charles. An emblem of stability and permanence, the cathedral survived the Blitz in World War Two with just minor damage to a side chapel. Time and again the dome has been used as a symbol for London, etched into our subconscious through its use, for example, by the BBC as a key studio backdrop. When Prince Charles intervened to halt the Paternoster master plan for redevelopment of the area round St Paul's in 1987, the question of the cathedral's lasting greatness seemed entirely rhetorical. 'Why does St Paul's matter so much?' the prince asked. 'Because it is our greatest national monument.' Nothing, he argued, must be allowed to crowd or overshadow this most revered and recognisable of London landmarks.

2

GOTHIC ARCHITECTURE

'The Saracen Style'

In his memoirs, Wren acknowledges the European debt to what he calls 'Saracen' architecture twelve times. His theories on architecture are detailed in what is known as 'Tract II' of the *Parentalia*, where he explains how his study of Europe's Gothic cathedrals had led him to believe that Gothic architecture was a style invented by the Arabs, imported by the returning Crusaders, and before that via Muslim Spain. 'Such buildings,' he concludes, 'have been vulgarly called Modern Gothick, but their true appellation is Arabic, Saracenic, or Moresque.'[1]

The first mention of this theory comes in 1713, towards the end of Wren's life when he was aged eighty-one, and thus based on a lifetime's study and experience. In a letter to the bishop of Rochester, talking about Westminster Abbey, which he had been asked by the king to repair, Wren refers to the abbey's Gothic style as:

> the mode which came into fashion after the Holy War. This we now call the Gothick manner of architecture (so the Italians called what was not after the Roman style) tho' the Goths were rather destroyers than builders; I think it should be with more reason called the Saracen style; for those people wanted neither arts nor learning; and after we in the West had lost both, we borrowed again from them, out of their Arabick books, what they with great diligence had translated from the Greeks.[2]

Evidently Wren, who attended Oxford during the peak of Arabic studies in the mid-seventeenth century under Chancellor Laud, had a clear understanding that while Europe was in its Dark Ages after the fall of Rome, the Muslim world was in its Golden Age, especially in Spain and in Sicily. For centuries our Eurocentric view of the world helped us to airbrush this inconvenient truth out of history, and only recent TV documentaries like Jim Al-Khalili's *Science and Islam* and Rageh Omaar's *An Islamic History of Europe*, both shown on the BBC in 2009, have helped bring this into the popular consciousness. In Spain, Toledo was the first Spanish city to be retaken by Christian forces in the Reconquista in 1085. It was made capital of Castille and became a famous centre of translation in the twelfth and thirteenth centuries, after its Christian rulers realised the importance of its notable Arabic manuscript collections. The works of Greek philosophers and scientists, lost to Europe for centuries, were translated from the Arabic, into Castilian Spanish (forming the foundation of modern Spanish) and into Latin (the official church language). The translators were Christians, Muslims and Jews all working together on hundreds of Arabic manuscripts, many of which had been translated from Greek during the Islamic Golden Age in the East (chiefly Iraq).

Examining the features of Europe's Gothic architecture, Wren calls to attention the contradictions of naming such a light, slender and delicately ornamented style after the heavy, rampaging Goths:

> Modern Gothic, as it is called … is distinguished by the lightness of its work, by the excessive boldness of its elevations, and of its sections; by the delicacy, profusion, and extravagant fancy of its ornaments. The pillars of this kind are as slender as those of the ancient Gothic are massive: such productions, so airy, cannot admit the heavy Goths for their author.[3]

He goes on to wonder at the coincidence of timing in the sudden appearance of Gothic architecture. This, he believes, provides even more reason to associate it with the Saracens:

> How can be attributed to [the Goths] a style of architecture, which was only introduced in the tenth century of our era? Several years after the destruction

of all those kingdoms which the Goths had raised upon the ruins of the Roman empire, and a time when the very name of Goth was entirely forgotten: from all the marks of the new architecture it can only be attributed to the Moors; or what is the same thing, to the Arabians or Saracens.[4]

So how valid is Wren's theory? To answer this question, we ought to start by examining the architecture around him as a young man and how that might have informed his views. It is worth taking a closer look at Wadham College, where Wren lived during his impressionable undergraduate years. The buildings of the first quad are still exactly as Wren would have known them. The college was built in the Jacobean style between 1610 and 1614 at extraordinary speed—in just four years—under the charge of Dorothy Wadham, who battled with builders and bureaucracy exactly as any owner or developer has to today. The architect was William Arnold, her choice, 'an honest man, a perfect workman, and my near neighbour.'[5] In the custom of the time, before the profession of architect existed, Arnold was referred to as a 'master mason'.

The first thing that strikes you about Wadham College is the symmetry and balance of the two-storey courtyard, built from the local stone of Headington quarry—the cheapest available material, finances always being tight. As you enter from the street, the tall frontispiece to the Dining Hall is directly opposite, in line with the entrance. It rises higher than the roof battlements in four sections. Below it is the gently pointed arched wooden door into the Hall, and on either side are two similarly sized wooden doors. One door leads to the chapel on the left, while the right-hand one is false, there purely to provide symmetry. This was unusual for the time and 'breathes a distinctly unmedieval air', as the Wadham College book describes it. The popular prevailing Gothic architecture of the time, as represented by wealthy colleges like Magdalen and Merton, dominated Oxford, the 'city of dreaming spires', as Victorian poet Matthew Arnold (no relation to the Wadham architect William Arnold) famously called it. English Gothic was characterised by vaulted ceilings, pointed arches, buttresses, elaborate tracery and spires, creating a very distinctive skyline when so many Gothic buildings were concentrated together.

Wadham's architectural design was therefore quite modern and 'with it', an unusual synthesis of classical and medieval. The central frontispiece carries stone-carved statues of Dorothy and Nicholas Wadham and above them a statue of King James I, ruling monarch of the time, with England's lion and Scotland's unicorn at the highest point, as well as the royal coat of arms created for James I in 1603 at the time of the Union of the Crowns. Each storey is flanked by columns of the four orders of architecture (Doric, Ionic, Corinthian and composite) in classical style. Yet the detailing everywhere is Gothic—what was called at the time 'traditional', since Gothic was the predominant style in most public buildings across the country.

The term 'Gothic' itself did not originate till the sixteenth century, when Giorgio Vasari first used the expression 'barbarous German style' in his 1550 *Lives of the Most Excellent Painters, Sculptors and Architects*, a highly influential book widely seen as the foundation of art history. Vasari attributed the style to 'the Goths', believing they had torn down Rome's beautiful classical buildings and replaced them with their own 'barbarous' architecture. An Italian painter, architect and historian, Vasari was also the first to use the term 'Renaissance' in print. Before Vasari's terminology came into use, Gothic architecture was simply known as *opus francigenum*, Latin meaning 'Frankish (i.e. French) work'. Westminster Abbey, the private abbey of the royal family, is a typical example of Anglo-French Gothic. The old St Paul's was in Gothic style, much loved by the clergy.

At Wadham, the first piece of unmistakeable Gothic is the intricate fan-vaulting of the entrance, below the tower. Then there are the battlement crenellations and the Gothic windows to the dining hall and the antechapel. These windows are pure Gothic, with their tall pointed arches, their tracery and their trefoil arches. The trefoil arch was the favourite adaptation of the pointed arch all across Europe because it represented the Holy Trinity. Start looking and you'll see it in virtually every Gothic church in Britain. Recurring themes of triples occur throughout Christian architecture—the triple nave, the triple window. Surrounded by these windows every time he ate or went to pray—daily prayers were obligatory at the time—Wren would have absorbed their feel. He would have noticed the details. His approach throughout his life was to function through observation and careful analysis.

Wren's graduate college All Souls, founded in the fifteenth century, though later amended by Wren's apprentice Nicholas Hawksmoor in the early eighteenth century, was likewise pure Gothic at Wren's time, with the popular Perpendicular style in the chapel, the same as in the Wadham chapel.

Wren was no fan of Westminster Abbey and bemoaned its weak Gothic structure where the pillars had been forced at least six inches out of true, bulging outwards—something he identified as a general problem in Gothic cathedrals—because the pillars were not strong enough to carry the load of the roof. In his letter to the bishop of Rochester in 1713, Wren writes:

> The Saracen mode of building, seen in the East, soon spread over Europe, and particularly in France; the fashions of which nation we affected to imitate in all ages, even when we were at enmity with it. Nothing was thought magnificent that was not high beyond measure, with the flutter of archbuttresses, so we call the sloping arches that poise the higher vaultings of the nave. The Romans always concealed their butments, whereas the Normans thought them ornamental. These I have observ'd are the first things that occasion the ruin of cathedrals, being so much exposed to the air and weather. … pinnacles are of no use, and as little ornament.[6]

Wren's son Christopher confirms how the origins of Gothic architecture intrigued his father, since it was so different to what had been typical of northern European architecture before, namely the heavy, thick-walled Romanesque, sometimes also called the Norman style after the rulers of Normandy. Wren junior wrote in the *Parentalia*:

> a discernment of no contemptible art, ingenuity, and geometrical skill in the design and execution of some few, and an affectation of height and grandeur, tho' without regularity and good proportion, in most of them, induced the surveyor [Wren] to make some enquiry into the rise and progress of this Gothick mode, and to consider how the old Greek and Roman style of building, with the several regular proportions of columns, entablatures, &c came within a few centuries to be so much altered, and almost universally disused. He was of opinion … that what we now vulgarly call the Gothick ought properly and truly to be named the Saracenic architecture refined by the Christians; which first of all began in the East after the fall of the Greek Empire by the

prodigious success of those people that adhered to Mahomet's doctrine, who out of zeal to their religion, built mosques, caravanseras, & sepulchres, wherever they came. These they contrived of a round form, because they would not imitate the Christian figure of a cross; nor the old Greek manner, which they thought to be idolatrous, and for that reason all sculpture became offensive to them. They then fell into a new mode of their own invention. ... As they propagated their religion with great diligence so they built mosques in all their conquered cities in haste.[7]

The quarries of great marble, by which the vanquished nations of Syria, Egypt and all the East had been supplied for columns, architraves, and great stones, were now deserted; the Saracens therefore were necessitated to accommodate their architecture to such materials, whether marble or free-stone, as every country readily afforded. They thought columns and heavy cornices impertinent, & might be omitted; and affecting the round form for mosques, they elevated cupolas in some instances, with grace enough. The Holy War gave the Christians, who had been there, an idea of the Saracen works, which were afterwards by them imitated in the West; and they refined upon it every day, as they proceeded in building churches.[8]

Wren consistently makes it clear in his writings that he favours symmetry and straight lines, and dislikes 'oblique positions' as he calls the chaotic asymmetry of Gothic: 'therefore Gothick buttresses are all ill-favoured, and were avoided by the Ancients, and no roofs almost but spherick raised to be visible.'[9] He was also a big critic of the Gothic roof, far too heavy and ill-supported, so that the pillars of the nave always bowed outwards. For this reason he refused to put a Gothic roof on the Sheldonian or on the new St Paul's, even though he came under pressure to do so since the old St Paul's had been built in that style.

Having made clear his dislike of the style and its inherent weaknesses, Wren then proceeds in the *Parentalia* to explain who he thinks the people were who actually built these Gothic cathedrals of Europe. His studies, he says, have led him to conclude that: 'The Italians (among which were yet some Greek refugees) and with them the French, Germans, and Flemings, joined into a fraternity of architects, procuring papal bulls for their encouragement, & particular privileges.'[10]

This account of how those returning from the Crusades formed themselves into Europe's first guilds is supported by other later scholars.[11] In medieval cities, craftsmen formed associations based on their trade, fraternities of masons, carpenters, sculptors and glass workers, each of whom passed down their secrets and skills to apprentices, often their sons. The founders were usually free, independent masters of their crafts, not tied to one employer or patron. It was common for commercial deals to be struck with the Vatican by such guilds at times of turbulence and religious unrest in the twelfth and thirteenth centuries. The pope would issue a favourable public decree and stamp it with his 'bull', the name given to his leaden seal, *bulla* in Latin.

The nationalities Wren lists here are interesting, as he names the Italians first. The Italians were the Europeans most closely linked to and influenced by the 'Saracens' through their trading connections in Venice, Amalfi and Sicily. When Wren refers to the 'Greek refugees' among them, these would not have been Greeks from Greece, but Byzantine Greek Orthodox Christians from Syria and the Holy Land, who stayed on and continued their trade under Muslim rule. These were craftsmen whose skills were honed in the Byzantine tradition. There are many well-known instances of such craftsmen staying on in their local workshops after the Muslim conquest, as evidenced in the mosaic work at the Dome of the Rock and the Damascus Umayyad Mosque, which will be described in Chapter 4. Wren then lists the French, the Germans and the Flemings, that is, the northern Europeans who were less familiar with the Muslim world before the Crusades, and lists them correctly in numerical order, since the French, the 'Franks' as they were known at the time of the Crusades, provided the most manpower for the Crusades and the Flemish the least, Flanders being a small country. The 'privileges' they were given by the pope were likely to be favourable terms, such as exemption from taxation, a kind of reward for their loyal service to the Church in fighting holy war on its behalf.

Wren continues: 'they stiled themselves Freemasons, and ranged from one nation to another, as they found churches to be built (for very many in those ages were every where in building, through piety or emulation).'[12]

This is a clear description of how the 'fraternity of architects' was formed as a guild of stonemasons, calling themselves 'Freemasons' because they were freelance, able to 'range', as Wren puts it, from country to country all over Europe. This ties in with their papal 'encouragements' and 'privileges', because they were not tied to a particular employer or master, but were free to move about to wherever their work was needed. As Wren explains, there was a rich vein to be tapped after the First Crusade (1096–9), with many cities wanting to erect churches quickly as symbols of their Christian faith, confirmations of their piety. Rich benefactors would have competed in trying to outdo each other in such pious endowments (just as wealthy members of society in Muslim countries did in donating funds for mosques, centres of learning and public fountains under the *waqf* system, a form of tax-free benefaction under Islamic law). The mood after the First Crusade was one of religious fervour all across Europe, hence the rash of church-building that spread quickly across Christendom.

Wren goes on to explain that the Freemasons organised themselves in a 'regular' well-disciplined manner, building themselves an encampment in the town, close to where the new church was to be constructed. Under the overall direction of a 'surveyor', they had a hierarchy of 'wardens' who supervised nine workers each below them. The local worthies would source the building materials and pay for them to be brought to the site, 'either out of charity or communication of pennance'.[13] Wren then comments on how diligently and thriftily the accounts were kept, the implication being that he has himself had sight of these accounts: 'Those who have seen the exact accounts in records of the charge of fabricks of some of our cathedrals near four hundred years old, cannot but have a great esteem for their economy, & admire how soon they erected such lofty structures.'[14] This is likely to be a reference to York Minster, which dates from 1220.[15] As master surveyor himself, needing to keep the accounts on his own projects and mindful of the importance of staying within budget, he would have been well placed to give an opinion on these 400-year-old accounts.

Wren also comments on the sheer speed with which the churches were erected, especially given how tall they were, writing:

Indeed great height they thought the greatest magnificence; few stones were used, but what a man might carry up a ladder on his back from scaffold to scaffold, tho' they had pullies, and spoked wheels … stone upon stone was easily piled up to great heights; therefore the pride of their works was in pinnacles and steeples.[16]

Here he begins to contrast these Freemasons' new building techniques with what had gone before: the Romanesque style. He explains that height became the defining characteristic of their building style, because of how they worked. They were itinerant workers, using smaller, lighter stones than the Romans and Normans. Their tools were minimal and they relied on what one man could carry on his back as he climbed up ladders and scaffolding. An occasional use of pulleys was all they needed to raise some of the bigger stones, but mostly they just laid ever smaller stones as the structures grew higher and higher. This was how they built the steeples of which they were so proud.

The Saracens, he explains, were the originators of this building style, thanks to the speed of the Islamic conquest of Christian territory in the seventh century:

They were zealots in their religion, and where-ever they conquered (which was with amazing rapidity) erected mosques and caravanserais in haste; which obliged them to fall into another way of building; for they built their mosques round, disliking the Christian form of a cross, the old quarries whence the Ancients took their large blocks of marble for whole columns and architraves, were neglected, and they thought both impertinent. Their carriage was by camels, therefore their buildings were fitted for small stones, and columns of their own fancy, consisting of many pieces; and their arches were pointed without keystones, which they thought too heavy.

The reasons were the same in our northern climates, abounding in free-stone, but wanting marble.

The Crusado gave us an idea of this form; after which King Henry built his church, but not by a model well digested at first.[17]

Wren's reference here is to King Henry III, who in 1245 had ordered the construction of the present Westminster Abbey, which Wren calls the king's church because it is a private church for the royal family, and not for official state functions like St Paul's. Westminster Abbey is where monarchs have historically been crowned, married and buried. The Abbey was completed in c. 1260. Before that it had been a Benedictine monastery under the abbot of Westminster, who was generally close to the monarchy and had a seat in the House of Lords.

Wren now explains how this vertical, 'perpendicular' style of the 'Freemasons' contrasts so markedly with the earlier Roman horizontal style:

> In this they essentially differed from the Roman way, who laid all their mould-
> ings horizontally, which made the best perspective: the Gothick way on the
> contrary carried all their mouldings perpendicular, so that the ground-work
> being settled, they had nothing else to do but to spire all up as they could. Thus
> they made their pillars of a bundle of little torus's.[18]

In geometry a torus is a surface of revolution generated by revolving a circle in 3D space, to produce a shape like an inner tube or a doughnut. Wren elaborates to explain that this is how Gothic tracery evolved, through the Freemasons' particular love of going ever higher with ever smaller stones or rings, 'which they divided into more, when they came to the roof; and these torus's split into many small ones, and traversing one another, gave occasion to the tracery-work (as they called it) of which this society were the inventors.'[19]

Next Wren comes to the Saracens' use of the pointed arch and how this enabled them to build structures that were higher than those that used the previous round Roman arches. He explains that the pointed arch is stronger than the round arch because it needs a lighter keystone to secure it at the central point. It is therefore able to carry more weight, and can carry another row of arches above it, centred over the keystone of the arch below:

> They used the sharp-headed-arch, which would rise with little centering,
> required lighter key-stones and less butment, & yet would bear another row

of doubled arches rising from the key-stone; by the diversifying of which, they erected eminent structures, such as the steeples of Vienna, Strasburg, and many others.[20]

It is interesting that Wren mentions the steeples at Vienna and Strasbourg, neither of which he would ever have seen, given that he never travelled beyond northern France. The steeple of St Stephen's at Vienna was built in 1304 and that at Strasbourg in 1190.

For Goethe too, Strasbourg Cathedral represented a Gothic pinnacle. Writing centuries later in 1773, the great German literary and scientific freethinker described Strasbourg as 'a sublimely towering, wide-spreading tree of God, with a thousand big branches, millions of smaller branches and as many leaves as there are grains of sand on the shore.'[21]

The cathedral was being built in Romanesque style following a fire in 1176, but the arrival of a team of masons from Chartres in 1225 revolutionised the look of the building through construction of the dramatic west facade, now acknowledged as a Gothic masterpiece, its construction apparently random, but based on rotating octagons.

In the next passage Wren contrasts the Gothic steeple with the Saracens' preference for the dome, observing that St Mark's in Venice was built in the Saracen style, with multiple domes (five in total): 'They affected steeples, though the Saracens themselves most used cupolas. The Church of St Mark at Venice, is built after the Saracen manner.'[22]

This is interesting since St Mark's was completed in 1092, just before the First Crusade of 1095. But Wren is referring specifically to the domes, which were later Gothic additions in the thirteenth century, by which time Venice had taken Constantinople as a kind of colony following the diverted and disastrous Fourth Crusade. By that stage the Venetians would have had ample opportunity to study the domes of their trading partners in Cairo, as well as to examine the structure of the Byzantine dome at Hagia Sophia. 'Glass began to be used in windows,'[23] he notes; stained glass was a Byzantine invention in churches, so again, the 'Greek refugees' Wren mentions earlier would have been familiar with this style and its technique.

Wren singles out the perpendicular steeples of St Stephen's, Vienna [left], and Strasbourg Cathedral [right] as typical speedily built 'Saracen' structures that contrast markedly with the heavier Roman horizontal style.

Wren sums up his study by assessing how this Gothic work, using smaller and lighter stones, was easier and faster to build than the old Roman way. The use of flat-moulds, he explains, made it even easier for the master masons, or 'wardens' as he calls them, to delegate and mass produce the materials. He admires the ingenuity of the technique, admitting that it would be much more expensive to build to the same height and magnificence using the old Roman methods:

> Thus the work required fewer materials, & the workmanship was for the most part performed by flat-moulds, in which the wardens could easily instruct hundreds of artificers. It must be confessed, this was an ingenius compendium of work, suited to these northern climates; and I must also own, that works of the same height and magnificence in the Roman way, would be very much

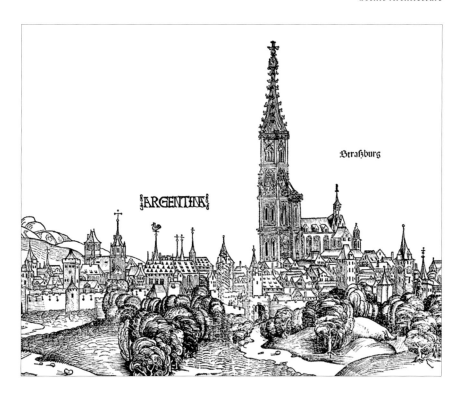

more expensive, than in the other Gothick manner managed without judgement.[24]

In the end though, he writes, it all went too far, getting completely out of proportion and over-elaborate, with a failure to use good geometry, thereby making the structures so weak that they required elaborate buttresses to hold them up. These European craftsmen were skilled stonemasons, yes, but they were not mathematicians and scientists like their Saracen counterparts. They lacked that knowledge. One glance at the highly advanced mathematics behind the Cordoba Mezquita,[25] explored fully in Chapter 5, is enough to make the contrast with the rather random and chaotic Gothic 'fancies':

> But as all modes, when once the old rational ways are despised, turn at last into unbounded fancies; this tracery induced too much mincing of the stone into open battlements and spindling pinnacles, and little carvings without

proportion of distance; so the essential rules of good perspective and duration were forgot.[26]

Wren's description of the masons in these passages from the *Parentalia*, their method of working, their hierarchies, tallies with most authoritative sources. The Encyclopedia Britannica entry for example says that Freemasonry evolved from the guilds of stonemasons and cathedral builders of the Middle Ages. A mason who was at the top of his trade was known as a master mason, just as the architect of Wadham College had been. The master mason supervised everyone, not just other masons but also carpenters and glaziers. He worked from a building on site known as the Mason's Lodge and all newcomers seeking work were tested and assessed to make sure that quality was maintained. Each master mason had an apprentice who moved around from site to site with him till such time as he was judged, through examinations that took place at the Master's Lodge, worthy to be admitted as a master mason into that lodge himself, whereupon he was given a mason's mark that was unique to him.[27] These are the masons' marks that can still be seen by the trained eye on stonework in Gothic buildings to this day.

With the aid of no more than elementary drawings and templates, master stonemasons meticulously directed the construction of the great medieval cathedrals of Europe. They worked intuitively, making calculations as they went along, based on simple geometrical and mathematical ratios and structural precedent, and this knowledge, born of experience and instinct, was kept a closely guarded secret, only passed down to trusted apprentices, who were often family members. The continuous demand from the church authorities for more and more churches and cathedrals, built ever higher and lighter, meant that the masons' skills were constantly improving and developing to meet new challenges.[28] Flying buttresses were developed as emergency repairs, to stop the buildings falling down.[29] One or two fell down anyway, notably the Cathedral of Beauvais (1225–72) north of Paris, just twelve years after completion, its collapsing nave pulling a few flying buttresses and part of the choir vault with it. Today it remains unfinished, an apse without a nave, but it still holds the record for the highest ceiling in a Gothic choir, an 'outburst of verticality'.[30]

What still stands of Beauvais Cathedral in Picardy, after its nave collapsed.

If we look at how masons operated in medieval England, it is clear that, like their European counterparts, they were highly skilled craftsmen who moved around in a nomadic manner to wherever someone would pay them to build churches, cathedrals or castles. One of the earliest Gothic constructions in England was Salisbury Cathedral, now a household name ever since the two Russian spies accused of poisoning Alexander Skripal alleged they were there to visit the cathedral's famous spire in 2018. It is certainly one of the very best examples of Early English Gothic, built over a fairly short period, mainly 1220–58. Apart from its fourteenth-century facade, tower and spire, it is relatively uncontaminated by other styles. Wren was as scathing about Salisbury Cathedral as he was about Westminster Abbey, listing 'some errors' in its structure and its faulty foundations:

> Almost all the cathedrals of the Gothick form are weak & defective in the poise of the vault of the ailes … there is scarce any Gothick cathedral, that I have seen, at home or abroad, wherein I have not observed the pillars to yield

and bend inwards from the weight of the vault of the aile … for this reason, this form of churches has been rejected by modern architects abroad, who use the better and Roman art of architecture.[31]

In England Gothic is generally divided into three periods. Early English (1180–1275) marks the first flowering, and as it evolved first in France during the twelfth century, it was originally called 'the French style'. Like the early forms of Gothic on the Continent, the English variety arose out of the efforts of cathedral architects and masons to redistribute the downward and outward thrust of the vault, so as to build higher without the danger of collapse. Before that the dominant style had been Romanesque, also known as Norman architecture, which crossed the Channel from France with the Normans.

After Early Gothic came 'Decorated Gothic' (1250–1350), separated into the 'Geometric' style (1250–90) and the 'Curvilinear' style (1290–1350), and then finally came 'Perpendicular Gothic' (1350–1520), also known in France as 'Flamboyant Gothic'.

An explanation of how the key features of these Gothic buildings—the pointed arch, the trefoil arch, the ogee arch, ribbed vaulting, the twin towers, the rose window, the spire—all have their origins in the Middle East and how they found their way westwards into Europe is coming in Chapters 3–9, but for now it is just worth giving a very quick summary of England's main Gothic cathedrals. The first large-scale application of English Gothic architecture occurred at Canterbury Cathedral (1174), while Durham Cathedral, otherwise Norman Romanesque, has the earliest-known pointed rib vault. An excellent example of English Decorated Gothic architecture is the nave and west front of York Minster, in particular the tracery on the main window. Other outstanding examples include sections of the cloister of Westminster Abbey, the east ends of Carlisle and Lincoln Cathedrals, and the west front of Lichfield Cathedral. A good deal of Exeter Cathedral is also built in this style, as is the crossing of Ely Cathedral. The structural and aesthetic development of the vault reached its pinnacle during the era of Perpendicular Gothic, in the form of elaborate star-shaped lierne vaults, culminating ultimately in the appearance of the fan vault, as seen in the chapel of King's College, Cambridge (1446–1515), which contains the largest fan vault in the world.

Several of the earliest examples of English Perpendicular Gothic architecture, dating back to 1360, can be seen at Gloucester Cathedral, whose cloisters' fan vaulting is particularly striking. Other examples include the nave, west transepts and crossing tower of Canterbury Cathedral (1378–1411); the choir and tower of York Minster (1389–1407); Manchester Cathedral (1422); the transept and tower of Merton College, Oxford (1424–50); and Eton College Chapel (1448–82). During the nineteenth-century Gothic revival, the Perpendicular style was used in the design of the rebuilt Houses of Parliament, discussed in detail in Chapter 9, and in the Wills Memorial Building, Bristol University (1915–25).[32]

The French Style

Art historians agree that the earliest example of Gothic architecture anywhere is to be found in the Basilica of Saint-Denis in north Paris in 1144, the historical burial site for the French kings. Wren describes how the masons, in their fraternity of architects, moved around from place to place according to demand, and the architect involved at Saint-Denis is known to have then moved on to work at Notre-Dame (1163–1345).

The reason for the appearance of the first clearly identifiable Gothic architecture here at Saint-Denis is, unusually, something we are able to trace and explain, due to a string of connections between individuals in the Church. This is explored in more detail in Chapter 7, but for now, a bit of important background about the abbot of Saint-Denis will suffice. Abbot Suger (c. 1081–1151)), born into relative poverty, was given, aged ten, to the royal abbey of Saint-Denis where the French elite was educated. A fellow pupil was the future King Louis VI, to whom Suger later became chief minister. Elected Abbot in 1122, he skilfully married the power of the Church to the prestige of the Crown, his career reaching its climax when Louis VII left on Crusade, leaving the trusted Suger as effective regent of France. Suger devoted the last fifteen years of his life to rebuilding and enlarging the abbey and wrote a famous account of the work and why the enlargement was necessary in order to cope with the crowds of pilgrims visiting the shrine on feast days. He tells us the old structure was so narrow that it 'forced women to run to the altar on the heads of men as on a pavement with great anguish and confusion.'[33]

The old church was in the Carolingian style, the dynasty of Holy Roman Emperor Charlemagne in the late eighth and ninth centuries, a north European pre-Romanesque architecture with thick walls, small windows and dark interiors. Carolingian churches often incorporated what were called 'westworks', fortification-like twin towers on the western entrance, which are the forerunners of the highly decorated western facades of the later medieval Gothic cathedrals and which had themselves been modelled on early Christian Byzantine architecture of the kind found throughout Syria and the Holy Land. Chapter 3 explains these links fully, taking us to Syrian churches like St Simeon's Basilica and Qalb Lozeh, important pilgrimage sites in the sixth and seventh centuries. Many churches were built in this and in the Romanesque style because the pope wanted to reorganise and standardise the Catholic Church with Charlemagne's help, ensuring they were all orientated with the altar in the east and the entrance at the west.

This orientation is closely linked to the sun and the symbolism of light, which is crucial to understanding the thinking and purpose behind Gothic architecture. To see why, we must turn to the work of a late fifth/early sixth-century Neoplatonist mystic philosopher calling himself Denys (or Dionysius), who believed in the divine power of light and whose work was an important influence on Abbot Suger, as well as on many other French clerics in the twelfth century. Denys's writings (in Greek) are a collection of treatises and letters, in which he claims to be a disciple of the Apostle Paul and says that he converted to Christianity following Paul's speech in Athens to the court of the Areopagus (Acts 1722–34). However, subsequent scholarship between the fifteenth and nineteenth century found this to be a false identity. As a result, he is now referred to in scholarly texts as 'Pseudo-Denys the Areopagite' — a bit of a mouthful. All this confusion was further compounded by the conflation of both Denyses with the patron saint of France, the legendary martyr Denis to whom the Abbey is dedicated. After decapitation in Paris by the Romans, this Denys is said to have picked up his head and continued walking, which is why Notre-Dame's west facade depicts him as a headless statue calmly carrying his own head.

None of this obscure theology would matter except that the work of this mystic Denys, who scholars now agree was writing between 485 and 528, became hugely influential—first in the East, as a source of inspiration for eighth-century theologian John of Damascus, and later, especially in the early twelfth century, in the West, where it went on to strongly influence Christian theology for several centuries. The real Denys, writing in the first century, is credited with spreading the gospel into the Greek world and was said to have become the first bishop of Cyprus or of Milan or of Athens, or maybe all three, so claiming to be him was a clever move and certainly did help Pseudo-Denys's writing gain attention. For his part, Pseudo-Denys attributed his inspiration to a fifth-century Syrian monk called Hierotheos or Stephen Bar Sudhaile.[34] It is now widely accepted that Pseudo-Denys was himself also Syrian, and in his most famous work, *The Celestial Hierarchy*, he describes Christian rites such as baptism and the Eucharist that conform to the practices of the Syriac Orthodox Church.[35] From now on we shall simply call him 'Syrian Denys' for the sake of clarity.

The *Celestial Hierarchy* codex was translated into Syriac, Arabic and Armenian before being translated into Latin in the ninth century, after a Greek copy of Syrian Denys's works was given by the Byzantine emperor Michael II to the Carolingian emperor Louis the Pious. Louis in turn gave the manuscript to the monastery of Saint-Denis, where it was translated (badly by all accounts) into Latin by the abbot.[36] This abbot, Hilduin, one of the leading scholars and administrators of the Carolingian Empire, was also bishop of Paris and chaplain to Louis. Hilduin therefore had an interest in promoting the legend that Denys (the real first-century one) had travelled to Rome, then preached in Gaul and been martyred there, hence the name Saint-Denis. From this point on, Saint-Denis became the burial place for all French kings.

The thinking of Syrian Denys reached a much wider audience after one of the monks of Saint-Denis, John Sarrazin, made a new translation and wrote a commentary in 1140 on *The Celestial Hierarchy*. Abbot Suger was very attracted to Syrian Denys's light symbolism—he called St Paul 'the light of the Church and the glory of Christianity'—and drew heavily on Syrian Denys's philosophy to explain how his new Gothic abbey church was built to raise the soul to God.[37] In Suger's own words, carved into the lintel at Saint-Denis after it was rebuilt: 'For bright is that which is brightly coupled with the bright, and bright is the noble edifice which is pervaded by the new light.[38] The church shines, brightened in its middle, enlarged in our time, I, who was Suger, having been leader while it was accomplished. Great Denis, open the doors of Paradise, and protect Suger through your holy defences.'[39] Suger credits no names other than himself, but records how he summoned the top master-craftsmen and paid them well. No expense was spared in the glory of God.

Syrian Denys invented the term 'celestial hierarchy', meaning a sacred order, explaining that the liturgy was not about the texts but about the ceremonies. Only a tiny fraction of the population would have been literate and able to understand Greek anyway at that time, so this was also a way of drawing ordinary people into the church and giving them a religious and spiritual experience. The movement of the bishop, or 'hierarch' as Syrian Denys calls him, in the Eastern Orthodox tradition, as he moves down the length of the church waving his censer and wafting incense over the congregation and then back again to the altar, represents, according to Syrian Denys, God moving out in life-giving love to embrace the congregation, then drawing the congregation back again into union with Him.[40] If people can understand the symbolism behind these rituals, he believes, they will feel closer to God, and have their souls uplifted, with no need to read religious texts. Anyone who has attended an Eastern Orthodox service will have experienced its much more 'physical' attachment to ceremony. It is not just meaningless ritual—there is a back story and every movement means something.

Here is a typical passage in Syrian Denys's writings, which expresses how important light symbolism is in his philosophy:

> But the most divine knowledge of God, that in which he is known and unknown, according to the union that transcends the mind, happens when the mind, turning away from all things, including itself, is united with the dazzling rays, and there and then illuminated in the unsearchable depth of wisdom.[41]

Here then is the entire thinking behind Suger's new 'Gothic' architecture suddenly made clear. He wanted to create a space where spirits could soar towards heaven and union with God and be raised up, just by entering the building. Light streaming in through tall, high windows represented God and His presence, so people instinctively looked upwards and felt their spirits uplifted, indeed exactly as most people do feel on entering a Gothic cathedral. In Abbot Suger's day, of course, the term 'Gothic' was not used—that

Choir of the Basilica of Saint-Denis in the northern suburbs of Paris. Built in 1144, it is the earliest example of Gothic architecture and its design was heavily influenced by the writings of Denys, a late fifth/early sixth-century Syrian mystic philosopher.

only came into common use in the nineteenth century when people were looking to call it something other than 'the French style'.

Suger began the rebuilding works by demolishing the dark, heavy Carolingian towers (known as the westwork, since it was always on the west), and then redesigned a lighter, thinner-walled west facade pierced by a rose window to let in more light above the entrance portal. He must have been directing the masons himself, explaining the effect he was trying to achieve, since he had seen at the Benedictine Abbey of Cluny how this taller, lighter style was possible through use of the pointed arch, as Chapter 3 will clarify further. The rose window was set within a square frame, the first such example in Christian Europe but a common feature in Islamic architecture, where decorative designs, be they windows or blind arches (decorative arches set onto a solid wall), are often set in rectangular or square panel frames (*alfiz*, from Arabic *al-hayyiz*, container), as we shall see in Chapter 4.

Suger's western extension at Saint-Denis was completed in 1140, and rose windows of this kind were soon imitated at Chartres and went on to become a dominant feature of Gothic cathedral facades in northern France. After finishing the western facade Suger supervised the reconstruction of the eastern end and the choir, which he wanted to be suffused with as much light as possible. To achieve this, he further developed the pointed arches he had already seen at the Abbey of Cluny. He also drew inspiration from the lighter ribbed vaulting that the masons already knew about through its use at the Cordoba Mezquita extensions of the late 980s, as Chapter 5 will explain in detail. Suger added large upper-storey clerestory windows, first seen in early Christian churches in Syria, as explained in the next chapter.

The final section of Saint-Denis was reworked by a later abbot, Abbot Odo, in the thirteenth century when the old, thick-walled Romanesque nave was transformed from a dark space, using the latest techniques of Rayonnant Gothic. The walled area was reduced to an absolute minimum and the windows were made as tall as possible, interrupted only by the slenderest stone tracery bars at the tops of the stained glass. This Rayonnant style had been first developed at Chartres, whose stained glass windows were seen as 'rays' of coloured light radiating out from the centre of the rose windows—the cathedral itself has been described as a museum of stained glass.

At Saint-Denis a pair of rose windows, 12 metres in diameter, were added in the transepts. It was the first time that all these elements were combined to produce a new synthesis, distinctive in the lightness of the structure and in the size of the stained glass windows. It was consecrated in 1144 in the presence of the king, and from that point on, the new style, with its tall pointed

West facade of Burgos Cathedral, which shows strong similarities with the west facade of Reims Cathedral.

windows, became the prototype for churches and cathedrals across northern France, embodying, thanks to Abbot Suger, France, its glory and its monarch. Over fifty Gothic cathedrals were built in France across the twelfth century— such as Saint-Denis, Noyon, Senlis, Laon, Notre-Dame de Paris, Tours, Soissons, Strasbourg, Bourges and Chartres—and the thirteenth century— such as Rouen, Reims, Bayonne, Auxerre, Amiens, Toul, Metz, Beauvais, Sainte-Chapelle de Paris, Clermont, Évreux, Limoges, Aix, Orléans and Saint Maximin la Sainte Baume. It was a race to build ever higher. Every city wanted one. From France the Gothic cathedral was introduced into England, where over twenty-five were built, and into Portugal, Belgium and the Netherlands during the twelfth century, and then into Germany, Spain and northern Italy in the thirteenth century.

Top masons were in constant demand and a team of masons from Chartres for example, under reconstruction from 1194 to 1250, was summoned to Strasbourg to replace the old Romanesque cathedral with the new style. A German master builder called Erwin von Steinbach was entrusted with construction of the facade of Strasbourg Cathedral in 1277. He and two of his sons, and after them his grandson, all became heads of the Strasbourg guild of stonemasons, whose influence subsequently extended as far as Bavaria, Austria and the Italian borders.

Wren talks of the new Gothic architecture and its dramatic spread, mentioning specifically the cathedral of Burgos (1221–60) as a model of Saracenic architecture:

> from all the marks of the new architecture it can only be attributed to the Moors; or what is the same thing, to the Arabians or Saracens; who have expressed the same taste as in their poetry; both the one and the other falsely delicate, crowded with superfluous ornaments, and often very unnatural; the imagination is highly worked up in both; but it is an extravagant imagination; and it has rendered the edifices of the Arabians (we may include the other Orientals) as extraordinary as their thoughts. If any one doubts of this assertion, let us appeal to any one who has seen the mosques and palaces of Fez, or some cathedrals in Spain, built by the Moors: one model of this sort is the

church of Burgos; and even in this island there are not wanting several examples of the same.[42]

The first stone was laid in the presence of King Ferdinand III of Castile and Bishop Maurice of Burgos. The pope granted 'indulgences', reducing the punishment for sins, to all contributors to the construction, and the architect is thought to have been brought to Burgos by Bishop Maurice himself after his trip to France and Germany to arrange the king's marriage to Elisabeth of Swabia. By 1240, a named master architect, Master Enrique, was employed. Enrique was later appointed for the construction of León Cathedral, also called 'the House of Light'. He must have been familiar also with Reims Cathedral, the west gable at Burgos showing many similarities with the west facade at Reims. Construction was completed in twenty years, an extremely short time span.

The story of the medieval confusion between the three Denyses gives an indication of how widely people moved around from country to country in the early centuries of Christianity despite the great distances involved. For ordinary people who were not travelling for reasons of business and trade, the main purpose was pilgrimage, encouraged by the Catholic Church as a virtuous deed for which the pilgrim would earn indulgences to mitigate his sins. He could even buy an indulgence from the Church for loved ones, to ensure their passage to heaven, a practice eventually outlawed in 1567. In medieval Europe the most renowned and popular pilgrimage was to Santiago de Compostela. The UNESCO map of the pilgrim routes to Compostela shows clearly how all the great cathedrals of the post-Crusader period, built first in the Romanesque and later in the 'Gothic' style, are on the route. Burgos and León were the last two in northern Spain before Compostela itself, hence the need to complete them quickly. The reason for the massive archway entrance of the Romanesque style was to cope with the arrival of huge crowds.[43] The pilgrimage was also a natural route along which guilds of masons would pass.

Pilgrims first started making the Santiago pilgrimage as early as the ninth century. By the early twelfth century it was a highly organised affair, attracting pilgrims who were no longer able to make the traditional Catholic pilgrimage to Jerusalem after the wars waged by the Crusaders made it more dangerous.

The plain Cistercian nave [left] contrasts with the elaborate Manueline sacristy [right] of the Alcobaça Monastery, Portugal, reflecting the slide from simplicity into decadence.

The important point to note is that the cult of Santiago, St James the Apostle, was sponsored above all by the super-wealthy Benedictine monks of Cluny, the most powerful monastic house in the Western world at that time, in delib- erate defiance of the hierarchy and dominance of the pope, who was of course sponsoring pilgrimages to St Peter's in Rome. It was a case of competing apostles. For Cluny, Spain was a second Holy Land and the Benedictines were keen to ensure that pilgrims were channelled through the major Cluniac shrines along the Camino. As the numbers grew, so did the wealth of the Abbey. At all the stopovers, board and lodging was required, and a range of merchandise was on offer, such as fine robes for the wealthy, or simple scallop shells for the poor, a souvenir according to your means to prove you had been on pilgrimage. The Muslim annual Hajj to Mecca is the same even today, a source of great wealth for the Saudi authorities, though Islam has no system of indulgences.

According to early medieval tradition, St James the Apostle was the first Christian evangeliser of Spain. His body had been miraculously transported back to Spain from the Holy Land after his martyrdom in Jerusalem in the year 44 and was 'rediscovered' at the end of the eighth century, by which time almost all of Spain was under Muslim rule—all except this extreme northwest corner of Galicia. It can hardly be accidental that the shrine was set up here, in what remained a bastion of Christianity and from where the Reconquista of Spain would later begin. In 997 the early church was reduced to ashes in a raid by Al-Mansur, *de facto* ruler of Andalusia. The booty of the church treasure was shared with his vassal Christian lords, while the bells and doors were carted back to be reused in a mosque, but the saint's tomb and relics were left untouched and undesecrated. During the Reconquista the bells and doors were recaptured and brought back again, while the Christian nationalist orthodoxy in Compostela promoted the iconography of St James as the Moorslayer—Santiago Matamoros—through paintings of the Apostle mounted and armed, trampling Muslims underfoot.

Politics and rivalries were never far away in twelfth-century Europe, with acrimonious theological polemics and mutual recriminations between the various orders.[44] The Alcobaça Monastery for instance, both the first and the largest in Portugal, was founded as a gift from the first king of Portugal, Afonso I, to the French abbot Bernard de Clairvaux, who formed the Cistercian order as a stricter breakaway from the Benedictines, whom they thought had lost their rigour. They wore white robes as opposed to the Benedictines' black robes. It was part of the king's strategy to assert his authority over the lands he had recently taken back from the 'Moors', or the 'Saracens' as Wren would have called them. The Cistercian monks started off 'on the straight and narrow' with a strict new regime of vegetables and manual labour in the fields, but within two centuries their wine cellar was the size of most churches and they diverted a river straight into the kitchen to cook fresh fish. Overindulgence was moderated by the size of the refectory door. If you were too fat to fit through it, you were meant to fast. In practice, there was a second, wider door further along.[45] The architecture reflects the progression from stern simplicity to luxuriant decadence; the first Gothic foundation of the Cistercians begun in 1178 was described as 'the architecture of light',[46] while the early-sixteenth-century sacristy added by King Manuel I to celebrate the Age of Discovery proudly crowns the elaborately carved vegetal foliage framing the doorway with the Portuguese coat of arms.

The 'fat waddling monks'[47] got their comeuppance in the various civil wars and revolutions against the wealth and power of the Church when many cathedrals across Europe were turned to secular uses such as garrisons, prisons and even stables.

Gothic was not born out of nowhere like some miracle. The political and religious power struggles of the late eleventh and twelfth centuries, not just between Muslims and Christians but also between the various Christian orders and the pope, created circumstances conducive to the building of many great cathedrals, not simply as emblems of faith but also as statements of authority by the monarchy and/or the Church. As for the Gothic style itself, it arose out of a succession of influences that started in the Middle East and Muslim Andalusia, blending with the earlier extant Byzantine and Romanesque styles; it was a creative combination, a synthesis. But it also needed the right combination of wealth and faith to bring such massive constructions to fulfilment.

All these strands in the complex story of how the Gothic style evolved in Europe via its contacts with the Middle East and the Islamic world will be treated in more detail in the coming chapters.

The sheer richness of Byzantine Christianity in Syria can be seen in the Dead or Forgotten Cities of Idlib Province, providing a missing link to the Romanesque architecture of Europe. Over 2,000 churches built from the local limestone are still spread across the remote, hilly terrain.

This decorative use of symbolic discs on a door lintel in the Dead City of Serjilla displays a high level of Syrian stone craftsmanship. Predating the sculptured ornamentation of Byzantium, it is evidence of a gradual transition from pagan temples to early Christian worship .

3

THE PRE-ISLAMIC INHERITANCE

Pagan and Early Christian Architecture in Syria

What we today call 'The Middle East' was the birthplace of civilisation. The transition from hunting/gathering to farming first took place here, followed by the building of the first temples and settlements, the first metalworking, the first kingdoms, the first empires and the first alphabet. What had shaped these civilisations' ideas of how to build? Clearly there were the constraints of their surroundings, the climate and the readily available building materials. Adaptation to climate in the Middle East was always key, because of the need to create effective shade, for example, and to manage a limited water supply successfully.

Once the pressures of survival were not so acute, there was time for reflection. People attempted to make sense of the world. The earliest known construction, one which has turned our understanding of man's early history upside down, is Göbekli Tepe (literally meaning 'the pot-bellied hill' in Turkish), 25 kilometres north of Urfa in what is today southeast Turkey. It dates back to the tenth millennium BCE. Far from being a village or a community, it seems to have been conceived as a type of religious sanctuary made up of several stone circles carved with animals. The individual blocks are enormous and the effort involved in dragging them to the top of this hill, which would have overlooked the grazing lands of the Fertile Crescent, is mind-boggling. Why did they bother? What drove them to spend so much time and energy in building this construction when they didn't even live there? It was to be another 2,500 years before they started to build communities where they lived and settled. The earliest known settlement is at Çatalhöyük in Central Anatolia, dated to around 7500 BCE.

It appears that the drive to build edifices as places of worship or tombs is what first forced people to become inventive. The wheel, the lever—such devices were essential to enable ambitious building projects to appease the gods and for a ruler to stake their claim to power.

In *Parentalia* in the Appendix of Architecture Tract I, Wren writes: 'Architecture aims at eternity'.[1] He had an instinctive understanding of man's purpose in his first constructions and his own approach was, in a way, equally reflective, as is revealed when he continues: 'Geometrical figures are naturally more beautiful than other irregular; in this all consent to a law of nature. Of geometrical figures, the square and the circle are the most beautiful, next, the parallelogram & the oval.'[2]

Göbekli Tepe, man's first temple, is round—a highly significant and deliberate choice. The circle was the sun and the moon, those inexplicable forces in the sky that man observed but did not understand. One appeared at night, the other in the day, at opposite ends of the sky. The mysterious cycles on which their lives depended, that brought heat and light, then sometimes rain out of dark clouds, led early humans to create a series of gods based round these primordial forces. The earliest gods were therefore always representations of the sun, the moon and the weather, usually thunder, bringer of rain, as rain tends to come in the form of storms in the Middle East.

Wren knew that, whereas the Eurocentric understanding of the world in England in his day looked only as far as Ancient Greece for its inspiration in building models, there was much more that predated Greek civilisation further east. He understood that the ancient Greeks had built upon what came before them, and that after Alexander's campaign to conquer the East, the Hellenistic legacy had been the blending of Persian and Mesopotamian influences in all fields, including art and architecture. So the stunning mosaics at Zeugma, in modern southeast Turkey, at the frontier of what was the Western Roman Empire, have decorative ziggurat patterns round their edges, and contain many abstract and vegetal patterns, all of which are pre-Islamic. Wren wrote:

Architecture aims at eternity; and therefore the only thing uncapable of modes and fashions in its principals, the Orders.

The Orders are not only Roman and Greek, but Phoenician, Hebrew, and Assyrian; therefore being founded on the experience of all ages, promoted by the vast treasure of all the great monarchs, and skill of the greatest artists and geometricians, every one emulating each other; and experiments in this kind being greatly expenceful, and errors incorrigible, is the reason that the principles of architecture are now rather the study of antiquity than fancy.

Beauty, firmness, and convenience, are the principles; the two first depend upon geometrical reasons of opticks and staticks; the third only makes the variety.[3]

Wren describes how he thinks that classical porticoes are derived from trees for shade, around temples and forums:

People could not assemble and converse, but under shade in hot countries; therefore, the forum of every city was also at first planted round with walks of trees … starting off with columnades in timber at first, then stone, to stop fire and make more durable as ambitions grew.

The Corinthian column and capital, he writes, forms the peak of 'grace',[4] representing the flowering of branches at the top of the trunk.

Of the Seven Ancient Wonders of the World, it is not surprising that all are spectacular architectural creations of lands bordering the eastern Mediterranean and further east.

Wren's early thinking on this theory of 'columns as groves of trees' is evident in the decorative detailing of the interior of the Sheldonian Theatre, one of the first buildings he designed in Oxford. The arcaded gallery is supported by fluted wooden columns painted brown and topped with Corinthian capitals highly foliated with acanthus leaves in typical classical style. Even the supports for the brass balustrade handrail round the gallery are in vegetal designs, reminiscent of exotic fruits opening up in ripeness and fertility. The cornice just below the ceiling is designed to look like branches or foliage supporting the roof or ceiling. An overhanging dentil frieze runs round the wooden colonnade carved with the classical egg and dart motif, dual symbol of life and death, as found in early classical sites such as Palmyra, together with the Palmyra rose carved just above it. Wren was aware of Palmyra, for in his *Parentalia* he mentions it, using its Arabic name 'Tadmur', thought by the Greeks and Romans to refer to *tamar*, meaning 'dates'. Maybe he had even dreamt of it, for his son tells us that while in Paris escaping the Plague, Wren was taken ill in 1665, with fever and kidney pain: 'He dreamt he was in a place where palm-trees grew, and that a woman in a romantick habit reach'd him dates. The next day he sent for dates, which cur'd him of the pain in his reins.'[5]

Each civilisation built with whatever building materials were to hand, hence the early Mesopotamian cultures learned to make bricks baked in the sun from the local mud mixed with straw. Stone quarrying came later under the Assyrians and the Egyptians, once they developed the tools to cut the stone. Stone was readily available and abundant in the Near East, and the people of the Levant were masters of building with stone in a tradition that went back thousands of years.[6] Their stone walls were dry-bonded and they hardly ever used brick and concrete. Rare examples like the brick-built sixth-century Byzantine palace of Qasr Ibn Wardan are exceptions.[7] The Nabateans of southern Syria and northern Jordan learnt how to make concrete-like materials, and hydraulic lime with self-cementing properties, to waterproof underground cisterns as early as 700 BCE, a technology that enabled them to survive in areas of flash floods and scarce rainfall. The ancient Egyptians discovered that adding volcanic ash to concrete allowed it to set underwater, as did the Assyrians and later the Romans, who developed the use of concrete in new and revolutionary ways. Arches, vaults and domes could be laid over moulds which quickly hardened to become rigid structures. The dome of the Pantheon in Rome is one of the most famous early examples, built of concrete using the new techniques of the second century. The Western Romans did use stone of course, but only rarely. Despite Emperor Augustus's boast that he had turned Rome into marble, most buildings just used stone or marble claddings on a bricks-and-mortar base, and in columns or decorative pediments.[8]

There were other big architectural differences between the Roman East and the Roman West. Roman temples in the East, as at Palmyra's Temple of Bel, for example, had an emphasis on vast walled spaces—open-air court-yards—which enclosed the small holy of holies room where the image of the god was housed and where only priests were permitted. This walled enclo-sure was an inviolate space for the public—the congregation—to gather and to take part in the ceremonies and rituals of the ancient Semitic religions. The earliest examples are in the Sumerian architecture of Ur and Babylon, both of them ziggurat temple complexes with large courtyards, dating back as far as the fourth millennium. Such a style was alien to both Iranian and Graeco-Roman religious architecture, where the public did not need to be accom-modated, but is found in third-millennium BCE Phoenician temples of the Levant like Amrit, just south of Tartous in Syria. As historian Warwick Ball tells us: 'The concept of a congregation is both fundamental and universal to ancient Semitic religion. … Ancient religious and architectural traditions were—and still are—extraordinarily tenacious in this region.'[9]

The tradition passed over into Christianity, with the early pilgrimage churches of northern Syria like St Simeon Stylites and Qalb Lozeh featuring large walled enclosures where pilgrims could gather safely. The Church of Bissos at Ruweiha was likewise known to be a place of protection. The Semitic tradi-tion of inviolability, also very important in the Arabian religious tradition with the *haram* or sacred enclosure, originally offered commercial advantages too, for places of worship were spaces where warring tribes or nations could come together to trade on neutral ground. The enormous open-air enclosure of Husn Suleyman, for example, located by itself high in the mountains of central Syria, boasts a temple compound measuring 134 metres by 85 metres dedicated to the local god Baal, which also served as a 'neutral tax-free market place.'[10]

When Islam, the latest Semitic religion, emerged at the end of the Roman period, this openness to the public continued into architecture with the con-gregational Friday mosque. Sometimes, as in Damascus, the same sacred space served consecutively as pagan temple, Christian church and Muslim mosque, making the transition seamlessly, with the architecture of each mani-festation simply repurposing the courtyard space.

Eastern Christianity

Near Eastern penetration and colonisation of Europe predates European colonisation of the East by a long way.[11] The Phoenicians, Persians, Syrians and Jews all established settlements and communities in the western Mediterranean long before the Greek and Roman expansion into the East, while the Arabs, Huns, Avars, Mongols and Turks did so after it. Warwick Ball tells us that substantial Syrian minorities were recorded in most of the ports of southern Spain—Malaga, Cartagena, Seville and Cordoba—from the first few centuries CE, while Syrian merchant communities were recorded in Spain and Gaul in places like Lyon, Grenoble, Orléans, Trier, Marseille, Bordeaux and Narbonne as late as 589. Ravenna, which sits on the Italian Adriatic coast and was capital of the Western Roman Empire from 402 to 476, was noted for its Syrian influence, both in its mosaics and its religion, with especially strong links to the Syrian port of Antioch.[12] All the bishops of Ravenna up till 425 were of Syrian origin, according to Abbot Agnellus's ninth-century history, the *Liber Pontificalis Ecclesiae Ravennatis*, and even Paris had a Syrian bishop in the fifth century. 'Such Syrian merchant communities became more influential,' writes Ball, 'after the adoption of Christianity, particularly in encouraging eastern forms of monasticism and the adoption of the crucifix as the Christian symbol.'[13] Ignacio Peña, in his comprehensive study of the Christian art of Byzantine Syria, tells us that the Lamb too was a favourite symbol of the Syrian Christians, carved on door lintels of fifth- and sixth-century churches to represent the expiatory sacrifice of Christ, and leading to the later Latin liturgy before communion: 'O Lamb of God who takes away the sins of the world, have mercy upon us.' Even more surprising perhaps is the fact that six popes were Syrian during the first 100 years after the Muslim conquest, and that Theodore, archbishop of Canterbury from 668 to 690, was from Tarsus, birthplace of St Paul, in the eastern Mediterranean. People often forget that the origins of Christianity and the first few centuries of its development were almost wholly oriental. The first original Christian architecture was born in the Byzantine East, not in Rome, in the fourth, fifth and sixth centuries, when Syria, Egypt and Byzantium were the centres of the civilised world. With the Latin West in full decline and Europe beset by social upheaval, emigration and unstable governance, Europeans looked east for inspiration in their art and architecture. St Adomnán, for example, abbot of Iona Abbey and biographer of the abbey's founder St Columba (521–97), tells us that Irish monks went to Syria to familiarise themselves with its monastic architecture, while Laurence Bishop of Siponte in Italy wrote to Emperor Zeno asking to be sent artists to decorate the churches of his Episcopal villa, a request duly granted.[14] All over Gaul in these crucial early centuries of Christian architecture there were monuments and funerary structures showing clear Syrian influence, such as the tombstone of Boethius, Bishop of Carpentras, dated 604.

Syria was annexed to the Roman Empire in 64 BCE, but despite its role as an economic powerhouse and the provider of several auxiliary regiments, the study of Syria as a Roman province has received far less attention than that of provinces such as Italy, Greece, Gaul and Egypt. Recent research has however highlighted how many pagan gods, such as Jupiter Dolichenus and Jupiter Heliopolitanus, and local fertility goddesses like Atargatis originated in Syria, and how Syrian influence penetrated all levels of Roman society, from private soldiers and ordinary citizens to priests and imperial families.[15]

Septimius Severus, Roman emperor from 193 to 211, was of Phoenician blood. He was born in Leptis Magna (today's Libya) and died in Eboracum (today's York in Britain). He married a Syrian, Julia Domna, daughter of the high priest at the famous Temple of the Sun in Emessa (today's Homs), who bore him two sons, both of whom went on to become emperors themselves. All would of course have been dark-skinned. The Roman Empire was one of history's most successful melting pots, generally tolerant of foreign cultures and religions, with no apparent prejudice regarding race or skin colour, so long as the empire's subjects did not challenge its rule. Julia Domna is said to have lobbied her son Caracalla to issue his famous decree of 212, which extended Roman citizenship to all free men of the empire, so that all distinctions between Romans and provincials were swept away. No 'go back where you came from' mentality, though of course some Romans felt otherwise, such as first-century poet Juvenal, who complained in his *Satires* that 'the Orontes has long since been emptying into the Tiber'.[16] Every Roman knew the Orontes was the Syrian river that flowed into the sea at Antioch.

The Sun Temple at Emessa was the major shrine in the region, drawing in many pilgrims, and with them much wealth for the town and its elite. The high priest's family was one of the oldest and richest families in Syria. Septimius, as a Phoenician, was familiar with the concept of an abstract deity—the sun god was represented on early coins as a black, conical-shaped stone, thought to have been a meteorite—just as he was familiar with the concepts of rebirth and resurrection. Julia Domna, who would have taken part in ceremonies of worship to the all-powerful, over-arching sun god, was equally familiar with the idea. She was known to enjoy the company of philosophers, notably Philostratus—a disciple of the mystic Apollonius—whom she commissioned to write his famous *Life of Apollonius*, sometimes seen as the Graeco-Roman challenge to the Gospels.[17] An ascetic from Cappadocia (central Anatolia, today's modern Turkey, east of Ankara), where Christianity and monasticism spread early, Apollonius preached against the evils of alcohol, meat, wool and any luxury. He venerated animals and birds and believed in reincarnation. By the early 300s his cult following rivalled that of Christ, and some scholars believe that Julia Domna's patronage played a key role in preparing the ground for Christianity to become the dominant religion in the Roman Empire.[18] Christianity spread from the eastern Mediterranean to cities like Carthage in North Africa, and from there to other Phoenician trading cities like Cádiz in Spain, Sicily, Malta and Sardinia. The first state to proclaim Christianity as its state religion is thought to have been the Kingdom of Edessa (now modern Urfa in southeast Turkey), reputedly the birthplace of Abraham.

All this is relevant to the early architectural development of the very first churches, which, unsurprisingly, began with the repurposing of the pagan temples. Syrians have always been open to religious experimentation and syncretism, and the eventual local transformation of the abstract sun god into one omnipotent god merged almost seamlessly into the cult of Christ, which was early on associated with the sun, hence the halo, just as early statues of the sun god had halos of the sun's rays.[19] Since the sun god temples faced east, towards the rising sun, it was a natural transition for early churches, following the concept of the resurrection, to remain orientated to the east, with the altar in the far east, where the sacrificial altar had always been. Ball writes that the sun cult 'not only paved the way for Christianity, it was later actually grafted on to Christianity to make it more palatable, and to this day Christian churches still face the direction of the rising Sun.'[20]

We are reminded of Abbot Suger, Syrian Denys and the new 'architecture of light' at Saint-Denis in Paris. Religious sites have always been repurposed in this way in line with changing beliefs in the eastern Mediterranean. The key Syrian mosques—like the Umayyad mosques at Damascus and at Aleppo—are among many examples. The monastery church of Deyrulzafaran, near Mardin in today's southeast Turkey, built at the time of the Byzantine emperor Anastasius (491–518), sits on top of a 2000 BCE temple dedicated to the Assyrian sun god Shamash. Like a kind of crypt below the current twelfth-century church, it is the pride of the monks there who show it off to all visitors. The east-facing window through which the pagan worshippers used to watch the sun rise was blocked up when it became a church, and the flat ceiling is made up of beautifully crafted enormous stone blocks fitted together without mortar.

The monastery of Mar Gabriel, east of Midyat, is the largest and oldest of the monasteries of the Tûr Abdin region in southeast Turkey. It has a community of around twenty monks and nuns and a bishop who is head of the Syrian Orthodox Church in Turkey. The monastery has two churches, and the older, very dark Virgin Mary church (no longer in use) boasts a fine but windowless ancient brick dome, built in around 512, a rare extant prototype for Justinian's brick-built dome of Hagia Sophia completed in 537. In the dome behind the altar of the main Forty Martyrs church are beautiful Byzantine mosaics in gold, green and blue, courtesy of generous donations from Anastasius and strongly reminiscent of the mosaics two centuries later in the Damascus Umayyad Mosque, with similar motifs of trees and vine scrolls, images of paradise and fertility. The bishop is justly proud of their recent restoration by a Frenchman, following lengthy struggles to raise the funding. The most exotic of all the Tûr Abdin churches can be found in the village of Khakh (Syriac Hah, Turkish Anıtlı). It is called Al-Hadra, The Virgin, or Meryemana, Mother of God, a graceful second-century Eastern Roman tomb topped with a decorated pyramid dome and two storeys of elegant, blind semi-circular arches.[21] The doorjambs and lintels bear Eastern Roman palm-tree decorations, garlands, pearls and acanthus leaves, and the whole ensemble illustrates well how blended the Roman and Byzantine cultures were and how similar their imagery was, which Islamic architecture then inherited and developed further.

Three Roman emperors were ethnically Syrian—Elagabalus, who ruled from 218 to 222, Severus Alexander from 222 to 235, and Philip the Arab, emperor from 244 to 249. Philip even allowed Christians to practise their faith openly. Some writers believe he was the first Christian emperor, based on his behaviour and tolerance of Christians, though he did not proclaim his faith publicly. The region of Greater Syria also provided seven popes, starting with Simon Peter, the later St Peter, he of St Peter's in Rome, who was born in Bethsaida, province of Syria.

When the Roman emperor Aurelian came east with his armies in 273 to quell the rebellion by Zenobia, queen of Palmyra, he credited his victory to the sun god, at whose temple he had prayed in Emessa before marching the final 150 kilometres across the Syrian desert to Palmyra. After a brief siege, Aurelian let loose his mercenary troops—a mix of Celts, Goths and tribal desert Arabs—who plundered and pillaged the rebellious desert oasis caravan city. Aurelian carried the treasures from the Temple of Bel—some of which came from as far afield as Palmyra's trading partners India and China—back to Rome, where he adorned his new sun temple with them. The temple's dedication ceremony (*natalis*) to Sol Sanctissimus (the most sacred Sun) took place on 25 December in the year 274. Aurelian went on to promote the cult of Sol as an official Roman national cult, elevating the sun god to the status of one of the most powerful deities in the empire and thus boosting the sun god further in the transition to the cult of Christ.[22] When Constantine the Great instituted the law in 321 making Sunday the day of rest, he explicitly linked it to the veneration of the sun, not the Christian God.[23] Christian and pagan art and architecture co-existed throughout the fourth century, and it took more than 300 years after the time of Christ before what we would recognise as churches began to appear.[24]

The world's earliest building thought to have been a Christian church, dated to 231, was found at Doura Europos in Syria, a multi-cultural, multi-ethnic and multi-religious trading city on the Euphrates right on the frontier of the Eastern Roman and the Parthian empires.[25] It is just a small square-shaped courtyard house, identified as a 'church' because of the murals of

Adam and Eve and depictions of various New Testament miracles and a shepherd tending his flocks. It was discovered in the 1930s by American excavators and then transported to Yale University Art Gallery in the USA.

The impressive synagogue at Doura Europos, dated by an Aramaic inscription to 244, makes a very informative comparison to this roughly contemporary church, for it demonstrates very clearly how much more artistically advanced and sophisticated Judaism, with a much larger following than Christianity, was at that time. Judaism too had originated in the Roman province of Syria. Christianity had started out under Jesus and his Jewish disciples as a sect within Judaism, but disagreements arose in the early years between Peter and Paul about whether or not the religion should be open to the Gentiles—non-Jews. Peter was in favour of keeping it for Jews exclusively, while Paul preached inclusivity for all, as explained in the Acts of the Apostles, an approach that won out.

Excavated at the same time as the church, the much larger synagogue was covered in highly coloured wall frescoes of scenes from the Old Testament with patriarchs and prophets in their human form, contravening Talmudic tradition. Painstakingly disassembled and recreated in a specially built annexe at the Damascus National Museum (where they are still viewable today), the synagogue frescoes are thought by art historians to show the origins of later wall paintings in the Romanesque churches of Europe. A total of sixteen temples were found at Doura Europos, a city in which Parthians, Greeks, Macedonians and Palmyrenes, be they pagans, Jews or Christians, all worshipped side by side in apparent harmony. The eastern Parthian influences evidently had a deep effect on the Mesopotamian Jews living here, freeing them from the traditional Talmudic injunctions against human and pictorial representation. The paintings were in near perfect condition as a result of being buried under the sand—Doura Europos was thereafter nicknamed the Pompeii of the Desert. Thanks to these frescoes, scholars have been able to trace the development of religious iconography before the Roman Empire officially converted to Christianity in 380 under Theodosius I.

The first Christians were a mix of ethnicities, blended, representative of the local population. The advent of Christianity was not a momentous revolution but a gradual transition, adopting many elements from the Eastern Syrian sun cult. Constantine was the first emperor to be fully persuaded of the potential benefit to the empire, and to himself as ruler, of enlisting the help of a Christian god,[26] but the empire's inhabitants did not suddenly become Christian as a result. Instead, Christianity grew slowly from a small base in Palestine. Periods of official imperial indifference and tolerance alternated with more or less severe persecution. Unsurprisingly given that Christianity is a Middle Eastern religion, much of the early development of the Christian church took place, thanks to fervent proselytising, in what are the present-day countries of Syria, Turkey, Israel, Palestine, Egypt, Jordan and Lebanon. It was in Antioch (modern Antakya, now in Turkey, but part of Syria till 1939), a vibrant and cosmopolitan centre known for its lavish lifestyle as depicted in the famous Roman mosaics now on display in its museum, that the followers of Christ were first called Christians, as the Bible tells us in Acts 11:26. The foundation of the church of Antioch is described in some detail in Acts 11:19–25, leaving us in no doubt of the city's significance in early Christianity. It is in Antioch, we are told, that Paul, after his conversion in Damascus, and his fellow disciple Barnabas begin their preaching, living in the city for a whole year and converting a large number of people. It is from Antioch also that the pair then set off towards Europe, converting Cyprus and much of Anatolia; according to Acts 9:15, Paul was God's 'chosen instrument to bring my name before pagans and pagan kings'.

By the time that Constantine the Great was finally baptised, on his death-bed, by Eusebius, bishop of Beirut, much of the groundwork had clearly already been laid by earlier events. Sun temples were adapted to Christian practices, continuing their orientation to the east. The official tolerance of Christianity with the Edict of Milan in 313 then gave Christians the right to practise their religion publicly within the Roman Empire and meant that churches could now be built openly, rather than being discreetly hidden within houses. The first purpose-built churches began from this point.

Part of the essential backdrop from then on—and as ever the architecture reflects the politics in visible form—was the start of what we now call the Byzantine Empire, which created a unique synthesis in art and architecture from the blending of the existing pagan Eastern Roman Empire and the new Christian religion. Its beginning is dated from the founding by Constantine the Great between 324 and 330 of his new imperial capital, the 'New Rome', renamed Constantinople, on the site of the ancient Greek colony of Byzantium. Constantine did not build a conspicuously Christian city. Its religious focus was his own circular mausoleum, next to which his son later built the cross-shaped church of the Holy Apostles in the 350s.[27] The first Hagia Sophia was only built in 360, also by Constantine's son, but there is no evidence that these churches had Christian mosaics on the walls of the type found from the fifth and sixth century onwards. Walls instead were covered with marble revetments, plaster, and painted and gilded stucco in decorative patterns.[28] Constantine, we are told, denuded virtually every city in the empire of its pagan statuary to adorn his new Rome.[29] In Rome itself it was the same, and his daughter Constantina, a devout Christian, has no Christian imagery on her porphyry sarcophagus, nor any obviously Christian content in the mosaics of her mausoleum, built c. 350, where there are instead scenes of harvest, with birds and fruit pickers among the vine scrolls. Though Christ did call himself 'the true vine' (John 15:1) and his followers fruitful branches, and likened the kingdom of heaven to a vineyard, these scenes were, to a contemporary public, much more associated with Bacchus, god of wine,[30] and vine iconography was in any case already common well before Graeco-Roman times in cultures of the ancient Near East and Ancient Egypt.

Theodosius I declared Trinitarian Christianity—the orthodox belief in the Holy Trinity—the official religion of the Roman Empire in 380. His death in 395 marked the all-important split between the Western Roman Empire, ruled from Rome, and the Eastern Roman (or Byzantine) Empire, ruled from Constantinople. The Arabs referred to the Byzantines as 'Al-Rum', meaning Roman Christians, and the Byzantines still called themselves 'Romans'. Latin remained the official language of the Byzantine army but the language spoken by most was Greek, used as a *lingua franca* to unite the many ethnic groups of the eastern Mediterranean populating Rome's eastern provinces. This has led many European writers, especially in the nineteenth century, to call the Byzantine Empire 'Greek', when in practice it was very ethnically diverse. Wren himself uses the term 'Greek refugees' when he describes the people returning from the Crusades with the Italians (see Chapter 2), in fact meaning Greek-speaking Byzantine Christians (their ethnicity unknown but who were almost certainly dark-skinned) who decided to leave the eastern Mediterranean and go to Europe with the returning Crusaders, taking their skills with them.

When the Western Roman Empire and Rome itself collapsed in 476, Constantinople became the largest and wealthiest city in Europe, and the influences upon it were wide and varied, including from the Roman Latin culture, the Egyptian Copts, the Thracians, Macedonians, Illyrians, Bythinians, Carians, Phrygians, Armenians, Lydians, Galatians, Paphlagonians, Lycians, Syrians, Cilicians, Misians, Cappadocians, Persians, and later the Arab Muslims. The Greeks composed only a relatively small portion of this multi-ethnic empire, and most of the Byzantine emperors themselves were not ethnic Greeks.

Constantinople continued as capital of the Byzantine Empire till 1453 when it fell to the Ottoman Turks under Mehmet the Conqueror. The Eastern Roman Empire was not only more densely populated and more agriculturally fertile than the Western Roman Empire had been, it was also becoming ever more powerful economically, thanks to its flourishing centres of trade. Rome's decline and fall was gradual, weakened by internal divisions, and hastened by the advent of 'the barbarians', Germanic tribes including the Goths who migrated from the north.

As part of his decision to reach an accommodation with the rising power of the Christians, Constantine sent his mother, Helena, already a convert, to Jerusalem to look for Jesus's tomb. With the help of local bishops she identified the spot believed to be Calvary, the crucifixion site. Two hundred years earlier, Emperor Hadrian had founded a Roman colony in Jerusalem and built a temple on the site over a cave containing a rock-cut tomb. In around 326, Constantine ordered the temple to be dismantled and replaced with a church, which led Helena and the bishops to discover the tomb and identify it as the burial place of Christ. Shrines were constructed around both holy sites—the site of crucifixion and the site of Christ's tomb. They were initially separated by a courtyard and later filled over the centuries with further constructions, along with many reconstructions, to become what is today known as the Church of the Holy Sepulchre. In 614 the shrine was destroyed by the Persian Sassanids, then rebuilt. It survived the Arab conquest of 638 but earthquakes in the tenth century destroyed it again. Then, in 1009, the Fatimid caliph Al-Hakim (996–

1021) set the tomb of Christ on fire. By the twelfth century Jerusalem and the Holy Sepulchre had receded from the memory of the Byzantine court in Constantinople. The Fatimid destruction was not mentioned. Jerusalem was simply thought of as 'a great city … built long ago … now in ruins through the passage of time'. Yet the continuing visits of pilgrims are well documented.[31]

In the early days of Christianity, the architecture of the Church of the Holy Sepulchre housing these two holy sites in the heart of Jerusalem naturally became very influential as a model for future churches. The concepts behind their design need to be explored and understood, since they form the basis of the church architecture that later found its way into Europe.

The religious associations of the Roman word 'basilica' came into usage in Byzantine times. Originally it meant an entirely secular structure, usually alongside the marketplace or forum, an oblong hall flanked with one or more colonnaded aisles, like the Greek *stoa* which ran alongside the *agora*. Modern writers have sometimes described it as a shopping mall. The roof was gabled and at the far end opposite the entrance was a raised platform from where an official might make public announcements. Sometimes that platform was covered by a semi-circular apse topped by a semi-domed vault, so that the authority figure could sit on his seat or 'cathedra' sheltered from the elements. At the other end was an atrium or gathering hall, the evident forerunner of the vestibule or narthex of what became the sacred basilica. For the Romans, this basilica was a building for public assembly or audiences, a space where meetings of local officials and legal hearings could take place, an administrative centre. It was not somewhere the divine emperor himself would generally have visited, but rather where his officials conducted business. Constantine did not see recognition of Christianity as a reason to surrender his own divinity.[32]

No one has been able to trace one single continuous line of development from the early Christian basilica to the domed, centralised space of Hagia Sophia in Constantinople, probably because there were multiple influences. Unlike other contemporary religions, it was a requirement of Christianity that all followers should gather together in church to take part in religious services, to share communion and to hear sermons and readings from the Bible. In ancient temples the cella was small and only ever accessible to the high priests, so when temples were converted to churches the cella was often removed, as happened at the Parthenon in Athens for example.

The earliest known dome shapes to appear in manmade structures were domed tents used by the Achaemenid Persian kings for royal audiences. The shape always had celestial associations thanks to the sun and the moon— eternity, the heavens, the power of the skies—which the Persian kings are thought to have used to project their own power and divinity. Alexander the Great adopted the practice, which was then inherited by Roman emperors, coinciding with their cult of 'divinification'.[33] The semi-domed apse in early basilicas often carried mosaic depictions of Byzantine emperors. The emperor's image was then promoted to occupy the main central dome, and gradually transformed into the image of Christ Pantokrator, 'the All-powerful'.

The Graeco-Turkish scholar of Constantinople architecture Stéphane Yerasimos tells us that the earliest known centrally organised domed churches in Constantinople date from just before Justinian came to the throne in 527, yet he also mentions that at the end of the fourth century, while longitudinal basilicas were still being built in Constantinople, 'numerous churches with a central or octagonal floor plan, with both niches and exedras, were already being built in Syria.'[34] He does not explore further, since his field is limited to Constantinople.

The Dead or Forgotten Cities of Syria

What Yerasimos is overlooking, however, is the largest group of ancient architectural monuments in the world, literally thousands of churches, extraordinarily intact, thanks to their fine limestone construction, concentrated in the hills west and southwest of Aleppo in northwest Syria. Known in Syria as 'the Dead Cities' or 'the Forgotten Cities', the top forty sites were belatedly recognised by UNESCO as worthy of World Heritage Status in June 2011, after the usual lengthy assessment—at least five years—completed just before the outbreak of the internationalised Syrian civil war. Most of the sites today fall within the province of Idlib, under rebel control at the time of writing, and subject to regular airstrikes by the fighter jets of the Syrian Assad regime and the Russian state.

Some have suffered damage, but most are still standing. Under the heading 'Ancient Villages of Northern Syria', the UNESCO website reads:

> Some 40 villages grouped in eight parks situated in north-western Syria pro-
> vide remarkable testimony to rural life in late Antiquity and during the
> Byzantine period. Abandoned in the 8th to 10th centuries, the villages, which
> date from the 1st to 7th centuries, feature a remarkably well preserved landscape
> and the architectural remains of dwellings, pagan temples, churches, cisterns,
> bathhouses etc. The relict cultural landscape of the villages also constitutes an
> important illustration of the transition from the ancient pagan world of the
> Roman Empire to Byzantine Christianity. Vestiges illustrating hydraulic tech-
> niques, protective walls and Roman agricultural plot plans furthermore offer
> testimony to the inhabitants' mastery of agricultural production.[35]

Having been fortunate enough to explore these north Syrian churches many times since the 1970s, most recently in 2010, I believe that they consti-tute a vital and largely unexplored link to the Romanesque churches of Europe. Not only that, but without the missing link of these churches, it is impossible to understand how Hagia Sophia itself, that most influential of domes, model for so many later European churches, was built. There is always a back story.

The sheer richness of Byzantine Christianity in Syria is overwhelmingly evident to anyone who has visited the so-called Dead Cities. With over 800 sites existing in total, and over 2,000 churches, the Dead Cities are spread over a hilly, sometimes mountainous area. Most are at an altitude of 400–500 metres, with some on outcrops as high as 800 metres.

Churches outnumber all other types of building in the ancient Roman East. Their sheer proliferation suggests a very devout population, testimony to the new Christian civilisation with all the confidence and energy of its early days, while there are maybe fewer than a hundred pagan temples in total.[36] The temples were massive and grandiose in ambition and statement, while the churches started out small and modest. Many centuries were to pass before Christianity would boast in the great Gothic cathedrals of Europe the same 'arrogant self-confidence, an unquestioning belief in the superiority of its own culture' as the pagan temples.[37] But what the early churches lacked in scale they made up for in quantity, with some small towns, like Al-Bara, boasting as many as five. Even villages, however small, had their own well-built stone church. This was to some extent because there was no shortage of money or patronage, but also because Christianity emphasised the importance of collective worship. People were invited to come and participate, so they needed a meeting place, a village hall equivalent. In Roman times this was the basilica or market hall, which from then on became the standard church form with a central nave and two side aisles.

Back in 2010, the days when Syria featured among the top ten destinations for European holidaymakers, talks were ongoing with the Syrian Ministry of Tourism to promote the area for walking holidays with home stays in the villages, a scheme which would have brought much-needed income to poor rural areas and encouraged local employment. Today it is virtually impossible for foreigners to visit the region, making it all the more important to highlight what a key role this forgotten region played in the evolution of churches in Europe.[38] Scholars like Emma Loosley Leeming have also been able to make connections between this region and the evolution of early churches in Georgia,[39] uncovering another route through which architectural influences no doubt passed.

UNESCO only focuses on the key sites, but all the settlements share the same characteristics. The scarcity of wood meant that most permanent buildings were made of stone, the prevailing local white limestone. Most buildings were two-storey, and only the supporting beams were made of wood, long since rotted away, just leaving the overall stone structures. Many of the simple village houses are made out of irregular polygonal blocks put together by relatively unskilled local people, with no mortar between the stones, but the more ambitious churches and public buildings show a surprisingly high level of stone craftsmanship, with careful well-crafted masonry displayed in decorative detailing on door lintels, arches and uprights, mouldings and cornices of facades, even mosaics, in a style we now associate with the sculptured ornamentation of Byzantium. As Howard Crosby Butler, former professor of architecture at Princeton University, tells us, this ornamentation is where Syrian 'native ingenuity', as he calls it, moves away from Hellenism, by intro-

The so-called 'drooping spaghetti' design seen here at Baqirha is unique to the Dead Cities of northwest Syria. Draped like festoons framing the windows and doorways, it is evidence of a distinct local style, unconnected to earlier classical motifs.

ducing into the architecture 'a host of charming motives, more Oriental than Classic, which unquestionably add much to the beauty of the Syrian style … the decorative use of ornamental and symbolic discs are, perhaps, the most salient features that represent the native genius.'[40] One such unique pattern can be found in the remote and rugged Jebel Barisha region (hiding place of the ISIS leader Abu Bakr al-Baghdadi, where he blew himself up in a tunnel during the US-led targeted raid on 27 October 2019), and has been nick-named 'drooping spaghetti' by modern writers thanks to its long curving lines. Butler called it 'mouldings as festoons and their spiral terminations.'[41]

These early settlements and their churches provide a missing link between the simple house church at Doura Europos and San Vitale and Hagia Sophia, the elaborate basilicas of Ravenna and Constantinople. They are the essential backdrop and give us a permanent record in stone of that all-important gradual transition from pagan temples to early Christian worship. They were first 'discovered' by French archaeologist and diplomat Count Melchior de Vogüé, who in between postings devoted his life to studying and cataloguing the archaeological remains of the Holy Land and Syria, providing detailed drawings which recorded for posterity how the buildings looked in the 1860s. In the introduction to his impressive two-volume *Syrie centrale: Architecture civile et religieuse du Ier au VIIe siècle* (1865–77), he sees parallels between these Syrian churches of the Byzantine East and medieval French religious architecture, specifically mentioning the exterior facade of Notre-Dame at Pontorson and the interior nave at Silvacane Abbey in Provence. Like all European scholars well into the twentieth century, he assumed their demise was the result of the 'Muslim invasion'. It was not till the 1950s that the French archaeologist Georges Tchalenko concluded that their demise may have predated the Arab incursions in the seventh century and occurred gradually during the sixth century, when Byzantine trade routes were disrupted by wars with the Persians.[42]

The wealth of the settlements was founded on the export of wine and olive oil, with olive and wine presses still clearly in evidence in even the smallest of villages. Tchalenko speculates that the first olive presses were set up in the second century under the auspices of the temple authorities, and later expanded considerably under private ownership when the price of olive oil boomed in the fifth century. Tchalenko's theories were further developed by historian Hugh Kennedy, who explained the decline as a gradual societal change, with rural decline exacerbated by severe bouts of bubonic plague, famine, and earthquakes.[43] Kennedy also makes the point that there is no evidence of town planning on the classical model during the fifth and sixth centuries. The streets are narrow, winding and uneven, showing their evolution to be local.[44] The fact that the inhabitants gradually emigrated—economic migrants as we would now call them—towards the Mediterranean coast and the port of Antioch makes it highly likely that their traditions, skills and crafts moved with them.

Serjilla and Al-Bara are two of the earliest settlements, with churches, monasteries, baths, meeting halls, wine and olive presses, tombs and necropolises. Private villas were designed around courtyards, some with up to sixteen rooms where one extended family would live together, inward-looking for privacy, exactly as we associate today with the Arab style of secluded family living, no windows to the outside. Tchalenko found that some of the earliest churches were in fact adapted from these private villas, a logical continuation of the house church of Doura Europos and one that would make sense as the easiest kind of adaptation to make while Christianity was gradually taking hold. It would also explain why the early Syrian churches here, in remote settings well away from urban settings and influences, did not have apses but had flat east walls. Some more minor settlements have other unique architectural features, such as the six-storey tower in Jeradeh with overhanging latrines (or defensive constructions), possibly for a stylite hermit living at the top.

The cult of the ascetic, a holy man who wanted to live away from the urban centres, seems to have played a big role in attracting the population of northwest Syria towards Christianity. Perhaps the loss of pagan gods left a vacuum that was then filled by the preachings of early holy men like St Simeon Stylites,

St Simeon's monastery shrine, northwest of Aleppo, was completed by 490, becoming the Santiago de Compostela of its day. No place of worship in Europe rivalled it until the cathedrals of the eleventh and twelfth centuries.

whose cult grew exponentially during the fifth century, drawing crowds of pilgrims from far and wide, even as far afield as Britain,[45] as his reputation grew. Son of a local farmer, Simeon seems to have been something of an attention-seeker, moving out of the monastery at Telanissos where he had lived as a boy and into a nearby cave where he would draw crowds by burying himself up to the chin in summer, wearing spikes which drew blood and chaining himself to a rock. The more outrageous his behaviour became, the more

This remaining stump of St Simeon's pillar, progressively chipped away at by souvenir-seeking pilgrims over the centuries, was heavily damaged by Russian airstrikes in May 2016.

people flocked to see him, ask him questions and seek miracles. He became a kind of oracle, and just as in pagan times pilgrims would visit shrines like the Sun Temple at Emessa to seek answers to their prayers, pilgrims now began to travel long distances to consult Simeon. Claiming the need to get closer to God and to escape for solitary contemplation, he began to stand on a pillar, first 3 metres tall, then 6 metres, then 11 metres and finally 18 metres, with a railing round the top to stop him falling off in his sleep. The Greek for pillar is *stylos*, hence his name Simeon Stylites, Simeon of the Pillar. Once a week his disciples would bring him food, climbing precariously up to him by ladder, a scene immortalised in a fragmentary local mosaic, last seen in the Hama Museum. There is also an immaculate and intact mosaic of St Simeon atop his pillar which can still be seen in St Mark's, Venice. Simeon's life was written up by Theodoret, the bishop of Cyrrhus, the closest metropolis. By the time of his death in 459 he had spent thirty-six years on his pillar, preaching to the assembled pilgrims twice a day, warning against the dangers of earthly vices and describing the heavenly rewards that awaited the virtuous.

Simeon's body was carried off to the port of Antioch by 600 troops sent by the emperor, to take the standard route by sea to the Byzantine capital of Constantinople. The Byzantine emperor Leo I (ruled 457–74), who was the first emperor to be crowned by the patriarch of Constantinople, authorised the financing of the vast complex of St Simeon's Basilica on top of the hill where Simeon had lived, centred around Simeon's pillar. Construction began in c. 480 and was completed by 490. At that time it was the largest and most important religious establishment in the world. Covering an area of around 5,000 square metres, it could hold some 10,000 worshippers, more than Notre-Dame de Paris or the Benedictine Abbey at Cluny. It held that accolade for nearly fifty years till the Hagia Sophia was completed in 537 at the end of an incredibly intense five-year period. No place of worship in western Europe rivalled St Simeon's until the eleventh and twelfth centuries.

Most of the hilltop complex is still standing, including the impressive arched gateway at the foot of the hill marking the ceremonial entrance. Known as the Via Sacra or the Pilgrims' Path, it is a wide dirt road that snakes ceremonially up the hill to arrive at the baptistery where pilgrims would immerse themselves in the walk-through font for mass baptism. A 200-metre-long courtyard then led across to the main church complex, whose magnificent triple-arched facade is a clear forerunner of what we in Europe now call Romanesque. Its grace and elegance, the delicacy of its proportions, and the golden limestone in which acanthus leaves are carved make it one of the most striking sights in all of Syria. Capitals with acanthus leaves blown in the wind were a common motif in fifth and sixth-century Syrian churches. In the Cathedral of St Helena (later Madrasa Halawiye) in Aleppo, six such capitals are still extant on marble columns, and the same distinctively Syrian swaying acanthus leaves can also be seen at Notre-Dame de Paris, in the central nave, on the capital capping the first pier on the left.

In another heralding of styles to come, fragments of stained glass have been found scattered on the St Simeon hilltop and analysed by scholars in order to track how their composition changed from the Roman mineral soda type to the Islamic plant ash type from the eighth century onwards. The same compositional range found at St Simeon's was seen in some of the twelfth-century blue cathedral glass from northern Europe, and blue glass from the windows of Abbot Suger's Saint-Denis Basilica has also been analysed to show 'clear Islamic compositions'. Glass that is slightly high in potash and magnesia suggests the practice of adding plant ash to cullet (recycled glass), a technique which originated in the Middle East after the Islamic conquest. The construction of St Simeon's was an imperial project undertaken on a huge scale, with architects and skilled artisans brought in from the two Byzantine centres of Constantinople and Antioch. Before construction work could even begin, a vast esplanade had to be created on top of the hill, large enough to accommodate the gigantic complex.

Simeon's pillar sits at the centre of a courtyard, surrounded by four separate basilicas, making a quatrefoil, a centralised cross-shape. The pillar was reduced to a misshapen stump, chipped away at by souvenir-seeking pilgrims over the centuries, but even this stump was then ignominiously blasted off its base by a Russian airstrike in 2016. A wooden dome originally covered the courtyard above the pillar, fitting with the idea that the dome should cover the holiest place in the complex. It collapsed in 528 as a result of an earthquake and was not replaced. The eastern basilica was the largest of the four, the one most used for religious ceremonies, while the others were mainly used as assembly halls for the pilgrims to gather. The altar end of the east basilica has beautiful floral stone-carved vegetal decoration in its semi-circular protruding wall, the first time such a protruding apse—known as a chevet—was used in church architecture, apart from at Qalb Lozeh, as we shall see.

The chevet became a typical feature of early Syrian church architecture from this point on, always topped by a stone semi-circular dome. It passed into Europe, where it was often found in Benedictine and Cluniac cathedrals. In England the only complete example is the eastern chevet of Westminster Abbey. The constraints of space on the esplanade, together with the need to incorporate Simeon's holy pillar, may well have led to the first quatrefoil, cruciform design, a natural adaptation to the plot available. St Simeon's became the first church centred beneath a dome.

As with all popular shrines, it was a major money-spinner for the authorities who controlled it, and the Byzantine officials were well aware of its potential. At the foot of the complex a large town grew up in the fifth and sixth centuries to provide accommodation and commercial services for visiting pilgrims, full of hostels where the pilgrims could stay and bazaars where they could buy souvenirs. The town continued to thrive on the pilgrim trade right through the period of Arab rule, with the monastery retaining its independence. The early Muslims did not interfere, respecting Christian monasteries and the learning they represented.[46] When the cult of Simeon died out in the twelfth century the buildings were abandoned, leaving them much as they look now. Nonetheless, the two-storey stone-built inns make an impressive collection of ruins.

It was, however, not only about money. The reasons for this level of imperial investment were also political. As Butler clarifies:

> Constantinople was the civil, but not at this point the ecclesiastical head of Syria, and the architectural aims of Constantinople and of Syria were almost diametrically opposed ... Antioch, ever proud of the Apostolic origin of her see, was jealous of any interference from the political capital. Her patriarchs were often opposed to the patriarchs of Constantinople; the emperors alone had power to control them, and often failed in their attempt to do so.[47]

The Eastern Church was at that time in a state of turmoil over internal disputes about the human and divine natures of Christ in what was known as the Monophysite schism. Monophysites believed Christ had just one nature, the divine. Our mystic monk from Chapter 2, Syrian Denys, was caught up in these controversies and is considered by some to have been a Monophysite himself. But the Council of Chalcedon, convened in 451, in its wisdom and representing the orthodoxy, decided that Christ had two natures, unmixed and unchangeable but at the same time indistinguishable and inseparable, and this remains the view of the Greek Orthodox, Roman (Catholic) and Protestant churches to this day. The issue may not seem very important, or even comprehensible, and in practice it was more of a slogan by which the churches of East and West denounced each other. But after the Council of Chalcedon, Monophysitism became a heresy in the eyes of Constantinople and Rome, and the churches of Egypt, Syria and Armenia were denied both spiritual communion with the Western church and military aid.

The emperor in Constantinople hoped that if he identified himself with the hugely popular St Simeon, the Byzantines' orthodoxy and power in this region would be reinforced against their rival Monophysites in Antioch. It is a situation which calls to mind the Benedictine monks of Cluny described earlier, who in their rivalry with Rome invested in the Santiago de Compostela shrine and channelled pilgrims along the way of the Cluniac shrines. In both cases, the pilgrims passing along the routes would be exposed to local influences, both cultural and architectural, and bring back new ideas to their own communities.

The true forerunner of Romanesque architecture can still be seen at the remote church of Qalb Lozeh, high in the mountains of northwest Syria at 670 metres. Olives continue to be grown in the surrounding area, and the name Qalb Lozeh, Arabic for 'heart of the almond', suggests something like the 'crème de la crème'. Today tobacco is a major local crop. Tchalenko estimated that the church was constructed in c. 450, observing that many of its innovative architectural features were refined and enhanced in the great basilica of St Simeon a few decades later, and that it was therefore likely built within Simeon's lifetime. The church, standing at the edge of a small village of the same name, is surrounded by a walled compound. Because its size is far

The twin-towered facade of Qalb Lozeh, flanking a monumental entrance, is the world's best preserved example of early Romanesque. Dated to around 450, it still stands on a hilltop in Idlib, northwest Syria.

too big to serve the local population, Tchalenko believed it must have served as a stopping place for pilgrims en route to see St Simeon preach from his pillar. The most striking aspect of the church is its twin-towered facade flanking a large decorated round-arched entrance, the classic Romanesque style which appeared in Europe at some point between the sixth and twelfth centuries—scholars are divided as to the exact date—because the technology of vaulting to create domes as seen in Rome in the Pantheon and the Domus Aurea seems to have been lost in Europe during this period, which is generally referred to as the Dark Ages. The other element seen clearly here is the southern porch entrance, a feature which also carries over first into Romanesque and then into Gothic architecture, as at Canterbury Cathedral. Commenting on the south facade at St Simeon's Basilica, Melchior de Vogüé wrote: 'It is impossible not to recognise in this construction the origin of all the elements that constitute the porch of the Romanesque churches.' There was a break in stylistic continuity, and these churches of northwest Syria provide the missing link as to the origins of the Romanesque style, together with the Norman buildings of Sicily, explored later in Chapter 7.

The huge round arch between the towers has largely collapsed today. The logic behind its size was to do with its function as the welcoming entry point for large volumes of pilgrims, as befits any important shrine. It was an idea that stuck in the later versions, and the highly decorated large rounded arch entrance became the defining characteristic of Romanesque. Pilgrims needed to feel they were arriving at somewhere suitably grand and special at the end of their long and arduous journey.

Stepping inside Qalb Lozeh, you are immediately struck by the massive square pillars, which divide the church into a central nave and two side aisles. This is the first time that square pillars, which would later go on to become a classic feature of European Romanesque, are seen inside a church, instead of the round columns that were usual in the Roman era. Indeed the arches throughout the church are the typical round regular shape, and another feature common in Roman basilicas is the set of smaller windows, separated by small elegant columns and regularly arranged to rise above the arches running longitudinally along the central nave. These are known as clerestory windows, and their purpose, apart from giving extra height to the nave, is to let in light from above, since it was too difficult, given the thickness of the walls, to create windows lower down.

This is a key characteristic of Romanesque—dark interiors with thick walls—and here at Qalb Lozeh we can see many other features: the twin towers flanking the huge arched entrance; the round arches; the sturdy pillars and the decorative arcading of the arches; the clerestory windows; the protruding semi-circular semi-domed apse (chevet) complete with its classical decorative cornice and framing in vegetal patterns. The overall design is symmetrical, each side a mirror of the other, with recurring threes supposedly to represent the Holy Trinity, though this was probably a post-rationalisation since the secular Roman civic hall from which the basilica evolved was likewise divided into a central area flanked by two side aisles. At Qalb Lozeh the trinity concept is taken further, as beyond the three aisles, there are three pillars on each side of the nave, three windows in the apse, three windows in the twin tower facade and three arches dividing the nave from the side aisles.

The prevailing wisdom of local people is that the heavy, thick, squat columns at Qalb Lozeh were designed to reinforce the structure, to enable it to bear the heavy weight of the stone roof and upper clerestory arches, and to help it withstand earthquakes, wreckers of so many structures in this region. One solid block of stone is at least 2 metres wide, itself hugely heavy, to bear the weight of the clerestory structure and the stone roof above. Some stone roofing slabs are still *in situ*, showing how the roof was flat above the side aisles. The roof above the nave was made of wood, long since disappeared. The giant capitals of the pillars are heavily carved in an attempt to lighten their appearance, but their strength can be in no doubt, since the structure has stood on this Syrian hilltop for over 1,500 years with no need of buttressing or any structural repair.

Qalb Lozeh is unique, but it is not the only church exhibiting this new style. While one of the best preserved, it is just one of hundreds of churches

The graceful church at Kharrab Shams northwest of Aleppo, dated to 372, is one of the oldest in the area. As well as its fine clerestory windows, its other distinctive feature common in north Syria was the *bema*, a special seating area for the clergy that evolved into the choir in later Romanesque churches. No damage has been reported in the current war.

scattered all over these hills of northwest Syria. Other examples of churches with the twin tower facade and arched entrance can be seen for example in the sixth-century Church of Bissos at Ruweiha (the second largest church after St Simeon in the Dead Cities), or in the monastery church of Deir Turmanin, both of which are settlements within a day's walk away. The churches of Ma'rata, Karratin, Al-Bara and Beyho also had two towers flanking their entrances but are now in a heavily ruined condition. Warwick Ball suggests the first prototypes for the twin tower may go back to an ancient Semitic practice, then copied by the Romans, of temples with two sacred 'high-place' towers joined by a classical pediment, as at the Temple of Baal-Shamin at Si' in southern Syria and at Baalbek in modern Lebanon.[48] The early Christian architecture of Syria then incorporated it into their church facades.

The Church of Bissos can also boast the only example in Syria of a domed saint's tomb made from cut stone, the precursor of domed Muslim saints' tombs which can be found all over Turkey, the Middle East and North Africa. The inscription above the door reads in Greek: 'Bissos, son of Pardos. I lived worthily, died worthily and rest worthily. Pray for me.'[49] The Basilica of St Sergius at Rusafa about two days' walk away was built between 480 and 500 and has the same heavy pillars as at Qalb Lozeh but supporting a much larger structure.

One of the earliest churches is Kharrab Shams northwest of Aleppo, dated to 372, in an isolated rural setting, a structure of wonderful grace and elegance, its five nave arches topped by ten clerestory windows still in near perfect condition. Kharrab Shams is also among the first settlements where the church has in its naves, tucked up close to the altar at the eastern end, a feature known as a *bema*, which went on to develop into what we today call the chancery of a church or cathedral, that is, the area where the choir and pulpit are situated. It is a slightly raised stone platform in the upper nave with seating for the clergy, arranged in a horseshoe-shaped stone bench. It passed into early church architecture from Jewish synagogues, where it was the raised area from which the rabbi delivered readings. In ancient Athens it was the orator's platform, and the word itself derives from the ancient Greek meaning 'platform' or 'step'. In Syria in the fifth century it evolved further, as at the large Rusafa pilgrim church of St Sergius, where the main *bema* seated twenty-eight and was covered with a central baldachin,[50] flanked by more complex additional (hierarchical) layers of seating of the type that our mystic philosopher, Syrian Denys (so influential in the 'light' theories that shaped later Gothic architecture), would have been familiar with when writing his *The Celestial Hierarchy*.

The readings and hymn-singing were led from the *bema*, like our pulpit and choir in the same location, in the nave, directly in front of the altar. The congregation was not permitted to enter the *bema*. St Ephrem the Syrian (c. 306–73), known as 'the Harp of the Spirit', is credited with writing the first church music, over 400 hymns, which would have been sung in Syriac from *bemas* like this. The most famous was entitled 'Hymn to the Light', still sung today. Born in Nisibis (today's Nusaybin in southeast Turkey, separated by the modern border from its other half in Qamishli, Syria), he became its first bishop, later settling in Edessa (today's Urfa, southeast Turkey). In Ephrem's day this was also a contested border region between Assyria under the Sassanids and Mesopotamia under the Romans. A champion of women in the church, Ephrem is said to have trained all-female choirs to sing his hymns set to Syriac folk tunes. He used his hymns, full of rich poetic imagery from the Mesopotamian and Persian tradition of mystic symbolism, early rabbinic Judaism, Greek science and philosophy, biblical sources and folk tradition, to warn his flock against heresies like Monophysitism which threatened to divide the early church.[51] The faithful, he lamented, were 'tossed to and fro and carried round with every wind of doctrine, by the cunning of men, by their craftiness and deceitful wiles.' Christ's unity of humanity and divinity, he asserted, represented peace, perfection and salvation. The Syrian hymn style, with clergy and congregation chanting alternately, was adopted in Rome by Pope Damasus I, via St John Chrysostom, a native of Antioch who later became archbishop of Constantinople.[52] The Syrian Pope Sergius I (687–701) spread the veneration of the Cross and of the Virgin Mary among the Romans, both popular subjects for devotion in Christian Syria. Literary sources tell us that the earliest known Marian festivals had their origins in Antioch around 370.[53]

Taken all together, these Syrian churches represent collectively the transition from late antiquity to early Christianity from the fourth to the sixth centuries. This critical 200-year period has been under-researched by scholars, who prefer to focus on the later Byzantine centuries, or maybe on the later Crusader period, if they are Western, and on the Islamic period if they are scholars from the Arab world. Governments too have neglected these areas, both in Syria and in places like Georgia, partly because the churches of this period are often in remote rural areas, partly because it is natural to focus on more touristic single spectacular sites such as Palmyra or Krak des Chevaliers. It is no accident that Syria's premier sites of Damascus, Aleppo, Palmyra and Bosra all achieved their UNESCO World Heritage Site status back in the 1980s, while the Dead Cities had to wait till 2011 for their belated recognition.

Work began on what would become the great landmark building of the East, the Hagia Sophia, in 532 on the orders of Emperor Justinian, in the heart of the Byzantine capital, Constantinople. But as we are consistently finding, nothing just appears by magic, and in the case of Hagia Sophia it is essential to see the Dead Cities as the great field of experimentation that took place over the 200-year period immediately before.

The residents of the settlements lost their prosperity gradually once the trade routes began to change over the course of the long, drawn-out wars with the Persian Sassanids. As they made their way west to the Mediterranean coast at Antioch in search of new livelihoods, there would have been among them stonemasons and craftsmen who had worked on the churches and learnt the practical skills, as well as the equivalent of what were called *mechanikoi* in Greek, the closest thing to what we would today called an architect. These were people who had an understanding of loads and stresses, like building engineers, though probably not yet of the complex geometry required to hold up vaults and domes—that would come later, thanks to the Golden Age of Arab, Jewish and Turkic mathematicians and scientists working together under the sponsorship of enlightened caliphs in the two rival courts, the western Mediterranean Umayyad court of Cordoba and the Eastern Abbasid court of Baghdad's, as explored in Chapters 5 and 6.

The decline of these communities in the early sixth century coincides exactly with the construction of Hagia Sophia, and whilst it will always remain impossible to prove, it is entirely possible, even likely, that some of the stonemasons who worked on Hagia Sophia came originally from the Dead

Cities of Syria. Byzantine craftsmen in the eastern Mediterranean were itinerant, just as they were in medieval Europe with their early guilds, and indeed later under the Mamluks of Egypt, bringing in new skills and ideas to new places as they travelled from project to project, often requisitioned by a new incoming ruler—or powerful abbot like Suger—wanting to make his mark. Highly skilled masons were always in demand.

The timing of the Dead Cities' decline also coincides with the spread of Romanesque across Europe, the first distinctive architectural style to be found all across the Roman Empire, even after Rome itself fell. There were regional variations, depending on local building materials and climatic considerations, but the overall concept and design was immediately recognisable as a Romanesque style, uniquely identifiable. As Warwick Ball concludes: 'The thousands of pilgrims who flocked each year to the holy sites of the Near East easily explains the transference back to Europe.'[54] Butler, at the end of his detailed study of the early churches in Syria, goes further, concluding that:

> Syrian art must have played a distinct part during the early centuries of Christianity in building up the culture and art of Western Europe, for, at the time when Syrian architecture was at its height, France and Italy were thronged with Syrians—both merchants and ecclesiastics—who held prominent positions in the economic and religious life of the West. ... We do not read about it in the ecclesiastic accounts, largely because their craft and its work were not considered important enough to be recorded, still we know that the itinerant builder was a common figure in the trade. Syrian workmen must have helped to restore the reviving art of architecture in Europe.[55]

The cult of St Simeon was known to be especially popular in Gaul; a fragmentary statue engraved with the name of Simeon was found in a seventh-century tomb in Poitiers, evidently a souvenir carried back by a pilgrim, and in Seine-et-Marne there is even a tiny village called Saint-Siméon to which we today can make a pilgrimage. Its church, rebuilt in the nineteenth century, is said to contain a relic of the saint, and also boasts a stained glass window of Simeon on his pillar, two frescoes depicting his life and a couple more statues identified with him. Three Templar commanderies have been identified around the village, suggesting that members of the Order, who would have been very familiar with Antioch and its hinterland, wished to conserve the saint's memory in their French homeland.[56]

In England Romanesque was generally known as Norman architecture, and the style persisted into the twelfth century when it was gradually superseded by 'Gothic'. Large numbers of Romanesque churches and cathedrals across Europe were rebuilt in the new highly popular style with its distinctive pointed arches, following other societal and political changes, which we will explore in more detail in the coming chapters.

The blend of Roman and Byzantine architecture from which Romanesque gradually evolved was neither Roman nor Greek, since, as we have seen, neither the Roman Empire nor the Byzantine Empire was mono-cultural. Both were for centuries multi-cultural and multi-ethnic, with emperors originating from many provinces all across the eastern Mediterranean, including Syria. Finally, as the place where both Judaism and Christianity began, ancient Syria was the natural field of experimentation with early religious architecture and styles, as the synagogue and first known church house show us in Doura Europos, the multi-religious trading city on the Euphrates in today's Syria. Since 2011, the site has sadly suffered extensive damage from illegal digging and ISIS looting during the Syrian civil war.

The early development of Christianity was accompanied by several centuries of serious divisions, both theological and political, and from the start of Justinian's reign in 527 began violent persecutions of non-Orthodox groups, particularly of the Monophysites, sometimes resulting in civil war. Orthodox pilgrims coming to the shrine of St Simeon from Constantinople for example were sometimes massacred by local Monophysites. The Monophysites finally founded a dissident church, known as the Jacobite Church after their leader, the monk Jacob Baradeus, which still has numerous followers in Syria and Lebanon today.

These schisms in the Christian church helped pave the way for the extraordinarily rapid spread of Islam across the lands of Egypt, Syria and Iraq. The Muslims armies met a series of weakened and incohesive Christian communities who readily accepted Muslim administrative control since they were allowed to practice freely whichever branch of Christianity they favoured. The

Arabs did not know written Greek, so had to rely on translations made in the early days by Nestorian Christians, who thus became the link between Hellenism and Islam, with much material having to pass first through a Syriac translation into Arabic. It was a situation to be paralleled later in Spain, when Arabic texts had to pass through a Castilian dialect into Latin so that Europeans could read them.

Throughout Muslim rule till the twelfth century, the pilgrimage to St Simeon's Basilica by Christians continued. The site was periodically sacked and looted—most notably by Fatimid armies from Egypt in 1017—and sometimes used as a fortress because of its commanding position, but never closed to pilgrims. At the time of writing in early 2020, it is in use as an observation post by the Turkish Armed Forces.

Domes and Cloisters of Southern Syria

Architectural religious developments in the southern reaches of Syria, an area known as the Hawran which also covers today's northern Jordan, evolved slightly differently to the northern Dead Cities. At Bosra, the ancient capital of the Roman province of Arabia from 106 CE (and before that the new Nabatean capital after displacement from Petra), Christians built a centralised church, known as the Cathedral of Bosra, dated to 512. Bosra also had an inner octagonal colonnade thought to have been modelled on Nabatean circumambulatory temples,[57] since the reverence for relics and ritual circumambulation was common in pagan, Christian, and later Islamic forms of worship.

Today only the foundations remain, but these reveal that the dome was 36 metres in diameter, comparable to the first version of Hagia Sophia.[58] A series of these domed centralised churches were built in the first half of the sixth century, such as the remarkable St George's at Ezra (515), still in use as a church today. At Ezra the base of the dome is ringed with a series of little windows, the earliest extant prototype of the lighting system fully developed later at Hagia Sophia. All these early Syrian churches may have taken their original inspiration from the fourth-century centralised Great Church (Domus Aurea) at Antioch, of which no physical trace remains today but whose architecture we know from written descriptions.

One final type of Christian building relevant to the future architecture of Europe in this pre-Islamic era of the Near East is the cloister. The only tangible evidence for the existence of a true cloister layout before the Age of Charlemagne, the Carolingian dynasty, comes from a few isolated Syrian monasteries of the fifth century, such as the convent of Saints Sergius and Bacchus at Umm al-Surab in what is today northern Jordan, not far from Dera'a and the southern Syrian border, in the Hawran. They are contemporary with the churches of northern Syria like St Simeon, none of which have such cloisters, but ground plans and 3D reconstructions at Saints Sergius and Bacchus using photogrammetric surveys have shown a square, highly symmetrical open paved courtyard attached to the church, ringed with about twenty rooms laid out over two storeys and colonnaded on all sides. Another convent simply referred to as Ad-Deir (Arabic, 'the monastery') in the same region has a similar semi-galleried courtyard attached to the flank of a church. The ubiquitous and plentiful building material here is the volcanic black basalt, with a complete absence of timber, which is why the ruins are still relatively intact. The only disturbance they have suffered, apart from earthquakes, is down to local Druze who settled here in the eighteenth century, inhabiting the ruins and adapting them to their needs, till they left in 1936.[59] As to the question of how this monastery design found its way into Europe, the answer lies in the Merovingian dynasty, France's oldest kingdom, ruling from the fifth century till 751, most of whose international trade was conducted with the Middle East. The Merovingians were overthrown by the Carolingians with the consent of the papacy, and Walter Horn tells us, in his authoritative study 'On the Origins of the Medieval Cloister', that Merovingia was full of Syrians.[60] These early Syrian cloisters therefore give us another link to Europe and to Romanesque architecture. As De Vogüé explained: 'The first artists arriving from the East at the request of the crowned barbarians were the inheritors of those fertile schools of which only Syria has preserved the monuments and whose influence, at the time of its greatest activity, surpassed the reduced limits of the Province (of Gaul).[61]

4

THE FIRST ISLAMIC EMPIRE

The Umayyads in Syria (661–750)

This chapter is by far the longest, a reflection of the remarkably large number of stylistic innovations that appeared during Islam's first century and which had a direct bearing on subsequent architectural developments in Europe. Since much of this material may be new to readers unfamiliar with the Umayyad Dynasty, this chapter is divided into sub-headings based mainly round the key buildings themselves, to help explain as clearly as possible.

Arab Presence in the Middle East Before Islam

It is important to note that many Arabs already inhabited parts of the Fertile Crescent well before the Islamic conquests began in 634, contrary to what is perhaps the common perception that Arabs swept out of the Arabian Peninsula for the first time in the seventh century. The Umayyads, a Meccan clan that would go on to conquer Syria and an offshoot of which would then go on to rule Spain from the eighth till the early eleventh century, already owned land there, thanks to their extensive trading links.[1] By organising caravans north to Syria and south to Yemen, they had been able to develop economic and military alliances with the nomadic tribes through whose historic territories they were carrying their goods. A powerful clan from within the tribe of Quraysh that lived in and controlled Mecca (the Prophet Muhammad was himself from a less powerful branch of the Quraysh), the Umayyads were descended from Umayya ibn Abd Shams (literally 'Umayya, son of the Sun-worshipper'). They went on to become the first hereditary dynasty of Islam, and the only one to rule over the entire unified Islamic world of its time, before rival dynasties splintered off.

As a powerful clan in their own right, the Umayyads had initially opposed the new monotheistic religion of Islam but converted before the Prophet's death and were rewarded with appointments to positions of power— Mu'awiya for example, founder and first caliph of the dynasty, had been given the governorship of Syria, so already had the loyal support of the Syrian Arab tribes, his allies from trade. Even before Islam, the Quraysh derived their power from their role as guardians of the sacred sanctuary in Mecca and as protectors of pilgrims who visited it annually. The original clansman from whom they were all descended, Umayya himself, had responsibility for over-seeing Mecca's military affairs during the regular wars against unruly nomadic tribes. This gave the sons of what came to be known as the House of Umayya considerable military, logistical and organisational skills,[2] which they were able to demonstrate fully in the rapid Arab conquests of North Africa, Spain, and Central Asia (today's Iraq, Iran, Uzbekistan, Tajikistan, Kyrgyzstan, Kazakhstan, Armenia, Georgia and even Sindh province in Pakistan).

Scholars such as David Graf[3] have studied the early epigraphy, which proves that Arab presence on the Fertile Crescent goes back as far as the seventh and sixth centuries BCE. Hellenistic sources rarely talk about the local indigenous population, but we now know that well before the arrival of Alexander in 333 BCE there was a cultural melange in Syria and the Levant—the 'Holy Land' in other words, where Christianity and Judaism both began—which was pre-dominantly Edomite and Arab, with only a sprinkling of Jewish, Phoenician, Persian-Parthian, Babylonian or Egyptian names. The region of Greater Syria—Al-Sham in Arabic—included Jerusalem, the Sea of Galilee and the Dead Sea right up till the end of the Ottoman Empire and the First World War. Archaeological evidence shows that many Arabs were not nomads, but part of the sedentary population, an essentially agricultural society engaged in the cultivation of fields and orchards. The harvest months—Tammuz and Ab—are still the Arabic (and Hebrew and Turkish) names for July and August used today, derived from the local Syriac Aramaic language, with their origin in the Assyrian calendar.[4] While Greek had been the written language of government since Alexander, Aramaic was the *lingua franca* of the Near East, with multiple dialects both written and spoken, such as Nabatean, Palmyrene and Syriac. A comparable parallel might be medieval England, for example, where court proceedings would take place in English but be recorded in Latin.[5]

The Old Testament of the Bible talks about the Philistines, the people who gave their name to the Palestinians (though the Palestinians in fact claim their descent from the Canaanites), but recent DNA tests on the origin of the Philistines shows that they came from islands in the Aegean, thereby adding weight to a long-held view that the Philistines are the mysterious 'Sea People' who arrived in the eastern Mediterranean over 3,000 years ago.[6] People moved around in the ancient world, just as they do in the modern world, and usually for the same reasons—war, overpopulation or better economic opportunity. Within two centuries the DNA of the Philistines was the same as that of the indigenous population, suggesting they were readily absorbed and had integrated well.

Again and again we are seeing that a strategic trading crossroad like the Middle East was always going to be a multi-cultural, multi-ethnic mix of all the earlier civilisations who had ruled there—the Babylonians, the Sumerians, the Arameans, the Assyrians, the Persians, the Egyptians, the Greeks, the Romans—each building on the inventions and innovations of the one before, be it through warfare or through cooperation.

Relations with Christians

When the Prophet Muhammad died suddenly in 632 without leaving or nominating an heir, it was left to his successors, the caliphs (Arabic *khalifa*, meaning successor), to fulfil his mission of spreading the new religion of Islam. Booty was certainly part of the incentive, as Syria to the north was known to be a land of fertility and wealth, but wholesale slaughter of the indigenous population was never endorsed. On the contrary, according to early Muslim historian Al-Waqidi (747–823), explicit instructions were given to the Muslim fighters:

> When you encounter the army of Unbelievers then do not flee for whoever flees, loses the battle. When you have obtained victory do not slay any small children, old people, women or pre-adolescents. Do not approach the harvests or trees. Crops should not be burnt nor fruit trees cut. Do not slaughter any animal which is impermissible. Do not break any agreement which you make with the enemy and after peace do not tear up your treaties. Remember that you will also meet such people who have undertaken monasticism in their monasteries, thinking this to be for the sake of Allah. Do not interfere with them for as long as they choose this isolationism—do not destroy their monasteries and do not kill them. You will also meet such a Satanic people who worship the Cross. They shave their heads in the middle to expose their skulls. Cut off their heads until they accept Islam or pay Jizyah disgraced. Now I place you in Allah's hands, may He protect you.[7]

In Jerusalem under Arab rule, the Church of the Holy Sepulchre remained a Christian church, with the early Muslim rulers protecting the city's Christian sites. It was prohibited to use churches as living quarters or to destroy them, unlike the Persian Sassanids who had set fire to the Holy Sepulchre church in 614 and captured the True Cross. The caliph Umar is said to have issued a decree prohibiting Muslims from praying at the Holy Sepulchre.

In Damascus, when the Muslim armies under their commander Khalid ibn al-Walid entered the walled city in 634 after a short siege, surrender terms were agreed differently, and the Cathedral of John the Baptist, the central Christian shrine of the city, was used by both Christians and Muslims for the best part of a century. Historian Hugh Kennedy tells us there were many similar agreements to share religious premises recorded in the contemporary sources. Like many city churches in Syria, it had been built on the site of a former pagan temple, in this case an Aramean weather god called Hadad who was then morphed into Zeus by the Greeks and into Jupiter by the Romans. Adaptation to local religions was the obvious way to keep the indigenous population content, but the gods underlying the Graeco-Roman temples were always essentially Semitic. Many of the elements of the Jupiter temple and the processional way leading to it were, and indeed are, still extant, and when Christianity took hold they were simply absorbed into the cathedral. Muslims and Christians shared the same entrance on the south side of the former temple. Once inside the temple precinct the Christians used the space to the west, the Muslims to the east. The head of John the Baptist (revered as a prophet in Islam) was said to have been buried under the cathedral, hence its name. Other churches in the city were also allowed to remain in use for Christian worship, and when the Muslims finally did rebuild the site as their main mosque, the Christians were given land for four new churches in compensation.

The First Muslim Dynasty

Damascus had long been famed as the Paradise of Syria. It was the obvious choice for Mu'awiya, already the governor of Syria, as capital of the new and rapidly expanding Islamic empire. When his son Yazid took over the title of caliph, followed by twelve further caliphs from within the Umayyad family, the first Muslim dynasty was born, lasting the best part of a century till 750.

At its greatest extent, the Damascus-based caliphate covered over 15 million square kilometres, from southern France to India and the frontiers of China, making it the fifth largest empire in history both in area and in terms of proportion of the world's population.[8] Apart from Arabic, which quickly became the official administrative language in which all documentation was issued, other languages spoken across the empire were Coptic, Greek, Latin, Persian, Aramaic, Armenian, Georgian, Berber, African and Spanish Romance, Sindhi, and the Pakrits. As well as a period of vibrancy and dynamism under new rulers who tolerated and even embraced the existing Jewish and Christian population—as long as they paid their special tax, *jizya*—it was to be a period of huge architectural innovation, as indigenous architects and craftsmen were given new impetus and energy to create new styles. The Umayyad caliphate was known for its unique synthesis of art and architecture, its blending of crafts and craftsmen from Eastern and Western origins.[9]

The Dome of the Rock

Some Western historians consider this iconic building—Islam's first architectural and political statement of its supremacy over a former Christian realm—to be an essentially Byzantine building. But while its octagonal domed shape is indeed derived from Christian martyria, and its inner colonnade may well be inspired by the sixth-century cathedral at Bosra,[10] that is where the resemblance ends, for no Byzantine building displays its colourful mosaics on the outer surfaces in this exceptional way—it is a first. The building also boasts two key innovations never seen before in Christian architecture: the pointed arch and the trefoil arch. Both were adopted so wholeheartedly by Christianity that they would end up as the defining architectural features of Christian Gothic churches and cathedrals. The octagon itself has meaning in Islam also, since the concept of paradise may be expressed through eight gardens with eight doors, and for this reason all courtyard fountains in residential Islamic architecture are octagonal in shape.[11]

As Islam's oldest religious structure to have survived largely unchanged, and as its third most holy sanctuary after Mecca and Medina, the Dome of the Rock's importance cannot be overstated. It was built in Jerusalem in 691–2 by the Umayyad caliph Abd al-Malik, who with his Umayyad predecessors had waited more than thirty years to start building in their own style. With a vast empire, wealthy from taxation and control of trade routes, now under Umayyad control, the Dome of the Rock represented their first power statement, a monument deliberately conceived to impress the mark of Muslim identity on Jerusalem and to proclaim Islam's dominance over the formerly Christian city. In the early years the Muslim victors had been on the whole content simply to use the local churches, or to share them with the resident Christians, a fact which has led some scholars to speculate that when the Muslim conquerors first arrived, the local population may not even have realised that they were bringing a new religion with them. Islam was after all presented as the last and purest of the world's three monotheistic religions, with the Prophet Muhammad described in the Qur'an as the last of the prophets, the 'seal' of prophethood. Jesus was recognised as a major earlier prophet, revered along with Mary, his mother.

Some consider this iconic building, the Dome of the Rock—Islam's first architectural and political statement of its supremacy over a former Christian realm—to be an essentially Byzantine building. But while its octagonal domed shape is indeed derived from Christian martyria, no Byzantine building displays its colourful mosaics on the outer surfaces in this exceptional way—it is a first.

To this day the Dome of the Rock remains the single most recognised symbol of Jerusalem, prominent and unmistakeable with its golden shining dome and its multi-coloured mosaic tiled walls. It rises above the Old City of Jerusalem on the raised platform known to Muslims as the Haram al-

Sharif, the Noble Sanctuary, and to the Jews as the Temple Mount. Also within this sacred precinct is the Al-Aqsa Mosque, opposite the Dome of the Rock on the south side of the sanctuary facing Mecca. Abd al-Malik built this too, but it has been much altered and rebuilt over the centuries, so that very few Umayyad features remain. It was originally a huge space, with fifteen naves and capacity for 5,000 worshippers. When the Crusaders captured Jerusalem 400 years later, they mistook Al-Aqsa for Solomon's Palace and used it as their headquarters and their stables. As for the Dome of the Rock, the Crusaders wrongly took it for Solomon's Temple and used it as a church, putting a cross on top and calling it the Temple of God.[12] Many people unfamiliar with Jerusalem still assume the Dome of the Rock to be a Christian or a Jewish building, since it is often used in publicity material as the icon of Jerusalem and sits above the sacred Jewish Temple of Solomon. But it is worth mentioning here that there have been no iconic buildings associated with Judaism since the destruction of the Second Temple in 70 CE.[13] The Western Wall or Wailing Wall is the focus of Jewish prayers, a retaining wall of Herod's Palace (separate to and below the Haram al-Sharif), which makes this the holiest site in Judaism. The Jews venerate the location where they believe God's divine presence manifests itself. Controversial Israeli excavations below the Haram al-Sharif have been ongoing for decades, with access and security to the Temple Mount controlled by Israel since the 1967 war, aimed at proving Israel's legitimacy. Religious sites rouse strong feelings and disputes can flare up quickly.

The proportions and geometry of the Dome of the Rock, with the unusual height of its central cylinder, were carefully constructed to make the dome itself as visually arresting as possible from a distance. To read its message you did not need to go inside, unlike the Holy Sepulchre. With no hierarchy and no clear function as a place of worship, the Dome of the Rock sets itself apart from the whole liturgical tradition of Christian churches and baptisteries. It is not a mosque—the mosque here was and is Al-Aqsa (literally 'the Furthest Mosque')—but rather a shrine, designed to surround the holy rock on which Abraham was said to have offered his son for sacrifice (the Feast of the Sacrifice is the biggest annual Muslim festival, analogous to Christmas in terms of importance). Much of the veneration for the site comes from its mention in Surah 17:

Glory be to Him who journeyed by night with His servant
from the Sacred Mosque to the Furthest Mosque.

According to Muslim tradition, Muhammad began his night journey up to
heaven on his winged steed, Buraq. This night journey, known as *Isra*,
together with Muhammad's subsequent ascent, known as *Mi'raj*, is celebrated
as a holiday in the Islamic calendar.

The Roman emperor Hadrian had built a pagan temple on the mount, but
this was destroyed, like all other pagan shrines in the city, on the orders of
Queen Helena, mother of Constantine, when she visited Jerusalem in the
fourth century. Strangely, the new Christians thereafter regarded the area as
cursed and abandoned it, so for the next three centuries it served as the city's
rubbish dump. The caliph Umar helped clear it with his own hands in 638 and
had a simple wooden mosque built there, on the site of the Temple Mount,
the same spot where Abd al-Malik later erected the Dome of the Rock. A
treaty was signed with the Christian patriarch to guarantee protection of
Christian holy places under Muslim rule, so the Church of the Holy
Sepulchre, some 500 metres to the west, was left to function exactly as
before, while Jews, excluded by the Byzantines, were allowed back. The
Umayyads also rebuilt and redecorated the Golden Gate and the Double
Gate, original entrances to the Temple Mount, both later walled up in medieval times. The battered Christian city, still recovering from indirect Persian
rule, was revitalised by the Muslims and their new commercial, military and
cultural presence. Islam always produced an atmosphere favourable to trade
in its cities—Mecca was after all a city of commerce and high finance, its
merchants extremely skilled and organised. Their new empire had now given
them a giant single market.

For our purposes here, to understand why the Dome of the Rock is so
significant for Europe, we need to go inside the shrine, to see the pointed
arches of the circular arcade within the octagonal arcade beneath the dome.
Islam uses the pointed arch here in a way that suggests it is about to become,
whether consciously or by chance, the single major feature differentiating
Islamic from Christian architecture. Up to that point Christian architecture
had been based on the round Roman or Byzantine arch. The pointed arch is

not a Muslim invention, as isolated scattered examples can be found across Syria and Persia that predate Islam, but the Muslims were the first to use it widely, along with many other shapes of arch. The arch is the clear favourite Muslim architectural feature—'the arch never sleeps,' runs the Islamic proverb—showing awareness of its dynamic power and flexibility, always changing, always adapting to what is required of it. This may indeed even have been how the arch first came to be used at the Dome of the Rock, an accidental discovery that arose from the desire to have a circular arcade around the eponymous holy rock, so that people could circumambulate it, like a shrine, as people did in Mecca.

The concept of a circumambulatory was taken from existing Christian architecture in Syria, where it occurs in the martyrium, the holy place where a saint was martyred. This was not a meeting place, so the basilica shape of a church was not suitable. A new design was called for, and since there was no precedent in pagan Roman architecture, what evolved in late antique Syria was a tradition of inner and outer central plans for martyria. They were usually domed and often octagonal, the shape representing the transition between the square, or the earth, and the circle, or heaven. St Simeon's Basilica is based on an octagon inside a square, while the cathedral at Bosra has an inner octagonal colonnade in an outer circular plan.

The Dome of the Rock was by far the most influential of these in Europe however, widely copied in medieval churches as we will see in later chapters, not only in the round Templar churches, but also in churches built with ambulatories to facilitate the movement of pilgrims through the church and round the altar where saints' relics were often kept. The Muslims were of course already familiar with circumambulation, because of their own pilgrimage rites at the Ka'ba in Mecca, the holiest shrine in Islam. Pilgrimage rites in Islam and Christianity share many concepts—only the direction of circumambulation is different, with Christians moving 'sun-wise' and Muslims going the opposite way.

Christian craftsmen skilled in mosaic work were almost certainly employed at the Dome of the Rock, but now working for new masters. There is no figural representation in the mosaic tilework, but the most important single message comes in the 240-metre-long inscription, quoting from Qur'an 4:171, admonishing Christians for believing in the divinity of Christ:

> O people of the Book, do not exaggerate in your religion. Do not say anything but the truth about God. The Messiah, Jesus, the son of Mary, is only God's messenger, and His word, which He cast into Mary, and a spirit from Him. So believe in God and His messengers and do not say, 'Three'. Desist. It is better for you. God is only One God. Far be it removed from His transcendent majesty that He should have a son. His is all that is in the heavens and all that is in the earth. And God is sufficient as Defender.

Scholars like Oleg Grabar have discovered there is also a unique system governing the Dome of the Rock's geometry, which contributes to its harmonious and magnetic effect. The supports of the central circular arcade and the columns of the octagon have been deliberately shifted by 3 degrees, a change in alignment that ensures that the visitor is able to see right through the arcades to the other side of the building.[14] Shafts of brilliant coloured light from the fifty-six stained glass windows under the dome illuminate the sacred rock in the central space beneath the dome, casting multi-coloured geometric patterns. The commonest glass colours used by the Umayyads were purple, light blue, light green, yellow and brown. Many scholars have calculated that it (along with other earlier buildings in the region, like the Church of the Virgin on Mount Gerizim and the archbishop's palace at Bosra) was planned according to standard ratios that approximate to the Golden Mean (the perfect aesthetic median) and that must therefore have been current in local building practices.[15]

The key innovation however may have come from an accidental discovery by the builders during construction, namely that the internal circumference of the built stone circle would necessarily be smaller than the outer circumference. Though the outer arcade today has pointed arches thanks to a nineteenth-century restoration, the original had the conventional rounded Roman-style Byzantine arches that were already in use all over the Byzantine Empire.[16] But on the inner circle, for the arches to align and to maintain a horizontal soffit—to match up in other words—the masons had to have a

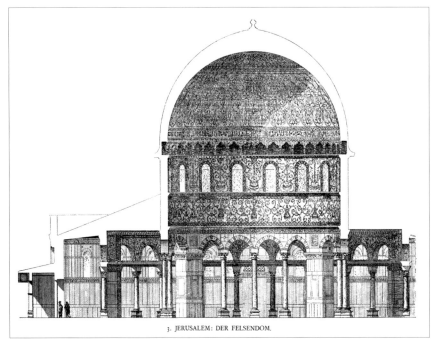

3. JERUSALEM: DER FELSENDOM.

The Dome of the Rock boasts two key innovations never seen before in Christian architecture: the pointed arch and the trefoil arch, both visible in this cross-section. They were adopted so wholeheartedly by Christianity that they would end up as the defining architectural features of European Gothic churches and cathedrals.

tighter arch, hence the need to make them pointed. It was an immediate difference in the way the architecture looked, but that did not mean that henceforth, all Islamic arches were pointed. Architectural changes take place very gradually, as with any deeply embedded tradition, though the exact pace varies according to the particular set of regional circumstances. The other innovation is harder to spot—high up in the dome, running round the circumference just above the windows of the drum where the cylinder moves into the curve, is a continuous arcade of tiny trefoil arches, the first appearance of this arch.

A few centuries later it was sprouting in profusion over virtually every Christian church. The Umayyad rulers in their building spree of the next fifty years continued to use a mix of pointed, round, horseshoe, whatever they felt like. They liked variety, as we will see—almost the exact opposite of the

In the Dome of the Rock's interior, gently pointed arches are visible in the ground floor circular colonnade, while trefoil arches can be seen high in the dome.

classical Graeco-Roman love of regularity, perfect angles and symmetry. Adhering to the rules never appealed that much to them.

The Syrian Niche

While Wren admired 'the Orders and proportions' and criticised 'the Saracen style' for its lack of structure and discipline, it is worth noting that even in the Hellenistic East the usually strict classical architecture developed its own more exuberant, flamboyant style, often called 'the Roman Baroque'. Wren himself was capable of a bit of flamboyance when the occasion warranted, such as his pointed ogee arches to decorate Tom Tower, the gatehouse of Christ Church College, Oxford, in a style that 'ought to be Gothick to agree with the founder's work.'[17] Gothic had gone out of fashion 150 years earlier in England by that point (1682), and some might even say that due to

Wren's Gothic Tom Tower, the gatehouse to Christ Church College, Oxford, decorated with an octagonal lantern and pointed ogee arches.

its immediate popularity, Tom Tower, ironically, given Wren's views on Gothic, may have been the precursor to the Gothic revival that began in earnest in the mid-eighteenth century.

Roman Baroque in the Near East was an oriental version of classical architecture. Most purists would dismiss it as 'decadent' for flouting the Vitruvian rules laid out in the purist's bible *De Architectura*, but it is undeniably more lively and experimental.[18] It showed a fondness for ornamentation and decoration which can still be seen in the ruins of cities like Palmyra, Baalbek, Jerash and Petra, even daring to jumble up the 'Orders' as at Apamea's colonnaded street which mixes Doric, Ionic and Corinthian and even spiralled columns. Anyone who has had the opportunity to visit classical sites in Greece and Italy then compare them with classical sites in the East will have seen and sensed this free-spiritedness—or lack of discipline, depending on your viewpoint.

One such decoration used to break up long plain wall facades is even called 'the Syrian niche', framed by a pair of colonettes and crowned by a miniature pediment. It can be seen at Baalbek and Palmyra in what architectural historians call 'elaborated walls'.[19] Palmyrene architecture is itself a blend of Assyrian, Phoenician, Babylonian, Persian, Egyptian, Hellenistic and Roman. Islamic architecture took on this Syrian niche enthusiastically, because it provided a frame that could then be decorated to suit each occasion and location. In Western classical architecture this type of framed decorative niche barely makes an appearance. But then it suddenly blossoms with great confidence all over Europe's Gothic cathedrals, as we will see later. What this shows us is, as Ball so clearly states: 'Ancient Near Eastern architectural forms had a tenacity which survived superficial Romanisation and still survive in the form of Islamic mosques to this day.'[20] The Romans were seen by the indigenous populations as transitory outsiders and their legacy proved to be ephemeral. It was the same, interestingly, with language, where Greek (and Latin) appeared in official inscriptions on public buildings, leading some Western historians to assume that the citizens were Greek-speaking. In practice the overwhelming majority spoke Syriac (a Christian dialect of Aramaic) and retained their Semitic character. Greek was never the predominant language in the Near East, and there are only a few isolated words of Greek in Middle Eastern languages today.[21]

The Great Umayyad Mosque of Damascus

The Dome of the Rock can boast the first monumental use of the pointed arch and the trefoil arch and the most influential ambulatory shrine, but we need to go to Damascus, the Umayyad capital, to see the single most important building sponsored by the Umayyads: the Great Umayyad Mosque. Its legacy to European architecture merits close examination. Like the Dome of the Rock, the Great Mosque of Damascus remains today architecturally unchanged despite fires, earthquakes and wars. Most constructions by the Umayyads were erected very fast—the Dome of the Rock was finished in two years, and Al-Aqsa Mosque in six months to a year, using craftsmen from Damascus, while the Damascus Umayyad Mosque took nine years from 706 to 715 and exhausted seven years' worth of the state coffers.[22] Wren was clearly aware of the 'Saracen' reputation for speed, when in his analysis of the Saracen style in *Parentalia* he comments: 'where-ever they conquered (which was with amazing rapidity) [they] erected mosques and caravanserais in haste; which obliged them to fall into another way of building.'

Certainly, what they built here was immediately recognised as 'another way of building', with medieval Muslim historians like Al-Tabari referring to the Damascus mosque as one of the Four Wonders of the World. Muslim geographer Al-Idrisi wrote in 1154: 'In Damascus, there is a mosque that has no equal in the world.' It was also considered the fourth holiest sanctuary of Islam, together with Qairouan, after the three *Harams* of Mecca, Medina and Jerusalem.

The church most likely to have influenced the design of the Damascus Umayyad Mosque is the Basilica of St Simeon, northeast of Aleppo, the monastery complex completed in 490 which was the largest and most important church in Syria, later surpassed only by Hagia Sophia in Constantinople. The caliph who built it, Al-Walid, was aiming to outshine St Simeon's, to show the Christian population that a new and more powerful religious force than Christianity had arrived. St Simeon's had been an imperial project on a huge scale, taking fourteen years, using architects and skilled artisans from the two Byzantine centres of Constantinople and Antioch.[23] Its dome collapsed centuries ago, but careful reconstructions of the roof by scholars show how reminiscent its front view, with the dome rising behind its gabled western narthex, would have been of the dome and gabled narthex of the Great Umayyad Mosque. The church of St George at Ezraa from the sixth century (515) also boasts a fine wooden dome, as did the cathedral at Bosra (512) before its collapse. The other influential dome of course, built by Al-Walid's father just fourteen years earlier, was the Dome of the Rock. Both these Umayyad domes, and the earlier Christian ones, were built of wood, a supply of which would still have been abundant at that time before the depletion of the forests of Lebanon, making the domes lightweight structures that did not require great buttressing. They simply rested on the walls beneath them.

Thus the Great Umayyad Mosque of Damascus had earlier inspirations to draw on, but what emerged on completion in 715 was unlike any previous building. The previous church was taken down to its foundations and the new mosque was rebuilt as a unique blend of Mesopotamian, Hellenistic, Roman, Byzantine and Muslim elements, which combine to give the whole space a timelessness that simultaneously conveys a sense of the deeply sacred. The high

The Prophet's Mosque in Medina, modelled on the Prophet Muhammad's courtyard house.

outer courtyard walls are topped with Mesopotamian merlons, a ziggurat-shaped decorative design used on Babylonian temples. The first minaret for the call to prayer was erected on the foundations of one of the square Roman towers at the corner of the original temple—the habitually square minarets of Syria are modelled on these square towers together with the square church towers of Christian Syria. Inside the vast marble-flagged courtyard stands an ablution fountain under a shaded roof, and a mosaic-covered treasury raised on pillars. The layout of the whole ensemble is modelled on the Prophet Muhammad's courtyard house in Medina, one of Islam's first mosques (still extant but altered beyond recognition), just as the first Christian churches were inside a house. The Prophet's early followers would gather in the courtyard to hear him speak and for communal prayers.

The prayer hall of the Damascus Umayyad Mosque is similar in shape to an elongated basilica, except that the two entrances are along the long northern courtyard side, not at the narrow west end. The space is divided into three by arcaded columns, but all parts are of equal size with no larger central nave. Instead of an altar at the far eastern wall, the prayer niche, called the *mihrab*, marking the direction of prayer, is on the long south wall. In other words, although the space inside is reminiscent of a church in some ways, the orientation of the space is completely different, as the congregation would have been spread out in long rows facing south, rather than in narrow rows facing east. The tomb of John the Baptist was incorporated into the space in the east end, away from the *mihrab*, as befitted a prophet revered by Islam as well as by Christianity.

Immediately above the *mihrab*, defining the central point of the mosque is a dome, known as the Dome of the Eagle because the architect was said to have visualised the dome as an eagle's head with the transept as its body and the aisles as its outspread wings. As an archetypal image this has distinct echoes of the pre-Islamic god Baal/Bel, represented as an eagle with outspread wings, as on the ceiling in the Palmyra holy of holies in the Temple of Bel (destroyed by ISIS in August 2015).

The main outer facade of the Damascus prayer hall dominates the courtyard, with another unique blend in the form of a Hellenistic gable framing a trinity of arched windows, separated with classical columns and capitals. The entire

The gable and pediment did not originate in Greek temple architecture, but were first seen far earlier in this 17-metre-tall stone-cut relief, dated to the sixth or seventh century BCE, in Central Anatolia at Midas Şehri in what was ancient Phrygia. It is known locally as the Tomb of King Midas, he of the 'golden touch'.

facade is covered with Byzantine-style mosaics in stunning greens and gold depicting a form of paradise, with stylised palm and cypress trees and gardens framing fantasised palaces and rivers and bridges. These palaces are another example of an orientalised 'Roman Baroque', as the style with its curved and broken pediments has been observed to be very similar to baroque classical facades in Pompeii wall paintings of the first century BCE, which in turn have been traced to Ptolemaic Alexandria of the second century BCE and so are Egyptian in origin, rather than Roman.[24] The mosaics, their distinctive buildings decorated with pearls and precious jewels, also bear a striking similarity to the Heavenly Jerusalem mosaic at Ravenna's Basilica of San Vitale.[25] There are no people or animals, since Islam very early on proscribed representation of the human or animal form (although they were sometimes depicted in secular art or architecture, such as in palaces, as we will see later). We tend to think of the gable and pediment as originating in Greek temple architecture, but stone-cut reliefs dated to the sixth or seventh century BCE, such as the one in Central Anatolia at Midas Şehri in what was ancient Phrygia (near modern Eskişehir), show it to predate the Greeks by centuries.

All these styles therefore represent blendings of what the Muslim rulers inherited from Syria's earlier monuments, such as Palmyrene temples and the thousands of churches covering Syrian soil. The conquering Muslims saw and learnt from all that went before. They are known to have employed Byzantine craftsmen, especially on the mosaics, but no one knows who the overall mastermind was and whether it was Al-Walid himself or a chief engineer figure like a master mason. Whoever it was, there are three distinct and important innovations which appear for the first time in this lavish building project, all of which have major implications for subsequent European Christian architecture: the minaret tower, the horseshoe arch and the geometric marble window grilles. All are still clear to see today, for in the case of the Damascus Great Mosque, despite suffering the depredations of two accidental fires in 1096 and in 1893 and a deliberate one in 1401 by Tamerlane, leader of the Turco-Mongols, we know that the repairs and restorations undertaken over the centuries have not substantially altered the original mosque design or layout, thanks to the accounts of early Muslim geographers and historians like Mas'udi and Yaqut.

The Minaret/Bell Tower/Spire

The first feature with relevance for European architecture is the minaret, since some architectural historians see in it the origins of the spire towers of churches and the decorated square towers built in sections or 'registers' of European castles and gatehouses. In the Damascus Umayyad Mosque today there are three minarets, on the southwest and southeast corners and on the centre of the north wall, all of them with strong plain bases, then rising in sections, becoming increasingly decorated as they reach the top. The original Roman temple enclosure had four towers, one in each corner, and the most likely explanation for the origin of the minaret in mosque architecture is that it evolved from the truncated bases of these towers. The call to prayer could obviously be heard best and carry furthest if delivered from a height, and here, on this site adapted from earlier religions, the extant towers enabled a more effective call to prayer. It was a natural development. The Roman

The Minaret of the Bride on the Umayyad Mosque of Damascus. Throughout Syria early minarets began to spring up on mosques, built as square stone-built towers, influenced by the existing square stone-built Byzantine towers of churches found all over the country.

masonry is clearly visible on all the lower walls. The Arabic word for mina-ret, *minaara*, supports this evolution, as it means lighthouse or watchtower. Towers were also used in Byzantine times for lighting warning fires as signals of enemy movements.

Minarets of mosques today are always positioned on the wall furthest away from the *qibla*, or direction of prayer, and it was the northeast Roman tower of the Damascus mosque, known today as the Minaret of the Bride, that was first used for the call to prayer. Architecturally it was considered inharmoni-ous to have the minaret off-centre like this, so it was later rebuilt in the ninth century in the centre of the north wall to give an axis of symmetry. The Great Mosque of Damascus can therefore claim to have the first minaret in Islam, and Al-Walid in his subsequent building spree then added four to the Prophet's Mosque in Medina, one in each corner. Throughout Syria early minarets began to spring up on mosques, all built as square stone-built tow-ers, likely to have been influenced by the existing square stone-built Byzantine towers of churches found all over the country. In southern Syria, the Church of Saints Sergius and Bacchus at Umm Al-Surab has two towers, and in the so-called Dead or Forgotten Cities, Byzantine stone-built ghost towns aban-doned in the seventh century, many examples can be seen of towers, often free-standing towers used by stylite hermits like St Simeon seeking places of solitary contemplation and meditation to escape the distractions of the world, as at Refade.

The first towers in a religious building appeared in Europe during the Romanesque period, and of course transferred into Gothic, especially cathe-drals, as we have seen from the Qalb Lozeh/Notre-Dame connection. The first spires came later still, a development that Wren firmly associated with 'the Saracens':

> the pride of their works was in pinnacles and steeples. In this they essentially differed from the Roman way, who laid all their mouldings horizontally, which made the best perspective: the Gothick way on the contrary carried all their mouldings perpendicular, so that the ground-work being settled, they had nothing else to do but to spire all up as they could.[26]

The Jesus Minaret in the southeast corner of the Damascus mosque is reminiscent
of a European church bell tower.

Becoming ever more elaborate with each register towards the top, the summit of the minaret was often crowned with a bulbous finial. The square shape was also almost certainly influenced by the towers of the fifth- and sixth-century Christian churches of Syria, but differed markedly from these simple early Christian churches in the style of its outer wall ornamentation, displaying a far more effusive and spontaneous type of décor as it tapered upwards in registers. The minaret that now rises from the southeast corner of the Damascus mosque is called the Minaret of Jesus, because popular Islamic tradition holds that Jesus will descend from this tower at the Last

The Cordoba Mezquita minaret, now the cathedral's bell tower.

Judgement to fight the Antichrist. In its current form it dates to 1247, but it is built on an earlier square Umayyad structure.

To our Western eyes it resembles a church campanile from southern Europe. The earliest surviving minaret on European soil is in Cordoba, not in the Mezquita there, but rather in the ninth-century Umayyad tower known today as the Torre de San Juan, which also carries the first twin windows that will be discussed in Chapter 5. The minaret at the Mezquita came later, built by the Umayyad caliph Abd al-Rahman III in 951–2 in exactly the same square Syrian style, in sections, highly decorated in panels, reaching to 47 metres in height and topped with silver and gold finials. Today it is repurposed in the Cordoba cathedral bell tower adapted in the sixteenth century after the Reconquista, as are many such minarets across Spain.

The same Umayyad ruler introduced square-shafted minarets to the mosques of Fez in Morocco as power statements to proclaim his victory against Fatimid incursions, and Andalusian origins are also evident in the Algerian Qal'at Bani Hammad square tower minaret built in 1007, richly decorated with ceramic tiles and various types of arches—semi-circular, trefoil, cinqfoil and multifoil—to lighten the structure and the weight. Extensive trade links between North Africa and Europe meant many merchants would have carried back ideas as well as goods, and strong similarities can be seen with the square Romanesque twin-towered Church of St Abbondio in Como, Italy (1063–95) and the Church of St Etienne, Abbaye aux Hommes at Caen in France (1066–1160), founded by William the Conqueror and one of the most important Romanesque buildings in Normandy, which ended up with over nine towers and spires added in later centuries to emphasise its dominance.

In England the very first spire was on the old Gothic St Paul's, finished in 1221, then destroyed by the 1666 Fire of London. The (Syrian) Cordoban type square-shaft minaret was further developed in the twelfth century under the Almohads, successors of the Umayyads, reaching heights of 70 metres, as at the Kutubiyya Mosque in Marrakech and the famous La Giralda, which defines the skyline of Seville. As well as becoming the archetype for later North African minarets, these minarets also decisively influenced the

The multi-spired Church of St Etienne, Abbaye aux Hommes at Caen in France.

developing form of the Spanish Christian bell tower, as numerous Mudéjar churches in Castile and Aragon show.[27]

Square minarets like the ones in the Damascus Umayyad Mosque, tapering thinner and ending in a bulbous finial dome at the top, are also thought to have heavily influenced Italianate towers like Florence's town hall, the Palazzo Vecchio at Piazza della Signoria (1299–1314), and the campanile of San Marco in Venice (originally 1173) where the square tower progresses through several sections to an ever thinner structure ending in a point. In mosques they were then crowned with the crescent moon of Islam while in European churches they were crowned with a cross, often in gold in both cases.

In Germany there seemed to be a general preference in medieval times, coinciding with the return of the Crusaders from the Holy Land, for very tall church towers, as in the Romanesque Holy Apostles Church in Cologne (1190), where the pointed spires crowning the tops are very reminiscent of minarets, and in the very tall twin-towered red sandstone Romanesque Worms Cathedral of St Peter (1130–81) in the Rhineland-Palatinate, which also stands on the highest point in the city.

The Romanesque Holy Apostles Church, Cologne.

This coincidence of timing in the Crusaders' return home with the sudden popularity of such minaret-like towers all over Italy, France and Germany in secular buildings like castles and gatehouses is the main factor that has led architectural historians to speculate about the possibility of influence from Islamic minarets. Whilst the connection cannot be ruled out, it seems equally difficult to draw definitive conclusions.

German scholar Wolfgang Born tells us that no bulbous domes were known in western and southern Europe till the Gothic period, when the most famous examples were the exotic onion-shaped domes that appeared on St Mark's in Venice. Their origin, he believes, lies in Syria, where Umayyad mosaics depict buildings with bulbous domes.[28] 'Venice was susceptible to oriental influences,' he writes.

The first printed map of Jerusalem, published in Mainz, Germany, in 1486, is also worth mentioning, since it shows the Dome of the Rock sporting a fine onion dome as the central point of the Holy Land. Meticulously drawn in pictorial style by Dutch woodcut artist Erhard Reuwich, who spent several months in Jerusalem accompanying the wealthy politician Bernhard

The west facade of the Romanesque Worms Cathedral of St Peter, Rhineland-Palatinate.

von Breidenbach on pilgrimage, all the other domes of the city are accurate—the Holy Sepulchre, for example—but most historians believe that the Dome of the Rock was never onion-shaped at any time. The Mamluk sultan Baibars was very keen on domes and restored it in 1263, along with the dome of the Damascus Umayyad Mosque in 1269–70. Baibars's own mosque in Cairo, built in 1267–69, is known to have had a monumental double dome (long since disappeared), the biggest ever seen in Cairo, made of wood and covered in lead, with space between the shells for a man to walk through.[29]

In true Mamluk tradition it was built with spolia from Jaffa after his victorious campaign against the Crusaders; Baibars in person, accompanied by his two sons, supervised the demolition of Jaffa's citadel in 1268, ordering its wood to be used for his dome and its marble for his *mihrab*. Two other smaller onion domes appear in the Jerusalem map on lesser buildings. The map itself was published as part of the illustrated travelogue by Bernhard (appointed dean of Mainz Cathedral on his return) at a time when the appetite in Europe for first-hand information about the Holy Land was so strong that the book became a best seller and was reprinted thirteen times and translated from the original Latin into German, French and Spanish. The map became one of the most influential maps of its time, continually reprinted into the eighteenth century. Ironically of course, its popularity perpetuated in the minds of most Europeans the Crusader myth that the Dome of the Rock was Christian, thereby clearing the way for it to remain a key influence in churches throughout Europe. The map may also have influenced the spread of onion domes across Europe in the sixteenth century, with church sponsors believing that they were copying the sacred Temple of Solomon.

This highly influential printed map of Jerusalem wrongly shows the Dome of the Rock sporting an onion dome. It also perpetuated the Crusader error that the Dome of the Rock was a Christian shrine by labelling it as the Temple of Solomon, ironically leading it to become a key influence in churches throughout Europe.

Wolfgang Born also makes a case that the bulbous finials of Egyptian and Syrian minarets, as seen in the Damascus Umayyad Mosque, were the models for the bulbous cupolas that began to appear on the Gothic spires in the Netherlands in the late fifteenth century. With German rigour, he traces the popularity of the feature as it spreads to Germany and Central Europe during the sixteenth century, looking at how it flourished in the Baroque period before finally receding into the rural architecture of village churches in the Alps. Still, despite his thorough approach, his theory seems a little far-fetched.

The origins and meaning of the ubiquitous Russian Orthodox church onion domes, like the sixteenth-century St Basil's Cathedral in Moscow's Red Square, remain much disputed, with Russian scholars arguing fiercely for their indigenous invention in the thirteenth century. Popular folklore claims they were built to resemble candle flames, a theory backed up, according to religious philosopher Prince Yevgeny Trubetskoy in 1917, by the Russian folk saying 'glowing with fervour' when people speak about church domes. Another American German scholar, Hans Schindler, believes the onion domes came about as a way of signalling a different identity to the prevailing Gothic, and to mark rural pilgrimage churches in southern Germany, Czechoslovakia, Austria and the Dolomites of northern Italy. He also makes the point that they could be easily constructed by a skilled carpenter, using carpentry manuals that have been found dating to the sixteenth century.[30]

Mosaics

At the Damascus Umayyad Mosque, the next most memorable feature after the striking shapes of blended temple/church/mosque elements, like the dome, the gabled facade and the minaret towers, are the mosaics. These in fact are likely to be the memory that stays with you the longest, so visually stunning are the scenes depicted and so breathtaking the level of craftsmanship involved. All the mosaics were covered with plaster by the Ottomans from the sixteenth century onwards, only being revealed again in the late 1920s by archaeologists brought in under the French Mandate. The mosque itself had also been impossible to visit as a Christian till after the French expedition in 1860.

The Damascus mosaics, originally covering all external and internal surfaces of the mosque, constituted the biggest passage of mosaics anywhere in the world, and are estimated to have covered an acre.[31] They are important to our narrative because of the influence they had in Spain when the craft was carried there by the Umayyads and deployed again in Cordoba, as discussed in Chapter 5. The two main controversies concerning the mosaics are firstly where the craftsmen came from to carry out this level of work, and secondly what the scenes were intended to represent. The sources on the first question are mixed. According to Al-Maqdisi writing in the tenth century, craftsmen were collected from Persia, India, the Maghrib (North Africa) and Rum (the Arabic for 'Romans', the word used for people living in Byzantine lands to the north controlled by the Roman Empire). The omission of Egypt seems curious, as Coptic craftsmen were also thought to have such skills. Several of the sources do however agree that some of the mosaic and marble materials used in these early mosques were recovered from ruined Byzantine towns of Syria. We can conclude from this that mosaic ornamentation clearly flourished in Syria, used in decorating palaces, churches and wealthy houses, and there is no reason to doubt that the skilled craftsmen who had carried out this work continued to be in demand under their new masters, the Umayyads. The likelihood is that Damascus had a school of mosaic and marble craftsmen, as did other centres like Antioch, Jerusalem, Madaba (in Jordan) and Cairo. No historian ever mentions that craftsmen were sent from Byzantium to carry out the mosaics of the Dome of the Rock, a fact which again suggests there were enough local Syro-Christian craftsmen to carry out the work without outside help.

German scholar Marguerite van Berchem conducted an exhaustive study of the Damascus mosaics spanning more than thirty years in the early to mid twentieth century after the Ottoman plastering was removed in 1929. She concluded that the Umayyad Mosque of Damascus represents the absolute pinnacle of mosaic craftsmanship, exceeding that of the Dome of the Rock. Fragments of mosaic remain too on the Church of the Nativity in Bethlehem, of a similar style and date. In Damascus, for the first time, the décor is not just stylised motifs of floral elements with scrolls covered in gems, necklaces and pendants as are found in the Dome of the Rock, but a visualisation of the beauties of nature, with gardens, trees and fantasy buildings like palaces with rivers flowing through them. The inspiration for these paradise scenes may well have been Damascus itself, exceptionally well-watered by its many springs and rivers and set in its verdant gardens, as well as Qur'anic descriptions of paradise: 'Gardens through which rivers flow to dwell therein and beautiful mansions in gardens of everlasting bliss.' (9:72)

Window Grilles

In the Damascus mosque, below the River Barada mosaic panel in the western arcade, there are still a few of the original carved marble window grilles to let in light. These represent the oldest examples in Islam of the use of geometric interlace. Today they no longer carry glass, which has been lost across the centuries through fire and war, but thanks to the writings of geographer Ibn Jubayr, we have a description of how they used to look in 1184. Bewitched by the magical effect of the coloured light from the mosque's seventy-four windows (known as *qamariyyat* from Arabic for moon, or *shamsiyyat*, from Arabic for sun) reflecting off the *mihrab*, he wrote: 'the rays of the sun pour through them such as to dazzle the eyes. It is all so grand as to beggar description, and words cannot express a part of what the mind can picture.'[32] The use of solar and lunar imagery continues the tradition first seen in the Syrian Dead Cities, where patterns like rosettes and whirling discs adorned the church facades, evolving slowly over the centuries into the circular rose windows of European medieval cathedrals. Medieval writers often compared them to the sun or the moon, and at Chartres, with its astonishing 167 stained glass windows, the structure of the West rose window has itself been described as resembling rays of light emanating from the central circle—the sun—containing the figure of Christ at the Last Judgement.

The delicate carving framed within a round arch and set within a rectangular frame was the earliest prototype of a design that then passed to Spain with the Umayyads and is widely used in the outer wall of the Cordoba

Mezquita, for the same dual purpose: to allow the entry of light in interesting patterns conveying a sense of the spiritual and at the same time to give ventilation. This concept of a window that is simultaneously functional and decorated—a common Islamic aim in architecture, as we will see later—was elaborated to new heights at Cordoba's Madinat al-Zahra palace and at the Alhambra in Granada. It also spread to Portugal, as seen in the Templar Church at Tomar.

Horseshoe Arch

The arches in the side chambers of the Damascus Great Umayyad Mosque show signs of a horseshoe shape, very slight, so slight that most people would not readily notice. The first person to study these and other early Umayyad arches in order to devise a dating system from the acuteness of their pointedness was respected historian Professor K.A.C. Creswell.[33] Before the evolution of the arch the Egyptians and the Greeks had used horizontal lintels to support openings in masonry walls, while the Romans, Byzantines and later Normans built round semi-circular arches with a capstone or keystone in the centre to hold them in place. Such arches were relatively easy to build but not very strong, especially once they reached a large size or had more heavy masonry to bear above.

The evolution of the arch towards the more and more pointed shape associated with Gothic architecture is very closely connected with architectural developments during the first 200 years of Islam in Syria, and though a few examples of early very slightly pointed arches can be found in Byzantine buildings (such as Qasr Ibn Wardan, a Byzantine church/palace/fortress outpost in the desert east of Hama built 561–4) and Persian Sassanid buildings, it was the Umayyads who, inheriting these earlier forms, enhanced them further. The tall double storey of arches inside the Umayyad Mosque was the prototype for the design of the double-decker horseshoe arches of the Cordoba Mezquita, explored in the next chapter.

The Damascus arch, as it is still called in Damascus by architects today, is known as *makhmous*, which means divided into five. It became the type of arch most widely used in early Islamic buildings, a kind of standard.

The space to be spanned by the arch is divided into five equal parts and the two centre ones are used as points of the compass (C1 and C2 in the diagram) to draw two circles. The point where they intersect will form the top of the arch and the sides of the arch are formed by the opposite circles as they move downwards. These are the same two circles that then bow inwards slightly at the base of the arch to create the horseshoe shape. The further the two centre points are moved apart, the sharper the arch becomes, so the arches which Creswell studied were divided into ten to form the slightest arch, moving up through seven, six, five and three to form the more pointed arches which he identified all over Umayyad Syria and listed in a table.[34] He gives the arched frame at the north end of the transept at the Damascus Great Umayyad Mosque (705–15) as the separation of the two centres representing an eleventh of the span, so a very slight arch.

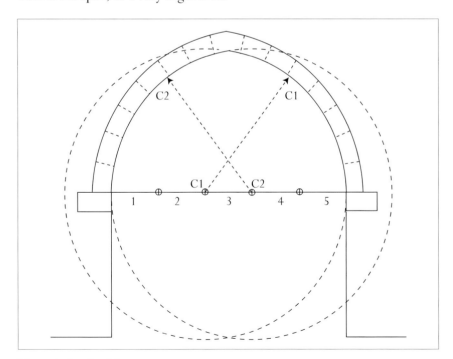

The typical arch of Damascus.

A round arch is formed from a single centre and is therefore much simpler. The two-centred arch can be divided again and by moving apart vertically can produce four-centred curves, which resulted in the later four-centred arch developed by the Umayyads' successors, the Abbasids. If a centre moves up and down a vertical axis of the arch it can produce a three- or five-centred curve, thereby resulting in a very wide variety of arches. As the shapes evolved into distinct styles, these enabled accurate dating. Arch experimentation was a clear passion in early Muslim architecture, much more so than in the earlier Byzantine and Sassanid eras. As the craftsmen working under Islamic rule, be they Muslim, Christian or Jewish, learnt how to make the arch more pointed, they also learnt how to reduce the thrust of the arch to just a few points that could then be easily reinforced, making it stronger. This left other areas free from support so walls could be built thinner and taller, an essential element of what was later to evolve into the Gothic style. Not only that, but as the skills improved, fewer and lighter building materials were needed, not only making it easier to build higher and create larger windows for light, but also making it cheaper to erect large buildings. As Oleg Grabar summed it up after his extensive studies as part of the team excavators at the Umayyad desert palace of Khirbat al-Mafjar:

> Its comparative cheapness and the rapidity with which it could be executed resulted in its becoming one of the main vehicles for the expression of a decorative art which might otherwise have used more elaborate and more expensive techniques. It is a constantly recurring principle in medieval oriental art that particular attention is given to a wealth of decoration and rapidity of execution, often at the expense of quality and solidity.[35]

It is exactly as Wren wrote in his *Parentalia* when he describes the 'Saracen' way of building, observing the further evolution in European cathedrals through the Early, the High, the Rayonnant, the Flamboyant and the Perpendicular as they reached ever higher with taller and taller windows and spires, perfected by the multi-cultural masons in the eleventh, twelfth and thirteenth centuries, who had learnt from the styles which had entered Europe via Muslim Spain, Sicily and Venice.[36]

Progressing through the later dates of the extant arches of the region, Creswell finds the Umayyad desert palace of Qasr Amra (712–5) to have arches of a tenth, the Umayyad palaces of Khirbat al-Mafjar (c. 740) and Qasr al-Mshatta (744) to both have a sixth, the mosque at Qairouan in Tunisia (862–5) to have pointed horseshoe arches and the Ibn Tulun Mosque of Cairo (c. 879) about a quarter, which is a noticeable curve. His theory has stood the test of time because the Umayyad buildings of Syria were able to evolve naturally during that period without disruptive foreign interference, so styles remained historically 'pure'.

Al-Walid lived only forty years and ruled for just ten of them, but had a passion for building and the leisure for it, since his rule was a period of comparative peace and opulence.[37] In addition to the Umayyad Mosque of Damascus, he enlarged the Great Mosque of Mecca, rebuilt the Mosque of the Prophet in Medina, and was perhaps the first medieval ruler to build hospitals for those with chronic diseases in Syria, as well as schools and institutions for lepers, the lame and the blind. Lazar houses for lepers in the West later followed this model from the twelfth century, after returning Crusaders first saw them in the Holy Land.

Religious Umayyad architecture in Syria was eclectic, drawing its inspiration from a number of existing sources, yet it took these earlier forms and fashioned them into a distinctive Umayyad style, recognisable in both its general shapes and its specific features. It is the earliest form of an art that can truly be called Islamic. The Great Mosque of Damascus represents the high point, whose influence can be clearly seen on the Umayyad palaces at Qasr al-Hair ash-Sharqi and Qasr Al-Hallabat, the Great Mosques at Aleppo, Hama, Harran, Diyarbakır, Cordoba and Ephesus, and the Cairo mosques of Al-Azhar, Al-Hakim and Baibars I.

The Umayyad Palaces

The secular architecture of the Umayyad caliphs is perhaps even more important to the subsequent development of the European Gothic style, as this section will explain. It can be quite clearly traced, thanks to the exceptionally thorough work of a handful of dedicated scholars, notably R.W. Hamilton, former keeper of antiquities at the Ashmolean Museum in Oxford. There are over twenty desert palaces, built between 660 and 750. Taken together, they constitute an extremely valuable collective grouping through which to trace not only the evolution of early Islamic art and architecture, but also the life-style priorities of these first Muslim rulers. Many were not just palaces for luxurious living (with extensive bath complexes and their own small mosques), but were multi-functional, serving as defensive forts, agricultural estates, relaxation centres, hunting lodges or even commercial centres. This matters so that we can clearly identify the priorities of the ruling Umayyads and therefore understand how, when they were forced to flee Syria and arrived in Spain in the eighth century, they chose to recreate their Syrian homeland and Damascus in Spain.

The Umayyad desert palaces have always excited controversy. Scattered across today's Syria, Jordan, Palestine and Israel, they show a variety of con-fusing architectural patterns. Sometimes they resemble Roman/Byzantine castles, sometimes Syrian Byzantine baths, sometimes Parthian/Sassanid halls or *khans* with four *iwans* or vaulted niches. The confusion is compounded by the fact that they were quite frequently adapted from existing buildings, such as old caravanserais or earlier fortresses, to suit new purposes. As a result, the palaces have been variously dated to 293, the fourth and sixth centuries and finally to the Umayyad eighth century, and it is perhaps because of the inventiveness required in repurposing these earlier structures that new dis-coveries were made.

Under their leader Mu'awiya, the Umayyads were the first settled dynasty of caliphs in Islam. They had conquered an empire at great speed. Finding themselves suddenly in charge of a huge machine with all its attendant head-aches and responsibilities, it was perfectly understandable, Bedouin horsemen as many of them were, that they longed to escape the tribulations of govern-ment and urban life, to return to their natural desert environment where they could build attractive bolt-holes—not unlike Londoners escaping to country cottages at the weekend.

Mu'awiya was a supreme administrator and laid the foundations of a sta-ble, orderly Muslim society in Syria. He was considered the first to introduce a registry system for recording the affairs of state, and he began the first proper postal system, using relays of horses. From among his many wives he chose as his favourite a Jacobite called Maysoun. Of Bedouin origin from the Christian Bani Kalb of Syria, with whom the House of Umayya had long been allies, Maysoun's tribe was known for camel-raising. She abhorred the rigid court life of Damascus and yearned for the freedom of the desert. Her wild spirit shows itself in this poem attributed to her:

> *A tent with rustling breezes cool*
> *Delights me more than palace high*
> *And more the cloak of simple wool*
> *Than robes in which I learned to sigh*
> *The crust I ate beside my tent*
> *Was more than this fine bread to me;*
> *The wind's voice where the hill-path went*
> *Was more than tambourine can be.*
> *And more than purr of friendly cat*
> *I love the watch-dog's bark to hear*
> *And more than any lubbard fat*
> *I love a Bedouin cavalier.*[38]

Maysoun's son Yazid, later to be Mu'awiya's successor, grew up in her mould, and she would take him to the desert east of Damascus, where they would roam with her tribesfolk, and where the young prince acquired a taste for hard-riding, hunting, drinking wine and composing poetry. He was nick-named Yazid al-Khumour, Yazid of the Wines. On becoming caliph he neglected affairs of state, and the empire threatened to fall apart. It was saved by Abd al-Malik, caliph from 685, through seven years of hard fighting against breakaway provinces to reclaim authority and re-establish supremacy, but the desert palace tradition continued.

Abd al-Malik and later his son Al-Walid built their country residences in the desert and called them *baadiyahs*, meaning desert retreats. One of the earliest and most controversial was Qasr Amra (in today's Jordan), built by Al-Walid in 712–15 and designated a UNESCO World Heritage site in 1985 thanks to the lavish frescoes decorating its baths, the best-preserved examples of Umayyad pictorial art in the world. Contrary to the strict Islamic view that the representation of human or animal forms in art was the prerogative of Allah alone, here at Qasr Amra there are paintings of naked women bathing, scenes of frolicking and dancing, hunting scenes with men chasing dogs chasing gazelles into nets, men on foot spearing horses, bears playing lutes, and camels and horses working in the fields.

The Umayyads were always fond of entertainment. Even Mu'awiya set aside the evenings for listening to tales of past heroes and historical anecdotes. The favourite drink, especially among women, was rose sherbet, still drunk today in Damascus and in many Arab cities. Wine drinking among the men was to become a weakness for some of the later caliphs. Abd al-Malik drank once a month, we are told, Hisham drank once a week after the Friday prayers, Al-Walid drank every other day, and Yazid drank daily. But Walid II was definitely the most committed, and Arab chroniclers have given us eyewitness accounts of his drinking parties, such as would have taken place at Qasr Amra, where he had the bathing pool filled with wine and would then swim in it, gulping enough to lower the level visibly. Accompanied by hand-maidens dancing and singing, he would frolic in the liquid till losing consciousness. These Umayyad soirées, be they in the desert palaces or in the city court itself, would also produce much by way of music and above all poetry, the genre most beloved by Arabs. The women of these early Umayyad days seem to have enjoyed what would now be regarded as an unusual degree of freedom. In Medina a proud and beautiful woman called Sukhaynah was noted for her beauty and learning, for her poetry, her song and her sense of humour. She once sent word to the chief of police that a Syrian had broken into her apartment. The chief himself rushed over to find her maid holding out a flea. Accounts of the number of her husbands range from seven to nine, and she frequently made complete freedom of action a precondition to the marriage.

Experts claim that the colourful murals in the baths at Qasr Amra were probably made by Christian and Sassanid craftsmen, but there is an almost child-like primitiveness in the human figures that makes this unlikely. The vine scrolls and complex geometry on the other hand were executed with great ease and dexterity, which suggests the artists may have been Syrian Arabs, highly skilled and practised in the latter but novices in the former, as was the case for many past generations living within the Near Eastern tradition.

The basis for the ban on representation lay not in the Qur'an but in remarks by the Prophet Muhammad that on the Day of Judgement the most severely punished would be the 'image-makers'. As a result of a strict interpretation of such passages, no human representation is to be found in any mosque, and almost all decorative motifs throughout the Islamic world derive from plants and abstract geometric patterns.

Beyond the scenes of frolicking and hunting at Qasr Amra is another striking scene showing six kings conquered by the Umayyads, identifiable from their names written underneath in Greek and in Kufic Arabic script. They are 'Caesar', meaning the Byzantine emperor, 'Roderick', the last Visigoth king of Spain before the Muslim conquest, 'Chosroes', the Persian Sassanid emperor, 'Negus', king of Abyssinia, and two other figures thought to be kings of China and India respectively.

Living in their desert palaces the caliphs and their families kept their pure Arabic language and escaped the linguistic changes that were happening in the cities and settlements. They also avoided the infectious plagues that befell the cities of Syria at regular intervals during the seventh and eighth centuries and decimated the armies. Here in the desert, each prince received what was held to be the perfect education: he learned to read and write Arabic, to use the bow and arrow, and to swim. In addition, he acquired the ethical ideals of courage, endurance of hardship, manliness, generosity and hospitality, regard for women, and the keeping of promises. After all this, he would be termed *al-kaamil*, 'the perfect one'. Things did not always go to plan though, and Caliph Hisham's young son was killed when he fell from his horse during a hunt. His father is said to have exclaimed: 'I brought him up for the caliphate and he pursues a fox!' Under Hisham's long reign (724–43) the empire reached the limits of its expansion. He was the last great statesman of the House of Umayya, whose ultimate downfall as a dynasty was triggered by the family falling out with each other and, some might say, by being too secular.

Fragments of the eighth-century Umayyad desert palace Qasr al-Hair al-Gharbi
were reassembled to form the facade of the Damascus National Museum. The stepped
merlon crenellations, blind niches, pointed and round arches, and geometric and floral
designs entwined in leaves, trees and rosettes are typical of the stylistic exuberance
of the Umayyads and their eclectic borrowings.

It was during Hisham's reign that two important palaces were built from
scratch in the desert east of Damascus, known as Qasr al-Hair al-Gharbi and
Qasr al-Hair ash-Sharqi, in around 727–8. Both are in today's Syria. The
names mean 'Western Palace of the Fenced-in Garden' and 'Eastern Palace
of the Fenced-in Garden' respectively, conveying their role as rural retreats
for the nomadic rulers who needed an escape from city life and the cares of
running an empire. The palaces did also serve a purpose as military outposts
to help cement relations with the Bedouin who were always rebelling against
authority. Both palaces were built on irrigated estates within military
encampments, and on trade routes east to the Euphrates and beyond. They
are far bigger than the simple hunting lodges to be found further south, in the
deserts of eastern Jordan, and both functioned more like self-contained towns

with gardens, markets, and populations of entertainers, servants and crafts-men. Those familiar with Islamic Spain will immediately realise the transfer-ence of this concept to the palace of Madinat al-Zahra near the Umayyad capital of Cordoba—something to be explored in detail in the next chapter on Muslim Spain.

The western palace, located some 37 kilometres west of Palmyra, is heavily ruined today, difficult to reach along dirt tracks and rarely visited. Fortunately for us however, the excavators working on the site between 1936 and 1939 during the French Mandate found the key architectural elements fallen in the sand in front of the collapsing towers—namely the highly elaborate stucco friezes from the facade of the twin-round-towered entrance to the palace, carved in a stylistic exuberance not seen before in this period. The finds were brought back to Damascus, where they were painstakingly reassembled and incorporated into a faithful, original-sized recreation of the twin round towers. Today this doubles as the facade of the city's National Museum.

The towers' almost effervescent motifs seem to reflect a love of life and luxury, which the palaces epitomise through patterns blending geometric and floral motifs entangled in leaves, trees and rosettes, with a rearing horse on top and the busts of young women on the capitals. The tympanum (the space between the lintel and the arch above the portal) is heavily decorated with niches, blind arches in alternating round and pointed shapes framed by colo-nettes. The eclectic mix shows clearly how the Umayyads borrowed from Byzantine, Hellenistic, Roman and Persian Sassanid designs to create their own uniquely busy, high-spirited style.

The location of the palace was determined by an earlier Palmyrene settle-ment in the first century, made possible in such an arid landscape thanks to the enormous Harbaqa Dam, 17 kilometres to the south, which collected rainwater from local flash floods and brought it to the site by underground canals and pipework. Under Emperor Justinian, the Byzantines and their local Arab allies, the Christian Ghassanid tribe, occupied the site in 559 and turned it into a monastery, one square tower of which survives to a height of three storeys and forms one corner of the 70-square-metre palace with its three round Umayyad towers.[39] Now largely collapsed, the rest of the palace was originally two-storeyed, made of mud brick walls built on a 2-metre-high limestone base, enclosing a colonnaded courtyard. Monasticism, as we saw with the cult of St Simeon Stylites in the fifth century, was flourishing in Syria, and the eastern desert saw several monasteries built around that time, most famously perhaps Mar Musa, a ruined monastery on a remote outcrop a little further west, restored and revived in 2005 by the Jesuit priest Father Paolo dall'Oglio, whose fate is, at the time of writing, still unknown since his kidnap by ISIS on 29 July 2013.

The Harbaqa Dam remains remarkably intact, the original Roman construction still standing 20 metres high and 18 metres thick at the base and running for a stretch of 345 metres. It was built of rubble infill behind solid stone facing, and the lake that once accumulated behind it has now filled up with sand. The Umayyads restored it and diverted the water to irrigate the palace gardens.[40]

The total command of water and irrigation systems at all the Umayyad desert palaces displayed their consummate skill in this field. As they were a people used to arid environments, water management was essential to their survival, and time and again we can see their ingenious solutions for guaranteeing the water supply. Much of the hydraulic engineering used by the early Islamic civilisations was of ancient Roman, Greek and Persian origin, but they repaired, extended and modified the existing wells, cisterns, channels, canals, aqueducts and dams. For example, the *qanat* system which originated in the Persian Achaemenid era (c. 550–330 BCE) was a series of subterranean channels that carried water from an elevated source. It was adopted by Islamic engineers and is still used today in Iran. The Umayyads adapted and improved the earlier Aramean and Roman water systems to supply Damascus with a water system unequalled anywhere in the world at that time and which still functions today. This skill is another accomplishment the Arabs brought with them to Spain. To this day in Granada one of the main streets in the Arab quarter is called Calle Agua del Albayzín, and the water supply to the Alhambra Palace was established by building a dam and aqueduct from the River Darro over 6 kilometres away. Recent discoveries suggest that complex hydraulic devices were used to draw water up to the palace.

Returning to Syria, at the eastern desert palace, located 120 kilometres northeast of Palmyra en route to Doura Europos on the Euphrates, on the trade route to Persia and beyond, the irrigation system is again clear to see, but here without the benefit of an earlier structure to capitalise on. A dam 18 kilometres away to the northwest at a place called Al-Qawm brought water to irrigate the extensive 6 by 3 kilometres of gardens and orchards stocked with rabbits and gazelle, and also supplied the bath house within the palace. Arriving here at this well-watered fertile oasis must have felt like paradise after the rigours of the journey across the barren desert. Avenues of palm trees shaded the approach to the palace, intimations of what was to come in the Cordoba Mezquita, where the exiled Umayyads tried to recreate their lost paradise in Spain.

The rest of the palace complex, with its two distinct castles 40 metres apart, is still remarkably well preserved, with a few recycled columns and capitals from Palmyra and even a piece of rare pink granite. The fortified appearance with 9-metre-high walls and defence towers seems modelled on Roman or Sassanid forts, built to accommodate large armies.

A feature not seen at the western palace, though, is a large machicolation box set above the monumental entrance gateway between the twin towers of the main facade. This is the first known use of a machicolation box in the world, dating from 729, designed as holes in the overhang of a parapet for defenders to fire arrows or to drop liquids or projectiles down onto their attackers. They were much favoured by later Arab military architects, and the Crusaders copied them and took the idea back to Europe, where they first appeared in Richard the Lionheart's favourite castle, the twelfth-century Château Gaillard near Rouen.

In other respects, the grandiose and elaborate facade set within the two round towers is very similar to the western palace, showing an eclectic mix of influences both local and foreign, such as Byzantine, Mesopotamian and Persian. The lower walls are of grey limestone while the upper levels are of Mesopotamian brick, probably added after 760 by the Abbasids of Iraq, who generally used brick more than stone since Iraq was naturally less endowed with stone than Syria. It is the earliest known use in Syria of these distinctively decorated bands of brick patterning, similar to a kind of dentil frieze, another style to make its way to Europe in later centuries. Brick was also used to build the vaults of the adjacent caravanserai, along with the domes

This facade from the eighth-century palace of Mshatta in today's Jordan, now in the Berlin Museum of Islamic Art, shows the complex blend of geometry and natural motifs so typical of Umayyad art.

that topped the twin towers, a technique imported from Iraq. Typically Syrian here and at the western palace is the use of cut stone. The carving of crosses in the stone of the quarries some 12 kilometres away from the eastern palace suggests that Christians were among the workers employed.

For those who cannot visit Syria, the spectacular facade of Qasr al-Mshatta (meaning 'Winter Camp') can today be closely examined in Berlin's Pergamon Museum, where it forms the monumental entrance to the Museum of Islamic Art. It was prised off the west wall of the palace—which still stands as a ruin beside the perimeter fence of Jordan's Queen Alia International Airport—and shipped to Germany in 1903 as a gift from the then Ottoman sultan Abdul Hamid II to Kaiser Wilhelm II in gratitude for the construction of the Hejaz Railway. Its complex ground plan shows a variety of styles, from high-vaulted brick domes, almost like baths, to colonnaded open-air sections, reusing fine marble pillars from Roman sites. The facade now on display in the Pergamon gives the chance to get right up close to a piece of Umayyad decorative stone-carved sculpture from the eighth century and to admire the elaborate ornamentation of its carved reliefs, with magnificent giant rosettes and octagons, together with animals and human figures entangled in vines. The dramatic zigzag motif harks back to an early Mesopotamian motif, and heralds the strikingly sharp-pointed arches of Notre-Dame's south facade.

The final palace known for certain to be Umayyad is Qasr Tuba, very remote in the eastern desert of what is today Jordan. It would have been one of the largest but was left unfinished when its builder, Caliph Walid II, was killed. Its name, Tuba, means brick, and indeed the main characteristic of the construction here is the mud brickwork, not found in other palaces. All decorative elements are gone, either stolen or broken up, with just one piece of a decorated lintel surviving in the Jordan Archaeological Museum in Amman.

The Umayyad Palace of Khirbat al-Mafjar (c. 740)

The architecture of these and other Umayyad desert palaces, notably Khirbat al-Mafjar, 5 kilometres north of Jericho in what is today the Occupied West Bank, was extensively studied by R.W. Hamilton, former keeper of the department of antiquities of the Ashmolean Museum in Oxford and director of antiquities in Palestine. He wrote:

> It is no surprise to find in these buildings, in their ashlar and timber construction, their arcaded columns, their mosaics and marble revêtements, and in many features of their plans, a perpetuation of well-established Syrian traditions, the accumulated inheritance of Phoenician, Aramean, and Hellenized Christian societies over the two thousand years preceding the Arab conquest.[41]

Hamilton notes the eclectic character of Umayyad architecture and says it is easy to explain since the Arab empire 'united under one sovereignty the contiguous provinces of the old Roman and Persian empires, as well as the semi-independent societies of the desert marches between them'. Oleg Grabar, also

involved in parts of the Khirbat al-Mafjar excavation, notes that many influences appear in the decoration of the palace—the *simurgh* for example, a
kind of phoenix or dragon, is Persian, he tells us,[42] and in other cases as with
rosettes, an Eastern tradition appears alongside a classical one. This kind of
synthesis of Eastern and Western styles, together with the juxtaposition of
older and more recent ones, is how art historians like Grabar define
Umayyad art. Grabar even calls it the ultimate art of improvisation (*improvi-
sierende Kunst*).[43]

Hamilton examines the workmanship of the carved plaster and the carved
stone and is certain in his conclusion that the sculptors were local: 'Syrians
or Palestinians endowed with the capacity of their Phoenician or Aramean
forbears for freely assimilating the artistic ideas of their neighbours and giving
them out again with a new look derived from their own traditional materials
and skills.'[44] Several teams of men were busy on different sections of the
building simultaneously, he is sure. One interesting finding relates to the
accuracy of the Umayyad masons—or rather, the lack of it. When they were
doing their measurements for the walls of the palace, they started off with
great precision, but then allowed discrepancies to stand without appearing to
be bothered about correcting them.[45] Measurements, it seems, were judged
by eye rather than by the use of rulers. Remember again what Wren wrote
after surveying the old Gothic St Paul's before the 1666 fire; he 'was
astonish'd to find how negligent the first builders had been; they seem'd
Normans, and to have used the Norman foot; but they valued not exactness.
Nor were they true in their levels.'

Khirbat al-Mafjar was probably destroyed by the earthquake of 746, but
despite the many Persian elements of the palace—the use of brick vaulting
and of gypsum plaster, more suited to the mud or rubble architecture of
alluvial lands than to the rocky landscape of Palestine, and the enclosing wall
with its half-round buttress towers similar to the military architecture of
pre-Islamic Persia—the proof of local workers rather than Persian immigrants comes from the graffiti.[46] The names written in Arabic script in red
paint on a number of stones in the western wing and elsewhere within the
palace are Qustantin, Yuhanna, Ali, Kulthum, Muhammad, Abdullah and
Ubayd Allah, in Greek and with Arabic and Aramaic letters. They signify that

the masons were a bilingual group of mainly Muslims, some Christians, and possibly some Jews. The carpenters, plasterers and mosaicists were likely to be the same general mix, since old established crafts, often hereditary and fostering a conservative mentality, would also have largely stayed in the same hands in Syria, Jordan and Palestine, where most of the Umayyad building activity had been concentrated for more than half a century by this stage. The unique collection of desert palaces and the flurry of building activity that took place between 700 and 750 in Syria gives us a remarkable record of the techniques used, and how they gradually evolved. These things take a surprisingly long time to change, as Creswell's arch study showed, where the arches only became a tiny fraction sharper every twenty-five years or so. It is why we can be so sure that the same techniques in use in Syria were carried over to Spain by the Umayyads later in the eighth century, and almost certainly some of the workmen themselves even migrated. Masters come and masters go, but techniques and repertoires take a lot longer to change than their masters.

We also know from papyri and other literary sources that workmen were on occasion conscripted or engaged, and material appropriated, by the caliphs or their agents for work on buildings far removed from their places of origin.[47] This is how new techniques like brick vaulting, stucco revetments, and the use of carved stucco appear for the first time in Umayyad buildings.

Carved stucco had been used for example on mud brick buildings in Iraq as a protective covering for at least six centuries before the Arab conquest, for the simple reason that they had no stone there. Gypsum plaster was portable and relatively hard. In Syria the same thing happened with the desert palaces. In areas where they had stone, they used that for construction, as at Qasr Kharaneh. But where there was no stone, mud bricks, protected and decorated with gypsum plaster carving, were heavily used instead. The Umayyad dynastic colour was white from the banner of Mu'awiya, and much of the stucco work remained white. The dynastic colour of their successors, the Abbasids, was black.

The magisterial study of Khirbat al-Mafjar conducted by R.W. Hamilton[48] nearly didn't see the light of day, as it fell victim to politics. Archeology is a frequent casualty with changes of power and government. The withdrawal of the British mandatory administration in 1948 prior to the creation of the state

of Israel brought a sudden end to what had been twelve seasons of very fruitful excavation and led to the dispersal of the staff. American business magnate
and philanthropist John D. Rockefeller came to the rescue and made it possible to collate the results of the digs into a single volume, so that what
Hamilton describes as 'the first architectural history of Islam and the last of
Hellenism' could be fully recorded. Khirbat al-Mafjar represents, he tells us,

> a wealth of detail in construction and ornament which time and chance have
> preserved ... at a critical and fleeting moment: a moment when the reviving
> stimulus of religion and empire, of wealth and passionate will, under the
> Umayyad caliphs seemed about to transform, by a new synthesis of Greek and
> Asiatic genius, the millennial art of Hellenistic Syria.[49]

Most of the finds can be viewed today in the Rockefeller Museum in East
Jerusalem.

With the sudden fall of the Umayyads in 750, all that dynamism was cut
short, but as Hamilton explains, 'not before the first architectural experiments of the Muslim Empire had revealed the creative and assimilative powers and the technical capacity that existed, still alive and ready to be called
forth, in Syrian workshops.'

A new religion and aristocracy had created, he tells us, in Umayyad buildings like those at Khirbat al-Mafjar, 'the chance of comparing the work of
craftsmen in at least four different media: stone, plaster, mosaic and paint.'
Through the tangible record of the buildings, all of which date to the second
quarter of the eighth century, the planning traditions, structural methods and
preferred building materials can be examined, which show clearly the versa-
tility and resourcefulness of the craftsmen, as Hamilton puts it,

> in turning their minds and skills to those novel problems with which the over-
> turning of society and revolution in economy, taste and manners confronted
> them. Finally, we can detect behind the work of these craftsmen and masons
> the ebullient eccentricity of a young society, sport-loving and aesthetic, which
> could delight in courtly ceremonial, admit the obligations of religion, and

throw itself uninhibited in pursuit of the most luxurious refinements of pleasure.[50]

It is precisely these qualities which the Umayyads took with them to Spain and which reappeared there in Cordoba, in Madinat al-Zahra, in Toledo, in Seville and finally in Granada at the Alhambra. Synthesis and revival were the two main characteristics of Umayyad art, along with a natural gift for improvisation in the decorative arts. In carving the palace stuccowork the Umayyad sculptors devised repeating patterns on the 'wallpaper' method, allowing the pattern to run off the edge wherever it wanted, unlike the earlier Christian designers in Syria and elsewhere, who generally made sure their patterns stayed within borders.[51] This 'wallpaper' approach shows similarities with Sassanid textile-weaving techniques with which some of the craftsmen would have been familiar, along with a mixture of fantasy and realism in the birds and animals that appear entangled in infinite variations of foliage based on rosettes and vines, fruits and acanthus leaves. Such an exuberant love of nature is one of the key characteristics that John Ruskin, influential Victorian art critic of the nineteenth century, would go on to describe in his definition of 'Gothic', which had its revival in his era in a new flush of faith, just as the original twelfth-century Gothic of Europe had represented an outpouring of faith to re-establish the Christian identity of Europe after the Crusades, as we will explore further in the coming chapters.

The Trefoil Arch

Among the discoveries by R.W. Hamilton at Khirbat al-Mafjar, perhaps the most significant is the trefoil arch, which comes to the fore again so prominently in the Cordoba Mezquita discussed in the next chapter, and which makes its way from there into northern Europe and all across the continent and into England to become a major hallmark of Gothic cathedrals and churches. We noticed its use high inside the Dome of the Rock, and Hamilton finds it again here in a panel of carved stucco plaster in the palace entrance hall, where it forms a repeating pattern of alternating three-lobed arches and round arches resting on twin colonettes. The spandrels (the gap between the bases of the arches) were filled with stepped crenellations, miniature upside-down versions of ones on the bath house gate tower, and reminiscent of the Mesopotamian merlons so favoured by the Umayyads and seen on the outer walls of the Damascus Great Mosque and all round the outer walls of the Cordoba Mezquita. Hamilton believes the panel was a kind of balustrade to support busts in the entrance hall and observes: 'In any case it anticipated by some centuries the lobed [trefoil] arches of medieval Saracenic architecture, and in the field of ornament, the three-lobed arcading sometimes found in early Abbasid stucco-work.'[52] He speculates that its origin may lie further east. In Sassanid Persia for example, similar decorative motifs were found, especially in stucco borders, such as a trefoil leaf intertwined with a swastika pattern or the very common beading—thought to be an imitation of strings of beads or even pearls—which would be stitched on to mark the edgings of luxurious clothing or textile furnishings. All these patterns he found in abundance at Khirbat al-Mafjar.

Vaulting Techniques

R.W. Hamilton conducted many detailed analyses with meticulous care and precision during his excavations, among which was a study of the vaulting techniques used in the palace. Most of the vaults and domes in the palace and the baths were constructed from kiln-baked bricks, showing a sophisticated grasp of the methods inherited from pre-Islamic Iraq and Persia where building in mud brick and rubble—the local materials to hand—had already achieved very high standards. The vaulting in the palace also shows competence in barrel vaulting and cross vaults sustained on transverse masonry arches, but the more surprising feature is the stone vaulting in the great archway entrance to the palace gate tower porch and its adjoining arcades. From elaborate reconstructions of the palace porch Hamilton's assistant, G. U. Spencer Corbett, drew a diagram showing the archivolt and vaulting system. Hamilton concludes: 'The construction of this vault, with its groins worked out with logical persistence, proves that masons in Palestine during the eighth century shirked none of the difficulties in cutting a true cross-vault.'[53]

Archivolts are decorative mouldings running round the face of an arch. The term is generally used to describe the features of medieval or Renaissance buildings in Europe, where archivolts are often decorated with sculpture, as in the archivolts on the west facade of Chartres Cathedral (1140–50). Used briefly by the Romans, they then died out till they were used again in Romanesque architecture, and elaborated further in Gothic, especially in the cathedrals. The basilica at Saint-Denis has them, in what we have learnt in Chapter 2 is widely regarded as the first truly Gothic church. The archivolt ornament of radiating niches strikes Hamilton as foreign, and the closest parallel he is aware of is the archivolt of the (now largely fallen) great *iwan*, or hall, at Ctesiphon, 'the pre-eminent monument of Sassanid brick building.' But given the Ctesiphon work is in stone, not brick, he concludes that the archivolts at Hatra, where radiating busts decorate the *iwan* arches, are more similar in effect. Hatra, in modern Iraq, was capital of Araba, the first Arab state to be established outside Arabia, and thrived in the second century as a caravan city controlling important trade routes on the frontier of the Roman and Parthian empires, before falling to the Persian Sassanids.

Hamilton finds convincing evidence of sophisticated cross vaulting to support the ceilings of the bath hall and its circular ambulatory and discovers that three different types of baked brick were identifiable in use at the palace. All were just 4 centimetres thick, but one type measured 33 by 33 centimetres, the next 25 by 25 centimetres, and finally a tapering one measured 34 centimetres on one side and 31 centimetres on the other. The tapering bricks were used for the dome while the square ones were used in barrel vaults laid alternately, first the large then the small, to make the arch. Hamilton concludes:

> The common Byzantine and Persian practice (which also appears at Mshatta and Qasr al-Tuba) of laying the bricks parallel with the vault thrusts (thus minimizing the use of timber formwork) does not seem to have been used at al Mafjar. Perhaps the reason was that the high standard of masonry building in Syria demanded the use of so much formwork for stone vaults in any case that economy of timber in brickwork became pointless.[54]

He is also able to deduce that the domes were brick-built, in a true hemi-sphere shape, resting on pendentives (curved triangles of vaulting that rise from the corners of a square base to support a circular dome). The Romans were the first to experiment with pendentives in the second and third centu-ries, gradually improving the techniques and the geometry till it reached its apogee in the sixth-century Hagia Sophia in Constantinople. The methods advanced for supporting ever larger domes will be explored, culminating in chapter 8 with the complete mastery of the technique used by Sinan in the domed mosques of Istanbul, which Christopher Wren says he then used in constructing his dome at St Paul's.

At Khirbat al-Mafjar, Hamilton's excavations reveal that the internal ceilings of all the domes were heavily decorated with gypsum plaster carvings of great ornateness. The inside dome of the bath hall porch for example was covered in one continuous scroll-work 'of majestic proportions', in which the coils of giant

This high-quality eighth-century floor mosaic can still be seen in situ at the Umayyad palace of Khirbat al-Mafjar near Jericho. Its self-contained border design and colourful nature symbolism share many motifs familiar to us from European Gothic buildings.

flowers composed a bunch of 'grape hyacinths' sprouting from the cleft of a split vine leaf and decorated further with floral medallions and sprays. Not a single surface was left unfilled, showing the same energy and exuberance as later Gothic would. Motifs used range from half-palmette flowers to fir cones, to the classical egg and dart, or egg and tongue motif, where the rims of the eggs have been combined with upside-down tongues to form three-pointed leaves, very typical of how early motifs evolve creating new forms. It is difficult to say whether or not domes used in a secular setting like this carried the same cosmic significance, pointing to the astral sphere of the afterlife, as they did in religious settings, such as the Dome of the Rock and Al-Aqsa in Jerusalem, and the small dome above the transept in front of the *mihrab* in the Great Umayyad Mosque. On the other hand, given the size of the Umayyad Empire when the palace was built, the domes must have lent a special sense of importance of which the caliphs certainly felt they deserved by that stage.

The Syrian Umayyads enthusiastically adopted the double-decker arcade in their palaces and mosques to lend light, grace and elegance, as here at Anjar, a unique early eighth century Umayyad city in the Beqaa Valley, Lebanon.

Serjilla, one of Syria's Dead or Forgotten Cities, showing the double-height arcade of the fifth-century public meeting hall, still standing in Idlib Province.

The fact that the most beautiful mosaic in the entire palace was found on the floor of the semi-circular *mihrab* apse of the ruler's audience hall (*diwan*), rather than in the much smaller open-air mosque that abutted the palace, tells us the Umayyad priorities. This audience hall was encrusted with carved plaster motifs of the highest standard anywhere in the palace, covering the entire inner surface of the walls. The mosaic is a magnificent ensemble composed within a semi-circular frame bordered to look like a tasselled carpet, of a superb tree in full leaf bearing golden fruits, perhaps apples or quinces, with gazelles beneath it, two nibbling peacefully at foliage to the left, another being caught by a lion sinking his teeth and claws into its back. Is it the circle of life and death? Is this the tree of life? Either way, it is another motif we see often in Gothic cathedrals and their stained glass windows.

The complex geometry of the decorations has been analysed by Hamilton; in their hundreds they are very varied, but one example will do here, which was found built into the facade of the palace gate tower. At least three arcade-patterned medallions composed of six triangular blocks form a twelve-lobed rosette in which the petals are replaced by radiating arches. The arches themselves spring from tiny columns, which emerge from a calyx-like capital and enclose alternating palmettes, grapes and pomegranates. As ever, it is contained within a border and then placed within a shaped frame, the typical Umayyad design that was subsequently transferred to Cordoba in the Umayyad buildings there, before finding its way northwards into France, where the subsequent Gothic cathedrals of Europe used the same styles and methods in their later stained glass windows.

The tools of the craftsmen consisted simply of a ruler, a compass/pair of dividers, a taut string and a sharp scoring point to draw out the patterns. Then each mason needed a pair of chisels, one narrow, one broad, to carve out the shapes.

More precursors of methods to come can be seen in the double-arcaded panel found in balustrades of the palace forecourt. The panel is carved in plaster, with a lower arcade of nine arches supporting an upper one of eight arches. The upper arches span the supporting pillars of the lower arches, as indeed they do in the double-decker arcade at the caliph's palace in the Umayyad city of Anjar in modern Lebanon in the Beqaa Valley, as if in anticipation of the double arches of the Cordoba Mezquita. The style had already been seen in the Dead or Forgotten Cities scattered over northern Syria, a well-preserved example of which survives today in the stone-built *andron* or men's meeting room at Serjilla, dating back to the fifth century.

The Rose Window

One final unique feature, which Hamilton was able to piece together through meticulous detective work and reconstruction following his extensive excavations at Khirbat al-Mafjar, is what he calls 'the round stone window'. He deduced from its position relative to surrounding fragments where it was found that it had fallen from the pediment of the roof gable in the palace, and its function was therefore likely to provide an interesting pattern of light to the central audience room of the palace. It was composed of 106 pieces of stone, about 85 centimetres thick and carved on both sides to represent six interlaced ribbons forming a six-pointed star within a circle.

Given its position high up within the gable pediment, some have specu-lated that we may have here the very first 'rose window', the feature so favoured high up in a similar position on Gothic cathedrals such as Chartres, Reims and Notre-Dame de Paris. Its purpose, to provide light and decoration for the special space from both inside and outside, and its round shape, are evidently similar. Predating it are single circular stone windows in the gables of several churches in the vicinity of St Simeon's basilica northwest of Aleppo, none of which, sadly, are still intact. From black and white photos in Butler's *Early Churches in Syria* however, we can see that the fifth- and

A reconstruction of the stone-carved Umayyad 'rose window' found at Hisham's Palace (Khirbat al-Mafjar) near Jericho. It had fallen from the pediment of the palace roof gable, where its function would have been to let in decorative patterns of light.

sixth-century churches at Simkhar, Qasr Iblisu, Deir Sem'aan and the Church of St Mary at Sheikh Sleiman, all had them, as did the gable of the Church of Bissos at Ruweiha in the Dead Cities further south, also now collapsed. Simkhar, Butler tells us, was 'as elaborately decorated as was possible within the limits of the Christian ornament of the period, and gives an effect which suggests the richest period of Gothic.'[55]

The most similar style of stone-carved rose window to the one at Khirbat al-Mafjar is found on the Romanesque facade of San Pietro church in Spoleto, Umbria. There are many other examples of decorative carved stucco window grilles, always in complex geometric patterns, found at the baths and adjoining palace of Khirbat al-Mafjar (and other Umayyad desert palaces like Qasr al-Hair al-Gharbi, fragments of which can be seen in the Damascus National Museum). Some give a sense of weaving, textiles, braiding on a garment or flowing inter-lace, sometimes in stucco decoration and similarly in the mosaics where the patterns form elaborate interlocking circles. All these patterns are built up using equilateral triangles and often form the borders as in a carpet design.

All this astonishing variety of vegetal and geometric decoration as found in the Umayyad palace of Khirbat al-Mafjar is preserved for us and for posterity by the incredible lifetime's work of Professor R.W. Hamilton and his defini-tive study published in 1959. The site is still there, and open to visitors, but the politics of the region discourages them because of Israeli signage implying it is dangerous to enter the West Bank. It is possible for foreign tourists to rent a car that can be legally driven in both the West Bank and in Israel, though all but the most determined are likely to be put off by Israel's draco-nian security restrictions. Even if you fight your way through the red tape, the Israeli Defence Force soldiers have instructions to obstruct you, as they obstructed me when I drove to Sebastea and was turned back by an Israeli jeep with two heavily armed IDF soldiers telling me it was dangerous that day. With the help of local Palestinians after the Israeli soldiers had gone, I found a back way to Sebastea avoiding their checkpoint, where there was of course no danger at all. It is simpler to visit by taxi from Jordan after crossing the Allenby Bridge. I would urge people to go and see for themselves. There is no substitute for being able to touch the stones yourself.

5

ANDALUSIA

The Umayyads in Spain (756–1492)

In June 2019, as part of my research for a new book on the history of Damascus, I visited Cordoba. Well aware that the Umayyads were the origin of the Islamic civilisation that lasted for nearly eight centuries in the Iberian Peninsula, I was surprised, not to say shocked, when I saw how little that fact seems to be known, let alone acknowledged, in today's Spain. Despite the hundreds of thousands of tourists flocking to Seville, Granada and other Andalusian cities each year, the Spanish appear unwilling to celebrate their Muslim past.

This chapter therefore begins by clarifying how 'Moorish' culture came about, before turning to the Cordoba Mezquita, described by early Castilian Christians as 'the most perfect and most noble mosque that the Moors have in Spain.'[1]

Syrian Beginnings

'Farewell O Syria, my beautiful province, what a paradise you will be for the enemy!' These are reportedly the words of Byzantine emperor Heraclius as his ship set sail from Antioch forever, returning to Constantinople. Byzantine rule in Syria was over, leaving the way clear for the first Muslim empire, the Umayyads, a family from the Quraysh of Mecca, the tribe of the Prophet

Muhammad, to establish itself in Damascus. But a little over a century later the Umayyads would lose their paradise too, when in 750 they were displaced by the rival Abbasid clan who claimed descent from the Prophet Muhammad's uncle. The Abbasids moved their capital east, first to Kufa then to Baghdad, and had all members of the House of Umayya assassinated—all but one, the twenty-year-old grandson of Caliph Hisham who managed a dramatic escape, first on horseback across the desert, then by swimming across the Euphrates. Known as Abd al-Rahman I, he was a remarkable young man who managed to survive numerous attempts on his life. For the next five years, he and the man historians call his 'Greek' freedman Badr made their way west across the whole of North Africa in disguise, penniless and friendless, outwitting their would-be captors. Heading towards the homeland of his Berber mother, they were finally given refuge by his maternal uncles in Ceuta. In 755 Abd al-Rahman I crossed the Straits of Gibraltar, arriving in Spain near Malaga at the invitation of Umayyad clients who still felt loyalty to the Umayyad clan.[2]

This young Umayyad prince, who would have learnt his horsemanship, hunted and received his formative education at the desert palaces like Qasr al-Hair ash-Sharqi, was described by the Arab historians Ibn Idhari and Ibn al-Athir as tall and lean, with sharp aquiline features and thin red hair. Proving himself a capable military and political leader, he established the Umayyad dynasty that went on to rule much of the Iberian Peninsula for the best part of three centuries. In Syria the Umayyad caliphate had lasted a little under 100 years before the Abbasid coup brought it to an abrupt end, but its energy and exuberance were to show themselves again in what came to be known as the Cordoba caliphate.

The Abbasid caliph Al-Mansur, arch-enemy to the young Umayyad prince, is said to have grudgingly given Abd al-Rahman I the exalted title 'Falcon of the Quraish'. The five-year journey to Spain would have been an extremely formative experience for the young prince. Not only was it challenging physically, on foot first through Palestine, then the Sinai desert and into Egypt, but also emotionally, as he had been forced to leave his young son and sisters behind, and to watch his fourteen-year-old brother be decapitated on the banks of the Euphrates. North Africa had been partially conquered by the Umayyads, but it was not safe to reveal his identity till he reached the

Maghrib. Even there enemies were still pursuing him and at one point a Berber chieftain's wife had to hide him under her rugs and possessions.[3]

Once he reached Morocco Abd al-Rahman I wanted to cross into Spain. The first Arabs had arrived there some decades earlier in 711, but a Berber revolt had left the province fraught with rivalry between the Berbers and various Arab tribes of opposing loyalties. Abd al-Rahman I could not have known if any might be loyal to him because of his Umayyad lineage but decided to risk it. From the tribes' point of view the young prince was also an unknown quantity, untested in battle. He struck an unlikely alliance with a group of 500 Yemenite notables, who agreed to hook up with him thinking they could use his Umayyad name to take control for themselves, only to find that the young prince took charge instead.

News of his arrival just east of Malaga soon spread across the province and waves of people, including other exiled Syrians, came from all corners of Andalusia to pay their respects. In Malaga a beautiful young slave girl was offered to him but he sent her back. There were schemes aplenty, trying to get him to marry into various rival chieftains' families, all of which culminated in a battle with the two sides facing each other near Cordoba on opposing banks of the Guadalquivir, in full flood. During the battles, plots and counter-plots that ensued, Abd al-Rahman I showed himself to be a skilful tactician and diplomat, as well as an able fighter and horseman.

After he had seen off his many rivals, he proclaimed himself head of the Emirate of Cordoba and let it be known throughout the Muslim world that Andalusia was now a safe haven for friends of the House of Umayya. His call was answered by waves of supporters, many of them also exiled Syrians, who came to join his ranks. Among them was his young son. His sisters were unable to make the long journey from Syria safely, but it is important to understand the extent to which Abd al-Rahman I's new emirate was begun with Syrians, whom he then put into positions of trust in his administration and who therefore helped shape the style and culture of Andalusia. In the context of the earlier colonisations of Europe by Phoenicians, Persians and others already mentioned in Chapter 3, the Syrian Arab conquest of Spain in the early eighth century and subsequent Arab expansion into Sicily, Italy, southern France and even Switzerland can be seen as the last in a tradition of

Near Eastern expansion into Europe. The fact that the Arab presence in Spain then lasted close to 800 years—longer than the Romans in Spain—is testament to the power of traditions stretching back thousands of years to the first colonisers, the Phoenician merchants from Tyre on Lebanon's coast.[4] Their colony of Cádiz, founded in 1100 BCE and thought to be the oldest city in Europe, grew rich on trading Spanish silver, Baltic amber and British tin.

The province of Syria had long been seen as a paradise, a coveted prize across the centuries, and certainly the Umayyads had loved and appreciated its many assets, its variety of landscape, its fertility, and its rivers, plains and mountains, especially when compared to their original desert homeland of the Arabian Peninsula. Spain and Syria have some geographical similarities in terms of size, landscape and climate, and when Abd al-Rahman I landed near Malaga and fought his first battle near the city of Cordoba, he is likely to have seen echoes of his Syrian homeland and Damascus with its fertile orchards and the River Barada flowing down from the mountains.

All exiles, refugees displaced from their home, instinctively seek to re-create what they have had to leave behind. It is a deeply rooted instinct, to form a new community. In London for example, communities of Cypriot Turks settled together in Green Lanes, Portuguese in Stockwell and Caribbeans in Brixton. Shops offering the cuisine of each community opened up, followed by restaurants. Abd al-Rahman I was even referred to in Spain as 'al-Dakheel', the immigrant.

That Abd al-Rahman I felt this nostalgia, not just on arrival but for many years after, is clear from a poem he composed in 770:

> *A palm tree stands in the middle of Rusafa*
> *Born in the West, far from the land of palms*
> *I said to it, 'How like me you are, far away and in exile!*
> *In long separation from family and friends*
> *You have sprung from soil in which you are a stranger*
> *And I, like you, am far away from home.'*

His poem was to set a precedent in Andalusia, in both literature and music, for nostalgic laments, a tradition that continues today through flamenco in Spain and fado in Portugal.

In Spain, a Syrian community quickly established itself around the exiled Umayyad prince, keen to make Spain into a 'New Syria' and Cordoba into a 'New Damascus'. The fertility of Spain had once been legendary but on arrival the Syrian newcomers found instead a land in which agriculture, under the last years of the Visigothic rule, had regressed and decayed from the high levels achieved under the Romans. In the sixth and seventh centuries the Visigoths had produced the best art in Western Europe, much of it inspired by earlier Syrian models. Visigothic churches show strong influence from Byzantine Syrian architecture, in their layout, basilical form, horseshoe arches, projecting apses, carved windows, wooden pitched roofs, crosses in circles and walls carved with symbols such as the rose with eight petals.[5] The same Syrian models influenced the development of Asturian architecture (from the late eighth to early tenth century, that is the pre-Romanesque period), since it was the direct heir, for political and spiritual reasons, of Visigothic architecture. The basilical layout of Asturian religious buildings, along with elements like the ornamentation above the north entrance and latticework windows of the ninth-century church of San Miguel de Lillo in northwest Spain, takes clear inspiration from the churches of the Syrian Dead Cities.[6] The Syrian Umayyads quickly absorbed the Hispano-Roman legacy, to which they added their own expertise in water systems, irrigation and agronomy in order to effect a great agricultural revival in Andalusia.[7] Among the plants and crops brought in from Syria were palm trees and pomegranates, powerful symbols of the decorative elements that had covered the stucco on the facades of their desert palaces and grown in their gardens.

Abd al-Rahman I had to fight and put down challenges to his authority for much of his thirty-two-year reign. He also had to combat external enemies such as Charlemagne, leader of the Frankish army that had been hired by the Muslim governors of Barcelona and Zaragoza who opposed him, and also against the Abbasids and the Berbers. To survive, he bought in his own massive mercenary armies of Berbers, so that his army totalled some 40,000. As with the original Umayyad caliphate of Damascus, religious tolerance was the norm, with Christians and Jews, seen as fellow monotheists referred to as 'People of the Book', paying a special tax but free to worship as they chose. By the tenth century a high percentage of Andalusis had converted to Islam, whether to escape the tax or out of belief it is impossible to know. Intermarriage was fairly common and followed the normal Islamic rules, whereby a Muslim man can marry a non-Muslim woman, but a Muslim woman cannot marry a non-Muslim man unless he converts. The granddaughter of the Visigoth king for instance married a Muslim whom she bore two sons, both of whom became high noblemen.

Abd al-Rahman I's successors went on to rule their remarkable empire till 1009 from their capital of Cordoba, which grew into one of the largest and wealthiest cities of the medieval world and certainly the most powerful cultural centre of tenth-century Europe. Christian communities were left unmolested, free to worship as they wished under their own ecclesiastical laws and jurisdiction, as long as they, along with the Jews, paid the poll tax, which had three bands according to the wealth of the payer. Women and children, the old and the destitute, monks and those with chronic illnesses were exempt. Spanish Christians were given land ownership rights they had been denied by their former rulers, the Visigoth elite, who had kept privileges for themselves.

Abd al-Rahman I had funded the building of new roads and aqueducts from the start of his reign, but finally as a man now in his mid-fifties, he had consolidated his control sufficiently to allow him to begin establishing a more Arab character for the Romano-Visigothic city of Cordoba. He built an aqueduct for the supply of pure water to the city, then in 784 replaced the Visigothic palace with a new Umayyad one, and the following year replaced the Visigothic Church of St Vincent with a new Great Mosque, universally known to this day as the Mezquita, Spanish for mosque.

The Cordoba Mezquita

Following the Umayyad tradition of speed in construction, the Cordoba Mezquita was completed in a single year from 785 to 786, helped by a large quantity of Roman and Visigothic stones available for re-use, and by abundant booty from the successful Narbonne campaign to provide the funds. Abd al-Rahman I devoted many hours each day to overseeing the work himself and was clearly closely involved in the design, consulting constantly with the stonemasons. The display of stones bearing masons' names and marks, on view inside the Mezquita along its southern wall today, shows them to have been overwhelmingly Arab.

Though he was not to know his mosque would be the subject of over 500 works[8] and become the icon of Muslim Spain for all future generations, Abd al-Rahman I clearly conceived it from the outset as a political statement that his dynasty was now the supreme power in the Iberian Peninsula and was here to stay. Viewed from the outside, encompassed by high crenellated walls, the Mezquita looks more like a fortress than a mosque, and the Great Mosque of Damascus too, the high walls of the Roman temple enclosure disguise the building's function as a mosque till you enter. Abd al-Rahman I also conceived the mosque as emulating the two sanctuaries of Islam, at Mecca and at Jerusalem. Enlarged by his successors, the Cordoba Mezquita did indeed become the Ka'ba of Western Islam, a rival site of pilgrimage. According to the tenth-century historian Al-Razi, the Visigothic Church of St Vincent had up till then been used by both the small Muslim population and the largely Catholic population. The original site had also been a temple, like the Damascus Cathedral of St John the Baptist. Just as his fellow Umayyad Al-Walid had done in Damascus, Abd al-Rahman I is said to have secured the agreement of the Christians to demolish the church, giving them land to build a new one in a different location.[9]

When Abd al-Rahman I died two years later in 788, his son succeeded him, and his grandsons later set about promoting a court culture in which Arabic poetry and music and the acquisition of scientific knowledge were prioritised. Cultural exchanges with the Islamic heartlands to the east continued and scholars, poets and scientists travelled in both directions. The mosque itself, together with the courtyard, formed the core of the city, its spiritual heart, a place of learning and teaching, surrounded by the bustling souks, just as in Damascus. The Mezquita was the first grand Umayyad mosque to be built in Spain and is the only one to survive today. All the other mosques in Spain perished in the

Christian Reconquista,[10] but of course the Mezquita survived because it was turned into a Catholic cathedral. A thirteenth-century chronicle relates:

> the Bishop of Osma, and with him the master Lope [de Fitero, first bishop of Cordoba after the Reconquista], who placed for the first time the sign of the cross on the tower, entered into the mosque, and preparing what was necessary so that the mosque could be made a church, expelled the Muhammadan superstition or abomination, sanctifying the place by the dispersion of holy water with salt; and what was a diabolical lair before, was made into a church of Jesus Christ, called by the name of his glorious Mother.[11]

To reach the mosque you have to walk through the narrow pedestrian streets of Old Cordoba, just as you have to wander through the narrow alleys of Old Damascus to reach the Great Umayyad Mosque at its heart. The so-called Gate of Forgiveness, completed in 1377, feeds visitors into the wide

The interior of the Cordoba Mezquita presents a dense forest of pillars crowned by double arcades of horseshoe arches in Abd al-Rahman I's dynastic colours of red and white.

spacious courtyard planted with orange trees and ablution fountains. The gate is part of the tall minaret, added in 952 by Abd al-Rahman III, which is square-shaped and divided into sections as it gets taller, like all Syrian minarets, and reminiscent of the Minaret of the Bride on the Damascus Umayyad Mosque. Nearby in Cordoba, in the Plaza de San Juan, a much smaller ninth-century Umayyad minaret that would have been contemporary with the Mezquita still survives, though the mosque to which it was once attached is long gone. Today called the Alminar (minaret) de San Juan, it is significant for the first known use of the twin window, both blind and open, divided by a slender column with a capital, decorating the square sides of the walls.

It was a look that went on to become a key tenth-century style, used on buildings by Andalusians and Mozarabs (Spanish Christians living under Islamic rule), and was later adopted as a defining feature of Romanesque architecture in Catalonia and in France, as seen in many churches such as Saint-Jean-de-Muzols in the Ardèche.[12]

In 1593 the minaret of the Mezquita itself was converted to a bell tower at the fourth section where the first windows appeared. Paintings of Christian saints now fill the blind arches, the first hint at what is to come. Distinctive Mesopotamian merlon shapes, so typical of the Umayyads, crenellate the tops of the mosque wall, exactly as at the Damascus Umayyad Mosque.

Inside, however, any echoes of Syria or Damascus today lie deep under the Catholic overlay. Cultural appropriation on a colossal, not to say shocking, scale has taken place. Church organ music plays constantly to impose the Christian identity on the space and to invade anything that might have remained from the original ethos of the mosque. Fat cherubs dangle from the domes, while ornate gilt frames hang round excessive numbers of Virgin and Child statues and crucifixes crammed into every available arch or space, creating a grand total of forty-two side chapels round the entire perimeter wall.

Yet, if you can rise above the Catholic overlay to see the real mosque underneath, in spite of the local authorities' efforts to thwart any such attempt, you will find some differences from but also many points of similarity with not only the Damascus Umayyad Mosque but also many other Umayyad buildings.

First of all, the ground plan which Abd al-Rahman I chose for his mosque is square, like the Umayyad desert palaces he grew up in, while the Damascus Umayyad Mosque is rectangular, more like a basilica style. The original area of the mosque was actually much smaller than the Damascus mosque, though by the time it had been extended by Abd al-Rahman I's successors, it ended up much larger. Each enlargement, however, respected the spirit of the original building, so that it is incontrovertible that Abd al-Rahman I in effect left his mark and that of the Syrian Umayyads on Hispano-Moorish architecture forever. The Mezquita without doubt set the standard for all other sacred architecture in Andalusia.

After the various extensions, the last of which was in 994, the Mezquita had the largest covered area of any recorded medieval mosque. For over six centuries, till the Blue Mosque was built in Istanbul in 1609–17, it was the second largest mosque in the world after Mecca. The single most remarkable feature of the Cordoba Great Mosque is the hypostyle hall, a veritable forest of pillars, achieved through the multiple extensions that took place over a 200-year period. There are 1,293 today in total, crowned by horseshoe arches in alternating red brick and pale limestone, no accidental choice, but Abd al-Rahman I's own dynastic colours. The effect is to make the worshippers almost lose their bearings in the space, to give a sense of the infinite power of the sacred.

Felix Arnold of the German Archaeological Institute in Madrid has conducted a remarkable mathematical analysis of this space,[13] which led him to conclude that in tenth-century Cordoba an entirely new mathematical approach to architecture was developed and put into practice, both in the tenth-century Mezquita extensions by Abd al-Rahman I's successors and at Madinat al-Zahra, their palace outside the city. He contrasts this approach with the standard Roman approach of architects like Vitruvius, who used mathematics to take measurements inside each separate element of a building—be it a courtyard or a hall or a large main room. The Roman approach was to then move to the next room and repeat the process to achieve symmetry within each separate space. In Cordoba, on the other hand, the architects used equilateral triangles and geometry to create a spatial web where all parts are equal and simultaneously part of a single, unified space. Arnold credits this almost revolutionary approach to the huge advances made in the field of mathematics in the Court of Baghdad during the Islamic Golden Age, where the Abbasid caliphs had encouraged scholarship under their patronage, attracting scientists and philosophers from the entire region, irrespective of ethnicity or religion.

These scholars were able to build on the knowledge learnt from classical Greek mathematicians like Euclid by combining it with sixth- and seventh-century innovations made in India, such as the decimal numeral system, with zero as a digit. The scholar of Turkic origin Al-Khwarizmi (c. 780–846), whose name was Latinised as Algoritmi, from which we get the Western word 'algorithm', worked mainly in Baghdad and invented the foundations of algebra. Such knowledge was not introduced to the West till the Latin translations of the twelfth century, but within the Islamic world it spread quickly across North Africa into Andalusia and into the Umayyad Court of Cordoba. The Indo-Arabic numeral system had already been introduced to Cordoba by the Andalusian polymath of Berber descent Abbas ibn Firnas (810–88), and geometry was employed in the design of ground plans, elevations, decorative patterns, and even to measure the human view. Tenth-century court mathematician Al-Maghribi worked on techniques of surveying and triangulation while also translating Ptolemy's star chart and improving the translation of his *Almagest*, so the fact that a revolutionary new development took place here in tenth-century Cordoba was no fluke—all the right conditions were in place, combined with the necessary knowledge.

The Mezquita is unquestionably a mosque and could never be mistaken for a church. There is nothing in the world that even closely resembles its unique hypostyle hall. It represents a major innovation in architecture, recognised as one of the greatest monuments of the medieval world and certainly the greatest Islamic building in the West. In Damascus, simple two-tier arcades were used in the prayer hall with the sole purpose of giving extra height to the space, but in Cordoba the arcades are supported on shorter columns and the two-tiered arcades become the dominant characteristic. The overall effect is an impressive intensification of the sense of space replicating itself, heightened by the alternating colours of the pale limestone and red brickwork of the arches themselves. The lower tier of arches is supported by smaller

The gates of the Cordoba Mezquita display the full gamut of arches so enjoyed by the Umayyads. Trefoil arches, blind arches and pointed arches had already appeared under the Syrian Umayyads in their desert palaces, but now interlocking arches, multifoil arches and even ogee arches were added to the repertoire, abounding over all surfaces. Stepped merlon crenellations on top of the walls complete the Umayyad ensemble.

columns, mainly in lavish pink and blue/black marble recycled from antiquity, while the upper tier sits on long and narrow piers that have been inserted between the arches of the lower tier, resting on the columns below.

The further innovation involves the arches themselves. At Damascus some of the arches have just the slightest hint of the horseshoe shape, while at

Cordoba the horseshoe arch becomes for the first time the shape of choice, used throughout. The Visigoths claimed the invention of the horseshoe arch for themselves, and a few of their churches in the northern part of Spain do have short, squat horseshoe arches sitting on blunt pillars. Examples are the church of Santa Maria, Quintanilla de las Viñas (Burgos), and San Juan de Banos (Palencia) but recent scholarship has disputed the pre-Islamic dating of their arches and claimed they are from the ninth or tenth century and therefore Mozarabic.[14] Whatever the accuracy of the dating, there is no denying that the grace and slender elegance of the horseshoe arches inside the Mezquita belong to another world entirely. Their ancestors are certainly pre-Islamic, with examples at Ctesiphon and across northern Syria as mentioned in Chapter 4, but here in Spain the form was developed to a whole new level. It became known throughout the West as the Moorish arch, and was popular in Victorian times to define the entrance of large public buildings like railway stations, as in Liverpool and Manchester.

In the later expansions of the tenth century, interlocking/intersecting arches appear for the first time, marking the location of the original eighth-century *mihrab* and the new *mihrab*. One important side effect of these arches is to create curves that are more pointed than any seen before. Interlocking arches also appear above the outer gates of the mosque on the west side.

During the tenth-century extensions, the multifoil arch emerged as a further evolution of the trefoil arch, breaking the arch into an uneven number of lobes, anything between five and eleven, so that there is still always a centred one flanked by an equal number of lobes on each side.

The feature would become exclusively Andalusian and continued to be widely used even after the Reconquista. Trefoil arches, blind arches and pointed arches had already appeared under the Syrian Umayyads in the desert palaces, but now interlocking arches, multifoil arches and even ogee arches were added to the repertoire, abounding over all surfaces on both inner and outer walls. The full range is perhaps best appreciated from the outside, where the mosque gates on the western wall facing the palace incorporate the full gamut—horseshoe, blind, pointed, interlocking, trefoil, multifoil and ogee. The earliest is Puerta de San Esteban (the Gate of St Stephen), the original entrance to Abd al-Rahman I's mosque, known at the time as Bab al-Wuzara', the Gate of the Viziers.

Early Ribbed Vaulting

Felix Arnold has speculated that the idea of intersecting or crossing arches may have itself been inspired by the view towards the *mihrab* of the pre-existing prayer hall. Both the Jerusalem Dome of the Rock and the Damascus Umayyad Mosque had already used double-decker arcades in their prayer hall to give extra height, but the width of the prayer hall at Cordoba meant that if the viewer looked diagonally across the rows of arches, one arcade appeared to cross over with those of the next arcade, 'creating a highly intricate web of arches.'[15] The result was to turn a three-dimensional effect into an extremely elegant two-dimensional form that could be used as decoration. Arnold also makes a convincing case for how the architects and master masons working on the extension to the mosque, once they had seen the pleasing aesthetic effect in both three- and two-dimensional forms, realised the advantages of extending this new geometry into the dome to provide decorative effect and strength simultaneously. The bases of four pairs of interlocking arches in each dome rest on eight sets of pillars that together distribute and carry the weight of the dome. Eight semi-circular windows are then cleverly inserted into the eight spaces created by the arches, letting in light through elaborately carved window grilles in geometric patterns. That is how for the first time load-bearing ribbed vaulting appears in the domes of the mosque, as a natural extension of the interlocking arches.

Robert Hillenbrand, emeritus professor of Islamic art at Edinburgh University, also singles out the Mezquita's 'unique array of domes and vaulting systems', which 'constitute some of the earliest Islamic examples still in their original form.' The three domes in front of the *mihrab* are positioned very deliberately in a row. All manage to project a bigger size than their actual quite modest size, and together they let light flood in to illuminate the glittering gold of the mosaics. Hillenbrand interprets this as the familiar analogy between the dome and heaven and wonders if the ribs themselves can even be read as rays of light.[16]

Gothic architecture, emerging some two centuries later when techniques had evolved and advanced further, makes extensive use of both devices, the interlocking arches and the ribbed vaulting, together with the side effect of the more pointed arch. The aesthetically pleasing result was used at much the same time in Arab-influenced Norman Sicily (see Chapter 7), but it does not really matter whether the devices began first in Cordoba or in Sicily; the end result and the Arab origin is the same. Whatever the symbolism, this use of geometry went on to influence the dome structure in many Spanish churches, such as the Church of the Holy Sepulchre at Torres del Rio (twelfth to thirteenth centuries) in Navarre.

The techniques and the architectural devices quickly found themselves in use in northern Europe in the great Gothic cathedrals and ultimately paved the way for such intricately geometric Baroque domes as are found in the Chapel of the Holy Shroud (1668–94) and the Cathedral of San Lorenzo (1668–87), both in Turin.[17]

Just as the Cordoba Mezquita did not just appear miraculously out of nowhere, so Notre-Dame de Paris did not appear by magic. The Cordoba Mezquita had evolved elsewhere, in the gestation whirlpool of Umayyad Syria at a time when Muslims ruled the largest empire in the world and had the energy and money to commission new mosques and palaces to reflect their supremacy. So too the Gothic cathedrals of northern Europe that suddenly sprang up had their own backstory: the coming together of skilled master craftsmen from Spain, Sicily and possibly even Syria, all of whom were now available to work for new Christian masters, just as Byzantine Christian mosaicists and masons had worked for new Muslim masters in Syria in the eighth century. Enthused with religious fervour from their victories in the Holy Land and Iberia, brimming with righteous zeal, these Christian masters had the money to give thanks to God and to immortalise their supremacy in churches, just as new Muslim rulers had poured state coffers into spectacular new projects like the Dome of the Rock and the Great Mosque of Damascus and just as Roman emperors before them, fresh from new conquests, had sponsored temples to their favoured gods.

The original thinking behind how and why these new architectural features were used was almost certainly different in Muslim Spain from how and why they were used in northern Europe. In the northern Gothic cathedrals, the vaulting, the pointed arches and the interlocking arches of the upper level all contribute to a sense of spatial hierarchy, division into separate areas used for specific purposes by certain people, while in the Islamic context it was the opposite. In the Cordoba Mezquita the aim was to create an organic web, a complex vision of infinity, from no matter where in the prayer hall the viewer was standing. From Arnold's mathematical analyses of the space inside the Mezquita,[18] he concluded that part of the thinking was to minimise the thickness of the columns in order to make the imam and the *mihrab* visible from wherever the worshipper might be standing—there is no furniture in a mosque, only floor space for prayer, and anyone can put themselves wherever they like—front, back, right, left or centre.[19] The space was multifunctional, also serving as school, law court and meeting place. There are some interesting parallels here, for in early medieval times the cathedrals too were communal spaces without chairs—people stood or knelt during services. They came not just to pray but also to socialise, even bringing pets like parakeets and falcons. The mayor of Strasbourg used his pew as his office while wine merchants set up shop in the nave of Chartres.[20] To illustrate how the decreasing column thickness is achieved, Arnold provides detailed diagrams and examines how the increasing arch height has the advantageous effect of making the supporting columns thinner. He measures the ratios between the thickness of the columns and the total height of the arches and concludes that from the Roman period to the tenth- and eleventh-century Islamic period, the thickness of the columns is halved. Compared to Roman architecture where horizontal lintels were used, sixth-century horseshoe arches raise arch height by 133 per cent, progressing to an overall increase of 150 per cent in the tenth century and 175 per cent in the eleventh century in buildings like the Aljaferia in Zaragoza. Such an approach had huge implications for the architects of Gothic cathedrals where the height was increased by the use of pointed arches.

The big difference in the Muslim and Christian approaches to the space comes in their view of hierarchy. In a mosque the only element of hierarchy is the *maqsoura*, the special enclosure for the caliph, found for the first time in the Damascus Umayyad Mosque and imitated here in Cordoba, where there is even a special passage for the caliph leading direct from the adjacent palace. Apart from that, there is no hierarchy, no special seating for important people as exists in a church. There is only the relationship directly between God and the worshipper, conveyed and highlighted by the sense of infinity and repetition in all directions. All spaces are equal and it does not matter whereabouts you are in the building. When inside the Mezquita this is how you actually feel as a visitor, unsure when you have reached the end or are back at the beginning. It is indeed a web. Western architects usually use a very different approach, namely the Vitruvian method of taking each room of a building one at a time and making all measurements follow a perfect symmetry from the centre of that room only. Then they move to the next room and start all over again. The whole is therefore created by sticking together a series of individual units, not by visualising the whole as one unit from the outset. This is a fundamental difference which you can sense on entering an Islamic building. When Gothic architects took on pointed arches, interlocking arches and ribbed vaults from their Islamic predecessors, they used them differently, to divide the space into hierarchies. You are never in any doubt in a church or cathedral where the important bits are, and once you start to look for it, it is easy to see how the architecture reinforces this.

In his *The Celestial Hierarchy*, our Syrian mystic Denys, whose thinking was so influential for Abbot Suger and the first Gothic architecture at Saint-Denis, describes the bishops as 'hierarchs', a concept of his own invention from a Greek word meaning the high priest in charge of pagan sacred rites. For Denys the hierarchs are the vehicles through which the Divine Light of God is passed to mankind. In the rites of the Syriac church described by Denys, baptism is called 'illumination'. The church space itself had a special screen at the eastern end behind which only priests could pass, through the 'holy doors'. Light and knowledge flowed from God, via the hierarchs, to each being who would then become radiant with light and pass the light on to beings lower down.[21]

Wren himself seems to have had a sense of rebelling against this hierarchy of the Catholic church, another reason he preferred the round shape of the

Ribbed cross vaulting of the Capilla de Villaviciosa, Cordoba Mezquita, a masterpiece of tenth-century geometry that has never needed structural repair.

dome, beneath which all worshippers could sit and actually hear the preacher. Circular shapes remove hierarchy, as in seating plans where round tables make everyone equal, no 'head of the table'.

> The surveyor [Wren] then turn'd his thoughts to a cathedral-form (as they call'd it) but so rectified, as to reconcile, as near as possible, the Gothick to a better manner of architecture; with a cupola, and above that, instead of a lantern, a lofty spire, and large porticoes.[22]

'In our reformed religion,' he wrote, 'it should seem vain to make a parish church larger than that all who are present can both hear and see. The Romanists, indeed, may build larger churches; it is enough if they hear the murmur of the mass, and see the elevation of the host, but ours are to be fitted for auditories.'[23]

Cross-vaulted Domes and Mosaics

Another area of similarity with Damascus, yet which also shows departure and innovation, is the main four domes of the Mezquita. The main ceiling dome in front of the *mihrab* keeps the conventional octagon supported by the squinch, but then it is carried on eight large ribs which rest on small colonettes fitted between the sides of the octagon. This has the effect of shortening it and giving the base of the dome an extraordinarily complex shape formed by twenty-four centripetal ribs, all of which are covered in mosaics. They are built of stone masonry and are both load-bearing and decorative at the same time, their useful function disguised by the decorative elements. Like all masonry structures, the most important element is in their equilibrium, not in their strength—in other words where the thrusts of the weight are contained within the load-bearing capabilities, so that the structure is self-supporting and will not collapse. The other three ceiling domes are similar, with the most striking one being in the Villaviciosa Chapel, where the ribs convert a rectangle into a square.

No structural study or survey of the Villaviciosa Chapel dome and its vaulting system had ever been conducted till 2015, when two Spanish academics gained special access and conducted a detailed analysis.[24] What they found was a masterpiece of practical geometry, so perfectly conceived and executed that it has never needed any structural repair in its thousand-year existence. It is also the first time that decorative ornamentation performed a structural role, a dual function. They concluded it represents one of the very oldest ribbed vaults ever built, a new type called the cross vault, which has such a degree of perfection both in its design and in its construction that

The most beautiful mosaics inside the Cordoba Mezquita are concentrated round the *mihrab*, whose horseshoe arch is surmounted by seven blind trefoil arches above the Qur'anic inscription. The Andalusian Umayyads inherited the trefoil from the Syrian Umayyads, developing it into a much more prominent decorative feature.

earlier samples must have been experimented with, though none of these have so far been found in Europe. The obvious early field of experimentation, as described in the previous chapter, was the Umayyad desert palaces, where Professor Hamilton marvelled at the technical competence he found in the vaulting of Khirbat al-Mafjar, which to him proved 'that masons in Palestine during the eighth century shirked none of the difficulties in cutting a true cross-vault.'[25]

Several similar ribbed domes were later built in a large number of Spanish buildings, especially in those by the Mozarabs, and then they started to be seen also in the churches built along the pilgrimage route to Santiago de Compostela in northern Spain and southern France, showing how readily styles spread from country to country. Examples of similar ribbed vaults can be found at the Almazán church in Castile, at Torres del Río in Navarre, in the Pyrenees church of Sainte Croix d'Oloron and in the hospital of Saint Blaise, as well as in the Templar church at Segovia and in the twelfth-century chapter house at Salamanca.

At the Cordoba Mezquita the mosaics are dominated by geometric borders filled with vegetal ornamentation based on the vine and acanthus, a classical element deriving from both Roman tradition and pre-Hellenistic tradition in the Middle East and found all over Syria in early Umayyad art. The most beautiful mosaics are to be found in the small dome above the recessed *mihrab* in the *qibla* wall. The design of the *mihrab* itself is unique; it becomes not just a semi-circular niche as it was in Damascus, but a small octagonal room covered with a scallop-shaped shell dome. The wall surfaces are covered in rich marble panels, but most interesting of all is the use of blind trefoil arches resting on delicate black marble columns inside the holy of holies-type octagonal room, and seven more blind trefoil arches positioned directly above the Kufic inscriptions forming a band above the main horseshoe arch of the *mihrab*. Inside each arch the flat wall surface is decorated with stylised 'tree of life' motifs. This trefoil form, so emblematic of the Syrian Umayyads, and developed here further by the Spanish Umayyads, was clearly associated with exceptional holiness.

When the trefoil arch was later taken up as the leading Gothic decorative arch throughout northern Europe—just look for it on any Gothic church in

England and you will find hundreds of them—the symbolism was as a reference to the Christian Trinity—it is another example, along with the dome, the importance of light, and the Resurrection, of the shared heritage of the sacred between Islam and Christianity.

Mosaics had not been seen in Spain since Roman times, and the use of these glass mosaics directly copies the mosaics at the Umayyad Mosque of Damascus, with their green and gold colours predominant, and their vegetal designs. In Cordoba, Byzantine craftsmen were sent for to execute the mosaics in 965 and Caliph Al-Hakam was said to have asked the Byzantine emperor to send him a mosaicist capable of imitating the mosaics in the Great Umayyad Mosque of Damascus. The emperor complied, even sending him as a gift several sackfuls of gold mosaic cubes, and the mosaicist was assigned various local apprentices and assistants to help him and to learn from him.[26] Local marble was quarried, as was local limestone, and Syrian stonemasons would have passed their skills on to local Spanish masons, enabling them to carve exquisite capitals and decorative plaster stucco work just as the Syrian masons had done in Syria at the Umayyad palaces, at the Dome of the Rock, at Al-Aqsa Mosque and at the Damascus Umayyad Mosque over the course of the late seventh and early eighth centuries. It is in the capitals of the older parts of the Mezquita that the best examples of their style and craftsmanship can be seen, 'far superior to Visigothic production',[27] whose carved capitals are much cruder, less detailed and less imaginative. It is difficult not to think again of Wren's words in the *Parentalia*:

> Modern Gothic … is distinguished by the lightness of its work, by the excessive boldness of its elevations, and of its sections; by the delicacy, profusion, and extravagant fancy of its ornaments. … it can only be attributed to the Moors; or what is the same thing, to the Arabians or Saracens.

The subject matter of the mosaics in Damascus and Cordoba share distinct similarities. At Damascus the scenes go beyond the stylised motifs of floral elements with scrolls covered in gems, necklaces and pendants as are to be found in Jerusalem's Dome of the Rock, and move to a visualisation of paradise, depicting the beauties of nature through gardens, trees, and fantasy buildings like palaces with rivers flowing through them. Damascus, exceptionally well watered by its many springs and rivers and set in verdant gardens, was often itself seen as a paradise. The Qur'an provides the strongest evidence of the imagery intended, with 140 references to gardens (Arabic *janna*, also meaning 'paradise' or 'heaven'), and descriptions like 'the God-

The green and gold mosaics throughout the courtyard walls of the Damascus Umayyad Mosque represent visions of paradise, with trees, rivers and gardens. The spreading palm tree laden with fruit, found here on the treasury, echoes the curved shapes of the Cordoba arches and suggests nature in all its abundance, the typical iconography of Islamic art.

fearing are among shade and springs and such fruits as they desire (77:41–2). The gardens imagery was carried over from Damascus to Cordoba, evident in the courtyard of the Cordoba mosque being planted with trees and perhaps even having water channels running through it, but also in the clear fact that Abd al-Rahman I, recalling his ode to a palm tree, conceived the entire interior of the mosque as a vision of paradise. The density of pillars is like a forest, and the elaborate superstructure of the arches can be seen as representing the spreading branches of a palm tree, while the poly-lobed arches resemble abundant foliage. A panel of the treasury mosaics in the courtyard of the Damascus mosque represents a date palm laden with fruit, its curved branches echoing the shapes of the Cordoba arches.

The sheer size of the Cordoba mosque, the lowness of the roof relative to the size of the space and the dimness of light all contribute to an air of mystery. Thousands of oil lamps would once have hung in the mosque, but the area of greatest natural light is beneath the four skylights above what is today called the Villaviciosa Chapel. The leaflet issued with your entrance ticket, in its customary style, airbrushes out the original purpose of these skylights and the area below them. Instead it simply states:

> the change to Christian worship led to the construction of a large Gothic nave with a basilica floor plan, which originally boasted ornate walls. What stands out here is the roof, where transverse arches were used to support a framework of gabled wooden coffers, on which plant motifs alternate with inscriptions in Latin and Greek.

What it fails to mention is that this area was specially designed as the *maqsoura* (area reserved for the caliph during Friday prayers) during an earlier enlargement by Al-Hakam II, and that it is therefore an entirely Islamic architectural device to enhance the power of light at this special location in the otherwise dimly lit mosque. Both Christianity and Islam share a symbolism around light, with many references to light in the Qur'an, as in 57:19, where the believers are promised 'their garden and their light'. There is even a whole chapter called 'Light', Surat al-Nour, in which verse 35 is the famous and much quoted 'Light Verse':

God is the Light of the heavens and the earth. The parable of His light is as if there were a niche and within it a lamp: the lamp enclosed in glass: the glass as it were a brilliant star: lit from a blessed tree, an olive, neither of the east nor of the west, whose oil is well-nigh luminous, though fire scarce touched it: Light upon Light! God doth guide whom He will to His light: God doth set forth parables for men: and God doth know all things.

The Gothic cathedrals of northern Europe can likewise be interpreted as temples to nature and to light, full of carved vegetal motifs conveying fertility and fecundity. The eastward orientation towards the sunrise even goes back to the conversion of pagan temples to the sun, as examined in Chapter 2 with our friend the Syrian mystic Denys, and chimes well with symbolism of the Resurrection as light streaming in from ever larger windows. In the words of Denys:

It is as if there were a great chain of light let down from the summit of the heavens and reaching down to the earth … for the ray of all-holy things enlightens purely and directly godly men, as kin of the Light.[28]

Christ is described as 'the Light of the World'. In both mosque and church, the sense of the sacred and God's power is enhanced by the chosen architecture.

Continuing the theme of light, the Cordoba mosque copies the Syrian Umayyad geometric lace marble window grilles that appeared for the first time in their desert palaces and in the Damascus Umayyad Mosque. A total of nineteen have survived in the Mezquita, using similar geometric patterns, and many are in the outer western wall. Their large panelled shapes served the dual function of letting in light and creating decorative interest, the same as stained glass windows in Gothic cathedrals. In fact, like the Dome of the Rock and the Damascus Umayyad Mosque, the Mezquita originally had coloured glass windows, which have been restored over the centuries. Even today some of its high windows are circular and are still known as 'Sunrise' or 'Sun' windows, designed to look like coloured rays emanating from a central yellow sun.

Abd al-Rahman I's original square mosque was about 74 metres on each side, including the courtyard. The east and west walls of his prayer hall, each about 37 metres long, were supported by four massive buttresses rising to the full height of the wall, and the two that supported the corners of the southern *qibla* wall were described as forming 'veritable corner towers'. This addition of buttresses to the outside wall of the Mezquita was adopted from Abbasid practice.[29]

It was in Andalusia that the most important ethnic and cultural fusion of East and West took place, in fields of science and mathematics, philosophy and mysticism, industry and agriculture and decorative arts and crafts. The technical advances were assimilated by the dominant powers, and at the same time imprinted with their own unique stamp. The Cordoba Mezquita, with its recycled Roman columns carrying Islamic arch systems and vaults, used together with Visigothic and Corinthian capitals and Byzantine mosaics, is a prime example of the capacity for synthesis. The Muslim artists and architects were able to combine these disparate elements to achieve not a fragmented

The delicate stucco work on the interior of the Cordoba synagogue is indistinguishable from the Islamic styles of the Mezquita, with geometric patterning and horseshoe and multifoil blind arches. The cultural overlap with the Jewish community in Spain was profound before the Christian Reconquista.

hotch-potch of shapes, but a perfect harmony of double arches over a forest of columns, along with beautiful cupolas linking all the elements into a cosmic significance.

Through explicit imitation of its counterpart in Damascus, the overtly Syrian character of the Mezquita was an open statement of where the loyalties of the Umayyad rulers lay in their multi-tribal and multi-confessional state. But the architects at Cordoba were responsible for several remarkable innovations in their own right, and it has also been observed by art historians[30] that the Cordoba Mosque is more like Jerusalem's Al-Aqsa Mosque than the Great Mosque at Damascus in its use of multiple aisles perpendicular to the *qibla* wall and of a transept in front of the *qibla*, while its vegetal mosaics have clearer links with Jerusalem's Dome of the Rock. A glance at any map will show that the overwhelming majority of the Umayyad desert palaces are far closer to Jerusalem than to Damascus, so maybe this is not surprising. The most lavish palace of all, Khirbat al-Mafjar, is barely 25 kilometres from Jerusalem, while Damascus is 200 kilometres away.

Inside the synagogue of Cordoba, open to the public and just a few minutes' walk from the Mezquita, the plaster stucco work shows exactly the same use of geometric patterning set in panels, horseshoe arches and blind arches with archivolt decorative mouldings and poly-lobed (multifoil) arches as in the Mezquita itself. There was evidently no sense that such decorative designs could only be used in an Islamic context, and in fact the favoured architectural style for nineteenth-century synagogues across Europe was Neo-Moorish, as considered later in Chapter 9.

It is clear that even after the Reconquista, the Spanish national style itself became precisely this 'Mudéjar' architecture, as it was called, using Islamic motifs and styles in non-Muslim settings. The word Mudéjar derives from Arabic *mudajjan*, meaning domesticated or subject, and describes Muslims who remained in Spain after the Reconquista. Their style spread all over the country. Mudéjar master craftsmen were highly skilled builders who continued to use the same materials, techniques and designs on many Christian buildings for new Christian masters, both churches and secular buildings through till the fifteenth century. Even in fiercely contested cities which changed hands many times, such as Girona in the north, the Arab baths were restored by a Christian ruler and heavily frequented by the Jewish community till practising Jews were expelled from Spain in 1492 under the Alhambra Decree. The Catalan Cultural Heritage website refers to the Girona baths as 'a medieval jewel of Saracen inspiration'.[31] In Cordoba, Muslim craftsmen had historically been in charge of maintaining the Mezquita, and even after the Reconquista, Muslim artisans, masons and carpenters represented the main pool of skilled workers—there were far more of them than Christians. Thirteenth-century Christian chronicles tell us how they were forced, as a tax, to work for free at the Mezquita for two days each year.[32] Cordoba evidently had resident Muslim master craftsmen

The brick-built miniature Bab al-Mardum Mosque in Toledo was modelled on the tenth-century extension to the Cordoba Mezquita, copying its arches and its ribbed vaulting. Today it is the church of Cristo de la Luz.

of some renown till at least the end of the thirteenth century, and in cities like Burgos and Valladolid Mudéjar carpenters held a monopoly. Ribbed domes were also typically identified with Mudéjar craftsmen.

In Seville, Mudéjar artisans were chosen by Christian kings Alfonso XI and Pedro the Cruel in the fourteenth century to build extensions and renovations to the eighth-century Muslim Alcázar (from Arabic *al-qasr*, fortified palace) because they were traditionally trained, father to son. These craftsmen were therefore quite simply the best and most highly skilled for carving the elegant *muqarnas* (stalactite vaulting) and the delicate stucco arcades. The Nasrid king Muhammad V in Granada, living in exile under Pedro's protection, is even known to have lent his Muslim artisans from the Alhambra in an amicable

Fifteenth-century fan-vaulted ceiling of King's College Chapel, Cambridge.

exchange.[33] The gardeners at the gardens of the Alcázar were Muslim up till the sixteenth century.[34]

The inexorable progress of the Reconquista evidently did not interfere with Christian rulers' enthusiasm for the artistic work of their Muslim subjects and they continued to commission the styles they liked, or else simply adapted the existing Islamic buildings to become churches, as with the Cordoba Mezquita and the Cristo de la Luz Church (Bab al-Mardum Mosque) in Toledo. The latter, a little church, was originally a private mosque built from brick, a miniaturised copy of Al-Hakam's extension to the Cordoba Mezquita in 961. Like that extension, it combines horseshoe and trefoil arches, blind arcades of interlocking arches, and is square in shape, just 8 metres along each side. The most remarkable feature comes in the nine ribbed vaults of its ceiling, each one different in the patterning of its ribs, as if the mason was conducting a kind of experiment. This unique form of rib vaulting, used here in Bab al-Mardum (998–1000) some thirty-five years after the Cordoba Mezquita ribbed domes, is thought to be the forerunner of the quadripartite vault. As in the Cordoba Mezquita, each one is a load-bearing vault, where the ribs are also decorative. It is a design where a pair of slimmer and therefore lighter crossed arches divide the space between the thicker ribs into four smaller segments which can then be filled in with lighter materials.

Here in Cordoba and Toledo the very first steps were taken towards the Gothic rib vaulting and fan vaulting that gradually became more and more sophisticated over the course of the twelfth and thirteenth centuries before reaching its apogee in the exquisite late Gothic fan vaulting of the fifteenth-century Chapel of King's College, Cambridge, the largest fan-vaulted ceiling in the world.

In Portugal, very few Islamic buildings have survived intact and virtually all mosques were rebuilt as churches and cathedrals after the Reconquista, so that their Islamic features are no longer visible. The sole exception is at Mértola in the Alentejo, now a church but with its interior still clearly a mosque in the Cordoba style, with five naves and a forest of slender pillars carrying arched cross vaults.

The fact that the Spanish language even to this day, well over 500 years after the Reconquista, contains some 4,000 words of Arabic origin, tells its own story. In the field of architecture, the proportion is much higher. Here are just a few, by way of example: *adoquín* (Arabic *kaddan*): paving stone; *alacena* (Arabic *al-khazanah*): cupboard; *andamio* (Arabic *ad-di'amah*): scaffolding; *azotea* (Arabic *as-sutayhah*): flat roof; *aljibe* (Arabic *al-jubb*, the cistern): ogive (pointed arch); *atabó* (Arabic *at-tabouq*): brick.[35]

Valencian builders were known for their excellent tile-vaulting techniques dating back to the Arab period, a very light type of thin-brick vaulting jointed with gypsum that can carry a very high load capacity and be built at great speed. It can be difficult to distinguish from other types of vaulting because it is usually plastered so the bricks are not visible.[36] The Spanish word *tracería* (as in English 'tracery', a major characteristic of Gothic window and spire architecture) means complicated mathematical patterns, which also reveals underlying Arab inspiration.

Spanish Umayyad Palaces

Alongside public buildings like the Cordoba Mezquita and the Seville Alcázar, a culture of recognisably Umayyad residential building also evolved in Andalusia, known in Spain as *munyas* or fortified country estates. While it is valid to say that in some ways they formed a continuation of villa culture from Roman times,[37] it is very clear from their garden design and layout that they were also explicitly Islamic, bearing close resemblances to the Umayyad desert palaces that Abd al-Rahman I and his Syrian followers would have known from their homeland. They were especially popular in the Cordoba area in the tenth century with senior officials in the administration. Today they are all in ruins and remain unexcavated. Photos of one of the most famous, Al-Munya al-Rumaniyya, can be seen in the Madinat al-Zahra Museum, where it is described as an 'orchard'. This tenth-century villa for the finance minister of Al-Hakam II was completed in 966 and is remarkable for its garden hall, built on a dam between the large reservoir and the garden. Arcades opened out on both sides, giving an unusually wide-angled view. Academic scholars have analysed this view and found it to be based on equilateral triangles and the human field of vision. It is a concept never seen before and not applied in Christian architecture till the Italian Renaissance. It became the prototype for later palatial halls of the eleventh century such as the Cordoba Alcázar, the Almería Alcazaba and the Zaragoza Aljafería.

Abd al-Rahman I began this trend himself in Spain in the eighth century; he is known to have built his own country estate near Cordoba and to have named it Rusafa, after the Syrian desert palace where he spent much of his childhood with his grandfather Hisham. He brought water to the estate and introduced exotic plants like peaches and pomegranates. The Phoenicians had brought the first palm trees to Spain, but the Arabs brought in new varieties that they knew how to propagate from offshoots. Before this knowledge, palms had only been grown from seed.

Here it is important to look closely at the architecture of the Syrian city of Rusafa. As the place where Abd al-Rahman lived throughout his formative years till he was forced to flee at the age of twenty, here were the buildings with which he was familiar and which would have shaped his creative imagination. It is highly relevant for our purpose to note Rusafa's history, first as a Roman, then as a Byzantine settlement at the very frontier of Sassanid Persia. The Roman emperor Diocletian (ruled 284–305) established the *Strata Diocletiana*, the Diocletian Line, along the empire's eastern border against the Sassanids, which ran from Sura on the Euphrates via Rusafa south to Palmyra, then southwest to Damascus via Dmeir.[38]

Hisham's new palace at Rusafa was in the traditional Umayyad square design, modelled on the Roman *castrum* or military enclosure,[39] as were the two Qasr al-Hairs (the Palaces of the Fenced-in Garden), Qasr al-Mshatta and Khirbat al-Mafjar. Located some 30 kilometres south of Raqqa in the middle of the Syrian Badia desert, Rusafa had been a huge Byzantine fortress city built round the shrine of St Sergius, one of the most popular pilgrimage shrines in Syria. It was guarded by the Ghassanids, a Christianised Arab tribe who had formed an alliance with the Byzantines to maintain control of the Syrian central desert tribes.[40] Their palace, built around 560–81 in a cross-in-square shape, remains visible, though largely buried in the sand outside the north gate.

The Byzantines called Rusafa 'Sergiopolis' in the saint's honour. The fortified city stands today, its walls so strongly constructed of stone in the sixth century under the Byzantine emperor Justinian that they still rise to their full height. Justinian was concerned to fortify this Christian frontier outpost as heavily as possible, both to protect the shrine and as a statement to the Persian Sassanids who were constantly threatening war along this eastern frontier. The huge sandy space inside the 2-kilometre-long walls remains unexcavated today, but the ruins of three basilicas are clear to see, along with a trio of vast and impressively constructed underground cisterns designed to catch the run-off rainfall from the mountain ranges to the south. The Persians eventually succeeded in overrunning Rusafa and sacking it in 616, part of the bigger picture of how Byzantine Syria was so weakened by constant Persian raids over time that the Arab conquest two decades later was made much easier than it might otherwise have been.[41]

The Christian city lay in ruins for over a century, but for whatever reason, it was Hisham, Abd al-Rahman I's grandfather (ruled 724–43), who took the decision to restore the site, to rebuild the cisterns and the churches, and to allow the pilgrimage to resume. Of course, he created extensive gardens round his new palace. He even died there. Hisham's palace and his tomb inside the city were utterly destroyed by the Abbasids soon after 750, maybe even as vengeance for Abd al-Rahman's escape, since they dug up his body, scourged it eighty times and then burnt it to ashes.[42] But it might not have been entirely personal, for they also desecrated the tombs of other Umayyad caliphs in Damascus and a few more cities.

Rusafa's remarkable feature architecturally is the local gypsum, hard and crystalline, creating a glittery building material, mined from a local quarry, widely used in construction as a kind of mortar between bricks or stones.

Given that Abd al-Rahman I would have grown up surrounded by Christian Syrians, it is not so surprising that the person who, according to some historians, accompanied him on his flight from Damascus was a Christian, called Badr. He may well have been an Arab Christian living in Rusafa. Accustomed to a multi-cultural environment such as Rusafa, and being of mixed Arab and Berber parentage himself, Abd al-Rahman I's natural inclination was always to be inclusive towards all groups, as long as they were loyal. He was therefore the initiator of the great movement of tolerance that encompassed Arabians, Syrians, Berbers, Jews, Hispano-Arabs, Goths and Numidians, and he turned Islamic Spain into one of the two centres of world culture from the ninth to the eleventh century. It reached its zenith under Abd al-Rahman III (ruled 912–61), the greatest in the long line of Umayyads and the first in Spain to assume the title of caliph in 929.

Madinat al-Zahra

Just as Abd al-Rahman I had wanted to live on his country estate modelled on the Syrian Rusafa, so Caliph Abd al-Rahman III, the seventh ruler of the Spanish Umayyads, decided he wished to distance himself from the intrigues of Cordoba and have space to relax. Beginning in 936, it took forty years to build the staggeringly beautiful Madinat al-Zahra, Zahra's City, just 10 kilometres outside the city of Cordoba on the south-facing slopes of Jebel al-Arus, the Mountain of the Bride, overlooking the Guadalquivir (Arabic Wadi al-Kabir, the Big Valley). Al-Zahra, the Radiant One, was Abd al-Rahman III's favourite wife.[43]

Abd al-Rahman III and his successors only enjoyed the estate for what were to be the final sixty-five years of Umayyad rule in Andalusia. Burnt, looted and plundered in 1013 by mutinous Berber troops, Muslims and Christians alike, its ruins slowly disappeared under the mud dragged down from the mountains by heavy rains. After that it lay buried and forgotten for nine centuries. Excavators began work in 1910, but still only a tenth of the palace has been uncovered. In July 2018, Madinat al-Zahra was finally recognised as a UNESCO World Heritage site, and it is described on the UNESCO website as the largest known city built from scratch in western Europe at that time.

The magnificent palace city was laid out over three terraced platforms, with elaborate gardens on the lower level. In their beauty and complexity one can again see the characteristic Islamic strivings to create an earthly paradise. The facades of Madinat al-Zahra were inspired by Umayyad art, using vegetal ornamentation and wide archaic elongated Kufic script, first employed to great effect above all in the Dome of the Rock, at a time when, elsewhere in tenth-century Andalusia, Arabic script was becoming taller and more elaborate. Fragments of the Umayyad Qasr al-Mshatta on display in Berlin's Pergamon Museum also appear to be the inspiration for tenth-century Cordoba ivories, crafted in the Madinat al-Zahra workshops, with scenes such as dancing figures floating over a vegetal garden paradise, bunches of grapes, a central tree of life and pairs of animals. The inheritance from the Syrian Umayyads is clear to see.

Eight-lobed frame of an ivory-carved medallion, Madinat al-Zahra Museum.

Stained Glass Motifs

In Madinat al-Zahra's Salon Rico, the grand audience hall where dignitaries were received, is a carved marble panel depicting the ancient oriental tree of life motif, with the trunk rising vertically in the centre giving perfect symmetry to the design. The internal patterns in the trunk, leaves and petals are cut with a hard outline, a typical Hispano-Umayyad feature, and the vertical axis gives a graphic, abstract quality. The border is a classical vegetal leaf stem design cut in the same way into the stone, creating a frame within a frame in the common Islamic style.[44]

The tree of life is often seen in a Christian context in the stained glass of Gothic chapels and churches, such as William of Wykeham's twin foundations of Winchester College and New College, Oxford, and St Margaret's Church in Margaretting, Essex. In the stained glass versions, the tree of Jesse, illustrating the descent of Christ from Jesse, father of David, showed itself to be a popular subject in England throughout the Middle Ages. The tree, its branches and its foliage lend structure to the composition of the window, often spanning three windows once these became tall and thin as in the Perpendicular phase. The branches and tendrils could carry the figures of David, Solomon and the rest, while the figure of Jesse lies on the ground as a foundation, with the tree trunk emerging from his body.[45] The concept of a tree of life seems to be shared widely by religions across the world, with the earliest examples originating in Mesopotamia, depicted in Assyrian palace reliefs as at Nimrud and on the helmets of Urartian warriors. In both the Qur'an and the Book of Genesis, there is a tree in the Garden of Eden depicted as a source of eternal life and immortality. Especially in the Qur'an's early surahs, the bounty and fecundity of nature are recurring themes explicitly mentioned as gifts from God to man, another reason perhaps why early Islamic art and architecture is so full of representations of nature, trees and flowers—religious beliefs created in architectural form as an act of worship, acknowledgement of God's gift to those who believe in Him.

Another parallel between Islamic and Christian architecture can be seen in the ivory-carved medallion, currently on display in the Madinat al-Zahra Museum, which shows the caliph attended by his servants and surrounded by abundant foliage and wild animals. The scenes are set within an elaborate eight-lobed frame, similar to the framing later used in European stained glass windows to depict biblical scenes, as at Saint-Denis and Canterbury.

In Andalusian ceramics, the influence of the Syrian homeland can also be seen in the colours used, the black of the Prophet, green of Islam and white of the Umayyads that were common in Damascus ceramics of the Umayyad period. In metalwork, the technique of 'damascene' work was further developed, and in Toledo filaments of gold and silver were inlaid onto metal, while workshops in Cordoba produced chests of carved wood, marble and magnificent glassware, inspired by their Damascus prototypes. The fact that knowledge of such commodities originating from the Islamic world made its way into Europe shows itself in the details of European stained glass windows of the fourteenth century, as in the rich blue patterned damask textile background border used at Merton College, Oxford.[46] Syrian silks and textiles were of legendary quality and style. One striped fabric imitated by the Arabs in Spain was traded under the name *tabi*, after an Umayyad prince called Attab. It became popular across Europe and survives today in our word 'tabby' for a streaked or striped cat.[47]

The similarities in the decorative details of Madinat al-Zahra with those of the Syrian Umayyad desert palaces are very striking. Effervescent nature is everywhere, bursting out from the stone and stucco carving, carried on slender columns and delicate arches.

Wren's words come to mind again:

falsely delicate, crowded with superfluous ornaments, and often very unnatural … let us appeal to any one who has seen the mosques and palaces of Fez, or some cathedrals in Spain, built by the Moors … such buildings have been vulgarly called Modern Gothick, but their true appellation is Arabic, Saracenic, or Moresque.[48]

At the court in Cordoba, intellectual life flourished and was encouraged by Abd al-Rahman III, as it had been by his forebears. This was Spain's Golden Age, where Muslims, Christians and Jews pooled their knowledge and intellectual abilities in the period known as Convivencia, 'co-existence'. Wren was aware of all this and understood well how such an influential and magnificent civilisation would have had cultural repercussions further north:

> This manner was introduced into Europe through Spain; learning flourished among the Arabians all the time that their dominion was in full power; they studied philosophy, mathematics, physics, and poetry. The love of learning was at once excited, in all places that were not at too great distance from Spain, these authors were read, and such of the Greek authors as they had translated into Arabic, were from thence turned into Latin. The physics and philosophy of the Arabians spread themselves in Europe, and with these their architecture: many churches were built after the Saracenic mode.[49]

In its heyday Madinat al-Zahra stunned visiting ambassadors and dignitaries arriving both from Europe and the East with its magnificence. Chroniclers give us details of diplomatic receptions held between 956 and 973 for these visitors, veritable queues of them, who would process from the lowest to the highest esplanade escorted by guards of honour and then be showered with exotic gifts such as jewels and textiles after their audiences with the caliph. Holy Roman Emperor Otto the Great first sent Johann von Gorze as ambassador to Andalusia in 956, and there followed myriad missions of important Christian dignitaries from León, Barcelona, Castile, Salamanca, Pamplona, Provence, Tuscany, Rome and Constantinople, as well as visitations from Berber princes and other North African and Arab delegations. These contacts illustrate well how interconnected the Umayyad Cordoba caliphate was with its close and its more distant neighbours, all of whom would have had ample opportunity to gaze at the lavish buildings, their designs and ornamentations, and return home with new ideas. The rest of tenth-century Europe, with its dark, thick-walled basilicas, had nothing that came even close.

Apart from Cordoba, the other Spanish cities with significant Islamic architecture are Seville, Toledo and Granada. Seville's Giralda Tower, a square tower of the Syrian style with Almohad influence, now the bell tower of Seville Cathedral but originally the minaret of the city's main mosque, was erected in 1184. It and the courtyard are all that remain of the original seventeen-aisled mosque, after a Gothic cathedral with eighty chapels was

Elaborate geometric window grilles within the Court of the Myrtles at the Alhambra, Granada. They were developed by the Umayyads, first in the Damascus Umayyad Mosque, then in the Cordoba Mezquita, before reaching their apogee here in the fourteenth century. They often carried coloured glass, since lost.

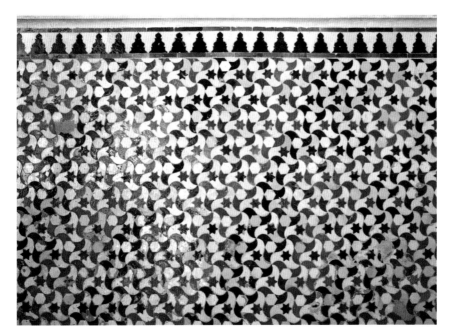

Tessellated tiles in the Alhambra, one of the designs that inspired M.C. Escher. Most of the seventeen mathematically possible endlessly repeating patterns have been identified at the Alhambra.

The Court of the Lions in the Alhambra evokes a perfect spiritual balance through geometry and rhythm, exemplifying the Islamic view of architecture as 'the clothing of buildings'. The cool simplicity of the white marble contrasts with the multiplicity of arches and their effusive ornamentation, in the final flourish of a dying dynasty.

imposed on the space in the late fifteenth century. At 104 metres tall, La Giralda still dominates the city skyline and is decorated with cusped arcading, anticipating later Gothic tracery.[50] Centuries later, La Giralda inspired many similar towers around the world between 1890 and 1950, especially in the USA as in Kansas City, Missouri, and even in Moscow's Seven Sisters, a combination of Russian Baroque and Gothic housing Moscow State University. Toledo Cathedral (1226–1493), built in High Gothic style, is modelled on Bourges Cathedral in France but with Mudéjar influence in some parts, such as the cloister (formerly the mosque courtyard) and the multifoil arches. The five naves of the cathedral were built over the prayer hall of the original mosque in defiance of King Alfonso VI's instructions. The king had promised the Muslim community it would remain a mosque, but his wife and the archbishop reneged on his word while he was out of the city on affairs of state, nearly causing a Muslim uprising.

Alhambra Palace Decorations

'Nothing in life could be more cruel than to be blind in Granada,' reads an Arabic inscription inside the Alhambra. From the outside, perched on its hill dominating Granada, the Alhambra (literally 'the Red One' in Arabic, named after the colour of its red bricks) looks like a fortress, austere and somewhat forbidding. But inside it is another world, filled with exquisitely designed gardens made possible by the remarkable 8-kilometre-long irrigation conduit, which still brings water to the city from the mountains today. The Nasrid palaces are what everyone comes to see, requiring a special ticket with a specific half-hour entry slot, such is the demand from visitors every day of the year. Numbers have to be limited to 6,600 per day, and tickets always sell out weeks in advance at high season.

The palaces together—the Court of the Lions and the Hall of Justice in particular—represent the last word in this level of workmanship, with effusive ornamentation covering every surface. Nowhere perhaps better exemplifies Arab poets' common view of architecture as 'the clothing of buildings', in which surface ornamentation is imagined as resembling a cloak draped over structural forms to disguise breaks and junctions in the underlying surfaces.[51] The dizzying tile patterns of the Alhambra have been analysed and shown to include most of the seventeen mathematically possible infinitely repeating 'wallpaper groups', the innovation thought to be based on textile-weaving techniques seen in the eighth-century Umayyad palace of Khirbat al-Mafjar near Jericho (see Chapter 4). The sense of repose and contemplation evoked by the patterns is a conscious aim of Islamic art, where the spiritual world is reflected in nature through geometry and rhythm; Muslim intellectuals defined these principles as *tawheed* (unity of being) and *mizaan* (order and balance). When M.C. Escher visited the Alhambra in 1922, the geometry of its tilework inspired his subsequent work on tessellation.[52] If ever Goethe's words 'architecture is frozen music' were to be applied to a single building, this would be it, the liveliest of scherzos yet still conveying an atmosphere of serene calm.

Construction of the Alhambra began in 1248 and was completed by 1354, too late to have been an influence on the Gothic cathedrals of northern Europe and thus irrelevant to our purpose here, except to note it as the final flourish of the dying dynasty, the last gasp of Muslim Spain, extinguished forever with the fall of Granada in 1492. When Ferdinand and Isabella took over the city, they kept the palace as their royal residence largely unchanged, but made sure to stake their ownership by putting their yoke and arrows 'brand' on the soffit of the arches, very visible today in the magnificent water- and flower-filled terraces of the Generalife (from Arabic *jannat al-areef*, 'garden of the architect'). They taxed the local silk industry so heavily that they eventually killed it; the ruined mills and mulberry terracing can still be seen in the mountains around Granada. Newly rich from this final victory over the Moors, they finally granted Christopher Columbus the funds to sail for the Americas, having previously refused him twice—a decision that would change European history forever.

The architectural legacy of the Alhambra lives on through subsequent Mudéjar building across Andalusia, but also through the profound impact it had on nineteenth-century European travellers, like the Welsh architect Owen Jones, who spent six months sketching the palace during his Grand Tour. He went on to become Britain's leading design and colour theorist and was a key figure in the foundation of what became London's Victoria and Albert Museum. The nineteenth-century Moorish revival of which he was part, explored in Chapter 9, developed into one of the most exotic architectural styles ever seen in Europe and the Americas, with the Spaniard Antoni Gaudí its greatest proponent and his Moorish Gothic Sagrada Família in Barcelona its most breathtaking achievement.

6

THE ABBASID AND FATIMID CALIPHATES

(750–1258)

With the end of the Umayyad dynasty in Damascus, the first truly Arab era in the history of Islam was over, but in that brief period of less than a century, an Islamic architectural style was born whose subsequent architectural legacy to Europe was immense, as explored in Chapters 4 and 5. From 750 onwards, Syria was eclipsed as the Abbasids took charge of the caliphate and power moved east to their successive capitals at Kufa, Anbar, Baghdad, Raqqa and Samarra. Henceforth, the many Muslim dynasties that ruled in the Near and Middle East all shared a clear architectural Islamic identity, distinguished aesthetically above all by the pointed arch and structurally by advances in roof vaulting.

The Abbasids in the East and the Spanish Umayyads in the West were always mutually hostile on the political front, but there were still myriad ways in which they continued to engage with each other's cultures and societies. Andalusi and Maghribi merchants, pilgrims and scholars continued to travel annually across North Africa to Mecca on the Hajj via Qairouan, Egypt or Syria, also welcoming visitors from Baghdad and Iraq.[1] This didn't stop the Abbasid East, with its glittering courts, its high Arabic poetic tradition, its steady appropriation of Greek scientific knowledge and its great cities of Baghdad, Samarra, Kufa and Raqqa, from considering Andalusia and the Maghribi lands as provincial backwaters, but the Umayyad response on the whole was simply to ignore the Abbasid court, never mentioning its name in the Friday prayer *khutba* or sermon.[2]

Despite their considerable political and ideological differences, the Abbasids did not, by and large, undo the architectural work of their Umayyad predecessors—the tombs of certain Umayyad caliphs like Hisham excepted. So when an Umayyad building such as the Dome of the Rock was damaged by earthquake, they repaired it, reusing Umayyad stones and capitals, and then simply appropriated it with a suitable inscription of their own. As with the Umayyads before them, they retained the presence of Christians and gained the return of Jews; before the Arab conquest, under the Christian Byzantines, 'there were no Jews in Jerusalem, which had become a Christian city on a Roman imperial canvas'.[3] Just as the Umayyads encouraged tolerance of race and religion, so too did the Abbasids. The three religious communities of Jerusalem— Judaism, Islam and Christianity—led parallel and reasonably peaceful lives for the next 300 years, crowded together in a small urban space, despite their 'vast array of internal distinctions and divisions' and the assertion by each group of its unique and divinely ordained right to practise its beliefs.[4] Of course, that all changed with the arrival of the Western Christian Crusaders in the late eleventh century. Plurality was later returned under the Mamluks and Ottomans, only to be lost once more post-1948 with the creation of the state of Israel in what had been Palestine, Syria and Jordan.

The Pointed Arch

The fact that the pointed arch began to have associations with an Islamic identity under the Umayyads was further confirmed when the Abbasids took it up with such vigour, notably at the early Palace of Ukhaidir (778), 100 miles south of Baghdad, where it is the dominant motif. Pointed arches were used again extensively in the city of Samarra, an Abbasid foundation of 836, where three pointed arches mark the triumphal entrance to a palace (Bab al-Amma) at the head of a flight of steps up from the Tigris. Samarra's major mosques, such as Al-Rafiqa, used pointed arches throughout, a clear decision and preference. In this region, where stone was in short supply and there were no Hellenistic or Roman columns to recycle, the arches were supported on brick piers. Pointed profiles were even chosen for domes, especially of tombs, as in the mausoleum of Caliph Al-Mustansir dated to 862.

By the ninth century, use of the pointed arch was prevalent across the Abbasid Empire. It was widely seen in Persia and carried into Egypt, where it appeared in a sophisticated form in the Nilometer of 861 in Fustat; Creswell measured the Nilometer arches and pronounced them to be 'tiers-point'—a third—the exact measure used in early Gothic architecture three centuries later. The pointed arch is also a major feature in the Mosque of Ibn Tulun in Cairo, built in 876. Ibn Tulun himself had been sent from Samarra to be governor of Egypt.[5] Son of a Baghdad slave, he was a highly ambitious man in his twenties who had risen through the ranks of the Abbasid army. Within two years of arriving in Egypt, he decided to break free from his Abbasid masters and build a Samarra of his own, creating a new capital on the outskirts of what is now modern Cairo with a magnificent palace, gardens and polo pitch adjoining the mosque. Nothing of his new city remains today except the mosque, which retains the distinction of being the largest mosque in Cairo in terms of ground area and the oldest that still exists in its original form. Although it was a bid for independence, the architectural similarities with Samarra are clear, with the same pointed arches on brick piers and very similar stucco decoration on the soffits of the arches. Al-Balawi, a tenth-century Egyptian historian, tells us that Ibn Tulun required 300 stone or marble columns to support the arches of the prayer hall, and was informed that the only way to get them was to ransack local churches. He decided that was a step too far, but the day was saved by a Coptic Christian prisoner, an architect, who volunteered to build the arch pillars from brick instead.

These are precisely the arches seen and admired by Italian merchants from Amalfi, who copied them in their eleventh-century reconstruction of the monastery of Monte Cassino, located 130 kilometres southeast of Rome. The first house of the Benedictine Order, originally established by Benedict himself in 529, the Monte Cassino monastery had been sacked by the Lombards in around 570, after which it was rebuilt, but sacked again by the Saracens in 883. It was rebuilt a third time in 1071 under the powerful Abbot Desiderius of Monte Cassino (later to become Pope Victor III). Monte Cassino reached its heyday in the eleventh and twelfth centuries, when it acquired land and received patronage from Byzantine emperors and even employed Byzantine and Saracen craftsmen to work on its many new building projects.

Meanwhile, just south of the Bay of Naples, in a stunningly beautiful location at the mouth of a deep ravine, backed by vertiginous cliffs, sat Amalfi, the capital of a small but powerful maritime republic known as the Duchy of Amalfi from 839 till about 1200. While most of Italy was still using barter trade, the Amalfi merchants used their cargo ships to sell grain from their neighbours, salt from Sardinia and slaves from the Italian interior to the Islamic ports where they enjoyed trading privileges. In return they received gold dinars minted in Egypt and Syria, which they then used to buy Byzantine silks to resell back into Europe. The Duchy of Amalfi reached its peak of prosperity around 1000, ahead of the rise of the Republic of Venice.

William of Apulia, a late-eleventh-century poet, wrote of Amalfi:

> No city is richer in silver, gold and textiles from all sorts of different places. Many different things are brought here from the royal city of Alexandria and from Antioch. Its people cross many seas. They know the Arabs, the Libyans, the Sicilians and Africans. This people is famed throughout almost the whole world, as they export their merchandise and love to carry back what they have bought.[6]

Accidents of timing have proved decisive throughout history, and it was at around this time, according to Leo of Ostia, a monk commissioned to write the *Monte Cassino Chronicle* detailing the history of the abbey and its possessions, that Abbot Desiderius made his visit to Amalfi in 1065. The abbot's purpose was to buy a gift of purple silks, a bribe in practice, for the fifteen-year-old King Henry IV of Germany, future Holy Roman Emperor. It was a shrewd move with an eye to securing the future financial health and influence of his monastery. At the port of Amalfi such luxury merchandise not available elsewhere could be purchased—highly suitable therefore for impressing future royalty. During this visit, Leo's *Chronicle* tells us, 'Desiderius saw the bronze doors of the cathedral of Amalfi and as he liked them very much, he

Exterior facade of the Amalfi Cathedral of St Andrew, an unusual synthesis of styles, showing its Syrian-style black and white striped stonework and its Arab pointed arches.

soon sent the measures of the doors of the old church on Monte Cassino to Constantinople with the order to make those now existing.'[7]

This is the same cathedral described by a church history pamphlet as 'more similar to an Arabic mosque than to a Christian church'. It still stands today in Amalfi as a basilica separated from the current cathedral, and a restoration carried out in the mid-nineties revealed tenth- and eleventh-century pointed arches marking the nave, with more pointed arches in the upper gallery. Abbot Desiderius was evidently smitten not only by the goods for sale at Amalfi, but also by the elegant architecture, choosing to copy the pointed arches in his Monte Cassino upgrade. Leo's *Chronicle* mentions that Desiderius hired builders from Constantinople, from Lombardy and from Amalfi to carry out his new building projects at Monte Cassino, since he was 'unable to find local artisans with the desired level of artistic skill.'[8] The craftsmen from Byzantium, according to Leo, then taught local novices, not only construction, but also 'the goldsmith's and silversmith's art, bronze casting, iron and glass working, ivory and wood carving, plaster modelling and stone carving.[9]

The Cloister of Paradise, Amalfi, a burial ground for local noble families, with its forest of slender pointed interlocking arches.

No traces of the window glazing, or indeed any of the other features described by Leo at Monte Cassino, survived the subsequent destruction of the monastery in World War II by Allied aerial bombardment. Just one echo of Monte Cassino's glazed screens and their decorative designs as described by Leo can still be seen, however, in the abbey church of the monastery of San Benedetto in Capua built in the late eleventh century, the last monument created under Desiderius's patronage.[10]

The heart and soul of Amalfi today is the Arab-Norman Romanesque thirteenth-century Cathedral of St Andrew overlooking the main piazza, built to house the relics of the apostle that were brought to Amalfi in 1206 after the sack of Constantinople in the Fourth Crusade. Providing another example of a unique synthesis of styles, its striking alternating black and white masonry facade (an imported Syrian style called *ablaq*, Arabic for of alternate colours), its Byzantine-style mosaics and its Arab pointed arches are clear evidence of the source of its inspiration.

Above the stairs leading down to the crypt where the saint's body is buried is another Islamic echo of Egypt and North Africa, in the distinctive form of a 'melon' dome resting on squinches. Cairo's City of the Dead where the Fatimid caliphs are buried and Damascus's tomb of Saladin beside the Great Umayyad Mosque are examples of how these 'melon' domes are used only to mark a tomb. Like many beliefs, the funerary symbolism of these domes is shared across Islam and Christianity. Before the Crusades, such cross-cultural exchange was common, as illustrated by the words of Pope Gregory VII writing in 1076 (shortly before the First Crusade) to the Algerian emir Al-Nasir ibn Alnas: 'We believe in and confess, albeit in a different way, the one God.'

Beside the cathedral, reached by a side door, is a further Islam-inspired building, the Cloister of Paradise, an exquisite garden courtyard, ringed with slender columns in white marble and built between 1266 and 1268 as a burial ground for noble families of Amalfi. The columns are topped by graceful interlocking pointed arches.

The splendour of Amalfi was doomed not to last, however, and in 1343 a tsunami destroyed the city and its port, bringing the prosperity to a sudden halt. But this was not before Amalfi had played its role in transferring many elements of Islamic architecture into Europe.

Just as Abbot Desiderius copied the pointed windows from Amalfi's basilica and took the design back to Monte Cassino, those windows were then copied from Monte Cassino and used in the Benedictine Abbey at Cluny. Abbot Suger then visited Cluny, saw and liked the windows and the way they let in more light, and immediately took the same design back to his Saint-Denis Basilica in Paris, as explained in Chapter 2. There's a good chance he even took some of the workmen, especially the master masons. What better way to make sure you get it right and achieve the same look? You wouldn't want a local builder, unfamiliar with the techniques, who would probably do a botched job and then make excuses.

Senior Catholic clergy in France seem to have consistently travelled far and wide. The Cardinal du Bellay for instance, who later became bishop of Paris in 1532, even travelled to Syria and brought back seeds of trees he liked, then got the gardener at the local chateau of Rebetz to plant them. Today the descendant of precisely such a tree, 30 metres tall and awarded the title of 'Arbre Remarquable' in 2015, still grows in Chaumont-en-Vexin near Beauvais.[11] The local ruler in the Middle Ages, a noble called Walo II, went on the First Crusade as part of Hugh the Great's army, so would have also visited Syria.

So too did the pointed arch make its way from Cairo across North Africa, where the famous mosque at Qairouan in today's Tunisia, built in the 870s, has pointed arches used in conjunction with slightly pointed horseshoe arches. The *mihrab* has a pointed profile, and its decorative tiles were made in Baghdad and imported specially. The Great Mosque at Mahdia, also in today's Tunisia, would have been well known to Amalfi merchants as a trading port. The mosque has been extensively destroyed and restored across its lifetime but still boasts an arcade of pointed arches built in 916 with quadrilateral groin-vaulting, a whole century earlier than this style first appeared in the Gothic churches of Europe. In England the earliest extant pointed arches can still be seen in the ruins of the Cistercian Roche Abbey in Yorkshire, dating to 1170.

Another example of how readily and how far architectural styles spread can be seen in Delhi, where pointed arches are used in the late-twelfth-century Quwwat al-Islam Mosque, the first to be built after the Islamic conquest of the city. The structure of true arches was unfamiliar to local Hindu craftsmen, but they managed by using a corbelling technique.[12] Their new masters must have instructed them to make the arches pointed, more evidence that this was by now a way of marking a building's Islamic identity.

The same thing happened under the Fatimid dynasty in Cairo during the twelfth century, when a slightly different form of pointed arch, known as the keel arch (sometimes called the ogee arch), was used by local craftsmen. It came to be associated with a uniquely Fatimid architectural style, a synthesis of Abbasid, Byzantine and Coptic elements. The Fatimids, who claimed descent from Fatima, daughter of the Prophet Muhammad, loved ornament and luxury. They built many exotic palaces, mainly of brick, none of which, sadly, survive. Contemporary historians tell us the palaces were adorned with furniture and ceramics often featuring motifs of birds and animals, thought to be symbols of good luck. Their style can however still be seen in their surviving stone-built mosques, with four-centred arches, squinches and arcades with keel arches. These keel arches are most prominent in Cairo's Al-Aqmar Mosque (1125), where they even feature in a very unusual chamfered corner form. The keel arch became a recognisable feature of Fatimid architecture that continued into the fifteenth and early sixteenth centuries.[13]

The Fatimids were an Isma'ili Shi'i dynasty that first came to power in 909 in Tunisia under Abdullah al-Mahdi Billah, originally from Salamiyeh on the edge of the Syrian desert halfway between Aleppo and Damascus. The Fatimids conquered Egypt in 969, ruling it and adjacent territories for the next two centuries and founding the city of Cairo, whose three gates—Bab al-Nasr, Bab al-Futuh and Bab Zuweila—all date from the tenth century. The Fatimid elite felt that they possessed esoteric knowledge setting them apart from the masses.

Islam has on its religious periphery a whole illuminationist philosophy, in which the notion of light was a way of exploring the links between God and his creation. The Fatimids in particular espoused Neoplatonism, a philosophy that would have reached them via translations made in Baghdad—the same way it reached the West. The Qur'an has many references to becoming 'enlightened' with divine knowledge and understanding. Even the names of the Fatimid mosques—Al-Azhar (the Radiant), Al-Anwar (the Shining) and Al-Aqmar (the Moonlit)—show how important the role of light was to them.

Many of the mosques, notably Al-Aqmar, had elaborately carved pierced circular medallions on their facades to let in complex patterns of light in stellar and geometrical shapes. The Qur'anic verses the Fatimids chose as decoration for their mosque interiors were often related to light or enlightenment. Pointed arches, apart from their structural merits of being able to bear more weight than a rounded arch, had the additional benefit of allowing in more light. Abbot Suger wanted to let in more light to his basilica, but it would be wrong to think of this as a Gothic monopoly, for light is equally important in Islam as in Christianity.

The arching to be seen at Samarra and elsewhere—as at the Baghdad Gate of Raqqa—showed that the four-centred arch was also slowly developing during the Abbasid caliphate. The distinctive profile of the ninth-century arch proved the initial clue to a significant cultural event—the removal/migration of the Alexandrian Greeks to Italy in the early ninth century.[14] This is how we can see their work in the first early church at St Mark's in Venice with its pointed arcades. Cresswell's arch dating system puts them at 829–36, which means that these arcades have survived from that early phase, incorporated as original elements within the subsequent eleventh-century rebuilding.[15] In the eighth century, too, the builders and architects of the original Church of St Moses in Venice were recorded by a contemporary chronicle as being Syrian: 'De Syria venerunt'.[16] This has been interpreted by scholars as coinciding with a wave of Syrian Christians emigrating to escape heavy taxation imposed on Christians under the caliphs Haroun al-Rashid and Al-Ma'moun. Many arrived in Europe, some taking refuge in Western monasteries, causing Byzantine scholar Ignacio Peña to speculate that this might explain why the facade of the great portico of the ancient abbey church of Cluny bears such a strong resemblance to St Simeon's Basilica in northern Syria—the position of their respective arches is identical, as are the fluted pilasters framing the arch.[17] The fame of St Simeon spread very quickly into Western Europe, where his cult, as evidenced by the many relics and images of him found throughout France and Germany, was highly influential. An imitation of his great Syrian basilica would have been entirely natural, and maybe it is not a coincidence that the monastery at Cluny is widely credited as the first example of Romanesque architecture on European soil.[18] This provides more evidence that men with the relevant skills and knowledge came from Egypt and from Syria to Byzantine Italy and to Western Europe more broadly, one of the many routes through which Islamic influences entered Europe. Peña, at the end of his exhaustive analysis of Christian art in Byzantine Syria, concludes: 'In short, the commercial, artistic and spiritual traffic between East and West which flourished during the Middle Ages resulted in a type of colonization of the Latin world by the peoples of the East and had a considerable influence on the material civilization of Europe, on its artistic conceptions and on the way it conducted its religious life.'[19]

Most writers on Western medieval architecture over the last fifty years have accepted that the pointed arch was imported into Europe from Islamic architecture. But when the Gothic revival fashion of the nineteenth century suddenly made it necessary to rediscover the origin of the pointed arch, many Western historians found ways of attributing it to northern Europe. In England, where it was regarded as part of the last phase of Gothic, it was even referred to as the Tudor arch due to its popularity during the Tudor dynasty (1485–1603). Some well-known examples are the Clock Court gatehouse at Hampton Court (c. 1520), the east window at St George's Chapel, Windsor (1475–1528), and King's College Chapel, Cambridge (1446–1515).

When used as a church window to cover a very wide space, as at St George's Chapel and King's College Chapel, the pointed arch lent itself to being divided vertically via tall thin mullions, which could then be filled with stained glass. This became typical of the Perpendicular Gothic style.

It does not greatly matter exactly how the pointed arch entered Europe—there were numerous possible routes, and indeed it could have come by many or all of them—via Spain into France with merchants, travellers and pilgrims to the Santiago de Compostela shrine; via Sicily, filtered through the Norman court of Roger II; via southeast Turkey through the Iranian-leaning Seljuks, or through the Crusaders returning from the Holy Land.

The cathedral at Le Puy for example, built in Romanesque style with rounded arches over a period of 200 years between the eleventh and the thirteenth centuries, has many incontrovertible Islamic features in its decoration. Its twelfth-century cloister has definite echoes of the Cordoba Mezquita: alternate red and white patterns on the arches, decorated multifoil arches,

Cloister of Notre-Dame du Puy Cathedral, twelfth century, showing two-tone stone arches and many Islamic features such as arcades, blind arches, and even a Kufic inscription. It is a UNESCO World Heritage site on the road to Santiago de Compostela.

pointed arches, and even a Kufic inscription. The use of Arabic calligraphy as a decorative element on stone and wood carvings in French and Spanish churches (as well as in borders of textiles) is another amusing example of misidentification by Crusaders. They saw the Arabic script on buildings like the Dome of the Rock—where the inscriptions are of course an explicit rejection of the divinity of Christ—and assumed it was the language of Christ and therefore holy, so they copied it. Sometimes it was gibberish, pseudo-Kufic, and sometimes it was legible, usually short repeated phrases like *al-mulk lillah*, meaning 'the kingdom is God's'.[20] Le Puy Cathedral has been a UNESCO World Heritage Site since 1998 as part of 'The Routes of Santiago de Compostela in France'.

Historians of architecture like Kenneth Conant, Jean Bony and Peter Draper concur in the view that the first prominent monumental use of the pointed arch in Europe occurred at the third church of the Benedictine monastery at Cluny (Cluny III), built between 1088 and 1120 under the energetic Abbot Hugh (1049–1109), where it is combined with horseshoe lobes on the arches of the triforium, together with classicising elements like fluted pilasters and Corinthian capitals.[21] Much of the money to build this vast and expensive structure, the largest church in Europe before St Peter's in Rome was rebuilt in the sixteenth century, came from the Spanish kings of León, Fernando and his son Alfonso VI, in the form of spectacularly generous donations to Cluny, money that had come from the tribute taxation of subjugated Muslim cities. In return the kings received advice and perpetual prayers for, among other things, further triumph over the Muslim enemy. The abbots of Cluny were statesmen on the international stage and the monastery of Cluny was considered the grandest, most prestigious and best-endowed monastic institution in Europe.

Like Cluny III, the slightly earlier Great Mosque at Diyarbakır, eastern Anatolia—built in 1091–2 by the Seljuk ruler Malik Shah from the local black basalt, but otherwise consciously modelled on the Damascus Umayyad Mosque—has Corinthian capitals supporting pointed arches, along with many classical recycled spolia in its two-storeyed facade. Clearly no

The courtyard of the Great Mosque at Diyarbakır, modelled on the Damascus Umayyad Mosque, shows effusive vegetal stone carving, with pointed arches supported on Corinthian columns like those of Cluny III, the largest church in Europe before St Peter's was rebuilt. Cluny III's pointed arches are recorded to have been copied from Egypt's Ibn Tulun Mosque via Amalfi and Monte Cassino.

contradiction was seen in either Cluny or Diyarbakır in combining pagan classical styles with the styles of their respective monotheistic religions.

Now that it had been so prominently used at the powerful and influential Cluny Abbey, the pointed arch became all the rage. Everyone wanted it. The Benedictines, who had already brought the arch to Cluny from Monte Cassino, began to transmit it in the Cluniac shrines they built all along the route to Santiago de Compostela. Kenneth Conant, whose life's work was the study of Cluny Abbey, argued that the monks had adopted the arch via Sicily.[22] It appears that by this stage, in their Benedictine Golden Age, there was no sense among the abbot or the monks that the pointed arch and other decorative techniques and styles were borrowings from the rival religion of Islam. And if it was good enough for Cluny, it was obviously good enough for the rest of France and Europe. The style spread with astonishing speed and became immensely popular.

Conant's lifelong study of Cluny, beginning in 1927 with the first of five Guggenheim fellowships and continuing till 1950, convinced him it was the pre-eminent building in all of architectural history. His studies led him to notice something that no Westerner before him seemed to have remarked upon—apart from, of course, Christopher Wren, 300 years earlier, whom everyone seemed to have forgotten about. This was that the pointed arch had structural advantages, and as well as giving what Conant called 'a more scientific profile' to the high vault, it also helped with vault construction in the aisles, permitting 'a cleverer and thinner groin vault, more easily built.' In short, the pointed arch was better at load-bearing, which had obvious implications for vaults in tall buildings of a monumental scale.

Jean Bony, a specialist in Gothic architecture and professor of fine art at the University of Cambridge and at the University of California, Berkeley, went further. After stating that the first appearance of the pointed arch in a 'properly Romanesque context' was at Cluny in the 1090s, and certainly by the 1120s, he argues that its use for the profile of the barrel vault had the effect of reducing the lateral thrusts by about 20 per cent—an astonishing calculation. For Bony, this technical advantage was the obvious reason for its 'rapid diffusion' across Romanesque Europe.[23]

Roger Stalley, professor of art at Trinity College Dublin, agrees with these points on the structural merits of the pointed arch, writing:

> Cluny is one of the first uses of the pointed arch in Western architecture, a form commonly thought to have been borrowed from the Islamic world … [The use of the alien form] must be linked to the scale of the building and to the realisation that the pointed arch offered structural advantages. Pointed forms were used only in load-bearing positions, not for windows or doors, indicating that the change was made for structural rather than aesthetic reasons.[24]

His conclusion may have been correct right at the beginning of its arrival in Europe, but it was not long of course before the pointed arch was used in all religious architecture. The Gothic style—or as Wren observed it should 'more rightly be called, the Saracen style'—had triumphed.

Quite apart from its structural advantages, Peter Draper, in his valedictory lecture as the president of the Society of Architectural Historians, stated that the other reason for the very rapid spread of the pointed arch in the twelfth century was that it marked an obviously differentiated form from the prevailing Romanesque and its round arches.[25] The new era heralded the post-First Crusade period of wealth and prosperity—exactly as the Umayyads had wanted to differentiate themselves from the earlier Byzantine round-arched style. What an irony.

It is an irony Draper seemed to feel himself, as he concluded his speech by noting that 'the history of Western medieval architecture, like that of Western culture in general, cannot be written without reference to the lessons learnt from Islamic culture, whereas the history of Islamic medieval architecture can be written largely without reference to the West.'[26]

Today less than 10 per cent still stands of Cluny III, which was demolished in 1810 after the French Revolution and used as a quarry, but thanks to the historical records and archives of the monasteries mentioned, facts about the rebuilding projects and the architecture have been unearthed.

Rib Vaults

The origins of rib vaulting can be traced back to the eighth-century Abbasid palace of Ukhaidir in today's Iraq, but the tenth-century rib vaults of the domes in the Cordoba Mezquita were the first time such vaulting systems were used on European soil. Though ruined, the Ukhaidir Palace still stands today and has eight transverse arches and rib vaults. The same system can also be seen in the tunnel vaults of the Ribat (fortress) of Sousse (821–2) in today's Tunisia, built by the Aghlabids, an Arab dynasty who ruled that part of Africa and southern Italy for about a century on behalf of the Abbasids. Exactly such vaults can also be found in the cross vaults of French Romanesque churches of the late eleventh and early twelfth centuries, such as the former Benedictine abbey of St Philibert at Tournus in Burgundy; the Benedictine and Cluniac abbey church of St Mary la Madeleine at Vézelay (1104–32), also in Burgundy, which stood at the start of one of the four major pilgrimage routes to Santiago de Compostela; and Fontenay Abbey (1139–47). The Vézelay Abbey was closely linked with the calls for the Crusades, and the tympanum above its portal, carved in 1130, depicts the 'ungodly' people against whom the Crusades were to be waged—Turks and Muslims—as deformed and repulsive in an attempt to dehumanise them. Pope Urban II had called on Christians to 'exterminate this vile race.'

The simplest kind of barrel vaulting may even go as far back as the Phoenicians, as a pointed arch entrance gateway has been reconstructed in the barrel-vaulted ramparts of Ugarit in modern Syria, once a powerful Phoenician sea port and trading centre. In what is today Israel, and open to tourists by rowing boat, a different type of early vaulting can be seen in the 10-metre-high stone cistern of Ramla built by the Abbasid caliph Haroun al-Rashid in 789. Ramla had become the prosperous new provincial capital of Palestine under the Umayyads in 715 thanks to its strategic location on the trade route between Damascus and Cairo. The population was mixed Muslim, Christian and Jewish, and when the Abbasids of Baghdad took over they endowed the small city of Ramla with grand mosques, mansions, gardens and fountains watered by an elaborate system of four underground cisterns fed by an aqueduct. Earthquakes destroyed most buildings in the eleventh century, but the cisterns survived. Only one of the four is open to visitors today, known as the Pool of the Arches, illuminated with eerie green and red lighting. It consists of pointed arches, still standing after more than 1,200 years, on cruciform (cross-shaped) masonry piers, then reinforced with six barrel vaults.

Sousse in today's Tunisia has two sandstone mosques which use a similar system—Bu Fatata (838–41) and the Great Mosque (850–1), for which the earlier Bu Fatata was a model, built on behalf of an Aghlabid prince by a master mason freed slave. This type of vaulting then appeared in Europe for the first time some 300 years later in the colossal twelfth-century Romanesque French cathedral of Notre-Dame d'Orcival (1146–78) in Puy-de-Dome, built as a pilgrimage site to venerate a statue of the Virgin Mary, supposedly carved by St Luke, still on display in the sanctuary.

Abbasid Mathematics and Geometry at Court

A major innovation under the Abbasids was the application of the equilateral triangle to architecture, generally as a way of framing the view. It first appears in the audience hall of the Abbasid palace of Al-Mahdia (916–21) and then in the palace at Asir (935), before being further developed in Spain in the tenth-century extensions of the Cordoba Mezquita, in Al-Munya Al-Rumaniyya and in the palace of Madinat al-Zahra just outside Cordoba. It is clear proof of the scientific and cultural contacts that continued between the rival caliphates at opposite ends of the Islamic world. What this application of the equilateral triangle did was to completely change the architectural approach, from Roman architecture with its axis of symmetry, to an approach based on what the human eye sees. It is an approach that would not have been possible without the significant advances made in the fields of mathematics and geometry by great Muslim scholars like Al-Khwarizmi (780–850). The use of equilateral triangles has clear practical advantages in architecture, especially in establishing accurate right angles in ground plans and in tying in exterior and interior space. They were later used in Romanesque and Gothic architecture in Europe too, though whether or not they were used in determining the proportions of cathedrals is still under debate.[27]

The human field of view was a unique way of combining architecture, geometry and optics and of making the individual the centre of the space, as opposed to some random point in the centre of the building. Such an approach also made it possible for the first time to convey, through extending our view to the horizon, a sense of infinity, that supreme sense which Islamic art and architecture evolved to express through complex geometry. The German academic Felix Arnold sees in this approach a similarity to how perspective is perceived for the first time in the European Renaissance, and gives the example of the paintings by Filippo Brunelleschi in 1425. Brunelleschi, deviser of the famous Florence Cathedral dome, is known to

There is clear Islamic influence in the Palazzo dei Papi in Viterbo, Italy, especially in the colonnade of interlocking trefoil arches of the loggia.

have read the writings of the Islamic scientist Ibn al-Haytham (965–1040), who worked on the principles of optics at the Fatimid court in Cairo in the early eleventh century.[28] His main work, *Kitab al-Manazir*, the Book of Optics, first written in 1028, was translated into Latin in Spain around 1200 under the title *De Aspectibus* or *Perspectiva*. Many researchers have recognised that Renaissance artists took the scientific principles of the human perspective from his writings, set down on paper four centuries earlier, having read Latin translations of the Arabic.

Arnold suggests that there are two missing links which explain and bridge this 400-year gap between the Islamic mastery of perspective and the later Italian Renaissance. The first is found in the architecture of the kings of Mallorca and the papal residency at Avignon. Mallorca had been under Islamic rule since 902, so when the Christian kings who were originally from Aragon (and were therefore already familiar with Aljafería, the eleventh-century Islamic palace in Zaragoza used by the kings of Aragon), arrived in Palma, they were happy to refurbish the existing Islamic palace, known as Zuda (Sudda), now called Almudaina (Arabic, 'the Little City'). There were similar palaces at Perpignan (1274–85) and at Montpellier, now lost. The popes who were based in Avignon from 1309 to 1377 were obviously aware of this palace architecture, and there are many examples of their incorpora-tion of some of its Islamic aspects into their own palaces, such as the creation of special gardens for the pope. When Pope Gregory XI eventually returned the papal residency from Avignon to Rome in 1377, he initiated the creation of the papal gardens at the Vatican, one of the first instances of Renaissance architecture in Rome.

The second missing link between the Islamic architecture of Spain and Renaissance Italy comes in the form of the papal legate and Cardinal Gil Alvarez de Albornoz (1302–67). He was born in Cuenca, Spain and had gone on to study in Toledo and Zaragoza and was therefore very familiar with Islamic palace architecture. It became his job to design and create the first papal residences outside Rome, and the Islamic influence is clear to see in the Palazzo dei Papi at Viterbo (1354–9); in the late Gothic palazzi and Loggia dei Mercanti in Ancona (1356–65); at the palazzi at Spoleto (1358–70); at the palazzo at Bologna (1365–7); and at Montefiascone (1368–70) on a hill overlooking Lake Bolsena about 100 kilometres north of Rome.

The scientist, philosopher and jurist Abu Nasr al-Farabi, of Turkic ethnicity, who died in Damascus in 950, was best known in the West for his commentaries and treatises on Aristotle and for his influence on Avicenna and Maimonides, but he also wrote a treatise on geometric constructions entitled *A Book of Spiritual Crafts and Natural Secrets in the Details of Geometrical Figures*. This book was later incorporated by Abu al-Wafa Buzjani (940–98), the Persian mathematician and astronomer who worked in Baghdad during the Islamic Golden Age, into a book called *On Those Parts of Geometry Needed by Craftsmen*, which gave full details and justifications for over a hundred geometric constructions.

Thanks to the enlightenment of Caliph Haroun al-Rashid, many advances in geometry were made at his Baghdad court during Abbasid rule, along with a huge translation movement of the Greek mathematical texts. The epoch of translation ran roughly from 750 to 850 and was followed by a period of creativity and invention, which, transmitted over the course of several centuries via Syria, Spain and Sicily, was to lay the basis for much of the canon of knowledge that dominated European thought from the Middle Ages. The scientists of the Arab world assimilated the ancient heritage of Persia, as well as that of India to some extent, along with the classical heritage of Greece through the study of geniuses like Aristotle, Galen and Ptolemy, while adding their own new contributions.

In the field of geometry and architecture the works of three Greek scientists were key. The first was Euclid's monumental and timeless *Elements*. The second was Archimedes, whose two major works were *On the Sphere and the Cylinder* and *On the Heptagon in a Circle*. The latter of these has been lost in the Greek and has only reached the West through Arabic translation. The third mathematical giant was Apollonius of Perga, whose difficult work *The Conics* was written around 200 BCE and appeared in eight books, but, as mentioned in Chapter 1 on Christopher Wren, seven came to the West via Arabic translation while only four survive in the original Greek.

Of these three *The Conics* was the most important for developing geometrical constructions, because the theory of conic sections could be used to solve construction problems that related to complex geometric shapes. Knowledge of conic sections was required in the accurate making of sundials—an early obsession of both Wren and his father.

Classical mathematical concepts underlie all Islamic abstract forms, and one of the reasons that geometry held such special interest for Muslim architects, as well as for Muslim artists and calligraphers, was their keen awareness of how mathematical equations and expressions seemed to have deep connections within the natural world. Algebra, from Arabic *al-jabr*, even means bringing back to normal, connecting (of broken bones), as if the overall concept is to restore natural balance and equilibrium. The Golden Ratio or Golden Mean, a ratio of measurements that appeal to the aesthetic sense and to the human eye, appears in nature, for example in mollusc shells and in plant leaves. The ratio works out at approximately 8:13, where 8 represents the width and 13 is the height, and once you start to look, you will notice it is widely applied in many forms of art, including architecture. Proportional ratios and balances were also analysed in cosmology, musicology and calligraphy from the tenth century onwards, and the natural harmony of the figure of eight for example meant that Muslim scholars used the number as the basis for musical scales, calligraphy and the geometric artistic patterns of what became known as 'arabesques', a phrase coined in Europe to describe interweaving stems branching into split leaves and secondary stems, which could cover any surface with a regular and rhythmical network capable of extending endlessly. The octagon was also favoured in Christian architecture, where most baptismal fonts have been octagonal since the Lateran Baptistery in Rome, built in 440. St Ambrose wrote that fonts and baptisteries were octagonal because the eighth day was the day where 'Christ loosens the bondage of death'. St Augustine also described the eighth day as 'hallowed by Christ's resurrection', so the octagonal shape came to be used in martyria as well, such as the remarkable St Philip the Apostle's Martyrium in Hierapolis, Pamukkale, modern Turkey.

Geometry, from Greek meaning 'measurement of land', is a science that fuses mathematics with the concept of space. While Europe lagged behind in its Dark Ages, Islamic scientists preserved Greek ideas and developed them further, creating ever-repeating patterns to convey infinity and, ultimately,

In this bold sixteenth-century portrait of Henry VIII, after Hans Holbein the Younger's painting, the macho monarch is standing on an Islamic Turkish carpet depicting a geometric star. The border of his cloak carries the Islamic 'knot' pattern, as does the curtain backdrop.

even a sense of union with the Divine as the patterns became more sophisticated. The designs can be purely geometric in shape or can be interwoven with stylised floral, leaf and stalk motifs that repeat, conveying a sense of the endless abundance of nature, ever-growing, ever-renewing. This is what is known as 'fractal geometry', where similar patterns recur in progressively smaller scales in nature, as in snowflakes or crystal growth, for example— something which Islamic architecture consciously recreates in its radiating patterns starting from a centre. It projects an acknowledgement that God is continuously creating and recreating the world, and that everything is therefore constantly hovering on the edge of change and even potential chaos if order dissolves completely.[29] This is the transition zone that, under the Islamic world view, man inhabits. The role of the Islamic architect, poet or composer is to reflect and express this uncertainty, this constant longing for something beyond this transitory world where material things are so ephemeral. In a building like the Alhambra, the pinnacle of the use of natural, fractal geometry, it is possible for most visitors to sense this poetry and music inhabiting the architecture. We may not understand why we respond to the rhythms of the ever-moving shapes and the ever-changing combinations of colours and textures, but on some intuitive level we are in tune with the themes of growth, change and order concealed beneath the veneer of chaos.

It is something which classical architecture rarely attempts, but many Western Renaissance, Baroque and Rococo artists have been inspired by Islamic geometric patterns. Leonardo da Vinci (1452–1519) revealed his fascination with arabesques in his drawings and is known to have spent long periods analysing the complicated patterns. Albrecht Dürer (1471–1528) used geometric patterns, as did Raphael (1483–1520). Italian painters of the sixteenth century called these patterns *rabeschi*, and in Hans Holbein the Younger's bold iconic painting (1536–7) of Henry VIII, legs astride, the macho English monarch has the Islamic 'knot'-style pattern on the border of his cloak, recurring in the curtain backdrop. He is standing on a Turkish carpet with a geometric Ushak star.

Even Andrea Palladio, widely considered one of the most influential architects in the history of Western architecture, showed in the groundplans and facades of buildings such as Il Redentore (the Church of the Holy Redeemer in

Venice, 1577–92) the same grasp of fractal geometry and how it can emphasise the spirituality of a space. M.C. Escher, the twentieth-century Dutch graphic artist, spent many days sketching the tile patterns of the Alhambra in Granada when he visited in 1936, declaring afterwards that it 'was the richest source of inspiration that I have ever tapped.' An insight into how craftsmen used these patterns was discovered in Istanbul in 1986 in a 30-metre-long scroll, consisting of 114 individual geometric patterns for vaulting and wall decoration. Known as the Topkapı Scroll and today on display in the Topkapı Palace Museum Library, they are the Timurid/Turkmen-style architectural drawings of a master builder working under the Safavid dynasty in Persia in the early sixteenth century. Turkish Harvard scholar Gülru Necipoğlu published a detailed analysis of the drawings in 1992, in which she demonstrated how the plans were read by trained masons and transformed into solid architectural forms. She also sees a relationship between Timurid and Gothic architecture in terms of the numerate handling of materials.[30]

Muslim scientists and engineers translated, studied and developed Greek treatises, many of which focused on things like designs for the construction of fountains, including the mechanisms for creating different patterns of jets and sprays to determine the shape of the water emitted. The shapes were then extended and combined to make ever more elaborate water displays, with lead pipes used to circulate the water, and automatic opening and closing valves in each pipe, centuries before Europe used decorative water systems in the same way.

Abbasid Glass

Syrian towns like Tyre and Sidon (in modern-day Lebanon) were survivals of the ancient Phoenician glass industry, the oldest in the world after the ancient Egyptian. Abbasid glass was proverbial for its clarity and thinness and Raqqa, infamous today as the short-lived capital of the so-called Islamic State (ISIS), was renowned in the late eighth and early ninth centuries as the site of the Abbasid caliph Haroun al-Rashid's recreational summer palace on the Euphrates. It also boasted famous glass factories which manufactured green, blue, brown and purple glass on a massive scale, with the raw materials made from the pure riverbed pebbles and local plant ash.[31] The enamelled and variegated types of Syrian glass discovered by the Crusaders became the forerunner of the stained glass Gothic cathedrals of Europe.[32] Fragments of the glass found from the palace alone, known as Qasr al-Banat (Palace of the Maidens) amounted to over eleven kilos.[33] Technical analysis of the glass from the Byzantine Chora and Pantokrator churches in Istanbul showed it to have a different chemical composition to that of Western glass, with an unusually high level of boron, pointing to a local sand source.[34] Eastern Byzantine glass preceded and influenced the western European tradition, and fragments of stained glass were also found at the Umayyad palace of Khirbat al-Mafjar by excavators working decades after R.W. Hamilton.[35] Syrian glass and metal vases were also highly rated for the standard of their workmanship, much in demand as luxury items in mosques and palaces, as well as in mosaics and tiles manufactured in Damascus workshops which survived into the eighteenth century. The famous 'Luck of Edenhall' in London's V&A Museum is a striking fourteenth-century enamelled Syrian glass goblet credited with magical powers, thought to have been acquired in the Holy Land by a pilgrim. The British Museum boasts what is known as the Hope Goblet, a similar glass copying the Islamic style, but probably made later in Venice, depicting the Virgin and Child and two angels with St Peter and St Paul. A curator at the museum comments: 'With spectacular technical skill and artistry, the Muslim cities of Aleppo and Damascus were producing between about 1250 and 1360 enamelled and richly gilded glass, the like of which could not be made in any European centre of glassmaking, not even in Venice.'[36] Glassmaking in Venice began in the tenth century; by 1224 there was already a glassmakers' guild, stimulated by trading contact with Fatimid Egypt and with the glass factories of the Crusader kingdom, especially Tyre.[37]

Glass production during Roman and Byzantine times had been highly centralised, with large tank furnaces in Egypt heating many tonnes of sand using natron—mineral soda—from the alkaline lakes of the Wadi Natroun (between Cairo and Alexandria) as the flux (soda-lime combination) to enable the melting process. The large slabs of glass were then broken into chunks and traded into Europe, where there was no known local source of soda. The earliest glass production, however, dates back at least to the Bronze Age, when the Phoenicians were already trading ready-coloured glass ingots round the Mediterranean, made not with natron, but with Mesopotamian plant ash as the melting agent.[38] The main source was the soda-rich plant known in Arabic as *ushnaan*, which grows around salt lakes such as Jaboul, south of Aleppo, and is still used today in both glass and soap production in Syria.[39] From the Abbasid period onwards, wider social, economic and political changes meant that Syrian plant ash glass gradually replaced Egyptian natron glass. Known in medieval times as 'the cinders of Syria', it was highly valued, being both easier to work with and cheaper to produce.[40] After heating in a furnace, the calcined residue of the Syrian plants solidified into hard chunks, and was shipped in this form to Venice.[41] Documents found in Venetian archives, and even a Venetian glassmaking recipe book dating from around 1400, testify that high-grade Syrian plant ash was considered superior to Egyptian natron ash, and all Venetian glass analysed from the eleventh to the sixteenth centuries shows its consistent use, by law. One recipe read: 'In order to make glass in the colour of any [precious] stone [you wish]. Take 10 pounds of pebbles from the Ticino [river], well crushed, and 10 pounds of soda ashes, well crushed; and [these] should be soda ashes from Syria.'[42] The export of Syrian soda ashes to other glassmaking cities was strictly forbidden by the Venetian Senate, in order to maintain the Venetian monopoly.[43] The Syrian ash was also extremely cheap, since, being heavy, it was used as ballast in Venetian cog ships bringing back cargoes of Syrian cotton, usually from the port of Tripoli. Again, contemporary documentation shows the vast quantities that were shipped—hundreds of tons, according to regular timetables, ensuring a reliable and constant supply of the highest possible quality of plant ash required to maintain Venice's pre-eminent position in the European glass industry, against its competitors like Genoa, Ancona, Vicenza, Verona and Florence.[44] Along with the raw materials came the glassmakers themselves, who were itinerant because the Venetian government imposed an annual five-month recess on almost all glass furnaces. During that recess the glass workers were not paid, so they would go elsewhere to practice their craft and earn money, sometimes settling at rival foreign glass centres, despite the Venetian Senate's attempts to lure them back with incentives.[45]

In the Middle Ages English workshops, using this imported glass, worked only with clear glass, while all coloured glass for the cathedrals was imported from Normandy. When the Norman French built Canterbury Cathedral even the limestone was imported from Caen in Normandy, along with the French masons themselves. Soft on quarrying, hardening on exposure, it was ideal for delicate carving,[46] so the masons knew and trusted it. Analysis of stained glass from 1200 to 1400 in the cathedrals of Canterbury, York, Chartres, Saint-Denis and Rouen all show the same high plant ash composition typical of Syrian raw materials.[47] The fact that mosques from Jerusalem's Dome of the Rock and Al-Aqsa onwards carried coloured glass ornament in their windows has been a lost dimension of medieval Islamic art, despite being an integral and innovative element of Islamic architecture from the start. Its connection with the stained glass of European cathedrals has therefore long been overlooked.[48]

For 200 years Syria's glass industry had been the world's leader, but it never fully recovered after the Mongol invasion of Tamerlane, when the glass furnaces of Damascus were burnt and its craftsmen taken to Samarkand in 1401.[49] Unfortunately only a relatively small fraction of the exquisite Raqqa glassware remains in museums today. This is because of the large-scale smuggling network not of ISIS but of much earlier Circassian immigrants, who had been settled there by the Ottoman authorities from 1885 onwards to help them flee from compulsory military service, forced religious conversion and imposition of the Russian language. The Ottomans gave the impoverished refugees land and permission to search for bricks among the town's ruins to build their new homes. An accidental smuggling epidemic was born, which the Ottoman Imperial Museum then did its best to stop through fines and confiscation, even conducting its own official excavations at the site in 1905–8, the first of their kind. A vast amount of priceless Raqqa ware still found its way onto the art markets of Europe and America, including the so-called 'Great Find'.[50]

Hard as it is to believe today, Raqqa on the Euphrates was, for a short moment in history (796–808), the centre of the world, when Haroun al-Rashid transferred his residence here and made it the seat of his caliphate. He set about building a huge imperial palace city which eventually extended over 15 square kilometres. What we today call Raqqa was built originally as a garrison city to house the caliph's troops and was called Rafiqa, the

Companion City. The German Archaeological Institute worked for over a decade with the Syrian antiquities authorities to excavate the stucco-fronted palaces, but their highly perishable mud-brick construction and the encroachment of the modern city have meant that little remains to the untrained eye. The horseshoe-shaped walls of the garrison city, graced with 100 semi-circular towers at 35-metre intervals, can still be seen in places. The University of Nottingham was conducting excavations—now interrupted by the war in Syria—on the main glass factories, which revealed both the scale of the industrial complex and the fact that the artisans were both Muslim and Christian, buried side by side. Abbasid society included Christians and Jews in high positions; in 985 the geographer Al-Maqdisi found most of the money-changers and bankers in Syria to be Jews and most of the clerks and physicians to be Christians.[51]

The vast construction enterprise at Raqqa required a huge workforce to be imported, and the caliph ordered the interruption of other building activities in central Mesopotamia so that the whole construction workshop could be sent to Raqqa instead.[52] The local workforce would not have been big enough or had the requisite high level of expertise to fulfil the sudden demand. On top of the numbers and the skill set, speed of construction was always demanded, not just by Haroun al-Rashid but by all imperial patrons. Speed required not just more workers but highly trained ones who could rise to meet the ruler's exacting standards. According to Islamic art and architecture historian Michael Meinecke, this pattern of a mobile workforce was in evidence from the last decades of the Umayyad Empire, though to a much lesser degree, and explains the absence of regional or urban schools of architecture.[53] It also explains how new stylistic syntheses emerged, since the combination of urgency and an inflow of new influences produced exactly the right conditions for innovative techniques and patterns to flourish.

Two centuries later in Europe, it was mobile workforces of this kind, formed by then into guilds of their own, that built our Gothic cathedrals, as Wren surmised: 'The Saracen mode of building seen in the East, soon spread over Europe, and particularly in France; the fashions of which nation we affected to imitate in all ages, even when we were at enmity with it.'[54]

7

GATEWAYS TO EUROPE

(800 – 1400)

The role of Muslim Spain as a conduit of ideas and architectural styles into northern Europe from the eighth to the tenth century was explored in Chapter 5, and that of the maritime Duchy of Amalfi in Chapter 6. But there were of course other significant channels through which Islamic architectural styles were passed, and these will be the focus of this chapter. Of all of these channels Andalusia was the most significant, while the Crusader states were arguably the least important, since by the time the Crusaders took Jerusalem in 1099, many key Islamic architectural influences had already reached Europe via other routes. The Crusader contribution came in the form of a few military innovations, together with the import of some skilled architects and/or masons, generally Arab Muslims.

Venice

The case of Venice and how it acquired its unmistakably oriental architecture has been convincingly clarified thanks to the immensely detailed decade of scholarship undertaken by Deborah Howard, professor of architectural history at the University of Cambridge. Her comprehensive findings were published in 2000 under the title *Venice and the East*, and the points made in the following pages are based largely on her work. Her book covers the four centuries from 1100 to 1500 which represent Venice's peak both as a trading emporium, 'a colossal suq', and as a station on the pilgrimage route to Jerusalem and the Holy Land. Venice saw the great multi-faith cities of the Islamic world—Cairo, Alexandria, Damascus, Tripoli, Tyre, Antioch, Aleppo and Jerusalem—as 'prosperous, colourful and civilised', so the Venetian adoption of Islamic styles was a deliberate and willing choice, unlike in Spain and Sicily, where it came from periods of Muslim domination.

Venice's location on a series of islands meant that the city had the opportunity to regularly refashion its urban architecture because of the constant programme of dredging and land reclamation that was necessary for its expansion. Not only that, but the great fire of 1105, immediately after the First Crusade, stimulated rebuilding in masonry at a time when Venetian merchants had just started to take over the homes of Muslim merchants in eastern Mediterranean ports like Tyre and Acre.[1] Later, when the Mamluks expelled the Crusaders, the relationship that Venice enjoyed with the Mamluk sultans was one between equal trading partners. Venice was never the superior, patronising coloniser, nor did Islam ever colonise Venice.[2] Their shared reverence for trade was genuine and deep-seated. The Qur'an sanctioned trade: 'It shall be no offence for you to seek the bounty of your lord by trading' (2:198). Christianity's relationship to trade had been more problematic in the Middle Ages, especially if it was with 'the infidel', but the Venetians had no such qualms. Trade in Venice was a 'quasi-sacred ritualised activity' and the Rialto (the main marketplace) became like 'a sacred precinct, virtually uninhabited, like an eastern bazaar.'[3] The main San Marco–Rialto axis was described by a pilgrim visiting in 1494 as 'the most beautiful street in the whole world and the one with the most beautiful buildings'.[4]

St Mark's Basilica

Two words sum up what the Venetians seemed to love most about the styles they encountered in the Islamic East—colour and curves. St Mark's Basilica, the icon of Venice that stands at the very heart of the city, is the perfect embodiment of both.

As a great maritime trading city state, Venice had enjoyed commercial contacts with Egypt and Syria for centuries, but the key moment for architecture began in 828 when Venetian merchants, with the help of a pair of local monks, smuggled the body of St Mark the Evangelist out of Alexandria

Tintoretto's highly fanciful sixteenth-century painting is based on the story of the theft of St Mark's body from Alexandria in 828 by Venetian merchants, with the help of two local monks. The Basilica of St Mark's was then built to house the body of the Evangelist.

and brought it to Venice, even hiding the body under a layer of pork and cabbage leaves to deter the Muslim guards from closer inspection, according to the scene depicted in one of the current mosaics in St Mark's. Mark, born in Cyrene (today's Libya), had founded the Church of Alexandria around the year 49, becoming the first bishop of Alexandria, and the Egyptian Copts are the successors to this original community. Martyred in 68 after being dragged round the streets by the city's pagans, who resented his attempts to turn them away from their traditional gods, he is symbolised by a winged lion and is most often depicted writing or holding his gospel.

The doge, elected ruler of Venice, ordered a special chapel to be constructed alongside his palace to house Mark's relics. Enhanced and elaborated many times over the course of subsequent centuries, this is the building known locally as San Marco, which came to symbolise Venice's wealth and power. Its unique appearance is an innovative synthesis of Byzantine and Islamic styles unlike anything seen before in Europe, an exotic blend of many oriental features, especially its thirteenth-century onion domes. It was nicknamed La Chiesa d'Oro, the Church of Gold, because of the profusion of glittering mosaics spilling out from the interior onto the exterior surfaces, projecting a sacred aura of kaleidoscopic brilliance. Charles Dickens, after a visit in 1844, wrote: 'Opium couldn't build such a place, and enchantment couldn't shadow it forth in a vision.'

Together with the fourteenth-century Doge's Palace, discussed later, St Mark's set the tone for the flamboyant style of Venetian architecture that has become known as Venetian Gothic, so eulogised by nineteenth-century Victorian art critics, like John Ruskin in his highly influential *Stones of Venice* (1851). Ruskin admired the Venetians' empathy with the East:

> The Venetians deserve especial note as the only European people who appear to have sympathised to the full with the great instinct of the Eastern races … While the burghers of the North were building their dark streets and grisly castles of oak and sandstone, the merchants of Venice were covering their palaces with porphyry and gold.[5]

There are no fewer than six ancient mosaics in St Mark's that show the Lighthouse of Alexandria in the background as a location marker, in the same way that Big Ben or the Eiffel Tower would mark London or Paris, and many of the mosaics feature Egyptian backdrops with the Pyramids, multiple domes, palm trees and camels.[6] The mosaic of Moses before Pharaoh features a building in the background whose gable strongly resembles the Damascus Great Mosque. Most of these mosaics depicting the martyrdom of St Mark in Alexandria are in the Zen Chapel, named after Pietro Zen, Venetian consul in Damascus.

An earlier version of St Mark's dating from 1063 was modelled in a consciously Byzantine style on the Church of the Holy Apostles in Constantinople, but the subsequent remodellings and enlargements added more and more Islamic features, notably the much higher thirteenth-century hollow double domes. They were made from lead-covered wood, in exactly the same way as domes in Cairo, like that of the Ibn Tulun Mosque, which Venetian merchants would have seen being repaired. They therefore understood how this additional height was achieved, with separate inner and outer layers; these 'great bulbous domes were certainly a conspicuous element in the Egyptian townscape by the thirteenth century' with 'the raised domes of San Marco [resembling] their Egyptian prototypes in construction as well as form.'[7] Not only was the construction and shape of the dome copied, but also the function, marking the tomb of St Mark. In Cairo such domes, with clear symbolism of the heavenly skies, were for centuries used above tombs of important figures—principally the Fatimid caliphs and the Mamluk sultans—in the vast necropolis known as the City of the Dead, which stretches for 4 kilometres just outside the historic city walls along the foot of the Muqattam hills, the quarry from which all Cairo's building stone was cut. The addition of these Islamic-style domes to St Mark's Basilica coincides with the Golden Age of Venetian trading activity with Muslim powers, and their distinctive style was 'absorbed into Venetian visual tradition … visible in the soaring domes of Santi Giovanni e Paolo, Palladio's churches and Santa Maria della Salute.'[8] Christopher Wren, who would only have seen sketches and read travel accounts, was in no doubt: 'The Church of St Mark at Venice, is built after the Saracen manner.'[9]

Once the Crusader Kingdom of Jerusalem was established, Venetian families would settle there for as many as three generations. Fulcher of Chartres, chaplain and chronicler of the First Crusade, observed the adoption of court-yard houses as Venetian homes, writing in 1124: 'Consider, I pray, and reflect how in our time God has transformed the Occident into the Orient. For we who were Occidentals have now become Orientals.'[10] A German pilgrim called Barchard, writing about his pilgrimage to the Holy Land in 1232, showed sympathies:

> The nation of the Arabs is closer to the will of the Christians than any other heathen nation. Our own people, the Latins, are worse than all the other people of the land, while Syrian Christians are stingy, giving no alms. By contrast, the Saracens, who preach Mahomet and keep his law ... are very hospitable, courteous and kindly.[11]

Dominican friar William of Tripoli wrote in 1272, 'their beliefs are wrapped up in many lies and decorated with fictions, yet it now manifestly appears that they are near to the Christian faith and not far from the path of salvation.'[12]

The Venetians were also known to greatly admire the Muslims' capacity for memorising large quantities of information—an ability developed through child-hood mastery of the Qur'an by rote. Very little was written down as there was mostly no need. Architectural information was likewise transmitted by memory via both Islamic patrons and itinerant craftsmen. Despite such sympathies, by the fifteenth century, discussion of religion with Muslims was strongly discouraged by the Church. Milanese pilgrim Santo Brasca wrote in 1480: 'Don't dare to discuss matters of faith with the Saracens, because that is a great sin.'[13]

Yet for all such views, the empathy of the Venetians with the Muslims of Egypt and Syria is clear, not only in the lifestyle and architectural borrowings, but also in the linguistic borrowings, where many Arabic words began to appear in Venetian dialect, especially words relating to trade and luxury goods—*fontego, zecca, doana, tariff, gabella, sofa, divan, caravan, damasco*—and even architecture, where the Arabic for dome, '*qubba*', becomes *cuba* in Venetian dialect.

Otto Demus was the first to point out many specific features in St Mark's that are directly borrowed from Islamic buildings.[14] The geometric-patterned stone window grilles above the Porta Sant'Alippio, on the extreme left as you face the facade, for example, are strongly reminiscent of those of the

The unique appearance of St Mark's in Venice comes from an innovative synthesis of Byzantine and Islamic styles unlike anything seen before in Europe.

LES PLUS BELLES EGLISES DU MONDE.

SAINT-MARC DE VENISE.

The two pillars in the Piazzetta, Venice, outside the south wall of St Mark's Basilica. Generally known as the Pillars of Acre, they were in fact brought from the church of St Polyeuktos in Constantinople after the Fourth Crusade as booty.

Damascus Umayyad Mosque, where they were first used in the early eighth century. They were also used at the eighth-century Umayyad desert palaces, such as Qasr al-Hair ash-Sharqi and Khirbat al-Mafjar, as described in Chapter 4, and they appear again in the Cordoba Mezquita, built with strong influences from the Syrian Umayyads, as described in Chapter 5. The same carved window grilles also appear in the narthex of the Venetian tomb of the Dogaressa Felicitas Michiel (died 1111), delicately carved with a tree of life motif.

Further borrowing is apparent in the relief panels at St Mark's, such as the peacock relief on the west facade, which are in the style of Egyptian Fatimid wood carvings.[15] Other decorative elements for St Mark's were shipped back as booty by the Venetians following the sack of Constantinople in 1204, like the famous Four Bronze Horses and the obviously oriental stone-carved *Pilastri Acritani* (Pillars of Acre) with their grape and vine designs. These pillars had once adorned the Church of St Polyeuktos (524–7), Constantinople's largest church until Justinian built the Hagia Sophia.[16]

More borrowings can be seen in the delicate metalwork lanterns, so typical of mosque lanterns of the Mamluks, and in the ogee arch relief set in a rectangular panel (a decorative feature known as an *alfiz* and first seen at the Cordoba Mezquita) above the entrance to the treasury, which contains 'no less than twenty-one Islamic objects … many of them in later Venetian mountings.'[17] Metalwork techniques in particular were so heavily borrowed that a special category of 'Veneto-Saracenic' was coined by art historians to describe the fifteenth- and sixteenth-century metalware thought to have been made by Muslim craftsmen working in Venice who also trained Italian craftsmen in the Islamic style. Subsequent research has shown that most of these works were in fact crafted in Egypt and Syria, and only later copied in Italy.[18] The Mamluks, as a warrior sultanate trained for warfare, had a strong interest in weaponry, which meant that craftsmen became highly skilled in metalworking, not just in armour, helmets, spurs and shields but also in everyday objects like metal lamps, ewers, basins and candlesticks, a tradition that lives on in Damascus especially. The Mamluks ruled over Egypt and Syria from Cairo in 1250–1517, defeating the Mongols twice and the Crusaders three times; their architecture reflected their military might with bold, heavily masculine designs that could hardly be further removed from Gothic.

In more general architectural style, Howard sees echoes of the courtyard of the Great Mosque of Damascus in the Piazza San Marco, with its double-arched arcade running round the piazza, enclosing roughly the same sized space. In the way San Marco brings exterior colour into the piazza, extending the realm of the sacred into the open space, she sees parallels with the multicoloured Dome of the Rock, projecting its colour out onto the Haram al-Sharif, the Sacred Enclosure, something that no Byzantine church had ever done. The exteriors of churches like Hagia Sophia in Constantinople and San Vitale in Ravenna, for all their colourful mosaics inside, are just plain brick walls.

There are also broad similarities in urban architecture between Venice and cities like Damascus in the dense labyrinthine residential alleys that have grown organically to infill the space between the main streets. The Venetians seemed to prefer the intimacy and social cohesion of Islamic cities, while the lack of wheeled traffic gave no incentive to widen the streets or to straighten the lanes. Residential mazes with narrow streets and dead ends brought privacy to families. For the same reasons of privacy, the Venetians adopted the typical Damascus-style screened-off roof terrace—which they called the *altana*—from the mid-fourteenth century, when it became a standard component of Venetian domestic building.[18] Women in Venice were generally veiled in public and dressed for the most part in black from head to toe, according to visitors from northern Europe, who were clearly surprised to note this Eastern habit. A fifteenth-century source commented: 'one cannot see their faces for all the world. They go about so completely covered up, that I do not know how they can see to go along the street.'[19]

Another fifteenth-century source counted 18,619 balconies giving onto the Grand Canal. In Cairo, many houses along the Nile in Fatimid times had *mashrabiyya* (wooden latticework) balconies overlooking the river above the main entrance, the favoured position in Venice too.[20] Venetian noblewomen were not allowed to circulate freely outside so balconies were used in the same way, to allow women to look out but not be seen themselves. From 1297, the Venetian nobility was closed to outsiders. Only hereditary members were allowed to enter their names in the Golden Book of the Great Council, yet nine families from Syria were permitted to join. They were refugees who came to Venice after the fall of Acre in 1291, and by 1522, eight of them boasted seven branches each.

The Church of Santa Fosca, Torcello

On the Venetian island of Torcello stands the tiny church of Santa Fosca, built beside the cathedral in the tenth century to house the relics of Santa Fosca along with her nurse from Sabratha near Tripoli. Most of the church is clearly Byzantine in inspiration, but there are two very non-Byzantine features. The first is the distinctive carved relief ornamentation that runs in a high band round the outside wall of the apse. Its stepped zigzag pattern is reminiscent of the dramatic Mesopotamian merlon crenellations which run round the outer walls of the Damascus Umayyad Mosque and the Umayyad desert palaces, as well as the Cordoba Mezquita. The second is also an Umayyad feature, namely the octagonal arcade running round the church which is instantly reminiscent of the Dome of the Rock in Jerusalem. Built as an Islamic shrine in 691, as explained in Chapter 4, the Dome of the Rock was given by the Knights Templar to the Augustinians, who used it as a church from 1118 to 1187 (when Saladin recaptured Jerusalem), believing it was the Temple of Solomon, 'wrongly of course', as Deborah Howard tells us.[21] Crusader pilgrims called it the Holy of Holies or the Temple of the Lord. The Venetians meanwhile believed that Helena, mother of Constantine, had built everything on the Temple Mount, and as late as the fifteenth century thought that Al-Aqsa Mosque, much modified by the Templars during the Crusader period, was the Temple of the Virgin and the Palace of Solomon.[22] The Santa Fosca church's ambulatory was a twelfth-century addition and the timing therefore coincides—maybe even more confirmed by the Crusader crosses inlaid in white, which are clear to see on the three gables of the church. The Templars had good connections in Venice and 'played an important role in east–west trade as bankers and custodians of valuables.'[23] Even if they had been aware of the earlier ambulatory at the cathedral at Bosra, it was the Dome of the Rock they saw as the most important model.

Round Templar Churches of Europe and Exotic Portuguese Spin-offs

The round Templar churches, all erroneously modelled on the Umayyad Dome of the Rock, the Templum Domini as they called it, can be found across Europe. Of the four in England, the most famous is the Temple Church in the City of London, which served as the Templars' English headquarters, consecrated in 1185. Its ground floor nave is ringed with an arcade of pointed arches topped by interlocking round arches, exactly as at the early Islamic Dome of the Rock in Jerusalem.

Under 'Bad' King John (1199–1216), London's Temple Church served as the royal treasury, supported by the very powerful and wealthy Knights Templar as independent proto-international bankers. Their status as quasi-supranational actors enjoying great wealth throughout Europe created many enemies, leading to their eventual undoing.

The church escaped damage in the Great Fire of 1666, but Christopher Wren gave it a new altar screen and organ, modifying the interior extensively—so extensively in fact that a Gothic revival makeover was performed on it in 1841 in order to return it to something closer to its supposed original appearance. Today the church is open to the public and is jointly owned by the Inner Temple, Middle Temple and Inns of Court, the core of the English legal profession. Noted for its excellent acoustics, in addition to holding masses and church services it has since the nineteenth century also hosted organ recitals and choral music performances. The whole area round it is still called Temple, including the tube station, though most Londoners have no idea it connects back to Islam's first monument, the seventh-century Umayyad Dome of the Rock.

In mainland Europe, one of the most famous round Templar churches is to be found at Tomar in Portugal. Built in the second half of the twelfth century and known today as the Convento di Cristo, it is an astonishing blend of Romanesque, Manueline (late Gothic) and Renaissance styles. Manueline architecture, unique to Portugal and named after King Manuel I, is itself a synthesis of Mudéjar elements blended with late Gothic. It forms a transition into Renaissance and Baroque styles, bearing all the hallmarks of the exuberant new wealth that resulted from the great Portuguese Age of Discovery and specifically Vasco da Gama's new sea route to India via the Cape of Good Hope in 1497.

The inside of the original Templar church at Tomar has an octagonal ambulatory of pointed arches that harks back to the Dome of the Rock with column capitals covered in vegetal and animal motifs, while the late Gothic additions are much more flowery, sponsored by King Manuel I in 1499. Like Lisbon's magnificent Jerónimos Monastery, it was financed by profits from the lucrative new spice trade with Africa and India.

This 1810 engraving of London's round Temple Church interior, modelled on the Dome of the Rock, clearly shows its Islamic influences in the pointed arches of the ambulatory, the rib vaulting and the blind interlocking arches.

Vasco da Gama is buried inside the great Lisbon Gothic masterpiece, built as a bold political statement by the Portuguese king to proclaim his new-found wealth and power. The decorative ornamentation was adapted to incorporate, along with the usual vegetal themes, exotic fruits like pineapples and strange

Late-Gothic Manueline cloisters of the Jerónimos Monastery, Lisbon, Portugal.

new animals like monkeys peeping out from the foliage. Around the door frames, coils of knotted rope and borders of coral carved in stone displayed the maritime roots of the wealth, with anchors and other nautical motifs. The sea journeys themselves were of course made possible through the technology of the astrolabe and the armillary sphere, perfected by Muslim scientists, which enabled the sea voyages that were so successfully conducted during the administration of Prince Henry the Navigator. The famous chapter house window (1510–13) at Tomar is dripping in ornate late Gothic décor, but at its centre is a simple rectangular stone-carved grille not so far removed from the early Umayyad window grilles of Syria and of Cordoba.

Above it is a rose window in the gable in exactly the same position on the facade as that of the eighth-century Umayyad palace at Khirbat al-Mafjar. Further Islamic influences show themselves in the ceiling of the nave, covered in elegant ribbed vaulting, and in the eight cloisters of the church complex, mostly of late Gothic fifteenth-century design.

The Doge's Palace in Venice

The lagoon-facing facade of the Doge's Palace is familiar to us as an iconic Venetian vista and has been immortalised in many paintings. It quickly set a trend that was copied by most fourteenth- and fifteenth-century Venetian palaces, even spawning copies five centuries later across Europe. Many of these copies are to be found in Britain, in buildings like the Bradford Wool Exchange, the Burslem Wedgwood Institute, the Scottish National Portrait Gallery in Edinburgh and the Templeton Carpet Factory in Glasgow, all nineteenth-century Venetian Gothic, inspired by John Ruskin's *Stones of Venice*, in which he declared the Doge's Palace to be 'the central building of the world'.[24]

The doge himself was the equivalent of the president, the foremost authority of the Venetian Republic, so his chosen style was always going to be a trend-setter. Like the Santa Fosca Church, the palace uses a stylised, Gothicised version of the merlon crenellations we have seen on so many Umayyad palaces to give the facade its bold, distinctive profile against the sky. In its overall shape and design Deborah Howard and other historians believe it to be modelled on Jerusalem's other major Umayyad building, the Al-Aqsa

The iconic waterfront facade of the Doge's Palace in Venice is modelled on the Al-Aqsa Mosque in Jerusalem, mistakenly thought by the Venetians to have been the Palace of Solomon.

Mosque, adjacent to the Dome of the Rock on the Temple Mount and thought by the Crusaders to have been the Palace of Solomon. The Crusaders occupied Al-Aqsa in the twelfth century and called it *Domus Salomonis*.[25] Howard bases this theory on a map dating to 1320, just two decades before work began on the Doge's Palace; the map appears under the title *View of Jerusalem* in the manuscript by Marin Sanudo the Elder called *Liber Secretorum Fidelium Crucis*.[26] Solomon's Palace would of course have been a highly fitting model for the ambitious doge seeking to project his authority to the world. In the Book of Kings I, 6:7–12, it is described as having three storeys of dressed stone with a portico of columns in front and an inner courtyard, and the doge seems to have followed this description. The palace facade is made from local red Verona marble and white Istrian stone. Inside, richly decorated wooden coffered ceilings, painted and gilded as in Mamluk or Persian palaces, were commonly used in patrician palaces, with many Islamic furnishings such as textiles, carpets and ceramics brought home by Venetian merchants.

Timing and context both become very important in explaining the further influences at this point, because the design of the palace was conceived soon after the fall of Acre in 1291, the end of the last vestiges of the Crusader kingdom. During the century of Crusader hegemony that began with the capture of Jerusalem in 1099, the opportunistic Venetians had made sure that their city was Europe's principal gateway to the Holy Land, organising not only galleys bearing merchandise for trade, but also 'pilgrim galleys' offering specialist 'package tours', inclusive of food on board, transportation to Jerusalem from the port of Acre, and all fees and tolls. Luxury voyages were organised for higher-status pilgrims, many of whom were from northern European countries that were Venice's trading markets, so the whole scheme was also a public relations exercise to foster good relations with customers. Needless to say, there were stopovers along the way at Venice's Greek colonies such as Corfu, Modon (Methoni) and Rhodes, and pilgrims were encouraged to stay in Venice as long as possible beforehand, venerating various relics in a specially devised circuit of votive churches. The wealthy dean of Mainz Cathedral, accompanied by the Dutch woodcut artist who drew the first ever printed map of Jerusalem in 1486, took this route, spending three weeks in Venice according to his best-selling *Peregrinatio in Terram Sanctam*.

A local axiom stated: 'Each one who goes on the voyage to the Sepulchre of our Lord has need of three sacks—a sack of patience, a sack of money and a sack of faith' (a pun on the Italian 'un sacco di', 'a lot of'). Venice was highly adept at cultivating its identity as a sacred city.[28]

This lucrative commercial venture controlled by the Venetian state was also encouraged by the Catholic Church, who granted 'indulgences' to the pilgrims. There were guides and interpreters for the pilgrim groups, employed by the ship's captain, and even a pocket guidebook setting out the various levels of indulgences, like a point scoring system. Ownership of the sacred sites in Jerusalem was contested between many denominations, including Catholic, Orthodox, Armenian, Coptic and Jacobite. The Franciscans were given guardianship of the holy sites, financed largely by donations from Western merchants based in Eastern trading cities like Damascus, Cairo, Alexandria, Tripoli and Aleppo, using Venetian bankers.

The military orders played an important role in the transfer of culture and resources between East and West, with the Templars having their main base in Jerusalem and the Hospitallers in Acre. The Templars, founded in 1118, had particularly good relations with Venice against Genoa, while the Hospitallers supported Genoa against Venice. The Templars offered a loan service to Venetian merchants and even operated their own ships to transport Italian merchandise and pilgrims. Once Jerusalem was lost to Saladin in 1187 and Acre instead became the centre of the Crusader kingdom till 1291, Venice quickly realised it needed to find alternative trading routes. As well as restarting trade with the Mamluks, they developed a new route east via the Black Sea, and by 1325 there were Venetian consuls in Tabriz and Tana. This brought Venetians into contact with further sets of Islamic rulers, the Mongol Ilkhanids, who ruled Persia from 1256, and the Seljuks of Rum (1077–1308), who ran a series of fully funded caravanserais controlling the Silk Road east across Anatolia so merchants could trade freely into Iran and Central Asia from their major cities in Anatolia.

The distinctive lozenge patterning of the pink and white marble inlay on the upper facade of the Doge's Palace mimics a distinctive geometric brick-work pattern that merchants would have seen on Seljuk buildings in their increasing trade with the Black Sea ports, Anatolia and Iran.

In its monumental scale, similarities have also been observed between the Doge's Palace and the Mamluk Customs House at Alexandria. The triumphant Mamluks transported the entire portal of the Crusader church of Acre to Cairo, where they reused it as conscious spolia to adorn the entrance of Sultan Al-Nasir Muhammad's dramatic new madrasa complex, which was under construction between 1295 and 1304, at the very time when the Venetians were consolidating their trading privileges with the Mamluks.[29] Another interesting parallel, possibly inspired by what they had seen in Islamic cities, especially Cairo and Damascus, is the fact that compared to other western European cities, Venice was in medieval times unusually well provided with charitable housing and hospitals for the poor, where the motive for wealth generation was honourable distribution in line with the Islamic *waqf* system.

But the most distinctive element that we have come to associate with Venice is the elegantly curved ogee arch appearing on the Doge's Palace, thirty-four of them in a row across the facade, in the exquisitely delicate *piano nobile*—the first floor where the main rooms are situated, with the best views. The ogival (tear-drop) medallion shape would also have been familiar to the Venetians at this time through its popularity as a fashionable royal Mamluk emblem in rich damask textiles imported from Egypt and Syria, often containing Arabic calligraphy.[30] Positioned below the thirty-four ogee arches, running along the ground floor level, is an arcade of seventeen pointed arches. Each ogee arch is framing a trefoil arch, an unusual combination which the Venetians would have probably have seen for the first time in the uppermost section of the 50-metre Seljuk square minaret of the Aleppo Umayyad Mosque. In that masterpiece of grace and elegance, added to the mosque in 1090 by the ruling Seljuks, the eight arches ran round the top just below the overhanging *muqarnas* balustrade, one on each facade and one straddling each corner, a design which made the point sharper and more exaggerated. The section immediately below was ringed with seven-foil arches, two on each side, so again a total of eight. The minaret also had a pierced stone window in a six-petal shape inside each arch, a more complex version of the four-petal window piercings above the ogee arches of the Doge's Palace. Aleppo's 900-year-old Seljuk minaret was considered one of the most important monuments of medieval Syria, with 174 steps to the top, but has been tragically lost in the Syrian civil war, collapsing in its entirety in April 2013. UNESCO described it as one of the most beautiful minarets in the Muslim world.[31] The pieces have been assembled in the mosque court-yard, with a view to future reconstruction, a challenging project that may be possible thanks to a detailed Italian photogrammetric study of the minaret conducted in the 1990s.

The minaret of the Great Mosque of Aleppo, added by the Seljuks in 1090, shows trefoil arches and possibly the earliest example of a blind ogee corner arch. Built of the local white limestone, it was tragically caught in crossfire during the Syrian war and collapsed in 2013, though will hopefully be reconstructed using the original blocks as far as possible.

All these elements combined together in the Doge's Palace represent yet another unique synthesis of styles, reflecting the many influences to which the Venetian merchants and noblemen were exposed during this period of exceptionally fast growth in trade with the East. Officially escorted ships were setting sail ever more regularly after 1303, when a state-protected convoy system was established, and even though the pope was in constant dispute with Venice over its trade with 'the infidel'—in 1320 the papacy imposed an embargo that lasted till 1343 on commercial exchange with any Islamic institution—the merchants continued nonetheless to travel to Constantinople and the ports of the Black Sea, to the Syrian ports of Antioch and Beirut and thence to Aleppo and Damascus respectively, and to Mamluk Egypt. It is as if, in this synthesis of Byzantine, Seljuk, Egyptian and Syrian, the Venetian nobility had found themselves a new and bold identity with which to project their independence from Rome and from the pope.[32] As a great trading nation they were proud of their relations with the Islamic world, which had made them rich.

It was therefore not altogether surprising that Venetian merchants should begin to imitate the Islamic 'cathedrals of commerce' in the architecture of their own palaces once they returned to their home city. All across the Islamic world, the *khan* (caravanserai) was designed as a two-storey enclosed building round an open courtyard with strong walls and a massively thick gate, giving it a slightly fortified feel. The courtyard had a well above its own cistern so its water supply was independent. It was vital to be self-sufficient and to protect the valuable commodities stored inside on the ground floor, which, in the case of Aleppo, would have been brought overland in a six- to nine-day journey loaded on camels or donkeys from Mediterranean ports like Syria's Lattakia or Tripoli. The first to institute a network of such *khans* were the Seljuks, converts to Islam in the eleventh century, as will be explained further in Chapter 8.

The upper storey of the *khan* was galleried and was where the merchants lived in a series of rooms all giving onto the covered portico that ran round the four sides of the courtyard, often referred to as *loza* (loggia) in Venetian dialect. They were however not just functional buildings. Mamluk *khans* such as Aleppo's Khan al-Saboun (Soap Caravanserai) and Khan al-Jumruk (Customs Caravanserai) for example boasted beautifully decorated polychrome stone-patterned inlay and tracery round the windows, with slender columns and pointed trefoil arches. Mamluk architecture itself was an eclectic mix of Iranian, Fatimid, Ayyubid and even Crusader elements blended to create deliberate evocations of early Islamic monuments. The 1285 complex of Sultan Qala'oun in Cairo, for example, incorporates a tomb which explicitly harks back to the Dome of the Rock.

Aleppo under the Mamluks was gradually recovering from the Mongol invasion of 1260, which had left much of the city in ruins and killed a third of its population.[33] Its famous commercial souks were beginning to revive. The Aleppan people had been steeped in commerce going right back to Roman times, the result of the city's location at the natural convergence of several overland trade routes east to Central Asia and Persia and south to Iraq and the Gulf. Although Cairo and Alexandria had bigger populations, Aleppo's level of trading activity was summed up in regional sayings like, 'What was sold in the souks of Cairo in a month was sold in Aleppo in a day.'

Damascus, however, was preferred by Venetian merchants as the more congenial Syrian city, where they had excellent trading privileges that were even inscribed at the request of the Venetian senate in 1421 on a stone tablet in the heart of the souks.[34] Damascus's caravan routes east via Palmyra to Central Asia and Arabia and to India via the Red Sea also made it the preferred trading hub. In the 1480s there were about forty Venetian residents in Damascus, allowed to rent accommodation wherever they pleased. A few even died *in situ*, their belongings then shipped back to Venice. Probate inventories reveal the rich array of Damascene ceramics, textiles, carpets and metalware that then found their way back into the heart of Venetian families.[35] Many Venetian merchants did not choose the Christian quarter, preferring instead to live among their Muslim trading partners, with whom they enjoyed close, even affectionate friendships. Damascus, like Aleppo, was never conquered by the Crusaders, something that gave stability to the local Venetian trading relationships, and the Venetians had always in any case been ambivalent about the Crusaders' aims.

Under the influence of the pope, the Crusaders had boycotted the Italian trading cities and kept trading privileges for themselves, but once the Mamluks booted the last of the Crusaders out, the way was clear once again for the Venetians. The Venetian commercial representative in Aleppo had previously been obliged to live outside the city walls, but from 1422 onwards Venice was allowed to establish its first resident Venetian consul inside the Old City. The *khan* itself, in the heart of the souk, doubled as their living quarters in the accommodation upstairs, with goods stored in the warehouse on the ground floor. Groups of about ten Venetian merchants lived fairly tough lives within their gated courtyard communities, though they had a doctor and a chaplain sent out from Venice to minister to their physical and spiritual health. Their aim was to make as much money as possible within a few years and then retire back to Venice and live on the proceeds.[36] Their major export was the extremely strong Syrian-grown raw cotton and their major import was fine English wool, traded via Venetian intermediaries, another reason why the Bradford Wool Exchange chose to model itself on the Doge's Palace centuries later.

No residential architecture survives in Venice from earlier than the twelfth century, because of a huge fire in 1105 that destroyed most of the houses. The rebuilding gave an opportunity for merchants to find themselves a new look, and, as many architectural historians have noted, the look they chose bears a remarkable resemblance to the Islamic *khan*.[37] In Venice the word *fondaco* was used to describe these buildings (Arabic *funduq* meaning hotel, inn), while in Arab cities they were referred to as *khans* (caravanserais), *wikaalas* (agencies) or *qaysariyyas* (roofed marketplaces). At this time Venetian dialect became infused with Arabic words instead of Latin or Greek, even in commercial documents—*corruptum latinum* as it was known. This coincided with what Deborah Howard describes as 'a dramatic expansion of Venetian oriental trade during the period of the Kingdom of Jerusalem and the Venetian colonies in the Levant.'[38] Venice had, as mentioned earlier, agreed to be used as a port of embarkation for the Crusaders, in exchange for generous trading privileges, and the wealth generated by this trade was therefore available for new and expensive building projects, as befitted the new status of the merchants. This ties in again with the desire of the Amalfi merchants to use their newly acquired wealth to fund new buildings, often for the Church. What better way to immortalise yourself and your family's name than as the generous donor of a famous monument? The building of so many Gothic churches and cathedrals within such a relatively short space of time in the twelfth and thirteenth centuries all across northern Europe likewise speaks volumes of the riches brought back from trade with the Islamic world. Not only, one could argue, were these Gothic buildings imbued with Islamic decorative detailing and built according to Islamic vaulting and arch techniques, they were also paid for with riches acquired through trade with the Islamic world, or, even more ironically perhaps, through the 1204 sack of Greek Orthodox Constantinople in the Fourth Crusade.

As always happened once a fashion took off, others imitated it, and archival records show that masons were often asked by new clients to copy certain details from other Venetian palaces. Ca' d'Oro, for example, built in 1421, copied styles from two other palaces and had its exteriors painted with gold leaf and ultramarine like the doorway in the Doge's Palace, possibly influenced by houses in Damascus, which a pilgrim from Milan, Santo Brasca, described as painted 'in gold and fine sky-blue'.[39] Palazzo Dario in 1480 copied the so-called 'telephone dial' motif from the 1337 Mamluk Palace of Bashtak, prominent in the Cairo streetscape.[40]

The extent to which the merchants themselves were consciously copying Islamic styles or were adopting them simply because the elegant styles appealed to their aesthetic sense will probably never be possible to prove. Whatever the reason, the end result is the same: a distinctive style we know as Venetian Gothic, mainly in secular buildings—which is in itself unusual in medieval times—whose hallmarks are beautifully decorated facades with delicately pointed and curved arches running in arcades and porticoes, elaborate stone-carved traceries, and two-dimensional decorative wall ornamentation often made from different coloured stones and marbles. All fourteenth-

Palazzo Dario (Ca' Dario) on the Grand Canal in Venice, showing the Mamluk 'telephone dial' motif. Many Islamic decorative styles were copied in Venetian residential architecture, often taken from *khans* or 'cathedrals of commerce'.

century construction in Venice was dominated by this style, which continued till the late fifteenth century. Even after the 1577 fire at the Doge's Palace, the Venetian state decided not to rebuild in the new and fashionable style of Renaissance classicism. They conducted difficult restoration of Venetian Gothic buildings to cling to their unique identity,[41] which had been forged through centuries of trade with the Islamic world.

John Ruskin fully sympathised with the Venetian nostalgia for their Golden Age. Within *The Stones of Venice* is a section called 'The Nature of Gothic', in which Ruskin defines the Gothic character as having six essential elements: savageness, changefulness, naturalism, grotesqueness, rigidity and redundance. He writes:

> It is one of the chief virtues of the Gothic builders that they never suffered ideas of outside symmetries and consistencies to interfere with the real use and value of what they did. If they wanted a window, they opened one; a room, they added one; a buttress, they built one; utterly regardless of any established conventionalities of external appearance, knowing ... that such daring interruptions of the formal plan would rather give additional interest to its symmetry than injure it. So that, in the best times of Gothic, a useless window would rather have been opened in an unexpected place for the sake of surprise, than a useful one forbidden for the sake of symmetry.[42]

He considered Gothic builders to be 'naturalists':

> To the Gothic workman the living foliage became a subject of intense affection ... The tendency to delight in fantastic and ludicrous, as well as in sublime, images, is a universal instinct of the Gothic imagination ... The cathedral front was at last lost in the tapestry of its traceries, like a rock among the thickets and herbage of spring.

Among all these definitions, he writes, 'by far the most important will stand thus: Gothic architecture is that which uses the pointed arch':

all good Gothic is nothing more than the development, in various ways, and on every conceivable surface, of the group formed by the pointed arch for the bearing line below, and the gable for the protecting line above … The modes of support and of decoration are infinitely various, but the real character of the building, in all good Gothic, depends upon the single lines of the gable over the pointed arch, endlessly rearranged or repeated.[43]

Ruskin's description of the Arab influence on Venetian Gothic is often conflicted; he talks about 'the mindless luxury of the East' on the one hand, while on the other hand praising the Arab 'love of colour; a seriousness rising out of repose'. If writing today he would be considered an imperialist and racially prejudiced against Arabs, yet he appeared to see no contradiction in admiring their architecture. He had of course never ventured east of Venice himself, yet thanks to his influence, the Gothic revival in Britain from 1850 onwards became heavily orientalised in the shape of Italian Gothic buildings, such as London's St Pancras, built in 1868, and the Manchester Reform Club of 1870. At Charles Barry's Highclere Castle, of *Downton Abbey* fame, direct echoes of the Doge's Palace with its 'blatantly decorative and indefensible array of pinnacles'[44] are also clear to see in the Venetian Gothic of its elaborate rooftop cresting. Barry was a little ahead of Ruskin in being a fan of Venice, having visited the city in his twenties, along with many Middle Eastern cities. Highclere was remodelled and rebuilt by Barry in 1842–9. He would no doubt have recognised the cedar of Lebanon in the grounds, already 100 years old by then, which had been planted from seeds collected by Bishop Pococke during his 1738 tour of Lebanon. A century before, Wren's contemporary the Arabist Reverend Edward Pococke (no relation) had imported the first cedar to England and planted it in 1646 on the rectory lawn at Childrey in Berkshire, now Oxfordshire, where it still grows.

Venetian Glass Mosaics, Syria and Ravenna

The Venetians imported the technique of making *smalti*, glass mosaic pieces, from Constantinople, especially after 1204 and the sack of the city in the

Fourth Crusade. The earliest production seems to have been in Egypt, from where it was transferred to Persia and the Byzantine Empire. The Venetian glass industry benefited from protectionist legislation and its craftsmen based on the island of Murano developed techniques and decorative styles inherited from Byzantine and Syrian glass from 1300 onwards. One Syrian secret worth protecting was the manufacture of colourless or deeply coloured glass that would then be painted with enamel colours and gold fused to the glass by refiring. Centred in Damascus, the technique developed in the mid-1200s. Through its merchant colonies in the crusader states, Venice also had privileged access to essential natural ingredients from Syria—a 1277 treaty between the doge and Bohemond VII, prince of Antioch, mentions duties on broken glass loaded at Tripoli to serve as raw material in Venice.[45]

While the most beautiful examples of glass mosaic in Venice are to be found in St Mark's Basilica, the earliest examples in Italy date from Ravenna's sixth-century octagonal Byzantine Basilica of San Vitale. Ravenna, dubbed 'the capital of mosaics', developed rapidly after replacing Rome as capital of the Western Roman Empire in 402. At its peak in the fifth and sixth centuries, the finest Byzantine churches outside Constantinople were built here. San Vitale's mosaics have survived intact and went on to inspire Emperor Charlemagne's Palatine Chapel in Aachen, built c. 800. The *ablaq* stonework in the arches of the chapel is also strikingly Syrian. Today the Palatine Chapel is a UNESCO World Heritage Site and has been incorporated into Aachen Cathedral. Its Carolingian throne came from spolia of the Church of the Holy Sepulchre in Jerusalem, and thirty-one German Holy Roman Emperors were crowned there between 936 and 1531.

Charlemagne visited Ravenna three times and also summoned artists, craftsmen, scholars and scribes from the eastern Mediterranean to his Aachen palace, ordering Greeks and Syrians to revise the text of the Gospels.[46] He is even thought to have imported materials from Antioch to build the chapel. The patron saint of Ravenna, Apollinaris, the city's first bishop, was a native of Antioch in Syria, appointed to the position by St Peter himself. Peter's disciples had established a cave church cut into the cliffs above Antioch, still viewable today as the Rock Church of St Peter. According to Abbot Agnellus in his ninth-century history *Liber Pontificalis Ecclesiae Ravennatis*, all of Ravenna's bishops were of Syrian origin up to and including Peter I (396–425).[47]

Antioch under the Romans had also been the main rival centre of mosaic production to Ravenna, and was renowned as one of the most important mosaic-producing areas in the entire Roman Empire. The city's famous mosaics remain on display today at the Antakya Archaeology Museum. Many historians such as Warwick Ball and Edward Schoolman have noted this strong Syrian influence in both the mosaics and the religious ambiance in Ravenna after the fourth century. In the iconography of the mosaics scholars have noted many oriental details, such as the four angels of the central vault in the Archbishop's Palace, which echo similar figures in the underground tomb of Yarhai in Palmyra holding up portraits of the deceased. In the Basilica of Sant'Apollinare Nuovo (completed 504), Jesus is depicted in the Syrian style as long-haired and bearded with brown eyes, while in the later Latin style he becomes short-haired, beardless and blue-eyed. As such, these mosaics of the Ravenna churches 'reflect the art of the Christian Orient sufficiently to serve as substitute for the lost mosaics and frescoes that once adorned in the fifth and sixth centuries, the churches of the East.'[48] They certainly resemble the mosaics still found in some of the early churches of the Tûr Abdin in today's southeast Turkey, such as Mor Gabriel (built 512) with its scrolls of vines in bright green, blue and gold. The octagonal Basilica of San Vitale itself, dedicated in 548, is thought to have been directly modelled on the octagonal Domus Aurea (Golden House), a magnificent church built in 327 during the reign of Constantine the Great in Antioch. Its exact location today is not known, since it was finally destroyed by fires and earthquakes in 588, a date which would corroborate its use as a prototype for San Vitale. The mosaics of San Vitale with their swirling vines animated by birds and beasts entangled in the foliage are also highly reminiscent of the mosaic pavements of Antioch villas.

Thanks to the Apollinaris link, Syrian monks were so numerous in Ravenna by the fifth century that the bishop of Clermont felt it necessary to complain about the strength of the Syrian influence in the city, bemoaning that 'the clergy lend money and the Syrians chant psalms.' By the sixth century, Syrians are recorded as holding key positions in the mercantile and banking sectors of Ravenna, leading to the opposite complaint—Syrian bankers and singing priests.[49] The two famous contemporary Ravenna basilicas of San Vitale and Sant'Apollinare in Classe (548 and 549) were both sponsored by a wealthy local banker/architect who was almost certainly of Syrian origin, since both the namesake saints of his churches are connected in faith and martyrdom to Antioch. As German scholar Christa Schug-Wille notices at Sant'Apollinare in Classe, 'there is a Syrian flavour to the architectural treatment of the buildings round the apse'. She also comments on 'the masterly handling of the mason's work.'[50]

Sicily

Sicily and southern Italy were under Islamic influence and partly under Arab Muslim rule from the eighth century onwards—hardly surprising, since the North African coast was only a day's sailing away, and Sicily, as the largest island in the Mediterranean, was always going to be a strategic and highly contested prize at a natural confluence of trade routes. It took the Arabs seventy-five years from their first arrival in 827 to conquer the island in full, displacing the Byzantines who were not popular due to their high taxation regime. Palermo was chosen as the Arab capital and Palermo Cathedral was turned into a mosque, as was the Church of San Giovanni degli Eremiti, but even the churches showed many Fatimid Islamic influences, like the Martorana with its recessed niches, carved wooden doors and elaborate stucco window grilles bearing coloured glass. The traveller Ibn Jubayr wrote in 1143: 'In its upper parts are well-placed windows of gilded glass which steal all looks by the brilliance of their rays, and bewitch the soul. God protect us from their allurement.'[51] Throughout the ninth, tenth and eleventh centuries, the Arabs turned Sicily into a thriving entrepôt and also introduced their advanced underground water systems, revolutionising agriculture and irrigation methods. Christians and Jews were taxed, but not too heavily, and were permitted to participate fully in society and to worship freely, as usual. The souks were full of new products like pistachios, couscous and spices.

Apse mosaic of Church of Sant'Apollinare in Classe, Ravenna, Italy, showing strong Syrian influence in its bearded saint, its predominantly green and gold colours and its central image of the cross enclosed in a sun-like circle of blue filled with stars.

But the Fatimid Arabs gradually lost what they called the Emirate of Sicily over a thirty-year period to the Norman Roger I, who by 1091, four years before the First Crusade, was in total control of the entire island. It was an enterprise sponsored by the pope and was the pattern across the western Mediterranean, as territory that had been occupied by Islamic rulers in Spain and in Sicily was taken back in the eleventh century by new Christian rulers and their armies. The Spanish Kingdom of León took Toledo from the Arabs at much the same time, in 1085. In both Spain and Sicily, the conquests resulted in more cross-cultural exchanges, with the French conquerors adopting many elements from the existing Islamic architecture. In Spain this produced the Mudéjar style and in Sicily the islamicised Norman style, which was for the first time a conscious copying of Islamic architecture—deliberate, unambiguous imitation. As Rageh Omaar put it in his documentary *An Islamic History of Europe*: 'In Sicily all the buildings that look Islamic aren't.'

It was inevitable that these styles would in turn influence the mainstream architecture of Christian Europe, and it is telling that what we now call the

This mosaic of the Lamb of God, a Syrian motif, in the presbytery of the Basilica of San Vitale, Ravenna, Italy, is very similar in colour and design to the mosaics found in earlier sixth-century Syriac churches, such as Mor Gabriel in what is today's southeast Turkey.

'Gothic' style was originally called the 'French' style, for it was in France that most of the Islamic influences coalesced. Already in late Romanesque buildings we start to see the interlocking arches, pointed arches and ribbed domes characteristic of Islamic buildings, but in Sicily, full-blown Gothic never took hold, only a kind of Romanesque Gothic hybrid that evolved gradually, mixing pointed arches with Romanesque features. In Sicily and southern Italy, the best known are the cathedrals of Cefalù (1131–1240) and Monreale (begun in 1174), while in Normandy an early example is the eleventh-century nave of the abbey of Sainte Honorine de Graville in Le Havre. The Normans introduced the style to England after 1066 with their victory in the Battle of Hastings, and the first example of pointed and interlocking arches and ribbed vaults appears in Durham Cathedral, begun in 1093. All this of course is a few decades before the Crusades, which shows that elements of Islamic architecture were already filtering into Europe via Spain and Sicily before the Crusaders started returning from the Holy Land in 1099. The German academic Felix Arnold also wonders if illuminated manuscripts might have played a vital role in the transmission of architectural ideas, as depictions of interlocking arches were common in manuscripts throughout the early medieval period in both England and the Iberian Peninsula.[52]

After the Norman conquest, the island of Sicily entered a remarkable period of its history through two very special Norman rulers, Roger II (1130–54) and his grandson, Emperor Frederick II, who was King of Sicily from 1197 till 1250. Both rulers became fluent in Arabic. They were intellectuals and patrons of Arabic literature, and their courts represented a fusion of Greek, Latin and Arabic culture that came to be the envy of Europe. Scholars from all over Europe were attracted here, as they were to Toledo. Roger II was an enlightened ruler who created a civil service based on Norman, Greek and Arab models. He gave power according to aptitude, hence his navy was predominantly Greek, while his army and financiers were predominantly Arab. His Sicilian subjects were mainly Muslim, and he took no part in the

At the Cappella Palatina in Sicily the complex Islamic vaulting style known as *muqarnas* is used for the first time in Europe, blended into a Christian context by the island's Norman rulers.

Second Crusade of 1147, since he hated the Frankish rulers of Jerusalem because of his mother's disastrous remarriage to King Baldwin of Jerusalem.

A wandering scholar called Michael Scot (1175–1232), who knew Latin, Greek, Arabic and Hebrew from time spent in Toledo, was employed as scientific adviser and court astrologer to Frederick II, translating many works and becoming one of the greatest intellectuals of his day.

There were two motives for the study of Arabic in medieval Europe: the pursuit of scientific knowledge, and Christian missionary activities. Frederick's son Manfred also presided over a period of active translation from Arabic, though this activity was never at the level of what took place in Spain. Perhaps unsurprisingly, the Crusader Kingdom of Jerusalem produced almost no translation works at all, though one of the earliest Western Christian translators, Adelard of Bath, famous for translating the astronomical tables of Al-Khwarizmi, is known to have visited Syria, Sicily and southern Italy soon after 1100.[53] The hybrid architectural style of Sicily is exemplified in the Cappella Palatina, the royal chapel of the Norman kings on the first floor of the Palazzo Reale in Palermo. Built c. 1132 by Roger II, it is a unique fusion of Norman architecture with Saracen pointed arches supported by recycled classical columns, and Byzantine-style apses covered in mosaics.

On the carved wooden ceiling, clusters of four eight-pointed stars, a typical Islamic design, are arranged to form a Christian cross. The Cappella Palatina is also the first building in Europe where the style of Islamic vaulting known as *muqarnas* appears in the ceiling. *Muqarnas* is sometimes called honeycomb or stalactite vaulting and creates a sense of weightlessness as it disguises the transition from the wall supports to the dome. In the Cappella Palatina, the facets of the *muqarnas* are painted with ornamental vegetal and zoomorphic designs reminiscent of Iraqi Abbasid art. *Muqarnas*, the most complex of all Islamic vaulting styles, originated in tenth-century Persia and was then spread by the Seljuk Turks all over Anatolia and Syria. In Europe *muqarnas* achieved its apogee in the fourteenth-century palace of the Alhambra in Granada, where it is employed to make the domes dissolve into weightlessness and infinity, symbolising the transition to paradise.

Cyprus

The easternmost of the large islands in the Mediterranean, a natural centre of seaborne commerce, Cyprus became the last bastion of Christendom in the eastern Mediterranean. The architectural evidence is still there in the form of abundant Gothic cathedrals and churches, the style imported from France—and even often the masons. Almost all of them, ironically, are in what has been since 1974 the northern Turkish side of the island, but all can still be visited. The island's strategic location has tended across the ages to make it a contested prize, and it changed hands eleven times in the 300 years that followed the Arab invasion of 647. 'Cyprus lived between the Greeks and the Saracens,' as Willibald, a visiting English pilgrim in 723, put it. The Byzantines recovered the island in 963 and the Greek Orthodox population thrived again, till it was overrun by Richard I on his way to the Third Crusade. He sold it first to the Knights Templar to raise money for his army, then presented it in 1192 to Guy de Lusignan, as compensation for his loss of the Kingdom of Jerusalem after his decisive defeat by Saladin at the Battle of Hattin, near Tiberias. Guy's father, Hugh VIII, lord of Lusignan (near Poitou in France), had died in Syria in 1165 on pilgrimage to Jerusalem. The Lusignan dynasty in Cyprus lasted till 1489 when it was ceded to the doge of Venice. The Venetians built magnificent defences to defend their ports, especially Famagusta, the deepest natural harbour in the Levant. Their efforts were to no avail, however, against the Ottoman Turks, who took the island in 1571 and held it till they gave it to Britain in 1878 in exchange for British military support against Russia.

The most remarkable relic of the Lusignans is the Cathedral of St Nicholas in Famagusta, consecrated in 1326, today known as Lala Mustafa Pasha. Topped with a small minaret, it bears the distinction of being the only Gothic cathedral in the world in use as a mosque, Famagusta's main mosque in fact. In its day it was a bold statement to the Greek Orthodox islanders that the Catholic Church was now in charge, and its twin towers are visible from most parts of the old city. Designed in Rayonnant Gothic style, it is sometimes called the Reims of Cyprus. Though damaged, it is still a beautiful building, its grace and elegance far exceeding that of its early Gothic sister St

Sophia Cathedral in Nicosia. Its more delicate tracery work and ornate design reflect the luxurious lifestyle and tastes of the ostentatious merchants of the port. The architects were brought from France, and a tradition tells that they were a master mason and his pupil. The master, seeing the pupil's genius in his work, was consumed with jealousy. Alleging technical error in the top of the towers, he led his pupil up to point it out in detail, and pushed him headfirst over the edge—the first of much blood spilt at St Nicholas.[54] Like all the Crusader and later Venetian buildings, it is built from the locally quarried soft brown limestone.

Conversion to a mosque in 1571 by the Ottomans meant the building was spared the usual Baroque embellishments and unfortunate nineteenth-century 'restorations', which, as Ian Robertson tells us in his *Blue Guide*, 'have destroyed the unity of many European cathedrals'.[55] It can be visited outside prayer times, a worthwhile experience since the cathedral's whitewashed walls (concealing the frescoes) serve to emphasise the superb proportions and height of the nave and its vaulting. Although its altars and stained glass were

Western facade of the Lala Mustafa Pasha Mosque, formerly St Nicholas Cathedral (1326) at Famagusta, sometimes called 'the Reims of Cyprus'.

The unadorned and simple whitewashed interior of the Lala Mustafa Pasha Mosque, the only Gothic cathedral in the world still in use as a mosque.

destroyed, it remains a fascinating example of French Crusader Gothic, albeit repurposed and with its human sculptures defaced. The Venetians later attached a loggia to the side, which today serves as the ablutions area.

This cathedral, now mosque, is the single most important monument in Famagusta and was where the Lusignan kings of Cyprus, already crowned at Nicosia in the St Sophia Cathedral, came to be crowned 'king of Jerusalem'— once Jerusalem was lost this was an entirely symbolic honour, but the exhausting procession on horseback was thought worthwhile since Famagusta was just that bit closer to the Holy Land. The Syrian coast is visible from the Kyrenia Mountains on clear days, and Cyprus is the only landmass visible from the hills of Palestine.

When the Crusader toehold of Acre fell in 1291, Henry II of Cyprus offered Famagusta as asylum to Christian refugees, the obvious choice as the largest natural harbour on the island and the closest to the Holy Land. Suddenly the European kings and merchants were all concentrated here, and Famagusta quickly grew rich from its new role as middleman between East and West, the import/export centre of the Mediterranean, trading in per-fumes, spices and ivory from the East and selling the island's produce of sugar cane, wine and silk. The ability to import labour to build the fine St Nicholas Cathedral reflected this wealth, as did the unusually large number of churches. Their abundance is also partly explained by the plethora of sects that co-existed in the city—Latin, Greek, Maronite, Armenian, Coptic, Georgian, Carmelite, Nestorian, Jacobite, Abyssinian and Jewish. Seventeen churches still stand today of what was said to be the original 365, each one paid for by a man or a woman intent on buying their place in heaven.[56] On the crest of the wave of wealth came the inevitable wave of sin, and the city's prostitutes were said to be as wealthy—and as numerous—as the merchants.

The Gothic masterpiece of the island is Bellapais Abbey in the hills above the port of Kyrenia. Founded around 1200, the abbey's first monks were Augustinians, displaced by Saladin in 1187 from Jerusalem, where they had custody of the Church of the Holy Sepulchre. Fleeing with them were some canons of the Order of St Norbert, whose white habits lent the abbey its other name, the White Abbey. The refectory, with its lovely fan-vaulted ceiling and perfect proportions, must have been one of the finest dining halls in the East,

The Crusader Gothic masterpiece of Cyprus is the Augustinian Bellapais Abbey in the hills above Kyrenia. Its elegant cloisters depicted here convey something of its hedonistic ambiance, where the monks enjoyed life.

with a rose window on the end wall casting an attractive patterned light. The cloister has delicate tracery windows onto the courtyard, and the chapter house boasts magnificent Gothic stone carving with wriggling sirens, mythical monsters, a monkey and a cat, all entangled in the foliage of a pear tree. By the mid-sixteenth century, the strict rules of the community had deteriorated to the point where many monks had wives, sometimes as many as three.

Cyprus is also the best place to see how Crusader architecture was influenced by exposure to Islamic styles and techniques. The pointed arch is a clear case of Crusader adoption of the 'Saracen' style, and they used it in their residential as well as their religious buildings, and in their palaces in Cyprus, Rhodes and Malta. The Lusignan palace at Nicosia is no longer extant, but contemporary accounts describe the admiration of Christian visitors arriving at luxury residences of the elite in the Kingdom of Jerusalem. The descriptions show clear Islamic taste, and it is evident that the knights had over the decades grown accustomed to a semi-oriental lifestyle, which they then brought back with them from the Holy Land. The bishop of Oldenburg for example wrote in 1212 of the Ibelin palace in Beirut:

> Its windows opened some on the sea, some on to delicious gardens. Its walls were panelled with plaques of poly-chrome marble; the vaulted ceiling [of the salon] was painted to resemble the sky with its stars [a common Islamic décor]; in the centre of the [salon] was a fountain, and round it mosaics depicting the waves of the sea edged with sands so lifelike that [the bishop] feared to tread on them lest he should leave a foot mark.[57]

Crusader Borrowings from Muslim Military Architecture

Cyprus is also a good place, along with Rhodes and Malta, to see some of the castle-building and defence techniques that the Crusaders encountered in the Holy Land and brought back to Europe. The island boasts a fine trio of Crusader castles built along the ridge of the Kyrenia Mountains, facing north and east towards the Mediterranean. From west to east they are today known as St Hilarion, Buffavento and Kantara, all in the eastern part of the island and in

The Queen's Window in the royal apartments of St Hilarion Castle, north Cyprus, hints at the luxurious lifestyle enjoyed by the Lusignan kings, Crusaders of French origin, after they retreated from Jerusalem to the island of Cyprus.

what is now Turkish Cyprus, but all readily visitable. Lawrence Durrell even used the word 'Gothic' to describe the Kyrenia Mountains with their sharp pinnacles. Kantara means 'arch' in Arabic, and the towers here are mainly round. All three castles use pointed arches—often referred to, misleadingly, as 'Crusader arches'—and all, especially St Hilarion, have a certain air of hedonism not normally associated with military architecture. Guy de Lusignan had never expected to be spared by Saladin after his crushing defeat at the Battle of Hattin in 1187—'kings do not kill kings,' Saladin is reported to have said to him—and maybe a more romantic side revealed itself in Cyprus, where the

Krak des Chevaliers, guarding the Homs Gap in Syria, was one of the first castles built with concentric rings of fortification. It is the world's best-preserved Crusader castle and a UNESCO World Heritage site.

royal apartments of the castles show a love of life perhaps gleaned from exposure to the East. Dieu d'Amour was the name the Frankish knights bestowed on
St Hilarion, and from afar, its extravagantly crenellated walls and towers tum-
bling over the craggy hilltop evoke a fairytale vision of bygone chivalry.

Guy's year spent in prison in the citadel of Damascus, key centre of Arab
resistance to the Crusader presence and Saladin's headquarters and residence
from 1174 to 1193, would have also given him the opportunity to observe
Saracen military architecture up close. Although we have no way of knowing
what exactly he learnt during this and his other experiences whilst fighting in
the Holy Land, there is no doubt that the Crusader Knights would have
observed the massive walls of Constantinople and other well-defended cities
in the Byzantine and the Islamic realm, which often used concentric fortifications. The Crusaders brought their own building techniques with them, of
course, as well as their own masons and craftsmen, but once in the Holy Land
they were exposed to new ways of thinking. New defensive tactics were of
necessity constantly evolving.

Imitation is clear in the machicolations, also called box brattices, that can
still be seen along the west side of the outer wall at the magnificent Crusader
castle Krak des Chevaliers in Syria, from when it had to be rebuilt after the
two serious earthquakes of 1157 and 1170. The Crusaders had copied these
devices for tipping hot oil or stones onto the attacker, not least because they
had been on the receiving end of this treatment during their three unsuccess-
ful attacks on the Damascus Citadel. Examination of the Krak machicolations
reveals they are clearly not yet up to the quality of Saladin's Ayyubid-style
box brattices.[58] Arab Muslims had a few centuries' head start in their refine-
ment, since their first appearance was in the Syrian Umayyad desert palaces,
at Qasr al-Hair ash-Sharqi in 729. Despite its inferior machicolations, 'the
Krak', as it was known, has been widely lauded. According to T.S.R. Boase,
'As the Parthenon is to Greek temples and Chartres to Gothic cathedrals, so
is the Krak des Chevaliers to medieval castles, the supreme example, one of
the greatest buildings of all time.'[59] In a letter to his mother, T.E. Lawrence
wrote: 'Crac, as a finished example of the style of the Order, and perhaps the
best preserved and most wholly admirable castle in the world, forms a fitting
commentary on any account of the Crusading buildings of Syria.'[60]

Saladin's brother, Sultan al-Adil, spent twelve years from 1206 to 1218 rebuilding the defences of the Damascus Citadel in response to the development of the counterweight trebuchet catapult by the Crusaders. He improved the design of both the arrow slits and the machicolation, and the construction today, with its 3- to 4-metre-thick walls, remains one of the best preserved Syrian fortresses from the time of the Crusades, still extant in the heart of Damascus. Its arches are all of the typical 'Damascus' *makhmous*, one-fifth, degree of pointedness (as explained in Chapter 4), and there is a trefoil arch above the interior door of the north entrance and a round oculus window with metal grillwork and a decorated stone edging. Technicians and stone-masons from Aleppo were summoned to help and their work is most clearly seen in the main northern gate, Bab al-Hadid, Gate of Iron, which has striking similarities with the entrance to the Citadel of Aleppo and its twisting access via five zigzags.[61] The Ayyubid masonry work is identifiable from its large rusticated blocks, massive regular towers and vaulted interiors. The three-storeyed structure was crowned with massive battlements in which even the merlon crenellations were equipped with arrow slits and shooting niches.

Machicolations feature commonly in many towers on Rhodes built by the Knights Hospitallers.[62] After the Knights were given rule over Malta, machicolations were also widely used on rural buildings such as Cavalier Tower, Gauci Tower, the Captain's Tower, Birkirkara Tower and Tal-Wejter Tower. They were routinely incorporated into European castles after the Crusades. The first prominent example is at Château Gaillard near Rouen, built by Richard the Lionheart on his return from the Crusades.[63] Here he had the opportunity to experiment with new techniques learnt in the Holy Land and to synthesise them into something even better. Richard is thought to have supervised the construction of the round-towered castle himself to make sure it was completed quickly, and construction was indeed finished in a remarkably fast two-year period from 1196 to 1198, but at a high cost of £12,000. Dover Castle, by way of comparison, had taken twelve years to build (1179–91) at a cost of £7,000. As Château Gaillard neared completion, Richard exclaimed: 'Behold! How fair is this year-old daughter of mine!' It became his favourite residence in his final years and documents written there bore the locator 'at the Fair Castle of the Rock'. In his classic *English Castles*, historian

R. Allen Brown described it as 'one of the finest castles in Europe',[64] while military historian Sir Charles Oman wrote that it:

> was considered the masterpiece of its time. The reputation of its builder, Coeur de Lion, as a great military engineer might stand firm on this single structure. He was no mere copyist of the models he had seen in the East, but introduced many original details of his own invention into the stronghold.[65]

Concentric castles like Château Gaillard were then widely copied across Europe. On his return from the Crusades, from 1277 onwards, Edward I (Longshanks) of England built a series of superb castles in Wales, including Caernarfon and Harlech, more than a century after the European Knights Hospitallers first built the Krak des Chevaliers in Syria.

The superbly elegant Gothic loggia that fronts the Krak's imposing twelfth-century rib-vaulted Great Hall is an addition that dates from the late thirteenth century. As Ross Burns tells us: 'The Gothic style was by then established in France and it was time for it to be tried out in the Frankish east.'[66] Boase writes: 'Apart from the cathedral of Tortosa, nothing of this period that survives in Syria can equal [the Krak des Chevaliers] in faultlessness of charm and elegance.'[67]

Château Gaillard, the first concentric castle in Europe, was built overlooking the Seine by Richard the Lionheart in 1196–98 on his return from the Crusades. Its poor state of preservation today, especially when compared to the Syrian Krak des Chevaliers, is because the French king Henry IV ordered its demolition in 1599 to ensure it could never pose a threat.

The elegant Gothic loggia of the Knights' Hall, Krak des Chevaliers, Syria, used to bear a Latin inscription on the window lintel reading: 'Grace, wisdom and beauty you may enjoy, but beware pride which alone can tarnish all the rest.' The loggia was damaged by Syrian regime aerial bombardment in 2014.

Together, this loggia at Krak (badly damaged in aerial bombardment by the Syrian regime air force in 2014) and the twin-towered Cathedral of Our Lady of Tortosa are the two easternmost examples of Gothic architecture in the world. Tartous, Syria's second port, is little visited these days, better known today for its Russian naval base, much expanded during the Syrian civil war, than for its Gothic cathedral. But set around 150 metres back from the seafront and looking distinctly incongruous, the cathedral's intricately carved stone Gothic west front still rises forlornly. Like the loggia at Krak, it dates from the late-thirteenth-century improvements, when the Templars reinforced the building's defensive role, adding fortified arrow slits in the now mainly missing twin towers on the eastern inland side. It has been described as 'the best preserved religious structure of the Crusades.'[68] The church was built on the site of a pre-existing Byzantine chapel, where an icon of the Virgin Mary said to be painted by St Luke was miraculously spared in a huge fifth-century earthquake; the original altar has been reincorporated. Construction of a cathedral first started in 1123, with flying buttresses added for earthquake protection, its design showing the transition from Romanesque to Gothic, exactly as was happening in mainland Europe, but a few decades behind the times, as would be expected in a provincial context.

It was the last point on the mainland held by the Crusaders till they were forced out, first to the island of Arwad just offshore, then in 1303 to the island of Cyprus. The cathedral was in use as a mosque in Ottoman times, was then converted to a museum under the French Mandate, and remains open as a museum today.

There are accounts of returning Crusaders bringing Muslim masons with them as prisoners, who were then able to build these various Islamic features into the defences of European castles. One such mason was identified as Lalys, whose master was Richard de Grenville, one of the Twelve Knights of Glamorgan. A Grenville family pedigree dated 1639 stated that de Grenville undertook a pilgrimage to Jerusalem and brought back with him a man named Lalys, who was 'well-versed in the science of architecture, who erected monasteries, castles and churches'. Lalys is credited with building Neath Abbey in South Wales in 1129. De Grenville died soon after, whereupon Lalys is said to have been summoned to London to become architect to Henry I, fourth son of William the Conqueror.

Notre-Dame de Tortosa, Tartous, Syria, built by the Crusader Knights Templar in the early twelfth century, shows the same transition from Romanesque to Gothic as in Europe, albeit a few decades behind the times, as was usual in the provinces.

More Crusader Borrowings from the Muslim East

The round tower at Krak's northeast outer wall is called Windmill Tower, copied from windmills seen with six or twelve sails covered in palm fronds or fabric, used for grinding grain and drawing water for irrigation. They had first been invented in 634 in Persia, before finding their way into Iraq and Syria. In Europe, windmills appear in Normandy, northern France, in 1180 and betray Crusader origin. In England, the first certain reference to a windmill dates from 1185, in the Yorkshire village of Weedley overlooking the Humber Estuary.[69] Waterwheels already existed in Europe, but the Crusaders brought back an improved Syrian version, an example of which can still be seen in Germany near Bayreuth. In Syria, it dated back to Roman times but was much improved at Hama, still famous for its waterwheels today, by local engineers working for the rulers to improve irrigation techniques on the banks of the Orontes.

The Frankish soldiers in Syria spent much of their time quartered in castles and barracks, rarely mixing with the intelligentsia, whose cultural level was undoubtedly higher than theirs—the Crusaders' failure to understand the origins of the Dome of the Rock or the Arabic script make that clear. But they did learn from 'the natives' how to train pigeons to carry military intelligence and also borrowed many features of knightly jousting tournaments, known locally as *jarid*, meaning a blunt javelin used in equestrian sport. As Philip Hitti tells us:

Several features of the chivalry institution developed on the plains of Syria. The growing use of armorial bearings of heraldic devices was due to contact with Moslem knights. The two-headed eagle, the fleur-de-lys and the two keys may be cited as elements of Moslem heraldry of this period. ... Most Mamluks bore names of animals, the corresponding images of which they blazoned on their shields. Mamluk rulers had different corps, which gave rise to the practice of distinguishing by heraldic designs on shields, banners, badges and coats of arms. Baibars' crest was a lion [cf. today's Assad in Syria, an adopted name meaning lion], like that of Ibn-Tulun before him, and Sultan Barquq's was the falcon. In Europe coats of arms appear in a rudimentary form at the end of the eleventh century; the beginning of English heraldry dates from the early part of the twelfth.[70]

The twin-headed eagle appears on coins of Sinjar minted by Zengi, ruler of Mosul, Aleppo, Hama and Edessa (1127–46) who fought the Crusaders, but the symbol was first seen in Sumeria, from where it was passed on to the Babylonians and the Hittites. It was adopted by the Seljuk Turks when they settled in the Hittite lands of Central Anatolia, and from the Seljuks it passed on into Byzantium, from where it reached Austria, Prussia and Russia.[71]

Both the French fleur-de-lys and the English lion royal symbols—as seen here in the backdrop to the boy King Henry VI of England's coronation as King of France in Notre-Dame de Paris—were used as blazons in 'Saracenic' jousting tournaments on the plains of Syria.

The fleur-de-lys was first known in Assyria and became a very widespread element of decorative art. Encyclopedia Britannica says it was an ancient symbol of purity, 'readily adopted by the Roman Catholic Church to associate the sanctity of Mary with events of special significance.' It was found on an ancient Egyptian cylinder seal of Ramses III, as well as on a wall decoration in Samarra and on fragments of pottery from Fustat, the first capital of Egypt under Muslim rule. It is of course related to the trefoil motif and also appears in abundance in the carved stucco of the Umayyad palace of Khirbat al-Mafjar near Jericho. It first appeared as the blazon of the Ayyubid sultan Nur al-Din ibn Zanki and on two of his monuments in Damascus, notably above the *mihrab* in his Damascus madrasa built in 1154–73. The German scholar L.A. Mayer, in his exhaustive ten-year study of Saracenic heraldry, concludes that the fleur-de-lys, 'in its true heraldic form' in the arms of France, where it consists of three separate leaves held together in the middle by a band, must be of Saracenic origin. His reasoning is that in the pre-heraldic form of the Western fleur-de-lys, the three elements are connected, growing as it were from one stem.[72] The established heraldic form in France, however, as it appeared in the arms of Louis VII, king of the Franks from 1137 to 1180, was in the Saracenic form with three separate leaves. Mayer also tells us that Mamluk helmets often had nasal guards terminating in a fleur-de-lys.[73]

Terms like 'azure' (Arabic for lapis lazuli, *lazaward*) used in heraldry also point to the link between European and Muslim heraldry. Today in the Islamic world, only the star and crescent, the lion, and the sun remain from those Mamluk heraldry symbols, probably, in the view of Hamilton Gibb, former Laudian professor of Arabic at Oxford, because there was no organisation corresponding to the European Heraldic Colleges to take them up with such enthusiasm.[74] Unlike in the West, where it conferred hereditary land tenure involving obligatory military service, no great importance was attached to the Saracenic blazon, and it conferred no special privileges.[75] Saracen knights did not use the Western-style helmet with full-face visor that made identification of the knight impossible without his symbol. It may be another example of where the Eastern approach was personal, based on simple preference, while the Western approach was preoccupied with registering status and legal protection.

This has relevance to architecture because in stained glass windows, the heraldic coats of arms of donors started to appear in churches from the thirteenth century onwards, as in the west window of Salisbury Cathedral. These motifs had the advantages of buying a form of immortality for the wealthy donors, and later of being immune to the charges of iconoclasm. From 1643 to 1660, Cromwell's armies smashed stained glass across the land, and in Kent, Richard Culmer, rector of Chartham, nicknamed Blue Dick, tried to break as much glass as possible at Canterbury Cathedral by standing on a ladder with pike in hand, 'ratling down proud Becket's glassy bones.'[76] Heraldry then became the subject matter rather than religion, together with 'branches, flowers or posies taken out of Holy Scripture' instead of saints and biblical stories, resulting in a big change in the style of craft. Stained glass began again after the Restoration, encouraged by Archbishop Laud. As a student at Oxford, Christopher Wren would have been familiar with the monumental east window of Wadham College chapel, created in 1622 by a Dutchman, Bernard van Linge, and depicting Jonah and the whale. Wren would not have known, however, that it was made using the revolutionary method developed in thirteenth-century Syria, where the enamel colours were painted on the glass like paint on a canvas. From then on, the leading became utilitarian, as the glass cutting took place after the painting rather than before, resulting in regular, usually rectangular shapes. The difference can be seen at a glance.

In Syria, where the technique originated, it was used on objects like mosque lamps and drinking vessels, with both colourless and deep blue glass. The multilingual Jewish traveller Benjamin of Tudela (1130–73) set off from Zaragoza on a long journey to the Muslim East and wrote extensively of the respect and intermingling that he encountered between Judaism and Islam, especially in Baghdad, where he praised the wisdom and virtue of the caliph. Considered by historians as a trustworthy source, he visited Antioch under the Franks and makes specific mention of its glass manufacture.[77] The clue again is in the timing, for stained glass windows became popular in churches from the twelfth century onwards, including the so-called 'grisaille' style whereby the window was mainly colourless, which was cheaper to make and would let in more light. York Minster's famous Five Sisters window, dating

'Jonah and the whale' stained glass window, Wadham College chapel, University of Oxford. The straight lines of the leading show it was made using the revolutionary Syrian technique of refiring with enamel paint, which entered Europe via Venice.

to c. 1253, is grisaille, with complicated geometric patterns of coloured weaving foliage suggestive of Islamic influence. The earliest grisaille window in England can be seen in the Norman village church in Brabourne, Kent, on the pilgrimage route to Canterbury from France; it has Benedictine connections and dates to the late twelfth century.[78]

This twelfth century stained glass window in the Kent village church of Brabourne is the oldest Norman glass to have remained intact and still in situ in England. Its thick Syrian glass full of bubbles and plant ash impurities lend it both strength and a mysterious light.

One older window which is similar to this one can be found at the church of Saint-Denis in Paris.[79] The very distinctive geometric pattern of the Brabourne window is also almost identical to that of a glazed screen in the abbey church of the monastery of San Benedetto in Capua, built in the late eleventh century as the last monument created under the patronage of Abbot Desiderius of Monte Cassino.[80] In addition, the window's colours of blue, violet, pink, green and yellow, painted with a dark grisaille, are near identical to the colours found in fragments of the stained glass windows at the Benedictine abbey church of Santissima Trinità in Mileto, Calabria, founded around 1080,[81] while the same colours and a similar geometric design based on interlocking circles can be seen in the eastern wall of the Hanbali Mosque in Damascus, one of the oldest surviving mosques in the city.

So intrigued was I by these connections that I invited my friend Zahed Tajeddin, a Syrian artist and glass expert, to come with me to inspect the Brabourne window in March 2020 and to conduct an elemental analysis of its composition using a non-destructive portable XRF analyser loaned from UCL. This would be able to tell us if it contained the high magnesia levels which would confirm the origin of its raw materials as Syrian. In the event, we were thwarted by the Coronavirus lockdown of the UCL laboratory before we had the chance. The best I could manage therefore was to go and inspect it on my own with an extendable ladder and a magnifying glass. This enabled me to see the telltale locked-in bubbles so characteristic of Syrian plant-ash glass—a feature which, incidentally, according to Austrian glass expert Gustav Schmoranz, makes the glass stronger and less liable to shatter. Maybe this explains why the window glass has survived intact for eight centuries in situ. It may also help explain the miracle of why Notre-Dame's 3,000 square metres of stained glass survived the April 2019 inferno. The plant itself, known as *ushnaan*, from Aramaic *shuana*, or *qily*, from which we get our word alkaline, still grows in abundance in Syria, especially round the salt marshes of Jaboul, south of Aleppo. Its ashes continue to be used in the local glass industry, and I myself still have a pair of goblets, bought in Damascus in 2010, whose thick, tough, deep-blue glass complete with bubbles appears to be unbreakable, despite frequent use and transportation.

Christian pilgrims sent or brought back Arab reliquaries of intricately carved ivory for relics acquired in the Holy Land, and the practice of using a rosary found its way into the Roman Catholic West during the Crusades.[82] Of Hindu origin, the device was first borrowed from the Eastern Christian churches by Sufis, the mystics of Islam, who then popularised the use of *sub-hah* (prayer beads) among Muslims. Mystics like Al-Junayd (died 910) used it to induce a trance-like state of ecstasy through repetition of prayer and the names of Allah, something also seen in the *dhikr* of the Whirling Dervishes.

The Crusaders' contact with local people in the Holy Land was mainly limited to merchants, farmers and artisans, so it is perhaps not surprising that most of the influences they carried back to Europe were practical rather than scientific or philosophical. As well as all the culinary delights, such as ginger (*zanjabil*), sugar (*sukkar*), lemon (*laymun*), shallot (Palestinian town of Ascalon), and carob (*kharrub*), they brought back and helped popularise new plants, trees and crops like sesame, millet, rice, melons, and apricots, which they called 'plums of Damascus'. Returning Crusaders also brought back luxury items that then found their way into stained glass backgrounds, like rich blue damask, baldachin, sarcenet ('Saracen stuff'), silk, satin and taffeta. Gradually, centres appeared in Europe, as at Arras, for manufacturing textiles and rugs copying these oriental products as they became ever more fashionable. The practice of public baths was reintroduced into Europe during the Crusades, an institution patronised by the Romans but discouraged by the Christians. Even the practice of wearing slick beards (hipsters take note), neatly trimmed by the bath attendant, was brought back to Europe.

The ways that all these things were transmitted are also deeply connected to the burgeoning trade links. Consular offices to deal with commerce, rather than diplomacy, appeared; the first consuls in history were Genoese accredited to Acre in 1180, followed by the Venetians in Alexandria in 1192. As Hitti puts it:

> The creation of a new European market for Oriental agricultural products and industrial commodities, together with the need to transport pilgrims and Crusaders, stimulated maritime activity and international trade to an extent unknown since Roman days. Marseille began to rival the Italian city republics as a shipping centre and share in the accruing wealth.[83]

The beginnings of our banking system developed to meet the needs of the rapid circulation of money, with firms of bankers appearing in Genoa and Pisa to offer credit, and the Templars using letters of credit (cheques, from Arabic *saqq*). Europe was getting rich, at exactly the time when all the necessary financial means, methods and styles were coming together to facilitate the building of a new kind of 'cathedral of commerce'—the magnificent Gothic cathedrals of Europe.

8

THE SELJUKS, THE OTTOMANS AND SINAN

(1075–1924)

The Venetians well understood the complex relationship between politics, religion and architecture in creating a national identity. So, too, did Christopher Wren when he wrote: 'Architecture has its political use, public buildings being the ornament of a country; it establishes a nation; draws people and commerce; makes the people love their native country, which passion is the origin of all great actions in a commonwealth.'[1]

It was a view shared by Wren's kindred spirit in Istanbul, Sinan, sometimes called the Turkish Michelangelo. His name is synonymous with what we think of now as the classical style of Ottoman architecture, a style that spread across the vast Ottoman Empire from the Danube to the Tigris and still embodies Turkish national identity today. Wren served as surveyor of the king's works under six English monarchs for forty-nine years from 1669 to 1718, while Sinan was chief royal architect under three sultans from 1539 to 1588, also for forty-nine years. Despite the geographical distance separating them, both Wren and Sinan were architects working to fulfil commissions for their wealthy rulers—be they kings, queens or sultans—and both men understood that their creations needed to dominate the skyline and send a message of power and control both to the capital city and the world beyond.

Size and height were vital, and this chapter is the story of how domes evolved to become ever higher and more imposing—for there is no denying that without the dome, St Paul's would be nothing remarkable. It is the iconic shape that stays in one's memory long after a visit.

For both Christians and Muslims, the symbolism of the dome was the same: the vault of heaven. From the inside, the worshipper could gaze up and marvel as his spirits rose, enjoying a sense of harmony and of the sacred. From the outside, the dome was the embodiment of God's presence and power. In both mosque and church, it also served to highlight or emphasise a certain part of the building—in mosques it was usually in front of the *mihrab*, and in churches it was generally positioned over the crossing, in the central part of the transept, towards the altar end of the nave. In both mosque and church, it also served to let in light, either through a central oculus or through windows in the vertical section supporting the dome, or indeed both, as at St Paul's.

Sinan was the architect of several hundred known monuments, and his ingenious experimentation with centralised domes pushed the boundaries of geometric structure, space and light to new limits. He was hailed as the Euclid of his time and the greatest engineer. His contribution to the advancement of dome technology was of huge direct relevance to European architecture, since it went on not only to inform the techniques of Christopher Wren in building the dome of St Paul's, but also to influence aspects of Italian Renaissance architecture. As eminent Turkish Harvard scholar Gülru Necipoğlu wrote:

> The global fame of Sinan, the most celebrated architect of the premodern Islamic lands, is bolstered by the affinity between his centrally planned domed mosques and Italian Renaissance churches: an affinity rooted in the shared Romano-Byzantine architectural heritage of the eastern Mediterranean basin that was concurrently being revived in Istanbul and Italy.[2]

Everyone built on everyone else's knowledge in a constant synthesis of all the techniques and materials to hand, but East and West each interpreted their Romano-Byzantine inheritance in entirely separate ways. While European architecture after the Renaissance became endlessly focused on designing facades using the antique orders so beloved of Wren, Ottoman architecture under Sinan instead concentrated on achieving perfectly central-ised unified domed spaces filled with light. Sinan's was a single-minded search for geometric purity of form, textured by masterful fenestration and the control of light and shade into a centralised space.[3] His inspiration was not simply the Hagia Sophia that already dominated Istanbul's landscape, but all the embedded memories of Ottoman cultural heritage reaching right back to the earliest Mesopotamian domed structures, Zoroastrian fire temples, Neolithic *tholoi* (corbelled stone 'beehive' structures) at Tell Halaf in south-east Turkey and northern Syria, and domed tombs of the Seljuks and the Armenians which blended with his Islamic vision.

The resulting synthesis produced a purity of style not equalled till the twentieth century, when the Swiss-French architect Le Corbusier (1887–1965) was inspired by Sinan's great Turkish mosques. As architectural histo-rian Godfrey Goodwin expresses it: 'Ottoman architecture after 1500 had already achieved that poetic interplay of shaded and sunlit interiors which pleased Le Corbusier.'[4] And Le Corbusier tells us himself, when describing his Villa Savoye (built 1928–31), one of his most famous works and now an icon of Modernist architecture:

Arab architecture gives us a precious lesson: it is best appreciated in walking, on foot; it is while walking, moving from one place to another, that one sees how the arrangements of the architecture develop. This is a principle contrary to Baroque architecture, which is conceived on paper, round a theoretical fixed point. I prefer the lesson of Arab architecture … which often erased the traditional difference between the inside and the outside.[5]

Like Wren, Le Corbusier makes no distinction between Turkish and Arab architecture, since it is all Islamic or 'Saracenic' in inspiration. What Le Corbusier calls his 'Free Plan' in his 'Five Points of Architecture',[6] in which the structure of the building is not visible from the outside, was inspired by Sinan's mosque design in which the unity of concept flows from the main dome. Sinan conceived his mosques from above, where the dome of heaven itself was the central focus. Everything else was subservient to this, so the challenge was to make the structural elements as invisible as possible, so that the dome appears to float weightlessly above. There was minimal superfluous ornamentation, as this would have constituted a distraction from the unity of space where the believer could feel immediately at one with God. This is the Islamic concept of 'oneness', *tawheed*, Arabic for 'making into one', as opposed to the Christian Trinity. Unlike in a church, in a mosque there is no hierarchy, no intermediary, no furniture or special places where only certain people can go or sit.

The first pioneering mosque where Sinan achieves this new vision— referred to by art historians as a 'single-domed central baldachin'—is the Mihrimah Sultan Mosque in Edirnekapı, Istanbul, commissioned by Mihrimah herself, the richest woman in the world at that time and the only daughter to Süleyman the Magnificent and Roxelana, his favourite wife. Here, for the first time, Sinan introduces windowed arcades on the side walls, which allow huge quantities of light to flood in—far more than in any church—in a complex interplay of light and shade. In European church architecture, the baldachin is a free-standing canopy over a holy space, such as the altar or relics of a saint.

The most famous baldachin is the ornate baroque Baldacchino of St Peter's, built in bronze in 1623–4, at the centre of the crossing directly under the dome of St Peter's Basilica in Rome. A highly elaborate canopy supported by four twisted columns, it forms the focal point of the space, and the underside of the mini-dome canopy is decorated with a radiant sun. The word 'baldachin' derives from a luxurious type of cloth from Baghdad with various spellings—usually baudekin in English—which was used to drape over an altar or throne, as befitted a special or holy place. The concept of creating a canopy of rich cloth over a king or ruler goes right back to the civilisations of the ancient Assyrians and Persians, where carved stone reliefs show rulers beneath shaded canopies. It was carried over into Byzantine Christian practices where it gradually became part of the architecture of the church, the focus of much rich ornamentation, as at St Peter's. In Sinan's Mihrimah Sultan Mosque the concept could hardly be more different—there is no furniture at all in the space, and the baldachin is the dome itself above you. It represents a completely different way of experiencing and conceptualising God—directly, not via all the decorative elements so loved in Europe. As Doğan Kuban puts it, in Sinan's domed structures:

The Mihrimah Sultan Mosque at Edirnekapı, Istanbul, where a perfect centralised light-filled space flows down from the dome as a 'single-domed central baldachin'. The design emphasises a oneness of space symbolising the unity of God, or *tawheed*.

There is nothing of the abstract scheme of superficially applied elements so characteristic of Western architecture throughout its history.[7] ...

After the Renaissance, all European buildings were an elaboration on the single theme of designing facades using antique orders. In Islamic architecture the functional elements were emphasised—gates, minarets, entrance iwans. Buildings are structural organisms, not facades.[8]

This is precisely what Le Corbusier, more than three centuries later, saw and understood, aged twenty-four, on his visit to Istanbul in 1911. Years later, he put those same principles into his utopian urban planning designs as far afield as India, as he explained in his 1935 book *The Radiant City*, a name

In European church architecture, the baldachin is a separate domed structure marking one important sacred spot, like the altar, as here in St. Peter's Basilica, Rome, thereby creating a sense of hierarchy in the space.

which even has echoes of Madinat al-Zahra. It is an approach that once again brings to mind the Cordoba Mezquita, with its unique structure where form is organic and embraces you. In 1907, aged twenty, Le Corbusier made sketches of the Mezquita from a book in the Sainte-Geneviève Library in Paris, and on visiting it in 1930 he sketched it and wrote postcards bought there, annotated in his own hand. Later notes dating from 1955 talk with wonder and amazement about the Mezquita's 'line of trees'. It has even been suggested that his alias, Le Corbusier, is derived from El Cordóbes, 'the one from Cordoba'.[9] His real name was Charles-Édouard Jeanneret.

Domes

Hagia Sophia (Turkish Ayasofya), Church of the Divine Wisdom

Earlier churches had stood on the site of today's Hagia Sophia in the Byzantine capital, all of which had been destroyed, generally by fire. The last had been damaged beyond repair during riots by angry crowds protesting against high taxes imposed by Emperor Justinian. He began the rebuilding quickly in 532 and commissioned two famous architects, both from western Asia Minor, 'where church architecture had been undistinguished in contrast to that of Syria.'[10] Anthemios of Tralles was a mathematician and author of several treatises, including one on conic sections. Isodorus was a professor of geometry and mechanics and a specialist in the works of Archimedes, Euclid and Heron. Both men enjoyed high status, with direct access to the emperor himself, and both 'ignored numerous stylistic quotations and detailed instructions from the emperor'[11] to come up with their own unique creation, universally recognised as the highpoint of Byzantine architecture and admired round the world for the stunning achievement of the central dome. A very different image is conveyed by the western European Latin manuscript now held in the Vatican Library, in which an enormous Justinian, many times bigger than the Hagia Sophia itself, is seen directing a small, rather nervous-looking mason who is balancing on a ladder. According to art historian John Lowden, Justinian was 'a person of vision and extraordinary energy, both

The Hagia Sophia, Istanbul, as it looks today, with added minarets and much buttressing to stabilise the dome, which has collapsed several times since the sixth century. Sinan himself was commissioned to supervise one such buttressing in the sixteenth century.

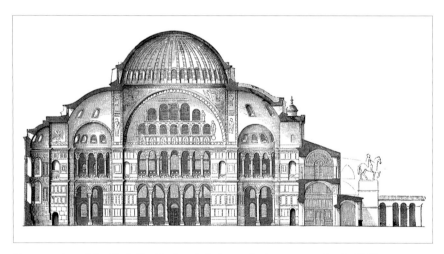

Cross-section of the Hagia Sophia, Istanbul, drawn during a restoration in 1908, showing the internal structure and the strengthened rib vaulting of the thin brick-built dome. The interior suffered the worst damage of its long history during the 1204 Fourth Crusade, at the hands of the Latin Christians.

Nineteenth-century lithograph of the nave of the Ayasofya Mosque/Hagia Sophia from
the period between 1453 and 1931 when it was in use as a mosque, serving as the
inspiration for many Ottoman mosques. It has been a museum since 1935.

intensely pious and utterly ruthless … his military ambitions matched by his grandiose building programme.'[12]

The overall size of the church was defined by the size of the previous plot, a near square of 77 by 72 metres. As in the case of the Syrian St Simeon's west of Aleppo, the biggest Byzantine basilica complex before the construction of Hagia Sophia, the space was centralised under the dome, though there was still a trace of the rectangular basilica in the central and side aisles. The dome was the unquestioned dominant element of the structure, 49 metres high and 31 metres in diameter, taller but less wide than the second-century Pantheon in Rome, where both the height and the width are 44 metres. But whereas the Pantheon's concrete dome is clearly resting on a huge circular base wall designed expressly for that purpose, the brick-built dome of the Hagia Sophia rests on a square base. Thanks to the first-time large-scale use of four spherical triangular pendentives (curved 3D triangular forms that effect the transition between the square and the circle, from *pendens*, Latin 'hanging', so named because they made the dome look as though it were hanging), the dome appears to float weightlessly by hiding the supporting pillars behind rows of pillars, exedras and coloured marble facings, relegating them to the side aisles, tucked out of view. The inspiration for Hagia Sophia was never Hadrian's Pantheon, as some Eurocentric historians like to suggest, nor the concrete vaults of Constantine's civil Basilica Nova of Maxentius, also in Rome (there are no historical links),[13] but rather much earlier Eastern traditions. The circular dome over a square base is a design rooted in Persian mausoleums and Zoroastrian fire temples. The pendentive too is thought to have originated in Persia or possibly even Armenia.[14]

The architects of Hagia Sophia cut forty windows into the vertical upright base section of the dome to relieve the weight and thereby relax the pressure on the pendentives. They then created two half-domes, each 31 metres in diameter (the same diameter as the main dome), five further half-domes above the apse, and niches in the arches. Taken all together, this enabled the creation of ninety-one more windows to illuminate the magnificent golden mosaics beneath the dome and on the walls. The dome, semi-domes and vaults created a far wider and more open basilical layout than would have been possible had even the longest roof timbers been used.[15]

Through this ingenious construction, the dome is in effect buttressed by the half-domes, which together help distribute the weight yet further. The dome is just 2 feet thick and made of bricks from Rhodes soil, which is light but durable, held together with mortar. It took nearly six years to complete, and on entering for the first time Justinian is said to have exclaimed: 'O Solomon, I have outdone you!'—a reference to Solomon's Temple in Jerusalem. For over a thousand years, Hagia Sophia was the largest cathedral in the world, a major influence on and inspiration for future religious architecture, both Muslim and Christian. Until the much later construction of the new St Peter's in Rome (1506–1626), it was the largest pendentive dome in the world.

Masterpiece or not, a series of earthquakes caused it to fall in 558, just twenty years after it was completed, by which time Justinian was seventy-six and both architects had died. A nephew of Isodorus was commissioned to repair it, and raised the dome by 7 metres to make the angle steeper and therefore reduce the outward thrust on the walls, using heavy external buttressing, which gives the church the look of a giant squatting insect from the outside but retains the weightless aspect inside. Isodorus also changed the design of the dome, adding forty ribs like the inside of an umbrella, which channel the weight to run down between the windows and onto the pendentives, and ultimately into the foundations. Sections of this second dome, completed in 562, collapsed again in 989 and in 1346, but were restored and repaired without material change.

It was a remarkable achievement, openly praised by later Ottoman historians—following the typical Byzantine tradition, they used language implying that the architect must have worked in direct union with God, with descriptions of a guardian angel watching over the church. Even before the Ottoman conquest of the city, Islamic tradition had identified Hagia Sophia as the heavenly temple that the Prophet Muhammad had seen on his nocturnal journey to heaven from Jerusalem's Dome of the Rock, which was understood to predestine the church's conversion to a mosque. In 1204, during the Fourth Crusade, Hagia Sophia was looted and sacked, along with the whole of Constantinople, thereby causing a major schism between the Latin and Greek churches—Roman Catholics against Greek Orthodox Christians:

The Latin soldiery subjected the greatest city in Europe to an indescribable sack. For three days they murdered, raped, looted and destroyed on a scale which even the ancient Vandals and Goths would have found unbelievable. Constantinople had become a veritable museum of ancient and Byzantine art, an emporium of such incredible wealth that the Latins were astounded at the riches they found. … The Crusaders vented their hatred for the Greeks most spectacularly in the desecration of the greatest Church in Christendom. They smashed the silver iconostasis, the icons and the holy books of Hagia Sophia, and seated upon the patriarchal throne a whore who sang coarse songs as they drank wine from the Church's holy vessels. The estrangement of East and West, which had proceeded over the centuries, culminated in the horrible massacre that accompanied the conquest of Constantinople. The Greeks were convinced that even the Turks, had they taken the city, would not have been as cruel as the Latin Christians. The defeat of Byzantium, already in a state of decline, accelerated political degeneration so that the Byzantines eventually became an easy prey to the Turks. The Fourth Crusade and the crusading movement generally thus resulted, ultimately, in the victory of Islam, a result which was of course the exact opposite of its original intention.[16]

Very few of the Crusaders continued on to Jerusalem, having become so rich so easily. Pope Innocent III, who had unintentionally launched the ill-fated expedition, rebuked them:

How, indeed, will the church of the Greeks, no matter how severely she is beset with afflictions and persecutions, return into ecclesiastical union and to a devotion for the Apostolic See, when she has seen in the Latins only an example of perdition and the works of darkness, so that she now, and with reason, detests the Latins more than dogs? As for those who were supposed to be seeking the ends of Jesus Christ, not their own ends, who made their swords, which they were supposed to use against the pagans, drip with Christian blood, they have spared neither religion, nor age, nor sex. They have committed incest, adultery, and fornication before the eyes of men. They have exposed both matrons and virgins, even those dedicated to God, to the sordid lusts of boys. Not satisfied with breaking open the imperial treasury and plundering the goods of princes and lesser men, they also laid their hands on the treasures of the churches and, what is more serious, on their very possessions. They have even ripped silver plates from the altars and have hacked them to pieces among themselves. They violated the holy places and have carried off crosses and relics.[17]

The pope's outrage however did not prevent him from accepting the stolen jewels, gold, money and other valuables, and the Church was of course much enriched as a result. A great deal of this wealth was in turn repurposed into huge building projects throughout Europe—some of it certainly would have helped to finance our Gothic cathedrals.

Remorse was expressed 800 years later by Pope John Paul II for the events of the Fourth Crusade. Writing to the archbishop of Athens in 2001, he said: 'It is tragic that the assailants, who set out to secure free access for Christians to the Holy Land, turned against their brothers in the faith. The fact that they were Latin Christians fills Catholics with deep regret.' In 2004, the 800th anniversary of the city's capture, he asked the patriarch of Constantinople: 'How can we not share, at a distance of eight centuries, the pain and disgust?' The patriarch formally accepted the apology.

When Mehmet the Conqueror took Constantinople in 1453, he permitted his armies three days of looting, as was the custom, but then called a halt. Most churches were allowed to continue functioning, but the Hagia Sophia was adopted as a mosque. Mehmet erected a minaret and subsequent sultans erected three more, so there is now one at each corner, but the interior remains largely as it ever was.

As discussed, there was much shared symbolism between Islam and Christianity in the meaning of the dome as the physical representation of heaven and the afterlife, but the flavour of Hagia Sophia as a building was always different to the sacred buildings of Rome like the Pantheon and St Peter's. Its design was rooted in Eastern traditions, where Persian mausoleums had a circular dome resting on a square drum. The transition between the circle and the square resulted in an octagon, which came to represent, both in Islam and in Christianity, the resurrection and the journey between earth and heaven, which is why so many tombs are octagonal in both religions.

As well as shared concepts, Muslims and Christians in the eastern Mediterranean enjoyed a common heritage of building materials, techniques and tools passed on from the Graeco-Roman, Persian and even earlier Etruscan worlds. They also shared workers, builders and craftsmen, who moved around according to demand, following the next or the most profitable commission from a wealthy patron, no matter what his religion. Byzantine mosaicists, for example, were frequently employed to decorate Islamic mosques, such as the Dome of the Rock, the Umayyad Mosque of Damascus, and the Cordoba Mezquita. By the eighth century, the figure of the architect himself mysteriously disappeared, and illuminated manuscripts and even mosaic panels simply show bands of builders all working together equally on a structure, as in the famous *Building the Tower of Babel* mosaic inside St Mark's, Venice.

In his astonishingly detailed study *Master Builders of Byzantium*, Robert Ousterhout concludes that the era of the theory-based *mechanikoi* (like the Hagia Sophia architects Isodorus and Anthemios) was by then over, and all training by this time took place in a workshop, where masons learned methods of wall and vault construction tested over time. The terms *maistor* and *protomaistor* for master mason or head of a guild came into use instead. Architecture became based more on practice, memory and experience than on theory, with itinerant bands of masons travelling round within the Byzantine Empire—to Jerusalem for instance to rebuild the Holy Sepulchre—while an Armenian called Trdat was summoned with his team to repair the dome of Hagia Sophia in the tenth century. Armenians also figured as architects in Istanbul post-1453. Speedy construction was often required by imperial patrons, which also meant large workforces, far larger than would have simply been on hand locally. One account of the building of Hagia Sophia, for example, talks of a hundred master masons directing a hundred apprentices, divided into two teams of fifty working on opposite halves of the church.[18] Apprentices were often sons or relations, starting out as boys, slowly working their way up in skill over five to ten years. Their skills and experience would in turn be passed down through the generations. By the tenth century, the artisans had organised themselves into guilds (*systemata*), privileged corporations with voluntary membership, protected from competition with non-members, who gradually became a political force in Constantinople. Western medieval guilds of Paris were similar, except they additionally had a clerk of works who was responsible for administrative and financial aspects, and who was paid more and enjoyed a higher social status. The master masons only took responsibility for the construction work itself; they were held accountable for their work for ten years if it was a brick construction, and for six years if it was mud brick.

The Double Domes of the Seljuk Turks

In Europe it was the Romans who built the first domes, like the Pantheon in Rome, using concrete, which was readily available, cheap, durable and malleable, but also heavy. To lighten the load, the Romans hollowed out wherever they could, by coffering the visible surface, and by incorporating unseen vases and jugs to create pockets of air. The Islamic world instead developed the technique of the double shell: that is, a lighter shell for the building's interior and a more durable shell for its exterior, with the entire space in between being hollow. This technique not only lightened the load, but also allowed for each shell to correspond perfectly to the building's interior or exterior proportions. It therefore gave the flexibility to adjust the building's profile both internally and externally, in order to project greater height outside and therefore greater visibility and a more imposing presence. Wren, as we have learnt from the *Parentalia*, was particularly aware of the importance of this, given the general resistance to the dome that he kept encountering from those who preferred the vertical thrust of the Gothic spire of the old St Paul's before the Great Fire of London. As well as these aesthetic considerations, and the lighter weight, the double dome system also had practical advantages. It substantially improved weather protection by keeping the exterior surface separate from the inner shell, and enhanced the acoustics beneath the dome, where a whisper could be clearly heard. In earthquake-prone regions like Istanbul, it also proved itself to be much more resilient.

The first to use the double dome technique were the Turkish Seljuks in their eleventh-century cylindrical or octagonal tombs topped by pointed cones or domes all across Anatolia and Persia. The Seljuks were originally nomads from the region of Samarkand and Bukhara, descended from Seljuk, who ruled the steppes of Central Asia. Renowned for their physical prowess, under their leader Alp Arslan the Seljuks surged out from their homeland into Persia, Iraq, Syria and Palestine, where they converted to Islam, before pushing north again via Antioch into Central Anatolia, where the Seljuks of Rum established their capital at Konya.

Architecturally, the Seljuks developed their own distinctive style based on conical domes, of which the most famous is Mevlana's Tomb at Konya, where they promoted the Mevlevi Order of the Whirling Dervishes. There are literally hundreds of Seljuk tombs all over eastern Anatolia, built of stone or red brick, with high plain walls contrasting with very elaborate decoration and carving in the doorways and niches.

The distinctive conical turquoise-tiled double dome of the thirteenth-century tomb of Mevlana (Jalal al-Din Muhammad Rumi), founder of the Whirling Dervishes in the city of Konya, Turkey. The Seljuks never built on pre-existing foundations, always starting afresh. The tomb became a museum in 1927.

Each architectural detail at the Divriği mosque/hospital complex in Central Anatolia has been executed with verve and passion. The style of this elaborately decorated north entrance portal, a typical feature of Seljuk architecture, might with good reason be termed 'Turkish Gothic'.

Most architectural effort was concentrated in the main entrance, with intricate carving and elaborate *muqarnas* stalactite vaulting. The most famous example, much lauded by art historians and now on the UNESCO World Heritage list, can still be visited at Divriği in Sivas Province, Central Anatolia, where a highly unusual blend of influences converged to produce a unique mosque/madrasa/hospital complex, all conjoined into one building. Divriği had been an important stronghold for the Paulician Armenians, a sect of iconoclast Christians founded in the seventh century, forbears to the later twelfth- and thirteenth-century Cathars in the French Pyrenees. Heavily persecuted as heretics by the Byzantines, they were given refuge in Divriği by the Muslim emir of Malatya in the ninth century to create a semi-independent state, but the Byzantines then retook it, before the Seljuks captured it from the Byzantines after the Turkish victory at the Battle of Manzikert in 1071, holding it till 1251.

Commissioned jointly in 1228 by a local emir and the daughter of another local emir, the Divriği Great Mosque and Hospital boasts three of the most elaborately decorated portals you are ever likely to see, the creation of an architect from Ahlat on the northern shore of Lake Van. Inside too, each column capital—like many Gothic cathedrals—boasts a different ornamentation, as if each mason spontaneously carved his design 'according to his own whims.'[19] Craftsmen from Tiflis in Georgia and Armenian masons are known to have worked on the carving, and all would have been familiar with Armenian church architecture, like the famous Cathedral of the Holy Cross on Akdamar Island in Lake Van. The sheer exuberance of the carving, however, with its garlanded fronds of foliage, goes way beyond the rather primitive carving on Akdamar, and also incorporates birds and animals entangled in the vegetal scrolls, which have definite echoes of what might with good reason even be called Turkish Gothic. The Central Asiatic Turks had always used animal figures, scrolls and fronds in their decoration, but after their conversion to Islam they also incorporated self-contained geometric panels within the foliage, such as twelve-pointed stars, hexagonal lozenges and circular medallion designs. More examples of this type of animal decoration used by the old Turkish tribes of central Asia can still be seen today on the

The Reception of the Venetian Ambassadors in Damascus, painted in 1511 by an unknown Venetian artist. The tall double-domed profile of the Damascus Umayyad Mosque can be seen rising in the background above its unmistakable gabled facade.

walls of Diyarbakır, on the Gök Medrese in Sivas, and in the Seljuk tombs at Niğde and Kayseri on the edge of Cappadocia.

Without exception the Seljuks built on new foundations, never using pre-existing temples, churches or mosques. Not a single Seljuk mosque was converted from a church or even built on the ruins of a church. They often marked their buildings with the symbol of the Seljuk state, the double-headed eagle, originally a Hittite symbol of power, later also used by the Mamluks, and subsequently adopted in Russia and in the Holy Roman Empire. There are traces of Persian influence in the Seljuks' elaborate tilework and carving, together with Syrian Arab influence in the strength of their castles and their minarets, the most famous of which graced the Aleppo Umayyad Mosque till 2013, when it was destroyed in the Syrian civil war. The pointed shape of Seljuk tombs is thought to hark back to the pointed tents of their nomadic origins, or else to have been influenced by the similar shape of the Armenian churches they would have seen in eastern Anatolia.

But the Seljuks understood that there were structural benefits to the conical dome, too. The taller, sharper profile meant that less outward thrust was exerted on the walls, exactly as was the case with the pointed arch. The two domes were of roughly similar thickness, and while the outside dome created the overall visual effect of magnitude, the inside one lowered the ceiling.

In the twelfth century, the structure of the double dome of the Great Mosque of Damascus was shown off to visitors, and Ibn Jubayr, a visiting geographer and poet born in Valencia in 1145, was allowed to enter the space between the two concentric shells, of which he wrote in 1184:

> This [inner] cupola is round like a sphere, and its exterior is of wood strengthened by stout wooden ribs bound by iron bands, each rib curving over the cupola. ... The Lead Dome enfolds this cupola. It is also strengthened by huge ribs of solid wood, bound in the middle by iron bands. These ribs number forty-eight, and the distance between each is four spans. They bend round in remarkable fashion, and their ends and meet at a central wooden disc at the summit.[20]

The brick-built ribbed dome of Florence Cathedral was the first in Europe to use the double-dome method. Completed in 1436, it became the largest dome the world had ever seen. The architect, Brunelleschi, kept his methods secret but drew his inspiration from complex Islamic geometric centring systems that made the structure self-supporting.

That double-domed timber cupola was destroyed after the fire of 1893, caused by a workman dropping his pipe, but its soaring dome can still be seen in the sixteenth-century painting *The Reception of the Venetian Ambassadors in Damascus* by an anonymous Venetian that hangs today in the Louvre.

The Mongol invasions caused a break in architectural creation from the early thirteenth century, with the destruction of many monuments and the murder of scientists by Mongol and Timurid troops. Tamerlane then brought all the craftsmen back to build his new capital in Samarkand in 1401.

In Europe, the first successful use of the double dome was in the Cathedral of Florence, built by the Italian Renaissance architect Filippo Brunelleschi. Though the first stone of the church was laid in 1296, the dome was not finished until 1436, leaving the rain to fall directly onto the congregation for over a hundred years, because the West lacked the technology to construct it. This dome was to be the largest the world had ever seen, larger even than that of the Pantheon. In 1418, an open competition was held to find a designer for the dome, won by Brunelleschi, who first went to Rome to study its ancient buildings. It is thought that he also travelled to the East,[21] since a number of the techniques he chose to employ were only known in the Islamic world at that time. He was also known, as mentioned earlier, to have read the works of Islamic scientists based at the Fatimid court in Cairo, where the double dome was in common use.

In 2007, an extraordinary practical experiment was conducted by a trio of academics—one Irish, two Italian—to build a one-fifth scale model of Brunelleschi's dome, and the Florence authorities permitted construction to take place in a park in the city's eastern suburbs. The key academic was Professor Massimo Ricci of Florence University's School of Architecture, who had already spent thirty years seeking to understand how the dome was constructed and had published papers on it since 1983.[22] The model was built between 1989 and 2007, longer than it took Brunelleschi himself, in terracotta brick. Brunelleschi's dome has an approximate internal diameter of 45 metres, and the model measured 11 metres across at the base and weighed hundreds of tonnes. The methods used were deliberately restricted to what Brunelleschi would have had available to him at the time.

What the academics discovered was that Brunelleschi had used a highly complex geometric centring system, devising a herringbone brick pattern and curved mortar beds, each ring of which was laid according to an inverted cone. This meant that the structure was self-supporting as it rose, because all weight was transferred down through the tip of the point, which was always positioned vertical to the ground. The base of Brunelleschi's dome was an octagonal drum with walls 4.25 metres thick. When he submitted his proposal to build the dome, he put forward the idea of building two concentric octagonal shells with a walkway and stairs in between. The two shells were tied together with twenty-four ribs, eight major thick ones along the curved lines of the octagon and sixteen smaller ones spaced regularly in between the others. He used no scaffolding, just a highly precise platform base spanning the spread of the gap, which could be used as a fixed reference point to check measurements and angles for the utmost precision. The system has been described as a 'radial methodology', based on the shared symmetry of each pair of opposite sides, where deviations from the desired curvature of the dome were constantly checked and corrected during construction using plumb lines.

The Florence Cathedral dome took sixteen years to build (1420–36) and Brunelleschi never disclosed his method, except to praise the importance of practical knowledge and experience in this sonnet he composed afterwards, three lines of which give the key:

One who has no practical knowledge is easily misled
And does not understand how art at its most profound
Taps into Nature's secrets to realise human dreams.

This seems to be a direct reference to the secrets of geometry, so closely tied to the properties of Nature, as described in Chapter 6, and as explored by the tenth-century scientists and mathematicians of the Abbasid court.

Once Brunelleschi adopted this technique for the Florence Cathedral, it became standard for monumental domes across Europe. The ovoid shape of the dome had both visual, aesthestic justifications—to achieve an imposing height—and structural reasons, because, as the Seljuks had already discovered from the pointed arch and the pointed dome, a steeper angle exerted less outward thrust on the walls than a hemispherical dome like that of the Pantheon. The ovoid shape was then adopted by Michelangelo for the dome of St Peter's Basilica in Rome, and by Wren for St Paul's Cathedral in London, where he even added a third, intervening shell. For the dome in Florence, Brunelleschi adopted additional Islamic techniques, such as the herringbone brickwork. In an age before the availability of modern materials like iron or steel, and when scaffolds were made of wood, another big issue was how to build a dome taller than the trees at hand, and how to provide support while it was still unfinished. The herringbone technique solved the problem, because the bricks in effect locked into place and supported themselves. Yet another influential Islamic technique employed in Brunelleschi's dome is the ribbing, which not only provided structural support but also emphasised the building's geometry. For structural support, ribbing would become essential to the development of Gothic architecture. In terms of using the ribs to bring out geometry, particularly in domes, such usage in the Cordoba Mezquita influenced the Church of the Holy Sepulchre at Torres del Rio (twelfth to thirteenth centuries) and other churches of Spain, and ultimately paved the way for Guarini's intricately geometric Baroque domes in the Chapel of the Holy Shroud (1668–94) and the Cathedral of San Lorenzo (1668–87), both in Turin, Italy.[23]

The Umayyads inherited the technique of supporting the weight of the dome on four pendentives from the Syrian Byzantines in the seventh and eighth centuries. These rested on four heavily built pillars in the four corners, but the Umayyads gradually improved the system by using squinches (small arches or corbelling) instead. To form the shell itself, the traditional Byzantine technique had been to mix small stones, debris and mortar, and then pour the mix into a timber-frame shell which held it in place till it was dry. This technique was time-consuming since the masons had to wait for the mixture to dry before the mould could be moved to the next spot; it also required a lot of timber for the frames, not always readily available. The Muslim architects therefore began using a more efficient, geometric solution, which meant replacing the wooden centring with courses of brick and using four squinches made from arched semi-circles straddling the four corners to produce a circular base for the dome. The earliest known squinch is

The Süleymaniye Mosque, commissioned by Sultan Süleyman the Great, was designed by Sinan to dominate the Istanbul skyline and to outdo the Hagia Sophia. Much of the buttressing was designed to be invisible, using semi-domes as squinches, a technique Wren also used a century later at St Paul's to create a sense of weightlessness in the dome when viewed from the inside.

found in the third-century Persian Sassanid palace of Ardashir in Firuzabad, Iran, built of brick.

The brick coursing was formed by laying an arch of bricks at an angle towards an end wall, then laying subsequent arches parallel to it and cementing the surfaces with mortar, until a vault or ceiling was gradually produced. The squinch then spread to western Europe and was used in Norman Romanesque architecture, as at the twelfth-century church of San Cataldo in Palermo, Sicily, whose three domes are supported by four doubled squinches. The other dome construction method was to use the rib vaulting techniques that the Umayyads had first developed at the Cordoba Mezquita in the late eighth century.

Parallels Between Sinan (1490–1588) and Wren (1632–1723)

Sinan, Islam's greatest architect, lived to be nearly a hundred, just as Wren did more than a century later. Like Wren, Sinan's preference was for classical simplicity over what he regarded as needless excess. His constant striving was to achieve the largest possible volume under a single dome. As Kuban tells us: 'Sinan was not prone to fantasy; he was a sober architect who avoided opulence, illusion-giving elements, architectural gimmicks and the exuberance produced by the addition of decorative elements.'[24]

Of his buildings, Sinan regarded the Şehzade Mosque in Istanbul as his apprenticeship, the Süleymaniye Mosque in Istanbul as his coming of age, and the Selimiye Mosque in Edirne as his masterpiece. As chief architect of the Ottoman Empire during its Golden Age, he had jurisdiction over all of Istanbul's craftsmen, who were organised into workshops under two broad categories: carpenters' guilds and masons' guilds. These guilds included timberjacks, adze makers, brick makers, lime burners, box makers, Iznik tile makers, carpenters, glaziers, lead sheet makers, water channel makers, stone cutters, marble cutters, plasterers, paint makers, painters, locksmiths, pavement makers, labourers and porters. Sinan took his duties towards his craftsmen very seriously and is known to have negotiated with the sultan for higher wages for dissatisfied masons and carpenters, always taking their side in grievances.[25] Like Wren, he even had to negotiate the costs and sizes of building materials like stones, timbers and bricks, often at times of monetary crisis in the empire, a crucial skill to make sure he stayed within budget of his imperial commissions.[26] Such was his respect for the heads of the artisanal guilds of Istanbul that his chief architect's office even built mosques for them as individuals.

The Süleymaniye Mosque was built as a commission from Süleyman the Great. Dominating the Third Hill in central Istanbul, it took eight years to complete (1550–8) and was seen as a direct challenge to the Hagia Sophia. In the event, the dome of the Süleymaniye was taller, at 53 metres, but not wider, at 26.5 metres, than that of the Hagia Sophia. Outdoing the great Byzantine structure was always the chief motivator of the Ottoman sultans, but this was not achieved till late in Sinan's life, when he was eighty years old, at the Selimiye Mosque in Edirne, commissioned by Sinan's next master, Sultan Selim II. The huge octagonal central dome, 42 metres high and 31.28 metres in diameter, was supported by eight gigantic piers of marble and granite topped with squinches instead of capitals, creating the optical illusion that the arches grew directly out of the piers. The semi-domes are set in the four corners of the square below the dome to provide invisible buttressing, so the weight of the dome and its supports are carefully concealed to give an elegant and airy feel to the vast open space, flooded by light from the myriad windows at the dome's base. These are all techniques appreciated and similarly used by Wren.

In his autobiography, which he dictated to the poet-painter Sai Mustafa Çelebi, Sinan makes clear that he felt it was his God-given destiny to become an architect: 'I wished to become an architect to leave with my perfect skills monuments in this world' (Verse 29). As he describes how he was taken from a village near Kayseri under the Ottoman *devşirme* system (forced Christian child conscription) as a youth, he uses geometrical language, imagining his travels as the movements of a compass:

> I was the first of the conscript boys. Being like a ruler, straight in character among the novice recruits, I was eager and aspired to the trade of carpenter. I became a steadfast compass in the master's service and kept an eye on the centre and the orbit. Later, I yearned to travel through regions like a moving compass drawing a circumference. For a time I traversed the lands of the Arabs and non-Arabs in the service of the Sultan, and I acquired a sought-after bit [of wisdom] from the crenellation of every *ayvan* and a provision [of knowledge] from every ruined dervish lodge.[27]

He was clearly a natural problem solver, able to apply his knowledge and practical experience to unexpected challenges, even building bridges:

> When Sultan Süleyman Khan set out for Moldavia [in 1538] and arrived on the banks of the river Prut, a bridge was needed for the army to cross. Many men worked diligently and for many days endeavoured to build a bridge. The bridge that they built sank in the mud and water and disappeared without

trace. Since it was a marshy place, they were bewildered and at a loss about how to build the bridge. His Excellency the late Lutfi Pasha said, 'My felicitous *padishah*, the construction of this bridge can be achieved with the skill and ability of your servant Sinan Subaşı … a master of the world and a skilled architect.' Upon his saying this, a glorious command was received by this humble servant, and I began the construction of a fine bridge over the above-mentioned river. In ten days I built a high bridge [and] the army of Islam and the shah of humankind crossed it with felicity.[28]

The kitchen, harem and supply room of the Topkapı, residence of the Ottoman sultans, was severely damaged due to a fire in 1574, and was restored by Sinan upon Selim's orders. Only the most accomplished architect was permitted to work on the imperial palace, just as Wren was regarded as the top architect to rebuild St Paul's after the 1666 fire. In 1573 Sinan was also commissioned to strengthen Hagia Sophia, which was starting to show signs of possible collapse. As Sinan was working on the Selimiye at the time, he delegated the work on Hagia Sophia to one of his chief assistants, who added extra buttressing to the outside to ensure its resistance to earthquakes, something Sinan would never have done to a building of his own construction. He disliked exhibiting the method that kept a building upright, as did Wren, who wrote that: 'Gothick buttresses are all ill-favoured, and were avoided by the Ancients, and no roofs almost but spherick raised to be visible.'[29] In talking of arches and vaulting, Wren says the Freemasons were 'not very solicitous about this, because they used buttresses on the outside of the wall … the Romans never used buttresses.'[30] In total, twenty-four buttresses have been added over the centuries to Hagia Sophia to ensure its stability, disfiguring it and making its external appearance quite different to how it would have looked originally.

Wren expressly tells us in his *Parentalia* that at St Paul's, he used the same vaulting technique as that used at Hagia Sophia, which is still used today 'in the present seraglio', that is the Topkapı Palace. This must be in reference to the two domes of the Topkapı's harem, the largest domes in the palace, rebuilt by Sinan after the fire. When it came to domes, Wren knew that the East had superior technology, as he explains:

The different forms of vaultings are necessary to be considered, either as they were used by the Ancients, or the Moderns, whether Free-masons, or Saracens. Another way, (which I cannot find used by the Ancients, but in the later Eastern Empire, as appears at St Sophia, and by that example, in all the mosques & cloysters of the Dervises, and every where at present in the East) and of all the others the most geometrical, is composed of hemispheres, and their sections only: and whereas a sphere may be cut in all manner of ways, & that still into circles, it may be accommodated to lie upon all positions of the pillars.[31]

Wren's use of these Islamic techniques was entirely new to England at the time, where no dome of such a size had been attempted before, and the use of semi-domes as a geometric solution to distributing the dome's full weight was revolutionary. If you stand beneath the dome at St Paul's and look up, you will see this technique in action. Wren used the same domed technique in the side aisle vaulting and in the central nave vaulting, as is clearly apparent in the dazzlingly colourful ceilings with their circular and semi-circular patterns.
Wren explains why he chose this method:

Now because I have for just reasons followed this way in the vaulting of the Church of St Paul's, I think it proper to shew, that it is the lightest manner, and requires less butment than the cross-vaulting, as well as that it is of an agreeable view. … [I] preferred it above any other way used by architects.[32]

Wren would have known about these 'Saracen' techniques and methods thanks to the travels and writings of Arabic scholars like Edward Pococke and John Greaves, mentioned in Chapter 1, who in 1637 travelled together by ship to Constantinople where they stayed for three years. Pococke stayed put in the Ottoman capital while Greaves travelled widely, recording what he saw. Wherever he travelled he took an interest in everything, not just mathematics and astronomy, the subjects that had earned him the Savilian professorship of geometry at Oxford. In earlier correspondence about his travels, Greaves describes himself as 'observing buildings, pictures, statues and antiquities'.

As a reader of the travel literature of his time with a replete library at home, Wren is likely to have seen images of some of the key buildings of the East at a young age. In 1677, he was sent a description of Hagia Sophia by Thomas Smith, a fellow of the Royal Society who had lived in Constantinople for two years. As noted in Chapter 1, Wren also benefited from drawings brought back from Constantinople by his friend John Chardin, which enabled him to sketch out his own versions of the ground plan and cross section of Hagia Sophia's dome. Correspondence also shows that he consulted merchant friends about dome construction methods used at Smyrna and at Constantinople, asking them about how lead was attached to domes.

Wren never talked about 'structural' problems, only about 'geometrical' solutions—geometry for him held the answer to all structural challenges. In collaboration with his friend Robert Hooke, he devised techniques that deflected the weight and tension of a dome so that it would be self-supporting, concluding that a 'cubico-paraboloid conoid' would solve all architectural problems to do with arches and butments.[33]

In the final dome of St Paul's, the inner brick cone structure supports the 70-foot stone lantern, which weighs a massive 850 tonnes. The outer dome is held in place by a light timber frame to give the profile, while the inner dome conceals the brick cone from inside the cathedral. The cone supporting the outer dome has a small oculus while the inner dome has a much larger oculus. It is the first triple dome structure anywhere on the planet and was the tallest building in London till 1963. All the practical workings are concealed from view, and the weight of all three shells is borne by buttresses hidden behind decorative screen walls. The hidden buttressing is another technique borrowed from Sinan, who used it to great effect at the Süleymaniye Mosque, where he masked the north–south buttresses, which supported the enormous porphyry monoliths holding up the dome, by incorporating them into the walls of the building, half inside and half outside. He then disguised the projecting parts by building colonnaded galleries on top of them, single storey inside, double storey outside. Another similarity was the viewing platform; Sinan provided access to a viewing terrace via the doorways of the southern minarets and from the doors of the unique 'small upper domes' that top the buttresses. In other words, he turned the buttresses, formerly considered an eyesore, into a virtue. Wren likewise provided access to his dome, first to the 'Whispering Gallery' inside the dome, 257 steps up from the cathedral floor, then to the Stone Gallery, the circular outdoor balustrade viewpoint at 376 steps, and finally to the Golden Gallery right at the top by the lantern at 528 steps, from which there are panoramic views all over London.

Approaching the age of seventy-six, Wren was too old to climb all the stairs to place the final stone on top of the lantern in the 'topping out' ceremony at St Paul's in 1708, so this was done by his son, together with the son of Edward Strong, Wren's master mason, who had followed in his father's footsteps as a mason and had himself built the lantern at St Paul's. Across both Europe and the Middle East, crafts tended to be passed from father to son. In 1691 Wren had joined the fraternity of London Speculative Freemasons, and in her biography of Wren, Lisa Jardine comments that the 'topping out' ceremony may even have included Masonic rituals.[34]

Like Sinan, Wren had a great deal of respect for his craftsmen and the guilds and clubs they formed in order to protect themselves. When his master carpenter, Richard Jennings, was accused of 'corrupt practices' and members of the St Paul's Commission called for his dismissal, Wren simply re-employed him under a sub-contract.[35] There was no question of sacking someone of Jennings's calibre; he had been responsible for erecting the wooden scaffolding frame against which the brick cone inside the dome was built, and whose precision in the centring had been so essential for the entire construction of the structurally complex triple-layered dome.

Wren was one of many famous people (including Admiral Lord Nelson, J.M.W. Turner, Lord Leighton, Florence Nightingale and Henry Moore) buried in the crypt of St Paul's—he himself disliked this practice, as it caused a disturbance of the foundations whenever someone died, and instead preferred burials outside cities in purpose-built cemeteries. His son Christopher wrote the epitaph: '*Lector, si monumentum requiris, circumspice.*' (Reader, if you seek a monument, look around.)

In his autobiography, Sinan wrote:

I resolved to become chief architect
To leave monuments in this world with my perfection.
I used to say, may God see me worthy
Of building a soaring sanctuary for Him.[36]

Sinan was buried in his own tomb in a corner of the Süleymaniye complex in Istanbul, a unique privilege acknowledging his status. Carved into the stone above the iron-grilled prayer window of the tomb, alongside its own public drinking fountain, facing out to the street and designed to be read by all passers-by, is the following inscription in Ottoman Turkish:

O you, who settle for a day or two in life's palace,
The world is not a place of repose for man.
Becoming the architect of Süleyman Khan, this distinguished man
Built him a Friday mosque that is a sign of the highest paradise.
With the sultan's orders he exerted great effort on water channels,
Like Hızır, he made the water of life flow to the people.[37]

[Hızır, or Khidr in Arabic, is a miracle-working saint, discoverer of the fountain of life. Sinan held two jobs together, chief architect and chief water engineer, more than doubling the water supply of Istanbul.]

Sinan's biographer, Sai Mustafa Çelebi, wrote that Süleyman once said of him:

If a person reaches mastery in his art,
The Gateway to Felicity opens up for him.
Thanks be to the all-forgiving God that,
He has given us such a perfect man.[38]

The perfect man (Turkish *insan kamil*) is the highest peak of spiritual station attainable by a human.

According to Islamic beliefs, the purpose of architecture was to create images of paradise on earth. Sinan himself wrote: 'with God's help, the righteous and pious architect-engineer may find divine guidance for the immortality of his work.'[39]

The two men, mentally and physically active into their nineties, both viewed themselves—and were in turn viewed by others—as possessed of God-given genius, 'blessed architects', instruments of God, acting out the wishes of their masters.

English architect and architectural historian Walter H. Godfrey (1881–1961) expressed it well when he said: 'The architect—the super-artificer—must possess an unusual type of mind, an insight into the potentialities of a hundred crafts, and he needs, more than any technical skill, the power of absorbing what is essential from each of these.'[40]

Both Wren and Sinan instinctively strove towards a seamless union of function and form, always looking for more. Sinan incorporated environmentally friendly features into his mosques in a way that still strikes us as ingenious today. At the Süleymaniye he designed the interior space so that the soot from thousands of candles and oil lamps would be funnelled by air circulation into a filter room before being released into the city. The collected soot was in turn channelled into a water fountain, where it was mixed and stirred to produce high-quality ink for calligraphy. The ink had natural insect repellent qualities, which protected the manuscripts and prolonged their life. It was recycling perfection, with sixteenth-century flair. Wren had no thoughts of recycling, but did intend St Paul's to be of dual purpose—cathedral and observatory. He designed the southwest tower to hold a giant telescope during the lengthy construction period so that a talented young astronomer might make scientific observations till the roof was put on. In the event the telescope, at 123 feet long, was found to be too long for the purpose, so the scheme was dropped, but the idea shows how Wren always thought creatively about maximising all possibilities. However 'divinely inspired' they may have been, both men also had their feet firmly on the ground.

9

THE REVIVALS

Neo-Gothic, Neo-Saracenic, Neo-Moorish (1717–2026)

The era of the Grand Tour, a rite of passage undertaken by wealthy young gentlemen to round off their education and explore the roots of Western civilisation, began in the 1660s, peaked in the eighteenth century and petered out in the 1840s when new rail and steamship transport brought Thomas Cook and the era of mass tourism. While many travellers were simply rich aristocrats enjoying themselves in European cities like Venice and Rome, others were highly educated multi-disciplinary scholars who travelled further east and wrote up accounts of their travels, often full of sketches, describing the cultures, customs and building styles they had encountered.

The study of Arabic also peaked across Europe in 1650, resulting in much previously unknown or forgotten knowledge finding its way back to the great European capitals. Architects were especially influenced by these new sources of inspiration and were endlessly curious about different techniques used in far corners of the globe. John Vanbrugh, the designer of Blenheim Palace, was inspired by a spell in India as an employee of the East India Company, and while Wren himself never travelled beyond France, he avidly read the ever-expanding specialist travel literature brought back by luminaries like Edward Pococke.

Since travel in Ottoman times was relatively safe, if you had the right connections and introductions, travel to the East continued to be popular throughout the eighteenth and nineteenth centuries. Among those whose trips, written accounts and drawings made a lasting impression on European tastes of the time were Robert Wood (1717–71), classical scholar, civil servant and politician, and James Dawkins (1722–57), a wealthy young Oxford scholar. They travelled to Palmyra together in 1750–1. Their detailed drawings of the ruins of Palmyra and Baalbek were published in 1753 and 1757 in English and in French, helping to stimulate the Neo-classical revival that was already sweeping across Europe and of which Wren himself was one of the earliest proponents.[1] Robert Adam, one of the most successful and fashionable architects in Britain and architect of the king's works from 1761 to 1769, developed the 'Adam style' based on his studies of antiquity. He designed the Sunburst Ceiling of the drawing room at Osterley Park, west London, a clear copy of the ceiling of the cella of the Temple of Bel in Palmyra, blown up by ISIS in 2015.

Cumulatively, these influences from abroad played a part in stimulating the period of revivals in European architecture. The Romantic era was also in full swing between 1800 and 1850 throughout Europe, and poets like Wordsworth, Chateaubriand and Goethe began to glorify nature and the past, partly in reaction to the Industrial Revolution and partly in reaction to the rationalism and classicism of the Enlightenment. Highly respected eighteenth-century French architect Jacques-François Blondel (1705–74) saw the influence of Arab/Islamic architecture on the European Gothic cathedrals clearly, writing in his *Cours d'Architecture* (1771–7) of 'the ingenious structures of the Arabs', but both Chateaubriand and Goethe fiercely resisted any suggestion of an Eastern origin, insisting that the source of Gothic was their own forests, setting in motion a literary trend where the Gothic cathedral took on a mystic-religious aspect as a 'forest of symbols'. Chateaubriand's *Le Génie du Christianisme* (1802) celebrated what he saw as the exclusively Christian origins of the French nation and its art, especially the Gothic cathedral built by 'nos pères' (our fathers). The overall result was an environment receptive to nostalgia for, and renewed interest in, an idealised medievalism.

Neo-Gothic

Known as Neo-Gothic, the revival began in England as early as the mid-1700s. Horace Walpole's newly restored Strawberry Hill House (1749) in west London is often seen as the revival's earliest example, with its imitation fan vaulting in the 'Gothick Long Gallery'. The style spread throughout England and its colonies, even reaching the United States. Art historian Kenneth Clark wrote that Gothic revival 'changed the face of England, building and restoring churches all over the countryside, and filling our towns with Gothic banks and grocers, Gothic lodging houses and insurance companies, Gothic everything from a town hall to a slum public house.'[2] Thanks to the influence of one Gothic revivalist par excellence, Augustus Welby Northmore Pugin (1812–52), it even spread to furniture, door knobs, and every household item imaginable. The illustrated catalogue for the 1851 Great Exhibition was full of Gothic detailing, and by then Gothic traceries and niches could even be inexpensively recreated on wallpaper. Gothic, it seemed, was suddenly everywhere.

Augustus Pugin

An only child brought up in a semi-itinerant fashion, Augustus Pugin did not attend school and instead accompanied his parents round the country whilst his French draftsman father toured the Gothic cathedrals of England, sketching both exteriors and interiors. Pugin drew his own Gothic cathedral sketch aged just nine. His first love was Lincoln Cathedral, where he was mesmerised by the pointed arches, the intricate profusion of the sculpted natural details and the flying buttresses. The soaring interior with its elegant vaulting made him feel as if the heavy stone had been somehow freed from gravity. His passion deepened further when the family toured northern France with his father's drawing school pupils and he laid eyes on Rouen Cathedral. His father taught his pupils they needed to touch the buildings, to connect with them, to feel the stone. At one small Gothic church in France, Pugin's father even knocked a hole in the vaulted ceiling and lowered his pupils down through it one by one, so that they could understand that the decorated ribs were structural elements and that what lay between was simply infill.[3] Pugin grew up imbued with Gothic, taking on his father's enthusiasm and admiration for it as a style that represented the honest hard work of devoted craftsmen. Medieval Gothic came to represent for him a moral vision of how life should be lived.

The opposite of his vision, however, was now on the throne, in the form of the dilettante hedonist prince regent, later George IV, whose favourite architect was the classicist John Nash. Under George IV, classical 'abominations' like Buckingham Palace and the British Museum were designed. Pugin felt these buildings were all for show on the outside, with their fake pillars holding nothing up and their stucco-fronted terraces mimicking stonework but concealing mean brick-built houses that were just one room deep. George also commissioned Nash to build the eccentric Neo-Saracenic/Neo-Mughal Royal Pavilion in Brighton between 1815 and 1822, a seaside pleasure palace topped with onion domes and minaret chimneys, in the exotic Indo-Saracenic style that was prevalent in India for most of the nineteenth century, based on a mix of Mughal and Islamic architecture. For Pugin, the Brighton Pavilion was the embodiment of debauchery and moral decay, and worse still, his father had been commissioned by Nash to paint a series of illustrations of it.

The only other example of Neo-Mughal architecture in Britain is Sezincote House in Gloucestershire, commissioned in 1805 by an employee of the East India Company on his return from Bengal.[4] It is a one-off fantasy creation in red stone, thought to have been dyed to mimic the typical Mughal red sandstone, with an orangery fronted by pointed arch windows in a fan shape and crowned with a green copper onion dome. It represented another form of romantic escapism from the realities of the Industrial Revolution, but Pugin would almost certainly not have approved, since its models were not Christian.

Pugin reacted violently against the Industrial Revolution, viewing it as a destroyer of society, an era that would reduce the labour force to no more than cogs in a wheel instead of proud craftsmen who had put their heart and soul into their creations of stone, wood or glass. The Gothic cathedrals, by contrast, he credited with a moral vision, whereby each craftsman was toiling

Brighton Royal Pavilion, East Sussex, UK, based on an oriental fantasy of onion domes and minaret chimneys derived from a mix of Mughal and Islamic architecture.

in his own corner of the cathedral, where he could leave his mark and gain satisfaction, compared to the factory workers of the Industrial Revolution, exploited by wealthy merchants and suffering shocking poverty in work-houses. The product of his anger was *Contrasts*, a book published in 1836 when he was just twenty-four. Within it he put his drawings of the facades of the classicists, like Buckingham Palace, the British Museum and St Paul's, side by side with the Gothic cathedrals of England and Europe.[5]

Pugin's parents and his first wife had all died in quick succession, leaving him alone in the world with only his baby daughter. His response was to convert to Catholicism, a reaction against what he felt to be the frigid Scottish Presbyterianism of his mother, and then to devote the rest of his short life to attacking the cold-fronted symmetry of Neo-classicism and championing the warm, energetic, physical beauty of medieval Gothic. He also treasured his relationship with his master mason, greatly valuing his skill, and wherever possible would use his own craftsmen. On one occasion when Pugin was forced to use a different mason, a belfry collapsed. He abhorred shoddy workmanship and the use of poor materials. For a church, everything had to be the best possible quality, since the creation of the church itself represented an act of worship. God inspired his every act, earning him the epithet 'God's architect'. Pugin believed that Gothic architecture was the product of a purer, more moral society, and in his second publication he boldly claimed that Gothic was the true Christian architecture. 'The pointed arch was produced by the Catholic faith,' he wrote.[6]

Pugin looked back to the medieval age but no further, so he had not the slightest notion that his pointed arches, detailed foliage, trefoil arches, ogival arches, vaulting, and decoration focusing on structural elements were all traceable back to the Arab and Islamic world—to what he would have called 'the Saracens'.

For Pugin, architecture was imbued with morality, and in his view Gothic was honest. He loved the physicality of the stone and felt that it was important to touch it and feel it. Every surface that was structural could be decorated, and Pugin loved the sheer exuberance and energy of the construction. In all these reactions, it is curious to think he was responding to exactly what the original creators of these Gothic details—the early Muslims—also loved about them. These were structures built by faith, and each craftsman would work with diligence on his creation as if it were an act of devotion. A metalworker in Damascus told me in 2010 that he would spend six months working on a single ewer, considering it an act of worship.

Pugin's own house, The Grange in Ramsgate, shows us more similarities in mentality and approach, for he designed it from the inside out. It creates a centripetal space where each room spins off from the other, no symmetry, like an organic creation of the individual. His mind would have been in total harmony with a Muslim boat-builder (Pugin did indeed do some sailing) or master architect, who saw their creations as products of their faith, expressions of their union with God. Pugin was not motivated by money or reputation, which was just as well, since he was airbrushed out of the picture and died largely unknown and unrecognised.

When the Seljuk minaret of the Great Mosque of Aleppo [left] suddenly collapsed during a fierce exchange of crossfire in 2013, I described the event as comparable to the loss of 'Big Ben' [right] from the London skyline. As well as being icons of their respective cities, the two square towers share other features. They each rise through four sections, becoming more ornate as they reach the top, and both are heavily decorated with trefoil, ogee and multifoil arches.

Thanks to Pugin's Tudor Gothic designs, Charles Barry, a respected architect aged forty-one, won the competition out of a total of ninety-seven entries to rebuild the Houses of Parliament after its 1834 fire. Pugin's Catholicism meant he was treated with suspicion, so his designs had to be submitted via Barry to get past the Royal Commission. Barry was given all the credit for the prestigious commission and most of the money, receiving £25,000 while Pugin got just £800.[7]

After a period confined to Bedlam, the notorious 'lunatic asylum', Pugin would die at the age of forty, worn out and bankrupt from building his private project, the St Augustine's Church alongside The Grange. But before Pugin's death, Barry had come to Ramsgate to ask him for one final favour: to design the Elizabeth Tower on the Houses of Parliament. Pugin, severely ill and already suffering from mental illness, produced one last flourish—the tower we now know as Big Ben (more strictly the name for the clock's bell), an emblem of Britain's parliamentary democracy. Pugin himself wrote of it: 'I never worked so hard in my life for Mr Barry for tomorrow I render all the designs for finishing his bell tower & it is beautiful'.[8]

For Pugin this was Neo-Gothic perfection, with none of Barry's classical 'Grecian' input at all. The Elizabeth Tower stands at 96 metres tall, twice the height of Aleppo's now collapsed Seljuk minaret built 750 years earlier (1090) under the Seljuk sultan Tutush, yet to the trained eye there are clear parallels. Each is a square tower with the main shaft composed of four distinct registers or sections, becoming more decorated as it reaches the top. The uppermost section then slightly overhangs the four registers, before continuing upwards in ever greater decorative detailing. Both towers are adorned in trefoil arches, and the ogee arch that sits at the uppermost section of Big Ben appears in the corner arches of the uppermost section of the Aleppo Seljuk minaret. Ross Burns calls the latter 'one of the first notable examples of a growing sense of assured style in Syrian Islamic architecture, heralding the developments of the Ayyubid and Mameluke periods in the next two centuries.'[9] Ernst Herzfeld described it as 'the principal monument of medieval Syria.'[10]

In a BBC Four documentary about Pugin, broadcast in 2012, art historian Richard Taylor gives a description of 'Pugin's Clock Tower':

It rises up from the ground in this stately rhythm, higher and higher, before you reach the clock face, picked out as a giant rose, its petals fringed with gold. Medieval windows above that, and then it hits the grey slate roof, its greyness relieved by those delicate little windows again picked out in gold leaf. And then rises up again in a great jet of gold to the higher roof that curves gracefully upwards to a spire with a crown and flowers and a cross. It's elegant and grand and has fairytale qualities.[11]

Alongside St Paul's at the other end of the city, Big Ben is London's other most iconic building—but what a contrast: one religious classicism, the other secular Gothic. They represent two sides of Britain's national identity—some might even say a split personality.

For his part, Pugin's partner Charles Barry had inherited enough money at the age of twenty-two to go on a Grand Tour for a full three years (1817–20), during which time he had sketched antiquities in the Louvre and the Vatican Museum. He then travelled on to Smyrna and Constantinople, where he much admired Hagia Sophia, and continued south to the classical ruins of Pergamon, Troy and Ephesus. He went on to Beirut, Baalbek, Damascus, Palmyra and Homs in Syria, then into Palestine, where he saw Jerusalem—including the Dome of the Rock and the Church of the Holy Sepulchre—followed by Jerash, Cairo and the Pyramids. During this time he produced over 500 sketches. On the return journey, he set sail from (Libyan) Tripoli to Cyprus, Rhodes, Malta, Sicily and Italy, where he particularly fell for Venetian Gothic and the Italianate architecture of Florence. Returning aged twenty-five, he would already have seen all the major classical sites of the eastern Mediterranean, along with the major mosques of the Ottoman Empire, including those of Sinan, dominating the skyline of Constantinople. In Cairo he would have seen the Fatimid and Mamluk mosques and the City of the Dead.

In his architecture, Barry produced a synthesis of the classical and Eastern styles to which he had been exposed as a young man, exactly as he had found at Venice. Aerial photos of the Houses of Parliament show that they are a unique synthesis of classical symmetry with Perpendicular Gothic pointed windows, trefoil arches, finials, traceries, vaulted ceilings and carved stone detailing. It is all straight lines with elaborate decorative ornamentation, as Pugin himself remarked to Barry when construction neared completion, before the addition of Big Ben: 'All Grecian, sir; Tudor details on a classic body.' By the word Tudor, Pugin is referring to pointed Gothic arches that were flatter, since they had first been popularised under the Tudors. Like most Europeans, Barry had little awareness of the Arab and Islamic character of what he was adopting.[12] The Tudor arch is the same as the four-centred arch, an elegant stylised evolution of the pointed arch first developed under the Abbasids in Iraq. This type of arch (also known as an ogee arch) also formed the mainstay of the distinctive Indo-Islamic architecture of the Mughals throughout the sixteenth, seventeenth and eighteenth centuries, finding its apogee at the Taj Mahal, voted one of the New Seven Wonders of the World in 2007.

By the time the construction of the Houses of Parliament, complete with 1,100 rooms, was finished in 1870, both Pugin and Barry were long dead. With delays and budget overruns, it had taken thirty years, and the final judgement was mixed. While Tsar Nicholas I of Russia called it 'a dream in stone', William Richard Hamilton, secretary to Lord Elgin during the acquisition of the Marbles, published a pamphlet decrying the fact that 'Gothic barbarism' had won out over 'the masterful designs of Ancient Greece and Rome.'

The Gothic revival in England was not just a romantic movement—it also had political drivers, once senior clerics in the High Church movement promoted it as a reaction against the rise of Evangelical Christianity. Thanks to its appearance in the Houses of Parliament, Gothic now represented, quite literally, the 'pillars of the establishment' and became associated with monarchism and conservatism. Gothic revival architecture was the most popular and longest-lived of the many revival styles of architecture, spawning copies all across the world. The Parliament Hill building in Ottawa, Canada's seat of government, is inspired by London's Houses of Parliament, as is Hungary's Parliament Building in Budapest on the banks of the Danube. Even in Australia there is a series of churches designed by Pugin after he met the first Catholic bishop of New South Wales at the official opening of his perfect Gothic church of St Giles' at Cheadle. The Australian vision of what a church should look like is still a Gothic building with pointed windows and arches, and even in outback towns with tiny churches of corrugated iron, Pugin's influence is clear to see. The United States has more architecture in the style of the Gothic revival in its universities, colleges and schools than any other country, and the style only died out in the early to mid-twentieth century, when modern materials like steel and glass began to take over. Pugin's revolutionary approach, however, in thinking of the user first, not of the outward look of the building, continues to inspire modern architects like Norman Foster and remains at the forefront of their work today. Thanks to the Gothic revival that he was so instrumental in inspiring, Gothic cathedrals can now be found all over the world. One of the biggest of them all is the Anglican cathedral of St John the Divine in New York, begun in 1892, sometimes nicknamed St John the Unfinished.

John Ruskin

The other great figure whose work was highly influential in stimulating the Gothic revival was John Ruskin (1819–1900), whose *Stones of Venice* (1851) was discussed in Chapter 7. Ruskin was openly hostile to Pugin, and, because he outlived him by fifty years, had plenty of time to dismiss Pugin's reputation and abilities, calling him 'one of the smallest possible or conceivable architects'. Ruskin was an Evangelical Christian, and his distaste for Pugin might have had its roots in Pugin's intense Catholicism. Yet, perversely, both men believed that Gothic was 'the true Catholic style'.

As many have observed, there seems to be an inherent contradiction in Ruskin's views, as expressed in *The Stones of Venice*, between his lauding of Gothic as the great embodiment of British and northern European identity, and his dismissal of the Arab Islamic world, whose architecture he so admires in Venice, as a place of languid indolence.[13] He makes abundantly clear that he has a low opinion of 'the Arab temper', yet as Daryl Ogden expresses it well: 'Ironically, in making clear his reverence for Venetian Gothic, Ruskin unravels the coherent Gothic self that he works so hard to wind together out of the disparate national strands of Northern European identity which he calls upon in "The Nature of Gothic".'[14]

The Cathedral of St John the Divine in New York City was started in 1892. Despite only being two-thirds complete, it is still the largest Protestant cathedral in the world.

Ruskin readily acknowledges the Arab influence on Venice, his 'Paradise of Cities', to the point where he even merges the Arab and Byzantine identities:

> During the ninth, tenth, and eleventh centuries, the architecture of Venice seems to have been formed on the same model, and is almost identical with that of Cairo under the caliphs, it being quite immaterial whether the reader chooses to call both Byzantine or both Arabic; the workmen being certainly

Byzantine, but forced to the invention of new forms by their Arabian masters, and bringing these forms into use in whatever other parts of the world they were employed.[15]

Yet the idea that the workmen might themselves have been Arab, or at the very least would certainly have learnt their craft from Arabs in Cairo, is something Ruskin, imbued with the characteristic imperialist mindset of the times, could never have contemplated.

Forming the central chapter in *The Stones of Venice*, Ruskin's 'The Nature of Gothic' is the most quoted piece of prose he ever wrote, his most influential work as the leading English art critic of the Victorian era. He was well aware of its influence himself, even complaining in a letter to the *Pall Mall Gazette* in 1872:

> I have had indirect influence on nearly every cheap villa-builder between this [Denmark Hill] and Bromley; and there is scarcely a public house near the Crystal Palace but sells its gins and bitters under pseudo-Venetian capitals copied from the Church of the Madonna of Health or of Miracles. And one of my principal notions for leaving my present house is that it is surrounded everywhere by the accursed Frankenstein monsters of my own making.[16]

The irony of the situation is summed up well by Ogden again, writing 125 years later:

> In the latter half of the nineteenth century, a period that witnessed the relentless acceleration of England's imperialism, particularly in what the Victorians called the Near East and over territory historically occupied by Arabs (especially Egypt), English architects and builders partially reshaped imperial Britain into an Orientalized Italy. Just as in Medieval Venice, Arab styles proliferated … The erstwhile arch-imperialist Ruskin begrudgingly played an unintentional part not only in bringing about the Orientalization of English architecture but also of Orientalizing the face of imperial England itself.[17]

Leighton House was specially commissioned by the painter Frederic Leighton as his London home. The Arab Hall shown here, its walls covered in original Damascus tiles of the 1500s, is often used in film sets and is open to the public as an art museum.

Ruskin went on to be appointed the first Slade professor of fine art at Oxford in 1869.

Like Pugin, Ruskin saw in medieval Gothic cathedrals a pure faith, an expression of the organic relationship between the artisan, his guild, his community, and the natural environment, and, ultimately, between the individual and God. He had a deep reverence for the way Gothic architecture reflected nature and natural forms. Like Pugin, he dismissed classical architecture as cold and dishonest, associating it with the demoralising effects of the Industrial Revolution. In his championing of nature, its beauty and its virtues, Ruskin has sometimes been viewed as the forerunner of environmentalism, the first 'Green'. His influence heralded the English Garden Cities movement of the twentieth century and the principles of the Green Belt.[18]

The Gothic revival produced other important related movements, such as William Morris's Arts and Crafts Movement, which began in Britain and flourished in Europe and North America from around 1880 to 1920. Morris acquired a textile factory and mill on the River Wandle in south London on what had been the site of the medieval Merton Abbey, repurposing the Gothic buildings and producing designs like 'Strawberry Thief' and 'Seaweed', which remain popular today in curtains, quilt covers, cushions, place mats and napkins. Inspired by the Neo-Gothic ideas of Pugin and Ruskin, for Morris medieval values and craftsmanship were seen as a positive way of resisting industrialisation. He grew dye plants in the abbey gardens and rinsed his fabrics in the river water. The overwhelming use of foliage, flowers and fruit in the twisting, entangled designs is immediately recognisable to the trained eye as Islamic in origin, synthesised once more into a new and distinctive style. Morris acknowledged the source of his inspiration as the Middle East, especially Iran: 'To us pattern designers Persia has become a holy land, for there in the process of time our art was perfected, and thence above all places it spread to cover for a while the world, east and west.'

Tile-maker and stained glass designer William de Morgan also moved his business to Merton Abbey, reproducing the fourteenth-century 'lustreware' techniques of Muslim craftsmen, inspired by Islamic and medieval patterns. His tiles also decorate the walls of Leighton House in London's Holland Park with its famous Arab Hall, a showcase of original sixteenth-century Damascus tiles procured on behalf of the painter Lord Frederic Leighton (1830–96).

Avowedly influenced by Islamic designs was another contemporary architect and designer, English-born Welshman Owen Jones (1809–74), who travelled on his Grand Tour to Cairo and Constantinople, before reaching Granada. There he spent six months, aged twenty-five, drawing detailed sketches of the Alhambra, acquiring a fascination with geometry, colour theory and the use of abstraction in decorative ornament. He was responsible for the interior design and layout of the great Crystal Palace in Hyde Park—made in cast iron and plate glass—that housed the 1851 Great Exhibition organised by Prince Albert, and for its subsequent incarnation when it was moved and reassembled in Sydenham. Jones went on to become a highly influential design theorist and a pivotal figure in setting up the South

Kensington Museum, which later became the Victoria and Albert Museum. His seminal work *The Grammar of Ornament* (1856) is still used as a sourcebook in design schools internationally.

Eugène Viollet-le-Duc

France was slower to get going than England in its Gothic Revival, but its key figure appeared in the form of Eugène Viollet-le-Duc (1814–79), a contemporary to both Pugin and Ruskin. He was an aspiring architect with no formal training who became, thanks to his father's high government connections and his own keen interest in Gothic, the country's leading restorer of Gothic cathedrals and churches. It was a time when many Gothic monuments had been damaged or abandoned during the French Revolution in the 1790s, associated as they were with the extreme corruption of the Catholic Church and the monarchy. In Paris alone, of its 300 churches in the sixteenth century, only ninety-seven were still standing in 1800. Many stones were carted off and reused in secular building projects. Repairs were therefore urgently needed, as the structures were often seriously weakened. Viollet-le-Duc's first project, when he was just twenty-four years old, was the restoration, as near as possible to its original state, of Vézelay Abbey, a twelfth-century Benedictine monastery.

Up to that point, no one had any idea how the medieval masons and craftsmen had built the huge cathedrals in the first place. There were no records, no studies and no schools of restoration. Without the benefit of original building plans, Viollet-le-Duc had to work out for himself how the building had held together and thus how to make it stable again. He began by lightening the roof, changing the shape of the vaults slightly, and sharpening the points of the arches to stabilise the walls.

Viollet-le-Duc's explanations about the structure of Gothic buildings are highly controversial even today, and there is still no consensus about how Gothic buildings stand up. He toured France widely, making detailed drawings of Gothic monuments, accompanied by extensive accounts of each site, which were later turned into books that made his reputation as the most prominent academic scholar on French medieval architecture.

In 1844, aged just thirty, he won a competition for the restoration of Notre-Dame de Paris. Like so many other Gothic churches, it had been badly damaged by angry mobs and revolutionaries, who plundered its interior treasures, declaring it wasn't a church at all, and smashing or beheading the statues of the biblical kings of Judah above the portals of the west facade. His mentor, Prosper Mérimée, noted historian and inspector-general of French historical monuments from 1833 to 1852, advised extreme caution: 'In such a project, one cannot act with too much prudence or discretion … A restoration may be more disastrous for a monument than the ravages of centuries.'[19]

Viollet-le-Duc heeded the advice. He removed much of the later Neo-classical decoration and reinstated over the transept the original medieval spire and bell tower, which had been removed in 1786 because it was

Heavily damaged by angry mobs during the French Revolution, Notre-Dame de Paris was carefully restored to its full Gothic splendour by Gothic revivalist Viollet-le-Duc. He reinstated the original medieval spire known as La Flèche, which collapsed during the April 2019 fire.

unstable in the wind. This was known as La Flèche, and it collapsed and fell through the blazing roof in the 15 April 2019 fire.

Viollet-le-Duc established a workshop in which masons and sculptors carved new statues of saints, gargoyles, chimeras and other Gothic decorative stonework, working from his own drawings of similar cathedrals of the same period. He designed stained glass in the Gothic grisaille patterns to replace the destroyed medieval windows of the ground floor, along with a new Gothic treasury. Some of the most precious stained glass had been dismantled and saved by the clergy before the Revolution, giving him originals to follow, and it is these that can still be viewed in the Louvre and the Victoria and Albert Museum. He rebuilt the sacristy and had new bells recast to replace the ones which had been melted down to make cannons in the Revolution.

The restoration took twenty-five years in total; while construction was in progress, Viollet-le-Duc also took on about twenty simultaneous smaller restorations commissions, including the Basilica of Saint-Denis, where Gothic had first begun in France. A different architect had already completed a restoration, but so badly that a rebuilt tower cracked and had to be demolished. Viollet-le-Duc was able to save the stones and concentrate on restoring the interior, including the original burial chamber of the kings of France. He went on to restore the cathedrals at Amiens (one of France's largest, built over several centuries) and at Clermont-Ferrand, and thanks to his efforts, Neo-Gothic became the accepted style for all church décor and furnishings across France.[20] He described his goal in restoration as being 'to save in each part of the monument its own character, and yet to make it so that the united parts don't conflict with each other; and that can be maintained in a state that is durable and simple.'[21]

Once the Notre-Dame restoration was complete, Viollet-le-Duc was criticised for going overboard with all these Gothic elements. Ruskin, meanwhile, disagreed with the principle of restoration *per se*, writing:

Neither the public, nor those who are responsible for the maintenance of public monuments, understand the true meaning of 'restoration'. It signifies the most complete destruction that an edifice can suffer; a destruction from which not a single vestige can be recovered; a destruction that comes from the false description of the thing destroyed. It is impossible, as impossible as it is to bring the dead back to life, to restore whatever might have been grand or beautiful in architecture. … the enterprise is a lie from the beginning to the end.[22]

Viollet-le-Duc's successor as restoration architect at Notre-Dame was Paul Abadie (1812–84), another devotee of medieval French monuments, whose design for a basilica on Montmartre beat twelve others and went on to become the striking white hilltop vision of Sacré-Coeur, the highest point in Paris after the Eiffel Tower. At the time of writing, following the fire at Notre-Dame in April 2019, it is the most visited church in France, a pilgrimage site where St Denys, first bishop of Paris, was beheaded. With its five domes and, according to its own website, modelled on Hagia Sophia and St Mark's in Venice, it could hardly be more different to the Gothic masterpiece

The Basilica of the Sacré-Coeur, Montmartre, Paris, France, completed in 1914, shows clear Islamic influences in its double domes, interior arcades of trefoil arches and blue and gold mosaics.

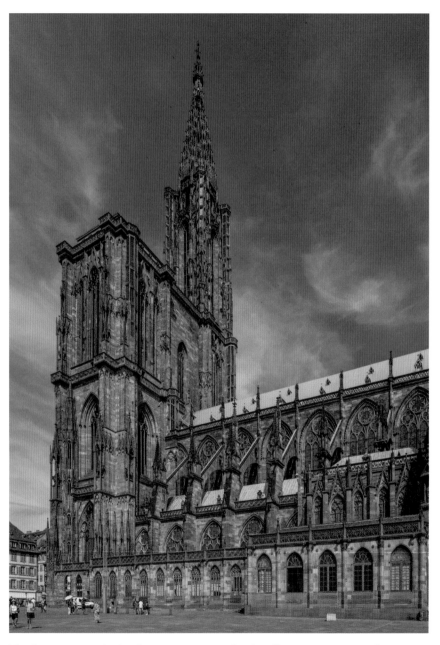

Thanks to its spire, the Strasbourg Münster is today the tallest extant structure dating from the Middle Ages anywhere in the world. For over 200 years it was the world's tallest building. Victor Hugo described it as 'a gigantic and delicate marvel'. Miraculously, though damaged, it survived the British and American bombing raids of 1944.

of Notre-Dame, yet it too shows Islamic influences in its double domes, its arcaded trefoil arches in its vast interior, and its blue and gold mosaics. Some have even seen similarities with the Taj Mahal.

Despite his critics, Viollet-le-Duc's reputation spread beyond the borders of France, and the German government invited him to comment on plans by a German architect to restore the roof and spire of Strasbourg Cathedral in a grandiose Romanesque style. It had been damaged by German artillery during the Franco-Prussian War but was now part of Germany. Viollet-le-Duc advised the Germans that such a restoration would be completely out of character. His advice was accepted and the church spire was restored to its original appearance.[23]

When criticised—as he was all his life by the academics at the famous École des Beaux-Arts in Paris, the leading architecture school of France—Viollet-le-Duc defended his decision to rebuild churches in the Gothic style. The École considered the Gothic style (rather like Wren) to be 'incoherent, disorderly, unintelligent, decadent and without taste', but Viollet-le-Duc rebutted:

> What we want, messieurs, is the return of an art which was born in our country … Leave to Rome what belongs to Rome, and to Athens what belongs to Athens. Rome didn't want our Gothic (and was perhaps the only one in Europe to reject it) and they were right, because when one has the good fortune to possess a national architecture, the best thing is to keep it.[24]

Like Pugin, he dismissed the symmetry of classical buildings as vain, considering it too concerned with outside appearance. Far more important in his view was concern for the individuals who would actually use a building. He went on:

> If you study for a moment a church of the thirteenth century, you see that all of the construction is carried out according to an invariable system. All the forces and the weights are thrust out to the exterior, a disposition which gives the interior the greatest open space possible. The flying buttresses and contreforts alone support the entire structure, and always have an aspect of

resistance, of force and stability which reassures the eye and the spirit; the vaults, built with materials that are easy to mount and to place at a great height, are combined in an easy manner that places the totality of their weight on the piles … all the parts of these constructions, independent of each other, even as they rely on each other, present an elasticity and a lightness needed in a building of such great dimensions. We can still see (and this is only found in Gothic architecture) that human proportions are the one fixed rule.[25]

This is the organic nature that Pugin and Ruskin also saw, the holistic quality of a Gothic building. Like Ruskin, Viollet-le-Duc loved nature, and as he grew older he spent more and more time writing about the Alps around Mont-Blanc, walking in the mountains, and advocating reforestation. For architectural inspiration, he also examined organic structures, such as leaves and animal skeletons. The wings of bats exerted a particular fascination.

In his later writings, Viollet-le-Duc drew conclusions from medieval architecture that he applied to modern architecture. He noted that it was sometimes necessary to employ an iron frame in restoration to avoid the danger of fires, as long as the new structure was not heavier than the original and kept the original balance of forces found in medieval structures:

The monuments of the Middle Ages were carefully calculated, and their organism is delicate. There is nothing in excess in their works, nothing useless. If you change one of the conditions of these organisms, you change all the others. Many people consider this a fault; for us, this is a quality which we too often neglect in our modern construction … Why should we build expensive walls 2 metres thick, if walls 50 centimetres thick [with reinforced supports] offer sufficient stability? In the structure of the Middle Ages, every portion of a work fulfilled a function and possessed an action.[26]

This consistency of view between Pugin, Ruskin and Viollet-le-Duc, the three key figures in the English and French nineteenth-century Gothic revival, is striking. All three were able to sense, through their intimate and personal exposure to these medieval Gothic buildings, their unique oneness, their unity of structure. It is as if they are somehow self-supporting, and if you tinker with one part, you will knock another part out of alignment somewhere else. This is the core concept at the heart of so many Islamic structures and creations, yet always backed up by highly accurate geometric and arithmetic measurements. It is exactly what Felix Arnold discovered when he analysed the mathematics of the space at the Cordoba Mezquita,[27] the ultimate Umayyad construction of tenth-century Moorish Spain, whose roots and inspiration are to be found in the original Umayyad constructions in Syria—the Dome of the Rock, the Damascus Umayyad Mosque and the Umayyad desert palaces—all built before the year 750 when their dynasty was snuffed out in Syria, only for the style to re-emerge irrepressibly in Spain and then to gradually make its way north in the eleventh and twelfth centuries in the shape of Europe's great medieval Gothic cathedrals like Notre-Dame.

Neo-Moorish

The Moorish revival reached the peak of its popularity in the mid-nineteenth century as part of the Romantic movement, which sparked a fascination with all things oriental and exotic. It was especially popular among Jews of Central

The restored New Synagogue of Berlin on Oranienburger Straße, Berlin, Germany.

Neo-Mudéjar became a popular style for housing and public buildings in Madrid around 1900, as seen in the 1931 Las Ventas bullring, with its arcades of horseshoe arches, double-colonnaded trefoil arches and unmistakeable merlon crenellations that could have been lifted straight off the Damascus Umayyad Mosque.

Sammezzano Castle, south of Florence in Tuscany, is one of the world's largest examples of Moorish revival residential architecture, each of its 365 rooms boasting unique Moorish decoration. It was in use as a luxury hotel till World War II but is today closed to the public, pending restoration.

Europe, for whom it represented a harking back to the Golden Age of Muslim Spain, when Jews were respected alongside Christians and Muslims throughout society at all levels. It therefore became the preferred choice for synagogue architecture, and throughout Europe synagogues were rebuilt in Neo-Moorish or Neo-Mudéjar styles. One of the most famous is in Berlin, the so-called New Synagogue, built in 1859–66, whose elaborate Moorish facade is modelled on the Alhambra. It was largely destroyed by British bombing in 1943, but the facade was rebuilt.

In Spain, Moorish revival architecture was also used in some new public buildings, such as the Gran Teatro Falla in Cádiz and the Plaza de España in Seville, built in 1928 for the Ibero-American World Fair Exposition of 1929. In Madrid, Neo-Mudéjar became a popular style for housing and public buildings around 1900; it was even used in the Las Ventas bullring, built in 1931. In Tuscany a wealthy Spanish nobleman built the Palazzo Sammezzano between 1853 and 1889, a fantasy palace in elaborate Moorish revival style.

In Bosnia, after the Austro-Hungarian occupation the new authorities decided to commission a series of Neo-Moorish public buildings in the hope of promoting a Bosnian national identity through 'Islamic architecture of European fantasy' that was neither Ottoman nor Slav. One example was the National and University Library of Bosnia and Herzegovina in Sarajevo, designed in pseudo-Moorish style with pointed arches. It was not, however, particularly successful, because the style had no previous connection to indigenous Bosnian architecture.

Antoni Gaudí (1852–1926)

Spain's greatest architect, Antoni Gaudí, like Pugin and Viollet-le-Duc before him, was a huge fan of Gothic architecture, admiring its organic qualities and its close connection with nature. Born in Reus, Catalonia, to a coppersmith father, he was the youngest of five children, of whom only three survived into adulthood. As a child Gaudí loved the outdoors, becoming a strict vegetarian in adolescence and later developing an interest in utopian socialism. He financed his degree course at the Barcelona Architecture School by working

Partially destroyed during the 1992 siege of Sarajevo, the National and University Library of Bosnia and Herzegovinawas designed in 1945 in elaborate pseudo-Moorish style, a misguided attempt to promote Bosnian national identity. As a strange hybrid fantasy with no connection to indigenous Ottoman or Slav architecture, it did not succeed.

as a draftsman for various local builders. On top of architecture, he also studied French, history, economics, philosophy and aesthetics, but achieved only average grades and sometimes even failed exams. Upon Gaudí's graduation in 1878, the director of the Architecture School is reported to have said: 'We have given this academic title either to a fool or a genius. Time will tell.'[28]

An instinctive improviser, Gaudí rarely drew plans for his buildings, preferring to work from a three-dimensional model which he translated into the living structure, conceptualising the detail and ornamentation as he went along. Like Pugin, he was sometimes called 'God's architect' because of his fervent Roman Catholic faith, which intensified throughout his life. Seven of his works were declared UNESCO World Heritage Sites between 1984 and 2005. His masterpiece, the Sagrada Família church in Barcelona (still incomplete nearly a century since Gaudí's death), is the most visited monument in Spain, described by American architecture critic Paul Goldberger as 'the most extraordinary personal interpretation of Gothic architecture since the Middle Ages'.

Gaudí's masterpiece, the Sagrada Família basilica in Barcelona, is an astonishing
visualisation of an organic building as act of worship. Gaudí was openly inspired
by Islamic architecture and its all-embracing, unifying connection to nature and God.

The theme of man entwined with nature and its creator is represented on many surfaces of the Sagrada Família, as here in this Nativity facade, which echoes the effusive foliage of medieval Gothic cathedral facades and the eighth-century eclectic ornamentation of Syrian Umayyad palaces. Like Islamic architects, Gaudí felt that God was to be found in the spatial uncertainties of a building, not in the precise formal perfection of classical facades.

Gaudí saw similarities between Gothic and Islamic styles in what he called their 'spatial uncertainty'.[29] Like so many Arab scientists before him, he found his main inspiration in nature, studying natural organic and anarchic geometric forms thoroughly with a view to finding ways of translating them into architecture. In his own words: 'Nothing is invented, for it's written in nature first. Those who look for the laws of Nature as a support for their new works collaborate with the creator.'[30]

Gaudí identified with and greatly admired the spirituality he observed in the infinite space encapsulated in Islamic art, its openness, unencumbered by barriers. He was deeply affected by Owen Jones's drawings of the Alhambra and also studied other Andalusian buildings, like the Cordoba Mezquita, where he experienced and then sought to recreate the feeling of being transported to another world through the total embrace of a building.

He intended the interior of the Sagrada Família to resemble a forest, with a set of tree-like inclined helicoidal columns dividing into branches, which in turn organically support a structure of intertwined hyperboloid vaults. He said:

> Gothic art is imperfect, only half resolved; it is a style created by the compasses, a formulaic industrial repetition. Its stability depends on constant propping up by the buttresses: it is a defective body held up on crutches. …
> The proof that Gothic works are of deficient plasticity is that they produce their greatest emotional effect when they are mutilated, covered in ivy and lit by the moon.[31]

Gaudí saw that the technology available to medieval Gothic architects had been wanting, but now, armed with new geometric knowledge and understanding, he determined to surpass them. Inspired by Islamic Moorish and Mudéjar styles, Gaudí perfected and went beyond Gothic to create a new architectural style, an utterly original synthesis. 'I am a geometrician, that is to say, I synthesise,' he said.[32] We might perhaps call it Hispano-Saracenic Gothic, the ultimate fusion of nature, geometry and religion. There is no perfect right angle to be seen anywhere in the Sagrada Família, inside or out. Gaudí himself said: 'There are no straight lines or sharp corners in nature. Therefore buildings must have no straight lines or sharp corners.'[33]

Nor is there anything flat in the interior of the Sagrada Família, and the surfaces are ever-changing, as in nature. Where Gothic (Islamic) vaults had their ribs, like leaves, Gaudí's new circular hyperboloid vaults had holes letting natural light in, allowing him to create the illusion of a starry sky, the whole achieved through highly complex geometry, using helicoidal shapes in the columns, together with cones and hyperboloids, which meant there was no need for buttressing and the structure would always be self-supporting.

The scale of the ambition is huge. Ultimately the finished building will have eighteen spires and hold 15,000 people and a choir of 1,000. Gaudí conducted both acoustic studies and light experiments; light and colour, unsurprisingly, were of fundamental importance to him as the key intangibles. He wanted the building to create a great symphony of its own colour and light that would be ever changing throughout the day as the sun moved across the sky. In his own words: 'Glory is light, light gives joy, and joy is the happiness of the spirit. … Architecture is the arrangement of light; sculpture is the play on light.'

For all its classical seriousness, Wren's St Paul's is also a celebration of the sun, symbolising the dawning of a new Copernican astronomical age. A golden sun is inlaid in the marble pavement at the centre of the cathedral beneath the dome (the traditional symbol for the sky-dome or heaven), Christ often traditionally being identified with Apollo, the sun god. The exact measurement from the cathedral floor to the top of the dome's cross is 365 feet, to reflect the astronomical year and the number of days it takes for the earth to rotate around the sun.

Like Wren, Gaudí is buried in the crypt of his masterpiece, but unlike Wren he died, tragically killed in a tram accident aged seventy-three, when the building was only 15 to 25 per cent finished. He had worked on the Sagrada Família for forty-three years, compared to Wren's thirty-six years on St Paul's, always knowing he would not live to see it completed.

Completion of the Sagrada Família, using Gaudí's 3D model and designs and funded by donations and the entry fees of visitors, is currently projected by 2026, the centenary of Gaudí's death. The team collaborating on the building is international and includes a Japanese artist creating designs in the gypsum workshop. The stone comes from all over the world—the UK, Germany, Spain, India, Brazil—and is hand-worked to achieve the final texture. There is only a 1-millimetre margin of error. In a short film made for *Time* magazine, the Spanish site construction manager, comparable to the medieval master mason, explained how he feels about his work: 'We aren't the kind of people that will end up in the history books, but inside ourselves, there is a part that is very proud to be here, to have contributed, and we are

This interior crossing and dome of the Sagrada Família was designed to resemble a forest, with a set of tree-like inclined heliocoidal columns dividing into branches, organically supporting intertwined hyperboloid vaults.

in the final stretch.'[34] When it is finished, in the words of the structural engineer in charge of construction, people will be able to go to the top of the 172.5-metre-tall Jesus Christ Tower, 'to feel what it might be like to be closer to God.'[35]

If Wren had been alive to see the Sagrada Família, he would surely have recognised all the same 'Saracen' qualities he wrote about so clearly in his 'Parentalia'—albeit at a far more advanced level, as befits a twenty- to twenty-first-century building. Through the giant circular jigsaw of this book, we have been unearthing Gaudí's backstory. For even his ideas, genius though he undoubtedly was, did not just emerge fully formed. Speed, indeed, was not his strong suit. When questioned why the pace of work was so slow, he is said to have replied: 'My client is not in a hurry.'[36]

10

ICONIC BUILDINGS OF EUROPE

A Gallery of Images with Key Influences

Key Architectural Features of Islamic / Middle Eastern Origin (chronological)

Twin towers flanking a monumental arched entrance

First seen in northwest Syria in the 'Dead Cities' in fifth- and sixth-century churches such as Qalb Lozeh, Deir Turmanin and the Church of Bissos at Ruweiha. It is the forerunner of the twin tower design further developed in Romanesque and then Gothic cathedrals across Europe, as at Notre-Dame and Westminster Abbey. Highly suited to pilgrimage churches.

Chevet (apse)

First seen in northwest Syria in the 'Dead Cities' in fifth-century churches such as Qalb Lozeh and at St Simeon's Basilica, the chevet is the semi-circular protruding wall at the eastern end of the church, often with elaborate stone-carved vegetal scrolling inside and out. The chevet became a typical feature of early Syrian church architecture from this point on, topped by a stone semi-circular dome, and developed into our semi-circular protruding apse in European churches, introduced into England from France by Henry III at Westminster Abbey.

Clerestory

First seen in religious architecture in northwest Syria in the 'Dead Cities' in fourth- and fifth-century churches such as Kharrab Shams and Qalb Lozeh, the clerestory is a set of smaller windows, separated by small elegant columns, rising above the arches running longitudinally along the central nave. Its purpose, apart from giving extra height to the nave, is to let in light from above, since it was too difficult, given the thickness of the walls, to create windows lower down. It became a common feature in Romanesque, Gothic and even later churches and cathedrals, as in St Paul's.

Bema

First seen in a Christian context in northwest Syria in the 'Dead Cities' in fourth-century churches such as Fafertin, Kharrab Shams and Barad cathedral, the *bema* is a slightly raised stone platform in the upper nave with seating for the clergy, arranged in a horseshoe-shaped bench. It passed into early church architecture from Jewish synagogues, where it was the raised area from which the rabbi delivered readings. In ancient Athens it was the orator's platform, and the word itself derives from the ancient Greek word meaning 'platform' or 'step'. In Syria in the fifth century it evolved further, as at Rusafa's pilgrim church of St Sergius, with more complex additional (hierarchical) layers of seating of the type with which Syrian Denys the Areopagite (so influential in the 'light' theories that shaped later Gothic architecture) would have been familiar when writing his *Celestial Hierarchy*. The liturgy and hymn singing was led from here, giving the origins of our chancel (choir and pulpit) in the same location, directly in front of the altar, as at Canterbury Cathedral.

Cloisters

First seen in a few isolated Syrian monasteries of the fifth century such as the convent of Saints Sergius and Bacchus at Umm al-Surab in what is today northern Jordan, not far from Dera'a and the southern Syrian border, an area known as the Hawran. Ground plans and 3D reconstructions at Saints Sergius and Bacchus using photogrammetric surveys have shown a square, highly symmetrical open-paved courtyard attached to the church, ringed with about twenty rooms laid out over two storeys and colonnaded on all sides. Toledo Cathedral (1226–1493) is built in High Gothic style, modelled on Bourges Cathedral in France, but took on Mudéjar influence in the cloister, which was formerly the mosque courtyard. Canterbury Cathedral and Westminster Abbey both have cloisters with ribbed vaulting, pointed arches and elaborate tracery.

Trefoil arch (sometimes also called lobed arch or cusped arch)

First seen in the Umayyad province of Syria-Palestine, where it appears inside the drum of the Dome of the Rock in Jerusalem, built by Caliph Abd al-Malik in 691–2, just above the drum windows, only visible from the inside of the shrine. More examples appear in the carved stucco work of the Umayyad desert palaces such as Khirbat al-Mafjar (Hisham's Palace) near Jericho, built by Abd al-Malik's son, Hisham, in around 740. It first appears in Europe in Umayyad Spain at the Cordoba Mezquita, built by the Umayyad prince Abd al-Rahman I in 785–6, and later became a defining feature of Gothic.

Pointed arch

First seen in monumental form in the Umayyad province of Syria–Palestine inside the Dome of the Rock in Jerusalem, in arches of the inner circle of the ambulatory arcade. Also seen with a *makhmous* (a fifth) angle at the Damascus Umayyad Mosque, built by Caliph Al-Walid in 706–15, it gradually became sharper and more pointed under the Abbasids during the late eighth and early ninth centuries. It moved to Europe via Spain and Sicily, becoming an essential feature of Gothic.

Merlons

A Mesopotamian, ziggurat-shaped decorative design to crown the walls on Babylonian temples, used at the early-eighth-century Damascus Umayyad

Mosque, then reused by the Umayyads of Spain on the late-eighth-century Cordoba Mezquita. The crenellated look became popular in later more delicate roof decorations, as at the Doge's Palace in Venice.

Horseshoe arch

First seen in slight horseshoe shape in Syria at the early-eighth-century Damascus Umayyad Mosque, then reused in a more developed and monumental double-arcaded form in Spain at the late-eighth-century Corboba Mezquita (also known as the 'Moorish' arch). It continued to be widely used in Spain in Mudéjar architecture.

Marble/stone window grilles

First seen in geometric lace form in the early-eighth-century Damascus Umayyad Mosque, then in Europe in the late-eighth-century Cordoba Mezquita. They were also later adopted at St Mark's in Venice, with similar geometric patterns.

Minaret/tower/spire

First seen in the early-eighth-century Damascus Umayyad Mosque, where the minarets were built on the foundations of the pre-existing Roman temple enclosure towers, one in each of the four corners. It was usually built in sections ('registers') and became more elaborate towards the top, the summit often crowned with a bulbous finial. The square shape was also almost certainly influenced by the towers of the fifth- and sixth-century Christian churches of Syria, but differed markedly in the style of its decoration, becoming much more effusive and elaborate than the more restrained Christian churches as it tapered upwards in registers. The shared purpose of minarets and spires was to proclaim religious power and to reach upwards as an emblem of faith. In England the very first spire was on the old Gothic St Paul's, and was finished in 1221.

Ribbed vaulting and cross vaults

Early example in stone seen in the palace porch at the Umayyad palace of Khirbat al-Mafjar (c. 740), and in the bath hall built of brick. The ruins of the palace can be visited today in the Occupied West Bank. Later developed by the Umayyads at the Corboba Mezquita in the tenth-century Villaviciosa Chapel dome. Its vaulting system is a masterpiece of practical geometry, never needing structural repair in its thousand-year existence. It is also the first time that decorative ornamentation performed a structural role. A 2015 survey concluded it represents one of the very oldest ribbed vaults ever built, a new type called the cross vault, which later spread via the churches of the pilgrimage route of Santiago de Compostela and further developed in the naves of Gothic cathedrals across Europe, reaching its peak in the fifteenth-century fan vaulting of King's College Chapel, Cambridge.

Medallion decorations

Early examples seen built into the facade of the palace gate tower in the decorations of Khirbat al-Mafjar, contained within a border and then placed within a shaped frame. This typical Umayyad design was subsequently transferred to Cordoba, as seen in the ivory medallion of the seated caliph (illustrated in Chapter 5) now on display in the Madinat al-Zahra Museum, before finding its way northwards into France where the subsequent Gothic cathedrals of Europe used the same styles in their later stained glass windows. A striking example can be seen on the facade of Westminster Abbey, called the Relief of Christ.

Double arcades

Early example seen in the double-arcaded panel found in the balustrades of the palace forecourt of Khirbat al-Mafjar. The panel is carved in plaster, with a lower arcade of nine arches supporting an upper one of eight arches. The upper arches span the supporting pillars of the lower arches, as indeed they do in the double-decker arcade at the caliph's palace in the Umayyad city of Anjar in modern Lebanon in the Beqaa Valley, as if in anticipation of the double arches of the Cordoba Mezquita. It is frequently used as a decorative feature in Romanesque and Gothic facades, as at Durham Cathedral and Notre-Dame.

Blind arch

First seen in Umayyad architecture on the entrance facades of desert palaces like Qasr al-Hair ash-Sharqi and Qasr al-Hair al-Gharbi in the mid-eighth century, then transferred to Umayyad Spain and used at the Cordoba Mezquita in the late eighth century. The blind arch frequently occurs as a decorative device in Romanesque and Gothic cathedrals, as at Durham and Canterbury.

Archivolts

Decorative mouldings running round the face of an arch, first seen at second-century Hatra (in modern Iraq), where radiating busts decorate the *iwan* arches. The Umayyads used them prolifically in the carved stucco and stone-work of their eighth-century desert palaces, as at the palace of Khirbat al-Mafjar near Jericho. The term is generally used to describe the features of medieval or Renaissance buildings in Europe, where archivolts are often decorated with sculpture, as in the archivolts on the west facade of Chartres Cathedral (1140–50). Used briefly by the Romans, they then died out till they were used again in Romanesque architecture, and elaborated further in Gothic, especially in the cathedrals. The basilica at Saint-Denis has them, in what is widely regarded as the first truly Gothic church.

Rose window

First seen as a high-placed oculus in a few early Syrian churches such as the cathedral at Brad (now collapsed) and at the Umayyad palace of Khirbat al-Mafjar, where it has been reconstructed and is composed of 106 pieces of stone, about 85 centimetres thick and carved on both sides to represent six interlaced ribbons forming a six-pointed star within a circle. From its high position within the pediment of the roof gable, its function was therefore likely to have been to provide an interesting pattern of light to the central audience room of the palace. The six-pointed star was common in Syria on fifth-to-seventh-century buildings, as was the rose with six petals, designs transferred to Europe by the many Syrian monks who settled in the Latin world, bringing their more advanced theological and artistic knowledge with them. There were more churches in Syria in the fifth and sixth centuries than any other Roman province. Both circular motifs, as well as the solar disc with twelve lines forming a spiral, were widely used in early religious settings as in the Visigothic church of Quintanilla de las Viñas. The Umayyad Cordoba Mezquita continued the tradition, with high circular coloured glass windows known as 'Sunrise' or 'Sun' windows, designed to look like coloured rays emanating from a central yellow sun. An early oculus appears in Europe on the Romanesque facade of San Pietro church in Spoleto, Umbria. It is unlikely to be a coincidence that a fifth century monk, Mar Isaac, arrived in Spoleto from Syria and built a monastery on the site where the church now stands. Rose windows became a key feature in Gothic churches, where they were similarly placed high up on main wall facades to let in light and colour, as at Notre-Dame and Chartres.

Twin windows divided by a slender column

First seen in the ninth-century Umayyad minaret known today as Alminar de San Juan in Cordoba and later adopted as a defining feature of Romanesque architecture in Catalonia and France, as at Notre-Dame.

Multifoil (poly-lobed) arch

First seen in the tenth-century extensions to the Cordoba Mezquita, the multifoil arch emerged as a further evolution of the trefoil arch, breaking the arch into an uneven number of five or more lobes, so that there is still always a centred lobe flanked by an equal number of lobes on each side. Widely used across Spain in Mudéjar architecture.

Intersecting/interlocking arches

First seen in the tenth-century extensions to the Cordoba Mezquita, inter-locking arches mark the location of the original eighth-century *mihrab* and the new *mihrab*. One important side effect of these arches is to create curves that are more pointed than any seen before. Interlocking arches also appear above the outer gates of the mosque on the west side. They went on to become a key feature in Romanesque and Gothic architecture, as at Durham Cathedral and Notre-Dame.

Ogee arch (also called keel arch, four-centred arch or Tudor arch)

Developed by the Abbasids and first used in their capital at Samarra in the ninth century. It appears in the eleventh-century Seljuk minaret (1090) of the Aleppo Umayyad Mosque (destroyed in 2013), from where it was exten-sively copied in Venice palace windows such as the Doge's Palace in the thirteenth century. Also developed further, possibly from Coptic keel-arched niches, under the eleventh- and twelfth-century Fatimid caliphs in Cairo in mosques like Al-Aqmar (1126). In England it was adopted with such enthu-siasm in Tudor times in the fifteenth and sixteenth centuries that it was referred to as the 'Tudor arch', appearing in profusion on later buildings such as the Houses of Parliament and Big Ben.

Tracery

Developed from the elaborate detailing found on wall surfaces and minarets in Muslim Spain, as at the 104-metre-tall minaret of the Great Mosque of Seville. Today known as La Giralda and repurposed into the bell tower of Seville Cathedral, the minaret still dominates the city skyline, decorated with cusped arcading, anticipating later Gothic tracery, as at the cathedrals of Chartres and Burgos, as well as the Houses of Parliament.

Stained glass

Analysis of stained glass in the 1200 to 1400 range in the cathedrals of Canterbury, York, Chartres, Saint-Denis and Rouen shows they all have the same high plant ash composition typical of Syrian raw materials. High-grade Syrian plant ash soda, known as 'the cinders of Syria', was considered superior to the pre-Islamic Egyptian natron ash, and all Venetian glass analysed from the eleventh to the sixteenth centuries shows its consistent use, by law. Continental Europe imported the raw materials for all its glass since there was no local source. Coloured glass windows have been an integral and innovative element of Islamic architecture from the start, with mosques from Jerusalem's Dome of the Rock and Al-Aqsa onwards carrying coloured glass in their many high windows, known as shamsiyyat ('like the sun') and qamariyyat ('like the moon'); the solar and lunar imagery of windows continued into European religious architecture.

The glass-painting technique used post-twelfth century originated in Syria. Syria's glass industry, based first in Raqqa, then in Damascus, entered a 'Golden Age' from the mid-1200s, when it introduced a revolutionary new method of decorating glass with enamel colour paints. The newly decorated glass was then refired to make the colour permanent. As a result, when making European stained glass, complete designs or biblical scenes could now be painted directly onto plain sheets of glass like paints on a canvas. The finished glass would then be cut into regular, usually rectangular, shapes, and slotted into leaded church windows. Before this technique, medieval stained glass creation was much more laborious, with each coloured piece having to be made separately and cut into complex shapes. You can see at a glance in Gothic cathedrals today which style has been used, from looking at the shape of the window bars. If it is regular, the Syrian method has been used, as at the Houses of Parliament. The Venetians and the returning Crusaders took the method (and often the raw materials) from Syria, and through them it spread across Europe, becoming especially popular with Dutch artists. After Damascus was sacked by the Mongols in 1401 and its craftsmen were taken as prisoners to work in Samarkand, the Syrian glass industry never recovered.

Heraldry

This is relevant to architecture because of the heraldic symbols used in stained glass and on public buildings to represent the coats of arms of rulers or important families, as at the Houses of Parliament. The concept of heraldry originated in Syria, where jousting competitions were first seen by Crusaders and where mounted Saracen knights using a *jarid*, a blunt javelin, held contests to knock each other off their horses. The Crusaders also saw the use of blazons, in a mix of designs including animals and plants, on Saracen knights' armour and shields. The symbol of Baibars, the Mamluk sultan, was a red walking lion/panther with its right forepaw raised and its tail curled back (similar to the royal English lion of the Plantagenets), which appeared on his buildings above the gateway. The same red lion in the same posture also features in a pair of heraldic badges which decorate the enamelled glass Baibars beaker on display at London's V&A Museum. Other sultans used the eagle, both single- and double-headed. The fleur-de-lys was widely used and appeared for the first time in Muslim heraldry as the blazon of Nur al-Din ibn Zanki before being adopted as the royal French symbol. It was also used on his buildings, for example over the *mihrab* in his twelfth-century madrasa in Damascus.

Double dome

The first to use the double dome technique were the Seljuks in their eleventh-century cylindrical or octagonal tombs topped by pointed cones or domes all across Anatolia and Persia. The technique of the double shell—that is, a lighter shell for the building's interior and a more durable shell for its exterior, with the entire space in between being hollow—not only lightened the load but also allowed for each shell to correspond perfectly to the building's interior or exterior proportions. It therefore gave the flexibility to adjust the profile both inside and outside to project greater height outside and therefore greater visibility and a more imposing presence. In Fatimid Cairo (973–1171) double domes were in common use, especially in the City of the Dead, crowning the tombs of the sultans. In Europe the first double domes in wood appeared at St Mark's, Venice, in the thirteenth century, while the first brick double dome was built by Brunelleschi at Florence Cathedral, completed in 1436. All of Sinan's sixteenth-century domes in Istanbul were stone double domes, and Wren used the technique at St Paul's, completed in 1708, going one further and creating a triple dome with three layers.

Machicolation box

First seen at Qasr al-Hair ash-Sharqi, the 'eastern desert palace', located 120 kilometres northeast of Palmyra en route to Doura Europos on the Euphrates, on the trade route to Persia and beyond. Dating from 729, the machicolation box appears above the main gateway, designed as holes in the overhang of a parapet for defenders to fire arrows or to drop liquids or projectiles down onto their attackers. They were much favoured by later Arab military architects, and the Crusaders copied them at Krak des Chevaliers near Homs and took the idea back to Europe, where they first appeared in Richard the Lionheart's favourite castle, the twelfth-century Château Gaillard near Rouen.

Windmills

The round tower at Krak's northeast outer wall is called Windmill Tower, copied from windmills seen with six or twelve sails, covered in palm fronds or fabric, and used to grind grain and draw water for irrigation. Windmills had first been invented in 634 in Persia, before finding their way into Iraq and Syria. In Europe they appear in Normandy, northern France, in 1180 and betray Crusader origins. In England the first certain reference to a windmill dates from 1185, in the Yorkshire village of Weedley overlooking the Humber Estuary.

The following gallery of images is arranged by country and in chronological order within each country.

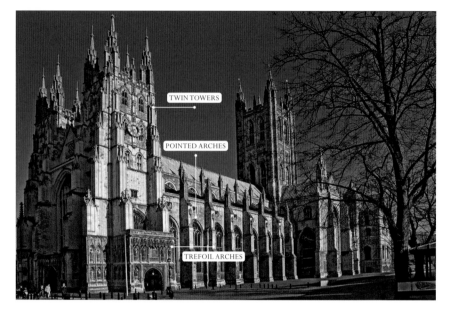

CANTERBURY CATHEDRAL

CANTERBURY CATHEDRAL, CHRIST CHURCH GATE

CANTERBURY CATHEDRAL, TWELFTH-CENTURY CHOIR

CANTERBURY CATHEDRAL CLOISTERS

CANTERBURY CATHEDRAL, FAN VAULTING OF THE CROSSING

YORK MINSTER, NAVE

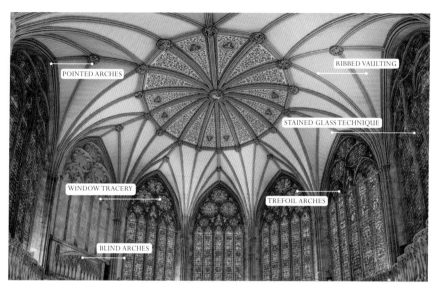

YORK MINSTER, CHAPTER HOUSE

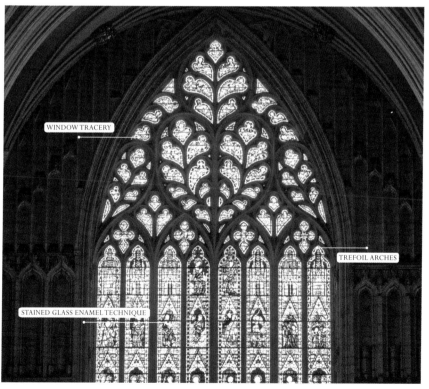

YORK MINSTER, GREAT WEST WINDOW

WESTMINSTER ABBEY (LONDON)

WESTMINSTER ABBEY, CLOISTER

WESTMINSTER ABBEY, RELIEF OF CHRIST (FACADE)

357

WESTMINSTER ABBEY, CHAPTER HOUSE

CONWY CASTLE

ST PAUL'S CATHEDRAL (LONDON)

PALACE OF WESTMINSTER (LONDON)

PALACE OF WESTMINSTER, NORTH FRONT

HOUSES OF PARLIAMENT (LONDON), CENTRAL LOBBY

BIG BEN (LONDON)

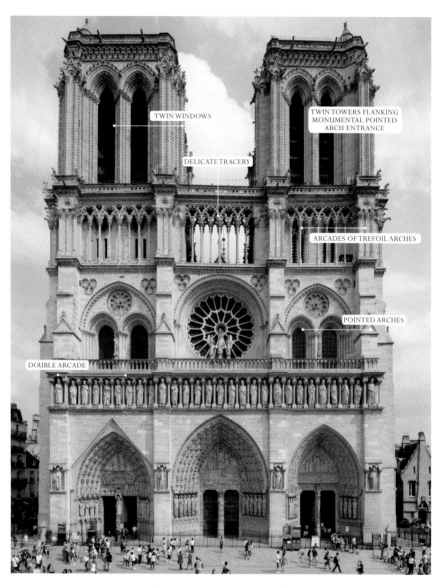

TWIN WINDOWS

TWIN TOWERS FLANKING
MONUMENTAL POINTED
ARCH ENTRANCE

DELICATE TRACERY

ARCADES OF TREFOIL ARCHES

POINTED ARCHES

DOUBLE ARCADE

NOTRE-DAME DE PARIS

NOTRE-DAME, NAVE

NOTRE-DAME, NAVE

DELICATE FINIALS

TRACERY WINDOWS

TREFOIL ARCHES

OGEE ARCH

TREFOIL ARCHES

CHARTRES CATHEDRAL, FLAMBOYANT GOTHIC NORTH TOWER

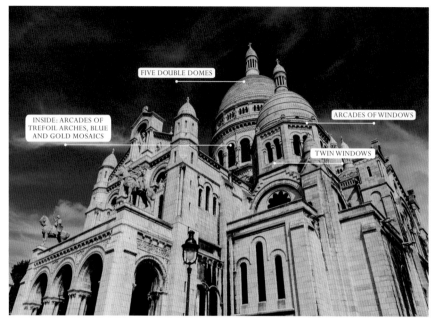

SACRÉ-COEUR (MONTMARTRE, PARIS)

CHÂTEAU GAILLARD (NEAR ROUEN)

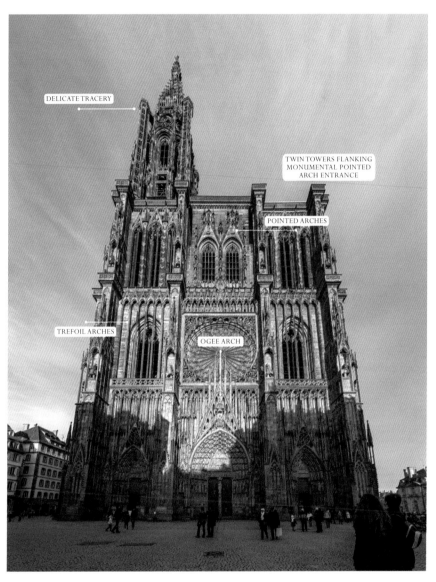

DELICATE TRACERY

TWIN TOWERS FLANKING
MONUMENTAL POINTED
ARCH ENTRANCE

POINTED ARCHES

TREFOIL ARCHES

OGEE ARCH

STRASBOURG CATHEDRAL

367

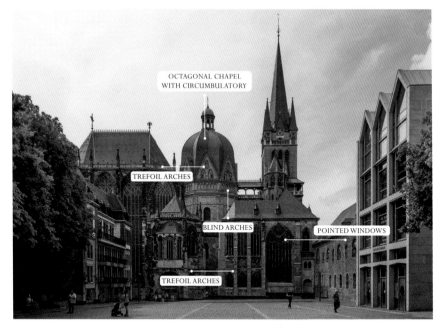

AACHEN CATHEDRAL WITH PALATINE CHAPEL

AACHEN CATHEDRAL, THRONE OF CHARLEMAGNE

CORDOBA MEZQUITA BELL TOWER/MINARET

PUERTA DE AL-HAKAM II, CORDOBA MEZQUITA

POSTIGO DEL PALACIO, CORDOBA MEZQUITA

DOUBLE-ARCADED
HORSESHOE ARCHES

ALTERNATING COLOURED VOUSSOIRS

CORDOBA MEZQUITA

PAVILION, COURT OF THE LIONS, ALHAMBRA (GRANADA)

MUQARNAS, HONEYCOMB, STALACTITE OR MOZARABIC VAULTING IN
THE HALL OF THE ABENCERRAJES, ALHAMBRA

ALHAMBRA, DETAIL OF ARABESQUES

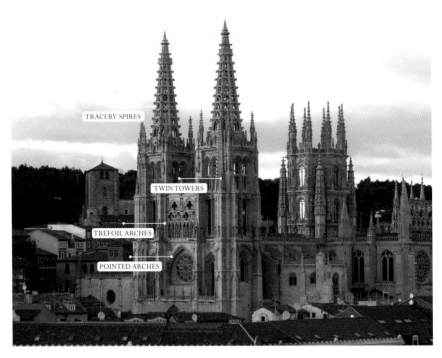

TRACERY SPIRES

TWIN TOWERS

TREFOIL ARCHES

POINTED ARCHES

BURGOS CATHEDRAL

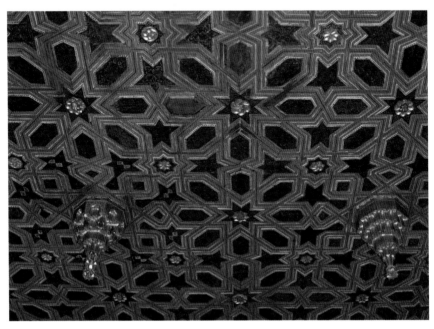

BURGOS CATHEDRAL, MUDÉJAR CEILING

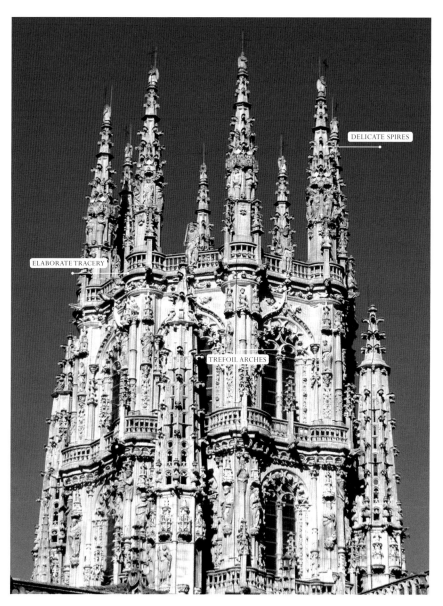

BURGOS CATHEDRAL, CIMBORRIO OCTAGONAL TOWER

SAGRADA FAMÍLIA (BARCELONA)

SAGRADA FAMÍLIA, NATIVITY FACADE

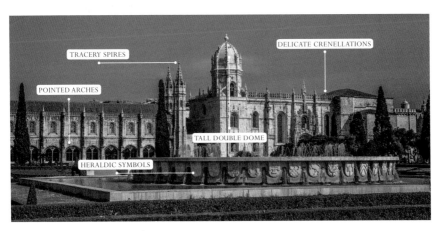

JERÓNIMOS MONASTERY (LISBON)

JERÓNIMOS MONASTERY, TWO-STOREY CLOISTERS

ST MARK'S BASILICA (VENICE)

DOGE'S PALACE (VENICE)

DOGE'S PALACE (VENICE)

CA D'ORO PALACE, VENICE

BRIDGE OF SIGHS, VENICE

CONCLUSION

A lifelong interest in the architecture of the Middle East has found its expression in this book. It has been my great good fortune to have had the opportunity to explore much of it over the course of successive decades since the 1970s. This has left me well placed to join the dots in the giant puzzle of how successive civilisations built on their predecessors' achievements, and how their inventions gradually entered Europe, changing our architecture forever, in ways that have been either wilfully overlooked or simply forgotten.

The built evidence is still there to see, though fewer people will be inclined to make the effort. The current political turmoil of the region and its associations with terrorism have pushed places like Jordan, Lebanon, Syria, Iraq, Iran and Eastern Turkey to the bottom of the must-see list.

This sad state of affairs made it perhaps all the more important to write this book, which I felt compelled to do after the fire at Notre-Dame de Paris. I must make clear that my aim is in no way to denigrate European architecture and its many brilliant achievements. My purpose has been to show that no one 'owns' architecture, just as no one 'owns' science. There is no property in a scientific discovery. Everything builds on what went before. Once made, a discovery can be used and built upon by people from other cultures, and where it came from is, in a sense, ultimately irrelevant. When people talk about 'Greek science', 'Islamic science' or 'European science', this does not change the fact that whatever Greeks, Muslims or Europeans discovered in the way of science is ultimately science, pure and simple. Double domes, pointed arches, ribbed vaults, etc. are all discoveries of architectural techniques that will, of course, subsequently be used and developed across cultures.

Except that architecture is not just a science. Neither is it just aesthetics. It is a deliberate choice, reflecting self-image, and in the case of public and historic buildings, it is closely tied to national identity. As such, architecture can be, and clearly already has been, co-opted into culture wars. Such wars can play out within cultures, such as the Neo-classicism versus Neo-Gothic war that Wren struggled with all his life when building St Paul's, which:

> being contriv'd in the Roman stile, was not so well understood & relish'd by others, who thought it deviated too much from the old Gothick form of cathedral churches, which they had been used to see and admire in this country. Others observed it was not stately enough, and contended, that for the honour of the nation, and City of London, it ought not to be exceeded in magnificence, by any church in Europe.[1]

But, far more serious, these wars can also be used to divide cultures—East versus West, Muslim versus Christian. This is what many in the West are caught up in today, with extremism on the rise across the globe.

Notions of racial superiority date back centuries. The ancient Greeks called anyone who didn't speak Greek a 'barbarian', someone who babbled incomprehensibly. The Crusaders were presented in European history as civilised people freeing Jerusalem from barbaric Muslims whom they called Saracens, 'people who stole things'. The concept of Europe was largely the invention of the Renaissance imperialist mentality, after the age of European colonialisation began from 1492 with the discovery of America. Such European superiority was explicit in Kenneth Clark's *Civilisation* TV series of documentaries in the 1970s. George W. Bush saw the 2003 US invasion of Iraq as a Crusade, using biblical quotes every day in his briefing notes. The American president was unflinchingly sure that God was on his side, just as sure as other leaders, both Eastern and Western, have been. Everyone has manipulated God to be on their side. What sense does it make—how can the same God be on everyone's side all the time?

We live in a time when culture wars are getting worse. A great deal of what people say in these wars is dishonest and intended to airbrush out the important contributions of others. Although the Islamic influence in Venetian architecture is patently clear to see, we still refer to 'Venetian Gothic' rather than 'Venetian Islamic'.

There is a tendency among academic historians to focus on distinct periods, to become specialists in this movement or that, a tendency that can inevitably lead them to ignore other, related periods. But the reality is, as I have discovered in writing this book, that everything is linked and related.

Just as the Crusades were a continuum of events that didn't just happen overnight when Pope Urban II made his call for Christians to regain the Holy Land in 1095, so Gothic architecture didn't appear magically out of nowhere in the twelfth century. The backdrop to 'the Crusades' included the Reconquista by Christian knights and warlords in Andalusia and the Norman wars in Sicily. The struggle in Iberia was a series of brawls and opportunistic seizures culminating in the conquest of Toledo in 1085. These Iberian Crusades led to the Holy Land Crusades, which were not just a complex web of battles, pacts, truces and alliances against the enemy. There was always Muslim–Christian interaction on many levels.

Granada's Inquisition Museum, housed in the sixteenth-century Palacio de los Olvidados (Palace of the Forgotten) in the former Arab quarter of Albaicín, displays a mind-bogglingly gory set of instruments of torture. Beheading, it explains, was the most humane and was reserved for the nobility and the aristocracy. The accompanying leaflet reads: 'The capital punishment and torture instruments selected are those most commonly used by the different inquisitional courts, both ecclesiastical and civil, from Spain and other European countries.' The civil courts, it points out, 'were particularly cruel, above all when dealing with certain groups that were considered dangerous for society.' It goes on:

> In spite of the fact that the name of Granada is of Jewish origin and that the
> Sephardic people contributed enormously to the splendour and development
> of the city, hardly any traces of their heritage are left to indicate the presence
> of this community in Granada. With the collection in the permanent exhibition

we are attempting to fill the cultural gap and demonstrate the historical presence of Jewish people in the city of the Alhambra.

No mention of the former Muslim presence is made, or of its cultural contribution. It appears there is guilt about the omission of the Jews, but not of the Muslims. The facade of the museum/palace bears an unidentified coat of arms, generally a give-away that the original owner, a Jew or a Muslim, had manufactured a nobility line to prove his 'pure' Christian lineage—what the Spanish of the Reconquista called *limpieza de sangre*, literally, 'cleanness of blood'. This led to the split between the so-called 'Old Christians'—those uncontaminated by Jewish and Muslim intermarriage—and the 'New Christians'—those that converted to Christianity to escape persecution. Muslim converts were known as Moriscos (little Moors), and Jewish converts were called Marranos (pigs, deviators or forced ones).

Over half the Jews in the Iberian Peninsula converted to Christianity to avoid the Decree of Expulsion of 1492. By the time the last Moors were expelled in 1609, the populations of Spain and Portugal were all nominally Christian. Ethnic cleansing on a grand scale had been achieved. Exact figures for conversions and expulsions are a subject of debate and can never at this distance be fully established, with estimates ranging from 10 to 60 per cent of the population. The first statute of 'purity of blood' appeared in Toledo in 1449. At first, such statutes were condemned by the Church and the monarchy, but then in 1496, Pope Alexander VI approved a 'purity' statute for the Catholic Order of St Jerome. Those with Muslim or Jewish blood were barred even from emigrating to America, and it was not until 1866 for example that the test of blood purity was outlawed for determining who could be admitted to college education. Spain, it seems, is the true home of Islamophobia and antisemitism, yet DNA studies of the current population show that 20 per cent still show a genetic makeup consistent with Sephardic ancestry, and also with Syrian and Phoenician ancestry.[2]

* * *

When I started writing this book, I never expected to find so much. Yes, I knew about the twin towers, the minaret/spire, the chevet, the pointed, horseshoe and ogee arches, the decorative stone windows, the vaulting techniques and the machicolations. But I had no idea that the trefoil arch, the multifoil arch, arcades of intersecting arches, cloisters, the chancel/choir area in cathedrals, tracery, double domes, stained glass techniques and the concept of heraldry, so important in the heraldic symbols used in stained glass and decorative stonework throughout Europe, had also originated in the Middle East, mostly in Syria, not to mention the raw materials for the actual glass itself. Perhaps I should not have been so surprised, since historic Syria, which included Jerusalem till 1923, was after all the birthplace of Christianity and its incubator for the first crucial centuries. Not only that, but all three monotheistic religions of the eastern Mediterranean also have a shared history of prophets and kings, with shared assumptions about eternal life and the proximity of hell and paradise. The concepts of ascension and resurrection are integral to all three faiths.

The next surprise was the discovery of just how much movement took place between Europe and the Middle East from the early centuries of Christianity onwards—pilgrims, abbots, monks, merchants, craftsmen. Everyone was on the go, it seemed—in spite of arduous journeys on foot, on horseback or by sea—from all levels of society. Influences and ideas travelled, even without the global economy and the internet. Maybe, in fact, because travel was difficult and people stayed far longer in their destinations, often for months or even years at a time, they had time to absorb and reflect on their new surroundings more deeply than we do, with our butterfly minds, flitting from one place to another, ticking them off our 'to do' lists.

But length of stay didn't always mean deeper understanding. The Crusaders of the Middle Ages captured Jerusalem but managed to misidentify the early Islamic Dome of the Rock as the Temple of Solomon, copying the design in their Templar churches. The Arabic inscription inside the Muslim shrine that openly chastises Christians for believing in the Trinity rather than in the oneness of God was misread by the new conquerors as the language of Christ, then copied in pseudo-Kufic calligraphic patterns on French cathedral stonework or on the borders of rich textiles. Such errors are telling, suggesting that the Crusaders may have liked the building style but held themselves aloof from the local population. They had little clue about the societies they ruled. Parallels with today spring to mind, where since World War One, the Western allies have carved up the region to suit their own interests, introducing sectarianism where before there was almost none. In 1923 the British and French mandates entered into force and partitioned the lands of the Levant against the will of the majority of the population. The 'divide and rule' tactic used in Lebanon and Syria by the French mandate authorities and in Palestine and Iraq by the British in the first half of the twentieth century laid the groundwork for so many of the current troubles in the Middle East.

The wealthy abbot of Monte Cassino thought nothing of travelling overland to the trading entrepôt of Amalfi to buy lavish silks as a gift/bribe for the future Holy Roman Emperor of Germany. While there, he was enthralled by the pointed arches (a style the Amalfi merchants had borrowed from their trading partners in Cairo) on the new cathedral doors, and promptly ordered a similar set for his own monastery. He even imported the materials and craftsmen from Constantinople. The abbot of Cluny was also smitten after seeing the completed work at Monte Cassino and adopted the same pointed arches in what is known as Cluny III, the largest church in the world at the time. Abbot Suger, his head full of Illuminationist philosophy from the newly translated works of Syrian mystic Denys (widely believed in medieval times to be the disciple of Paul known as Dionysius the Areopagite and also confused with Denis the decapitated patron saint of France), then arrived at Cluny on a visit from his basilica at Saint-Denis, where he seems to have been struck by an epiphany—the tall pointed windows let in much more light. Bingo! The architectural style we today call 'Gothic', what Wren calls 'Saracenic' and what at the time was simply known as 'French', was born.

The abbots of Cluny were statesmen on the international stage and the Benedictine monastery of Cluny was considered the grandest, most prestigious and best-endowed monastic institution in Europe. Where did the money come from? Much came from generous donations by the Spanish kings of León, money they had collected as taxation from subjugated Muslim cities. In return for their generosity to the Church, the kings received advice and perpetual prayers for, among other things, further triumph over the Muslim enemy. So sure were the Benedictine elite of their superiority as Christians during their Golden Age that it never occurred to them that their architectural adoptions in fact represented the identity of a different religion entirely, the very religion they saw as the enemy. They simply appropriated the styles as Christian.

It has been enlightening for me to learn how differently Muslims and Christians relate to space and to buildings, as is seen in the comparison between the Cordoba Mezquita and Notre-Dame de Paris, the former conceived as a complex radiating web and the latter a linear hierarchy. If the choice of house is said to reflect the mind of the owner, then surely the choice of public architecture is likewise a reflection of the mind of the sponsor. The same phenomenon occurs centuries later in Istanbul, when Sinan was seeking to perfect unified domed spaces filled with light at a time when European architects after the Renaissance were instead endlessly obsessed with classical facades—the way the building looked from the outside, not the way it felt from the inside. Le Corbusier sensed this essential difference between Baroque 'conceived on paper' and Arab architecture, which blurs the distinction between inside and outside. He was profoundly inspired by Sinan's holistic approach, where the unity of concept flows down from the main dome. When it comes to hierarchy of space, the Western Christian seems to crave certainty and consistency, while the Eastern Islamic priority is to create a space devoid of hierarchy, an uncertain transition zone in which the worshipper feels closer to God because there is no intermediary.

Following the money gives us many insights. Pilgrim package tours to the Holy Land, for example, were run by the Venetians, using their own galleys, cramming as much trading merchandise on board as possible, and making stopovers in their own colonies. It was an extremely lucrative industry, encouraged by the Catholic Church. There was even a guide book of purchasable 'indulgences' to smooth the passage of the faithful to paradise. Ownership of the sacred sites in Jerusalem was squabbled over by the various rival Christian denominations till Jerusalem was lost to the Mamluks. Undeterred, the Venetians continued, in spite of papal bans, to trade with 'the infidel'. The Arabic word for gun or rifle is *bunduqiyya*, meaning Venetian. Within Europe it was much the same, with a network of Cluniac shrines erected all over

France on the pilgrim route to Santiago de Compostela, at a time when the Benedictines were promoting this as their own pilgrimage in rivalry to that of the pope in Rome.

The burgeoning of so many Gothic churches and cathedrals in the twelfth and thirteenth centuries all across northern Europe speaks of serious wealth. Not only were these Gothic buildings imbued with Islamic decorative detailing and built according to Muslim vaulting and arch techniques, but they were also paid for with riches acquired in one way or another through links with the Islamic world, or, even more ironically perhaps, through the 1204 sack of Greek Orthodox Constantinople in the Fourth Crusade.

More than 700 years have passed since the last Crusades. While the political rights and wrongs of how all parties involved conducted themselves will no doubt be forever debated, the cultural interchange that took place then—and in earlier centuries via Muslim Spain and Sicily—between the Franks, the Spanish and the Normans and the Byzantines, Armenians, Seljuk Turks, Arabs and others is incontrovertible. The medieval Europeans themselves were, as far as we can tell at this distance, largely unaware of how great the impact was and how it led to the cultural and architectural flowering witnessed in Europe in the twelfth and thirteenth centuries.

My architectural parallels between Big Ben and the Seljuk minaret in Aleppo will no doubt draw howls of protest in some quarters, as will my comparison of Wren to Sinan. But I like to think that Wren himself, open-minded and tolerant of difference as he was, would have found the comparisons of interest, and would, I hope, have enjoyed reading my defence of his theory that 'what we now vulgarly call the Gothick ought properly and truly to be named the Saracenic Architecture'.

After this exploration of the origins of Islamic art and architecture, as manifested above all in the ancient province of Syria, I believe that he was right. Unlike Wren, I have had the benefit of being able to visit, on numerous occasions since the 1970s, buildings today scattered across modern Syria, Jordan, Lebanon, Palestine, Israel and Turkey, such as the Damascus Great Umayyad Mosque, the Umayyad Dome of the Rock, the Umayyad desert palaces, and the Umayyad city of Anjar. I have been able to touch their stones and absorb their essence. But thanks to Wren, when I now look at the trefoil arches and pointed windows in so many of our churches and cathedrals, the fan vaulting, the elaborately carved wooden choir stalls busy with twisting vines, curvaceous leaves and ripening fruit, I look at them with new eyes and appreciate them more deeply. Knowing where the style came from has enriched my understanding. I can now see what lies behind it and what it represents.

* * *

London's Imperial War Museum ran an exhibition from July 2019 to January 2020 called 'Culture Under Attack', asking the question: Is it ok to attack culture to win a war? It covers ISIS in Syria and Iraq, the Nazis, the Bamiyan Buddhas and Coventry Cathedral. 'Destroying cultural heritage often strikes at the heart of our communities,' the blurb tells us, but it makes no mention of Britain's bombing of Berlin in 1943 or of Dresden in 1945, when the iconic Frauenkirche was destroyed. It is another example, perhaps, of how it's never comfortable to look too close to home when it comes to questions of national identity and pride in heritage. Ferdinand and Isabella didn't see their attack on the cultural identity of Muslim Spain as vandalism. In their eyes it was entirely justified by their conviction that Catholicism was the true path and that the infidels of Islam and Judaism were to be killed or pushed out, their culture obliterated. It is little different, I could argue, to how ISIS felt entirely justified in killing anyone who didn't believe what they believed and in destroying Shi'a mosques, Sufi shrines and pre-Islamic sites like Palmyra.

* * *

In July 2019, a report called 'Housing Britain—A Call to Action' was published by the Prince's Foundation, a charity run by Prince Charles, the heir to the British throne. It describes the culture of house-builders in the UK as one of 'cost-cutting for short-term profit'. It goes on to explain that this is why 'the new housing estate has become a stain on the landscape and unwanted by the locals.' The action plan calls for homes to be better integrated with workplaces. Terraced housing, it maintains, can be a more effective way of creating a community than 'fields of detached houses'. Prince Charles has long been critical of modern architecture, which he once lambasted as enormous 'energy-guzzling glass boxes'.[3] As an alternative, he proposes that heritage buildings in cities like London should be repurposed. 'High-rise buildings,' he said in the report, 'in cities like London rarely make good contributions to public spaces at street level nor the skyline itself. Some of the most attractive places in London are made up of mid-rise mansion blocks. They are ideally suited to hosting a wide range of unit types, making them highly flexible.'

There is much in this report that chimes with the Islamic approach to housing, the organic growth of communities living round the key religious and commercial buildings of a city. That is what Venice learnt from its contacts with Islamic cities like Damascus, Aleppo, Alexandria and Cairo, as it developed its own residential areas in closely knit networks of houses side by side. In Syria today, alas, the Assad regime is intent on the opposite, destroying the old city centres and building faceless uniform tower blocks in the suburbs. The last thing Assad wants is a cohesive society.

If only architecture, instead of being manipulated in divisive culture wars, could instead be used positively, with the help of enlightened government policies. A move away from monotone suburbs—the detritus of the modern age—towards resettlement of central areas of the cities, where communities can once again build organically and evolve, could shape the future way forward—the Saracen Way, maybe—to a more cohesive and integrated society where people once again know their neighbours. That would be an architectural borrowing all might celebrate.

ACKNOWLEDGEMENTS

Sometimes I wonder if my entire life could be viewed as an apprenticeship for writing this book. Much of it has been in my head for years, ideas I'd never dared voice before. Now, suddenly, the incentive was there, after a coincidence of events, as explained in the Introduction.

My first acknowledgment must be to Michael Dwyer of Hurst, for running with the idea from the start. He allowed me to structure the book as I wished and his flexibility has been liberating. The excellent team at Hurst commissioned the stunning front cover where you can lose yourself looking up into the dome of St Paul's Cathedral, your eye drawn to the title in the oculus, where the light floods in. The obviously Christian and Neo-classical imagery in the dome paintings makes for a very strong contrast with the word 'Saracen'—not what you expect. In my mind this hints at the pre-Islamic inheritance that the Arabs built on, the multi-layered influences that passed to and fro depending on the politics and the trade routes of the time. The circular shape also encapsulates the importance of geometry, and the dome technology is where Wren really did use the 'Saracen' geometrical methods, as he himself freely admits. I am also grateful to Farhaana Arefin, my editor at Hurst, who has been patience personified in decoding my many complex messages and who took enormous care in steering the final choice from among my hundreds of supplied images.

Childhood family holidays spent roaming round Europe, exploring cathedrals, churches and archaeological sites, must have laid the foundations for an early interest in architecture. For this I am deeply grateful to my German mother and to my English father, a professor of German. He would make the church visits memorable by playing the organ, invariably unlocked in those days. At university, inspired by a new passion to explore the birthplace of civilisation, I switched from studying German and philosophy to Arabic, loving it from the start. Learning the language, literature and culture of the Arab world broadened my horizons beyond Europe, and I will be forever grateful to Wadham, my college, for allowing that switch. There followed extensive independent travel across the Middle East and Turkey for both work and pleasure.

Gradually, over the decades, I acquired a first-hand familiarity with most of the key monuments—and many of the lesser-known ones—especially in Turkey, Syria, Lebanon, Jordan and Egypt. Remarkably, after a gap of over forty years, I then chanced to meet up with my former Arabic admissions tutor, Alan Jones, now emeritus professor of classical Arabic at Oxford. It transpired he shared my interest in Sinan and in Ottoman architecture, and he offered to read my manuscript once it was complete. To my immense relief, he did not pronounce it all to be 'rubbish', a word that he was renowned for using when we were students. I am deeply grateful to him for taking the trouble to read it so carefully, and within such a short timescale. His discerning cat Layla adopted my gift of a 1486 Jerusalem map tea towel as her royal rug. Specially merchandised by the British Museum shop for their 2019–20 'Inspired by the East' exhibition, it perpetuates the erroneous labelling of the Dome of the Rock as Solomon's Temple, which misled European Christians for centuries. Treating it with the disdain it deserves, Layla now spreads herself over the image.

Several Syrian friends are owed a particular debt of gratitude: Dr Rim Turkmani for her stimulating talks at the Royal Society, where she spoke about Wren's theories on 'Saracen' architecture many years ago, and about the many Arabic manuscripts collected by seventeenth-century travellers returning from the East; Beshr al-Barry, a restoration architect still in Damascus, for his diagram and enlightening background on the Damascus horseshoe arch; Dr Zahed Tajeddin, an artist and sculptor from Aleppo, with whom I discussed many ideas and who lent me his books; and Wesam Al Asali, a PhD candidate in architecture at the University of Cambridge, for interesting discussions about Valencian vaulting techniques—his field of speciality—and for providing me with a list of Hispano-Arabic construction terms.

Crusades scholar and family friend Paul Chevedden has been, as always, an encouragement and source of in-depth knowledge, even sending books from across the Atlantic.

Rose Hadshar, the daughter of family friends, must get special mention for coming up with the book's title. Quick as a flash, after I'd explained the derivation of 'Saracens' over a Chinese dinner in Oxford, she thought of 'Stealing from the Saracens'.

My brother, Mark Taylor, and his wife, Deborah, were full of many suggestions from their own extensive European travels, pointing me to places like Girona in northern Spain and '*arbres remarquables*' in France with Syrian ancestors.

My husband, John McHugo, has, as ever, been an excellent sounding board, always happy to listen to my theories and discuss them with me critically. Apart from Alan Jones, he was the only person to read my manuscript before submission to the publishers.

My children, Chloe Darke and Max Darke, and my daughter-in-law, JiHae Shin, and her family were always supportive and willing to be consulted on various thoughts and ideas. Max's classics library on Roman Syria was especially helpful, as was Chloe's aesthetic sense in photo selection.

My thanks are due to historians Ross Burns and Warwick Ball for allowing me to use some of their excellent photos gratis and for always corresponding by email from geographically distant locations so promptly.

Finally I must make a huge acknowledgement to the London Library in St James's Square, W1. It has been an invaluable resource, allowing me to borrow essential texts like Christopher Wren's *Parentalia*, Howard Crosby Butler's *Early Churches in Syria*, R.W. Hamilton's *Khirbat al-Mafjar* and Deborah Howard's *Venice and the East* for months on end. Its vast online catalogue of academic articles has enabled me to pinpoint specific areas often researched already for decades by specialist scholars and to zoom in on other detailed studies, gradually helping me to join the dots and fill in the gaps in tracing this wonderful, multi-faceted puzzle. I hope future readers enjoy the journey as much as I have.

I cannot end without making special reference to the conditions under which this book was produced. With publication postponed from early June to late August by the extreme challenges of the Coronavirus pandemic, with staff furloughed and sick from COVID-19, the Hurst Production Director, Daisy Leitch, has managed all eventualities with supreme skill and care. The fact that the book exists at all is a triumph over adversity and a testimony to her professionalism. I owe her a huge thank you for bringing it to fruition.

GLOSSARY

Abbasids	Arab-Islamic dynasty who ousted the Umayyads from the caliphate in 750, retaining it till 1258. The Abbasid Islamic empire was centred on Iraq and the Abbasid caliphs resided mainly in Baghdad which they founded in 762.
Ablaq	Striped masonry (Arabic, of alternate colours).
Alcázar	Spanish from the Arabic *al-qasr*, a fortified house or palace.
Alfiz	Spanish, a rectangular frame for an arch, probably derived from the Arabic *al-hayyiz*, 'container'.
Ambulatory	Covered walkway encircling a temple or shrine.
Andalusia	The area of Spain under Muslim rule, also Al-Andalus.
Apse	Semi-circular structure at the east end of a church nave.
Archivolt	Decorative mouldings running round the face of an arched window or door.
Ayyubid	Dynasty founded by Saladin that ruled from 1169 to 1250. Ayyubid rule was marked by economic prosperity and a period of Sunni revival, with Damascus turned into a city of fine schools and hammams, many of which are still extant.
Bab	Door, gate (Arabic).
Baldachin	Free-standing canopy above an altar, tomb or throne.
Barrel vault	Vault in the shape of a half-cylinder.
Basilica	Building of Roman origins in the form of a central nave flanked by two aisles.
Bema	Raised platform with seating arranged in a horseshoe shape, found in the main nave of a Byzantine church.
Blind arch	Arch built against a wall as a decorative feature, not as a window or door.

Caliph	From the Arabic *khalifa* meaning 'successor', used as the title for Muslim leaders who succeeded the Prophet Muhammad.
Cella	Central sacred chamber in a Syro-Phoenician temple.
Chancel	Area, often raised by steps, in front of the altar.
Chevet	Semi-circular structure at the east end of a church nave.
Clerestory	Upper storey of windows flanking the nave of a church, to let in more light.
Deir	Monastery.
Dhikr	Sufi ceremony aimed at achieving mystical union with God.
Double dome	Dome where the exterior and interior profile are different, creating two shells with a hollow space in between, enabling much higher, stronger dome profiles from the outside.
Emir	Commander, prince.
Funduq	Building serving as an inn, warehouse and trading centre within a town. The word is Arabic and derives from the Greek *pandocheion*, meaning 'inn'.
Hajj	Pilgrimage to Mecca, to be undertaken at a specific time in the Muslim lunar calendar, at least once in the life of every Muslim, one of the Five Pillars of Islam.
Hammam	Public bath house with steam room, adapted from the Roman baths but with no pool.
Haram	Sacred enclosure, related to the word meaning forbidden under Islamic law.
Imam	Spiritual and general leader in Islam.
Insan kamil	'Perfect person', a Sufi concept, the final stage in man's evolution.
Isma'ili	A sect within Shi'a Islam, Isma'ilism has many offshoots, the largest of which is Nizarism, whose titular head is the Agha Khan.
Iwan	Roofed but open reception area, often north-facing and thus the coolest place in summer, with an arch giving directly onto the courtyard.

Jizya	Tax levied on non-Muslims living under Muslim rule, as stipulated in the Qur'an.
Keel arch	Pointed, keel-shaped arch, same as ogee arch or Tudor arch.
Khan	Caravanserai, a place where merchants could stay and trade their goods, often fortified for security, built round a court-yard with shops and workshops on the ground floor and residential rooms on the upper floor.
Kufic	A type of Arabic script used in the early Arab period, with square-shaped lettering.
Machicolation	Box-like projection from a masonry wall with holes for dropping stones or hot liquids onto the enemy, also called brattice box.
Madrasa	School for teaching Islamic law, often endowed by a prominent citizen, usually alongside a mosque.
Mamluk	Arabic meaning 'owned'. The Mamluk Sultanate of Egypt and Syria which lasted from 1250 to 1517 was based on 'slave' soldiers, trained to be part of a military elite and therefore free from family feuds because succession could not pass on in hereditary fashion.
Maqsoura	Special place reserved for the caliph near the *mihrab* in the prayer hall of the mosque, often domed or enclosed with a low rail.
Maronite	The dominant sect of Christianity in Lebanon, named after a fifth-century saint called Maron. Some claim descent from the Phoenicians.
Medallion	Shaped frame used decoratively on walls to enclose a special scene or design, especially in cathedral stained glass.
Melkites	Syrian Catholics, sometimes confusingly also called the Greek Catholics. Today they are in full communion with Rome and belong to the Patriarchate of Antioch.

Merlon	Step-sided triangle used as an ancient Mesopotamian architectural decoration, found throughout modern Syria (including crowning the walls of the Damascus Umayyad Mosque), and even in Petra, modern Jordan.
Mezquita	Spanish for 'mosque'.
Mihrab	Prayer niche in a mosque indicating the direction of Mecca.
Mi'raj	The Prophet Muhammad's ascent to heaven.
Moors	From the Greek *mauros*, 'dark'; used by the Greeks for the Aboriginal inhabitants of northwest Africa. In English usage, the Muslim inhabitants of medieval Spain, whether of African or Near Eastern or mixed descent.
Mozarabs	From Arabic *musta'ribun*, 'Arabised'; Christian communities in Islamic Spain.
Mudéjar	From Arabic *mudajjan*, 'domesticated'. Term used for Muslims who stayed in Spain after the Spanish Reconquista, paying tribute to the Christian rulers.
Multifoil arch	Also called poly-lobed arch. An arch that has been divided into an odd number of five or more foils/leaves/lobes/cusps spreading out from the arch centre. An example is the cinqfoil arch, with five lobes.
Munya	Fortified country estate or villa.
Muqarnas	Honeycomb-like decorative motif in wood or stone consisting of numerous geometric niches first seen in the Islamic world in the eleventh century, used in transitional zones between domes and their supports, conveying a sense of infinity.
Nilometer	Structure on the island of Roda, Cairo, to measure the Nile flood.
Ogee arch	Curved, pointed, four-centred arch, introduced to Europe via Venice where it became the defining feature of Venetian Gothic; also called keel arch or in England the Tudor arch.

Orthodox	Indigenous Syrian Christians of the Eastern Church (as opposed to the later Catholic arrivals who first came to the region at the time of the Crusades). They are not in communion with Rome and do not follow the pope, but follow Constantinople and their own patriarchs.
Ottoman	Turkish dynasty with its capital in Istanbul which ruled through regional appointed governors from 1516 to 1918.
Pendentive	Triangular segment of a sphere, used to carry the transition between a square base and a round dome.
Qibla	Direction of prayer towards Mecca.
Qur'an	Also Koran. Literally meaning 'recitation', the Qur'an comprises the collected revelations made to the Prophet Muhammad orally by God over a twenty-three-year period, written down after his death to form the Muslim holy text, the main source for Shari'a or Islamic Law. Considered 'the word of God', so only ever recited in Arabic, the language in which it was 'revealed'.
Quraysh	Arabian tribe which ruled Mecca in the early seventh century. The Prophet Muhammad, the Umayyads and the Abbasids all belonged to this tribe.
Reconquista	Spanish, the Christian reconquest of the parts of Spain controlled by the Moors.
Rib vaulting	Structural and decorative roof support system achieved by geometric division into a framework of diagonal arched ribs.
Rose window	Circular stone window decorated with stained glass held in place by elaborate stone tracery.
Saracens	A term used by Christians in Europe to denote Muslims in Syria, Palestine and Egypt during the period from the First Crusade (1095) till the Ottoman conquest (1453).
Seraglio	Palace, headquarters of a governor.
Shari'a	Literally meaning 'the road to the watering place, the clear path to be followed', the canon law of Islam derived from the Qur'an and the Hadith.

Shi'i	Follower of Shi'a Islam, the second largest Muslim sect, which accounts for less than 10 per cent of Muslims worldwide. The sect split off from Sunni orthodoxy, believing that 'Ali was the rightful successor to the Prophet Muhammad.
Souk	Market of stalls, bazaar.
Spandrel	The roughly triangular area between two arches.
Squinch	Small arch or niche placed across a corner to carry the transition to a domed or octagonal structure, first invented by the Persian Sassanids (224–651).
Sufi	Muslim mystic.
Sunni	The largest Muslim sect, Sunnis follow the Prophet Muhammad's 'path' (Arabic *sunna*, meaning custom or wont) and account for nearly 90 per cent of Muslims worldwide. Syria's population is estimated at 70 per cent Sunni.
Syriac	Ancient Semitic language related to Aramaic, which was the language of Christ. Syriac is the liturgical language used by the indigenous Syriac Christians (also called Assyrians), who are today much smaller in number than the Syrian Orthodox, who use Arabic as their liturgical language. Syriac was once the lingua franca of the region.
Tawheed	The Islamic doctrine of the unity and oneness of God, literally meaning 'making into one' in Arabic.
Tracery	Elaborate decorative stonework supporting stained glass in a Gothic window.
Transept	Section of the church that crosses the nave, forming a cross, usually in front of the altar.
Trefoil arch	Three-foiled cusped arch widely used in church architecture on windows to represent the Trinity.
Umayyads	The Islamic dynasty of caliphs reigning from 661 to 750 from Damascus. They were largely wiped out by the Abbasids in 750, but one of them, Abd al-Rahman, fled across North Africa and into Spain, where he founded the Umayyad dynasty that ruled from Cordoba from 756 to 1031.

Voussoir	Wedge-shaped stone used to form the components of an arch; alternate-coloured voussoirs are an important motif in Islamic architectural decoration, usually black and white or red and white (Arabic *ablaq*).
Waqf	Religious endowment, system of Islamic trusts used to maintain a religious building.

NOTES

INTRODUCTION

1. @dianadarke, Twitter, 16 April 2019,https://twitter.com/dianadarke/status/1118051834973892608, last accessed 27 January 2020.
2. Diana Darke, 'The heritage of Notre Dame—less European than people think', 16 April 2019, https://dianadarke.com/2019/04/16/the-heritage-of-notre-dame-less-european-than-people-think, last accessed 27 January 2020.
3. Chris Baynes, 'Most Americans say "Arabic numerals" should not be taught in school, finds survey', *The Independent*, 17 May 2019, https://www.independent.co.uk/news/arabic-numerals-survey-prejudice-bias-survey-research-civic-science-a8918256.html, last accessed 27 January 2020.
4. Christopher Wren, *Life and Works of Christopher Wren: From the Parentalia or Memoirs by his son Christopher*, London: Edward Arnold, 1903.
5. Ibid., p. 247.
6. Warwick Ball, *Rome in the East: The Transformation of an Empire*, London: Routledge, 2000, p. 334.
7. Ibid., p. 335.
8. Wren, *Parentalia*, p. 236.

1. CHRISTOPHER WREN: THE ARCH-SYNTHESISER

1. C.S.L. Davies, 'The Youth and Education of Christopher Wren', *The English Historical Review*, Vol. 123, No. 501 (April 2008), p. 303.
2. Davies, 'The Youth and Education of Christopher Wren', p. 304.
3. C.S.L. Davies and Jane Garnett (eds), *Wadham College*, Oxford: Wadham College, 1994, p. 24.

4. Ibid., p. 26.

5. Ibid., p. 35.

6. Ibid., p. 12.

7. Ibid., p. 20.

8. Lisa Jardine, *On a Grander Scale: The Outstanding Career of Sir Christopher Wren*, London: Harper Collins, 2003, p. 108.

9. Ibid., p. 106.

10. Ibid., p. 62.

11. Wren, *Parentalia*, p. 319.

12. Ibid., p. 129.

13. Ibid., p. 172.

14. G.J. Toomer, *Eastern Wisdom and Learning: The Study of Arabic in Seventeenth-Century England*, Oxford: Clarendon Press, 1996, chapter 4.

15. Ibid., chapter 7.

16. Ibid., p. 235.

17. Ibid., p. 166.

18. Ibid., p. 137.

19. Ibid., p. 176.

20. Ibid., p. 177.

21. Wren, *Parentalia*, p. 128.

22. Ibid., p. 129.

23. Ibid., p. 130.

24. Ibid., p. 137.

25. Ibid., p. 143.

26. Ibid., p. 143.

27. Ibid., p. 245–7.

28. Gülru Necipoğlu, *The Age of Sinan: Architectural Culture in the Ottoman Empire*, London: Reaktion Books, 2005, p. 92.

29. Ibid., p. 92.

30. Henry A. Millon and Craig Hugh Smyth, *Michelangelo Architect: The Facade of San Lorenzo and the Drum of the Dome of St Peter's*, Milan: Olivetti, 1988, pp. 94–155.

31. Necipoğlu, *Age of Sinan*, p. 92.

32. Ibid.

33. Jardine, *On a Grander Scale*, p. 415.

34. Ibid.

35. Necipoğlu, *Age of Sinan*, p. 92.

36. Jardine, *On a Grander Scale*, p. 421.

37. From the nineteenth-century map of London exhibited at the British Museum exhibition 'Inspired by the East', October 2019–January 2020.

2. GOTHIC ARCHITECTURE: 'THE SARACEN STYLE'

1. Wren, *Parentalia*, p. 172.

2. Ibid., p. 160.

3. Ibid., p. 172.

4. Ibid.

5. Davies and Garnett (eds), *Wadham College*.

6. Wren, *Parentalia*, p. 162.

7. Ibid., p. 172.

8. Ibid., p. 160.

9. Ibid., p. 237.

10. Ibid., p. 173.

11. Joann Jovinelly and Jason Netelkos, *The Crafts and Culture of a Medieval Guild*, New York: Rosen Publishing Group, 2006, p. 8.

12. Wren, *Parentalia*, p. 173.

13. Ibid.

14. Ibid.

15. Revd Neville Barker Cryer, *York Mysteries Revealed*, Surrey: Ian Allan Publishing, 2006.

16. Wren, *Parentalia*, p. 173.

17. Ibid., p. 160.

18. Ibid., p. 173.

19. Ibid.

20. Ibid.

21. Susan Bernstein, *Goethe's Architectonic Bildung and Buildings in Classical Weimar*, Baltimore: John Hopkins University Press, 2000.

22. Wren, *Parentalia*, p. 173.

23. Ibid.

24. Ibid., pp. 173–4.

25. Felix Arnold, 'Mathematics and the Islamic Architecture of Córdoba', *Arts*, MDPI (August 2018).

26. Wren, *Parentalia*, p. 174.

27. Michael Johnstone, *The Freemasons: An Ancient Brotherhood*, London: Arcturus Publishing, 2005, pp. 101–20.

28. 'Guild', Encyclopedia Britannica, https://www.britannica.com/topic/guild-trade-association, last accessed 1 April 2020.

29. Roger Stalley, *Early Medieval Architecture*, Oxford: Oxford University Press, 1999, p. 139.

30. 'Beauvais Cathedral: the gravity-defying church', French Moments, www.frenchmoments.eu/beauvais-cathedral, last accessed 27 January 2020.

31. Wren, *Parentalia*, p. 172.

32. Martin S. Briggs, revised by Stephen Platten, *Cathedral Architecture*, London: Pitkin Publishing, 2006, p. 23.

33. Abbot Suger, *On What Was Done in his Administration, Chapter XXV: Concerning the First Addition to the Church*, accessed via Fordham University Medieval Sourcebook.

34. Arthur Lincoln Frothingham, *Stephen bar Sudaili, The Syrian Mystic and The Book of Hierotheos*, Eugene, OR: Wipf and Stock, 2010 [Leiden: Brill, 1886].

35. Andrew Louth, *Denys the Areopagite*, London: Geoffrey Chapman, 1989, p. 14.

36. Jean LeClercq, 'Influence and noninfluence of Dionysius in the Western Middle Ages', in Paul Rorem (ed.), *Pseudo-Dionysius: The Complete Works*, trans. Colm Luibheid, New York: Paulist Press, 1987, pp. 25–33.

37. Louth, *Denys the Areopagite*, p. 122.

38. Bruce Watson, *Light: A Radiant History from Creation to the Quantum Age*, New York: Bloomsbury, 2016, p. 52.

39. Abbot Suger, *On What Was Done in his Administration, Chapter XXV: Concerning the First Addition to the Church*, accessed via Fordham University Medieval Sourcebook.

40. Andrew Louth, 'Apophatic Theology: Denys the Areopagite', *Hermathena*, No. 165 (Winter 1998), p. 79.

41. Ibid., p. 73.

42. Wren, *Parentalia*, pp. 172–3.

43. 'Romanesque Architecture', Durham World Heritage Site, https://www.durham-worldheritagesite.com/architecture/romanesque, last accessed 27 January 2020.

44. Gary Dickson, 'Encounters in Medieval Revivalism: Monks, Friars and Popular Enthusiasts', *Church History*, Vol. 68, No. 2 (June 1999), pp. 265–93.

45. Paul Everett Pierson, *The Dynamics of Christian Mission: History Through a Missiological Perspective*, Pasadena, CA: William Carey International University Press, p. 101.

46. Rolf Toman (ed.), *The Art of Gothic: Architecture, Sculpture, Painting*, Königswinter: Tandem Verlag, 2007, p. 9.

47. William Beckford, *The Life and Letters of William Beckford of Fonthill*, London: Heinemann, 1910, chapter IX, pp. 174–84.

3. THE PRE-ISLAMIC INHERITANCE: PAGAN AND EARLY CHRISTIAN ARCHITECTURE IN SYRIA

1. Wren, *Parentalia*, p. 236.
2. Ibid., p. 237.
3. Ibid., p. 236.
4. Ibid., p. 242.
5. Ibid., p. 233.
6. H. Dodge, 'Impact of Rome in the East', in M. Henig (ed.), *Architecture and Architectural Sculpture in the Roman Empire*, Oxford: Oxford University Committee for Archaeology, 1990, pp. 108–20.
7. Ball, *Rome in the East*, p. 376.
8. Ibid., p. 376.
9. Ibid., p. 334.
10. Ibid., p. 335.
11. Ibid., p. 397.
12. Edward M. Schoolman, *Rediscovering Sainthood in Italy: Hagiography and the Late Antique Past in Medieval Ravenna*, London: Palgrave Macmillan, 2016, p. 4.
13. Ibid., p. 398.
14. Ignacio Peña, *The Christian Art of Byzantine Syria*, Garnet Publishing, 1997, p.235.
15. John D. Grainger, *Syrian Influences in the Roman Empire to AD 300*, London: Routledge, 2018.
16. Juvenal, *Satires*, 3.62.
17. Diana Darke, *The Merchant of Syria: A History of Survival*, London: Hurst Publishers, 2018, p. 56.

18. Ball, *Rome in the East*, pp. 440–4.

19. Ibid, p. 414.

20. Ibid.

21. Diana Darke, *Eastern Turkey*, Chalfont St Peter: Bradt, 2014, p. 287.

22. Ball, *Rome in the East*, p. 444.

23. John Lowden, *Early Christian and Byzantine Art*, London: Phaidon, 1997, p. 33.

24. Ibid., p. 44.

25. Carly Silver, 'Dura-Europos: Crossroads of Cultures', *Archaeology*, 11 August 2010, https://archive.archaeology.org/online/features/dura_europos, last accessed 27 January 2020.

26. Lowden, *Early Christian and Byzantine Art*, p. 32.

27. Ibid., p. 33.

28. Ibid., p. 38.

29. Ibid., p. 33.

30. Ibid., p. 43.

31. Jelena Bogdanovic, 'The Rhetoric of Architecture in the Byzantine Context: The Case Study of the Holy Sepulchre', *Zograf*, Vol. 38 (2014).

32. Stéphane Yerasimos, *Constantinople: Istanbul's Historical Heritage*, Königswinter: Tandem Verlag, 2007, p. 39.

33. Michele G. Melaragno, *An Introduction to Shell Structures: The Art and Science of Vaulting*, New York: Van Nostrand Reinhold, p. 8.

34. Ibid., p. 38.

35. 'Ancient Villages of Northern Syria', Observatory of Syrian Cultural Heritage, https://en.unesco.org/syrian-observatory/news/ancient-villages-northern-syria last accessed 27 January 2020.

36. Ball, *Rome in the East*, p. 358.

37. Ibid., p. 356.

38. Diana Darke, 'Syria War: Forgotten amid the bombs: Idlib's ancient, ruined riches', 8 February 2020, https://www.bbc.co.uk/news/world-middle-east-51177433, last accessed 10 February 2020.

39. Emma Loosley Leeming, *Architecture and Asceticism: Cultural Interaction Between Syria and Georgia in Late Antiquity*, Leiden: Brill, 2008.

40. H.C. Butler, *Early Churches in Syria: Fourth to Seventh Centuries*, Princeton, NJ: Princeton University, 1929, p. 262.

41. Ibid.

42. Georges Tchalenko, *Villages antiques de la Syrie du Nord: Le Massif du Bélus à l'époque romaine*, Paris: Paul Geuthner, 1953.

43. Hugh Kennedy, 'From Polis to Madina: Urban Change in Late Antique and Early Islamic Syria', *Past and Present*, No. 106 (February 1985), pp. 3–27.

44. Hugh Kennedy, *The Byzantine and Early Islamic Near East*, Farnham: Ashgate, 2006, p. 14.

45. Lowden, *Early Christian and Byzantine Art*, p. 72.

46. Ball, *Rome in the East*, p. 229.

47. Butler, *Early Churches in Syria*, p. 263.

48. Ball, *Rome in the East*, p. 354.

49. Ross Burns, *Monuments of Syria: A Guide*, London: I.B. Tauris, 1999, p. 212.

50. Ibid., p. 264.

51. Diana Darke, *Syria*, Chalfont St Peter: Bradt, 2014, p. 123.

52. Peña, The Christian Art of Byzantine Syria, p. 235.

53. Peña, The Christian Art of Byzantine Syria, p. 234.

54. Ball, *Rome in the East*, p. 354.

55. Butler, *Early Churches in Syria*, p. 264.

56. Georges Tate in Béatrice Hemsen-Vigouroux (ed.), *Syrie*, Guides Bleus, Paris: Hachette Livre, 2004, p. 356.

57. Ball, *Rome in the East*, p. 359.

58. Burns, *Monuments of Syria*, p. 68.

59. Piero Gilento, 'Ancient Architecture in the Village of Umm al-Surab, Northern Jordan', *Syria*, No. 92 (2015).

60. Walter Horn, 'On the Origins of the Medieval Cloister', *Gesta*, Vol. 12, No. 1/2 (1973).

61. Melchior de Vogüé, *Syrie centrale: Architecture civile et religieuse du Ier au VIIe siècle*, Paris: J. Baudry, 1865–77, Vol. 1, p. 22.

4. THE FIRST ISLAMIC EMPIRE: THE UMAYYADS IN SYRIA (661–750)

1. Wilferd Madelung, *The Succession to Muhammad: A Study of the Early Caliphate*, Cambridge: Cambridge University Press, 1997, p. 45.

2. Della Vida and Giorgio Levi, *Banu Umayya*, in Bearman, Bianquis, Bosworth, van

Donzel and Heinrichs (eds), *The Encyclopaedia of Islam*, Volume X, Leiden: Brill, p. 838.

3. David F. Graf, 'Arabs in Syria: Demography and Epigraphy', *Topoi: Orient-Occident*, Vol. 4 (2003).

4. Ibid., pp. 331–2.

5. Michael MacDonald, from a lecture given on 25 November 2019 at Wolfson College, Oxford, entitled: 'Nomads, soldiers, musicians and hairdressers: some thoughts on language and identity in the Roman Provinces of Syria and Arabia'.

6. Ariel David, 'Ancient DNA Solves Age-old Mystery of Philistine Origin', *Haaretz*, 3 July 2019, https://www.haaretz.com/archaeology/.premium.MAGAZINE-ancient-dna-solves-age-old-mystery-of-philistine-origin-1.7433390, last accessed 27 January 2020.

7. Al-Imam al-Waqidi, *The Islamic Conquest of Syria*, trans. Mawlana Sulayman Al-Kindi, London: Ta-Ha Publishers, 2000, p. 13.

8. Dawn Chatty, *Syria: the Making and Unmaking of a Refuge State*, London: Hurst Publishers, 2017, p. 16.

9. Ibid., p. 16.

10. Ball, *Rome in the East*, p. 359.

11. My own house in Damascus has an octagonal fountain in the courtyard, and local architects have explained the Qur'anic symbolism to me, as derived from Surah 55, 'Al-Rahman'.

12. Deborah Howard, *Venice and the East: The Impact of the Islamic World on Venetian Architecture, 1100–1500*, New Haven: Yale University Press, 2000, p. 200; and Oleg Grabar, *The Shape of the Holy: Early Islamic Jerusalem*, Princeton, NJ: Princeton University Press, 1996, p. 107.

13. Gerard Heuman, 'No such thing as "Jewish architecture"', *Jerusalem Post*, 5 May 2015, https://www.jpost.com/Opinion/No-such-thing-as-Jewish-architecture-402192, last accessed 27 January 2020.

14. Grabar, *Shape of the Holy*, p. 107.

15. Ibid., p. 108.

16. Peter Draper, 'Islam and the West: The Early Use of the Pointed Arch Revisited', *Architectural History*, Vol. 48 (2005), p. 7.

17. Christopher Wren, 'Tom Tower, Christ Church, Oxford (1681–2)', *The Wren Society* 5, Oxford: Clarendon Press, 1928.

18. Ball, *Rome in the East*, p. 382.

19. Ibid., p. 390.

20. Ibid., p. 396.

21. Ibid., p. 447.

22. Al-Maqdisi, quoted in K.A.C. Creswell, *Early Muslim Architecture*, Vol. 1, Part 1, Oxford: Clarendon Press, 1969.

23. Butler, *Early Churches in Syria*, p. 98.

24. Ball, *Rome in the East*, p. 385.

25. Laurence Hull Stookey, 'The Gothic Cathedral as the Heavenly Jerusalem: Liturgical and Theological Sources', Gesta, Vol. 8 (1969), p. 35.

26. Wren, *Parentalia*, p. 173.

27. https://www.oxfordartonline.com/groveart/abstract/10.1093/gao/9781884446054.001.0001/oao-9781884446054-e-7000058348, last accessed 27 January 2020.

28. Wolfgang Born, 'The Introduction of the Bulbous Dome into Gothic Architecture and Its Subsequent Development', *Speculum*, Vol. 19, No. 2 (April 1944), p. 208.

29. Doris Behrens-Abouseif, *Cairo of the Mamluks*, London: I.B. Tauris, 2007, p. 124.

30. Hans Schindler, 'Concerning the Origin of the Onion Dome and Onion Spires in Central European Architecture', *Journal of the Society of Architectural Historians*, Vol. 40, No. 2 (May 1981), pp. 138–42.

31. Creswell, *Early Muslim Architecture*, p. 177.

32. Finbarr Barry Flood, Palaces of Crystal, Sanctuaries of Light: Windows, Jewels and Glass in Medieval Islamic Architecture, PhD thesis, University of Edinburgh (1993), p. 244.

33. Ibid., p. 151.

34. K.A.C. Creswell, J.W. Allan (ed.), *A Short Account of Early Muslim Architecture*, Aldershot: Scolar Press, 1989, p. 116.

35. R.W. Hamilton and Oleg Grabar, *Khirbat al Mafjar: An Arabian Mansion in the Jordan Valley*, Oxford: Clarendon Press, 1959, p. 325.

36. H.W. Freeland, 'Gleanings from the Arabic: The Lament of Maisun, the Bedouin Wife of Muâwiya', *Journal of the Royal Asiatic Society of Great Britain and Ireland*, New Series, Vol. 18, No. 1 (1886), pp. 89–91.

37. Philip K. Hitti, *History of the Arabs*, London: Macmillan, 1974, p. 221.

38. Wren, *Parentalia*, p. 173.

39. Burns, *Monuments of Syria*, p. 200.

40. Ibid., p. 130.

41. R.W. Hamilton, 'Carved Plaster in Umayyad Architecture', *Iraq*, Vol. 15, No. 1 (Spring 1953), p. 43.

42. Hamilton and Grabar, *Khirbat al Mafjar*, p. 325.

43. Ibid.

44. Ibid., p. 292.

45. Ibid., p. 41.

46. Ibid., p. 42.

47. Ibid., p. 44.

48. Ibid.

49. Ibid., 'Preface', p. v.

50. Ibid., 'Preface', p. ix.

51. Ibid., pp. 280–1.

52. Ibid., p. 168.

53. Ibid., p. 13.

54. Ibid., p. 41.

55. Butler, *Early Churches in Syria*, p. 149.

5. ANDALUSIA: THE UMAYYADS IN SPAIN (756–1492)

1. Thirteenth-century Castilian *Crónica Latina*, p. 98.

2. Hugh Kennedy, *Muslim Spain and Portugal: A Political History of Andalusia*, New York: Longman, 1996.

3. Ibid., pp. 58–61.

4. Ball, *Rome in the East*, pp. 398–9.

5. Peña, The Christian Art of Byzantine Syria, p. 236.

6. Peña, The Christian Art of Byzantine Syria, p. 238.

7. Expiración García Sanchez, 'Agriculture in Muslim Spain', in Salma Khadra Jayyusi (ed.), *The Legacy of Muslim Spain*, Leiden: Brill, 1992, p. 987.

8. Heather Ecker, 'The Great Mosque of Córdoba in the Twelfth and Thirteenth Centuries', *Muqarnas*, Vol. 20 (2003), p. 113.

9. Amira K. Bennison, 'Power and the City in the Islamic West from the Umayyads to the Almohads', in Amira K. Bennison and Alison L Gascogine (eds), *Cities in the*

Pre-Modern Islamic World: The Urban Impact of Religion, State and Society, New York: Routledge, 2007, pp. 67–9.

10. Hitti, *History of the Arabs*, p. 594.

11. Ecker, 'The Great Mosque of Córdoba', p. 118.

12. Katherine Watson, *French Romanesque and Islam: Andalusian Elements in French Architectural Decoration c. 1030–1180*, Series 488, Oxford: BAR, 1989, p. 15.

13. Arnold, 'Mathematics and the Islamic Architecture of Córdoba'.

14. George R.H. Wright, *Ancient Building Technology, Vol I: Historical Background*, Technology and Change in History, Leiden: Brill, 2000.

15. Felix Arnold, *Islamic Palace Architecture in the Western Mediterranean: A History*, New York: Oxford University Press, 2017, p. 112.

16. Robert Hillenbrand, '"The Ornament of the World": Medieval Cordoba as a Cultural Centre', in Salma Khadra Jayyusi (ed.), *The Legacy of Muslim Spain*, Leiden: Brill, 1992, p. 132.

17. Theresa Grupico, 'The Dome in Christian and Islamic Sacred Architecture', *Forum on Public Policy: A Journal of the Oxford Round Table*, Vol. 2011, No. 3 (2011), p. 7.

18. Arnold, 'Mathematics and the Islamic Architecture of Córdoba'.

19. Women, however, tend to stay at the back of the mosque, for reasons of public propriety when they prostrate during prayers. Mosque congregations are overwhelmingly male, with most women praying at home.

20. Wim Swaan, *The Gothic Cathedral*, Elek, London, 1968, p.30.

21. Louth, *Denys the Areopagite*, pp. 38, 54, 85, 101.

22. Wren, *Parentalia*, p. 139.

23. Ibid., p. 319.

24. Paula Fuentes and Santiago Huerta, 'Geometry, Construction and Structural Analysis of the Crossed-Arch Vault of the Chapel of Villaviciosa, in the Mosque of Córdoba', *International Journal of Architectural Heritage*, Vol. 10, No. 5 (2016).

25. Hamilton and Grabar, *Khirbat al Mafjar*, p. 13.

26. Henri Stern and Dorothea Duda, *Les Mosaiques de la Grande Mosquee de Cordoue*, Madrider Forschungen, Berlin: De Gruyter, 1976, p. 53.

27. Marianne Barrucand and Achim Bednorz, *Moorish Architecture in Andalusia*, Cologne: Taschen, 1992, p. 46.

28. Louth, *Denys the Areopagite*, p. 91.

29. Amira K. Bennison, 'The necklace of al-Shifa: Abbasid borrowings in the Islamic West', *Oriens*, Vol. 38 (2010), p. 257.

30. Hillenbrand, '"The Ornament of the World"', p. 131.

31. 'The Arab Baths of Girona', Patrimoni Cultural, http://patrimoni.gencat.cat/en/collection/arab-baths-girona, last accessed 27 January 2020.

32. Ecker, 'The Great Mosque of Córdoba', 2003.

33. D. Fairchild Ruggles, 'The Alcazar of Seville and Mudéjar Architecture', *Gesta*, Vol. 43, No. 2 (2004), pp. 87–98.

34. Ibid.

35. I am grateful to Wesam Al Asali, Syrian PhD candidate in architecture at the University of Cambridge studying vaulting techniques, for this list of Hispano-Arabic construction terms.

36. As above, for the information on Valencian tile-vaulting techniques.

37. Glaire D. Anderson, *The Islamic Villa in Early Medieval Iberia: Architecture and Court Culture in Umayyad Cordoba*, Farnham: Ashgate, 2013, pp. 49–50.

38. Burns, *Monuments of Syria*, p. 207.

39. Ibid., p. 210.

40. Ibid., p. 209.

41. Ibid., p. 208.

42. Hitti, *History of the Arabs*, p. 286.

43. Ibid., p. 595.

44. Barrucand and Bednorz, *Moorish Architecture in Andalusia*, p. 67.

45. Michael Archer, *Stained Glass*, Andover: Pitkin Pictorials, 1994, pp. 17–18.

46. Ibid., p. 9.

47. Hitti, *History of the Arabs*, p. 345.

48. Wren, *Parentalia*, p. 172.

49. Ibid., p. 173.

50. Hitti, *History of the Arabs*, p. 595.

51. Jo Tonna, 'The Poetics of Arab-Islamic Architecture', in Oleg Grabar (ed.), *Muqarnas*, Vol. 7 (1990), p. 187.

52. Fatih Gelgi, 'The Influence of Islamic Art on M.C. Escher', *The Fountain*, No. 76 (July–August 2010), https://fountainmagazine.com/2010/issue-76-july-august-2010/the-influence-of-islamic-art-on-mc-escher, last accessed 1 April 2020.

6. THE ABBASID AND FATIMID CALIPHATES (750–1258)

1. Bennison, 'The necklace of al-Shifa'.

2. Ibid., p. 251.

3. Grabar, *Shape of the Holy*, p. 170.

4. Ibid., p. 171.

5. Draper, 'Islam and the West', p. 10.

6. William of Apulia, trans. Graham A. Loud, *The Deeds of Robert Guiscard*, 1096–9, https://ims.leeds.ac.uk/wp-content/uploads/sites/29/2019/02/William-of-Apulia.pdf, last accessed 27 January 2020.

7. Leo of Ostia, *The Monte Cassino Chronicle*, 1075.

8. Francesca Dell'Acqua, Enhancing Luxury through Stained Glass, from Asia Minor to Italy, Dumbarton Oaks Papers, Harvard University, Vol 59, 2005, p.204.

9. Ibid.

10. Leo of Ostia, *The Monte Cassino Chronicle*, 1075.

11. 'Le platane de la Foulerie', Chaumont-en-Vexin, http://mairie-chaumont-en-vexin.fr/le-platane/, last accessed 27 January 2020.

12. Draper, 'Islam and the West', p. 11.

13. Ibid.

14. John Warren, 'Creswell's Use of the Theory of Dating by the Acuteness of the Pointed Arches in Early Muslim Architecture', *Muqarnas*, Vol. 8 (1991), p. 65.

15. John Warren, 'The First Church of San Marco in Venice', *Journal of the Society of Antiquaries of London*, Vol. 70, No. 1 (1990), pp. 327–59.

16. Peña, The Christian Art of Byzantine Syria, p. 232.

17. Ibid.

18. Ibid.

19. Ibid., p. 239.

20. Watson, *French Romanesque and Islam*, p. 66.

21. Jean Bony, *French Gothic Architecture of the Twelfth and Thirteenth Centuries*, Berkeley: University of California Press, 1983, p. 18; Kenneth Conant, *Carolingian and Romanesque Architecture 800–1200*, The Pelican History of Art, Harmondsworth: Penguin, 1966, p. 118; Draper, 'Islam and the West', p. 17.

22. Conant, *Carolingian and Romanesque Architecture*, p. 118.

23. Bony, *French Gothic Architecture*, p. 18.

24. Stalley, *Early Medieval Architecture*, p. 139.

25. Draper, *Islam and the West*, p. 18.

26. Ibid., p. 19.

27. Arnold, 'Mathematics and the Islamic Architecture of Córdoba', p. 3.

28. Arnold, *Islamic Palace Architecture in the Western Mediterranean*, pp. 118–9.

29. Tonna, 'The Poetics of Arab-Islamic Architecture', p. 185.

30. Gülru Necipoğlu, 'Geometric Design in Timurid/Turkmen Architectural Practice: Thoughts on a Recently Discovered Scroll and Its Late Gothic Parallels', in Lisa Golombek and Maria Subtelny (eds), *Timurid Art and Culture: Iran and Central Asia in the Fifteenth Century*, Leiden: Brill, 1992.

31. Flood, Palaces of Crystal, Sanctuaries of Light, p. 352.

32. Hitti, *History of the Arabs*, p. 346.

33. Finbarr Barry Flood, *Palaces of Crystal, Sanctuaries of Light:Windows, Jewels and Glass in Medieval Islamic Architecture*, University of Edinburgh PhD Thesis, 1993, p.352.

34. Robert Ousterhout, *Master Builders of Byzantium*, Princeton, NJ: Princeton University Press, 1999, p. 154.

35. N. Brosh, 'Glass Window Fragments from Khirbet Al-Mafjar', *Annales du 11e congrès de l'Association international pour l'histoire du verre*, Amsterdam, 1990, pp. 247–56.

36. 'The Hope Goblet', British Museum, https://research.britishmuseum.org/ research/collection_online/collection_object_details.aspx?objectId=27590 &partId=1, last accessed 1 April 2020.

37. Howard, Venice and the East, p. 155.

38. Approximately 175 glass ingots of cobalt blue, turquoise and lavender, the earliest known intact glass ingots, were found in the cargo of the famous Uluburun ship-wreck dated to the late fourteenth century BCE, now on display in the Bodrum Museum, southern Turkey.

39. I am grateful to Syrian glass expert Dr Zahed Tajeddin of UCL for this information.

40. Matt Phelps, Ian C. Freestone, Yael Gorin-Rosen and Bernard Gratuze, 'Natron Glass Production and Supply in the Late Antique and Early Medieval Near East: The Effect of the Byzantine-Islamic Transition', *Journal of Archaeological Science*, Vol. 75 (2016), p. 67.

41. David Jacoby, 'Raw Materials for the Glass Industries of Venice and the Terraferma,

about 1370–about 1460', *Journal of Glass Studies*, Vol. 35 (1993), p. 68.

42. Ibid., p. 76.

43. Ibid., p. 67.

44. Ibid., p. 70.

45. Ibid., p. 71.

46. Wim Swaan, *The Gothic Cathedral*, Elek, London, 1968, p.74.

47. Robert H. Brill and Patricia Pongracz, 'Stained Glass from Saint-Jean-des-Vignes (Soissons) and Comparisons with Glass from Other Medieval Sites', *Journal of Glass Studies*, Vol. 46 (2004), p. 127.

48. Flood, Palaces of Crystal, Sanctuaries of Light, p. 352.

49. Rosamond E. Mack, *Bazaar to Piazza: Islamic Trade and Italian Art, 1300–1600*, Berkeley: University of California Press, 2002, p. 113.

50. Ayşin Yoltar-Yildirim, 'Raqqa: The Forgotten Excavation of an Islamic Site in Syria by the Ottoman Imperial Museum in the Early Twentieth Century', *Muqarnas*, Vol. 30 (2013), pp. 73–93.

51. Ibid., p. 356.

52. Michael Meinecke, *Patterns of Stylistic Changes in Islamic Architecture: Local Traditions Versus Migrating Artists*, New York: New York University Press, 1996, p. 18.

53. Ibid., p. 25.

54. Wren, *Parentalia*, p. 162.

7. GATEWAYS TO EUROPE (800–1400)

1. Howard, *Venice and the East*, p. 151.

2. Ibid., p. 218.

3. Ibid., p. 113.

4. Ibid., p. 134.

5. John Ruskin, *The Stones of Venice: Volume the First*, London: Smith, Elder & Co., 1851, p. 13.

6. Roderick Conway Morris, 'Venice's Love Affair With Egypt', *The New York Times*, 8 November 2011, https://www.nytimes.com/2011/11/09/arts/09iht-conway09.html, last accessed 1 April 2020.

7. Deborah Howard, 'Venice and Islam in the Middle Ages: Some Observations on the Question of Architectural Influence', *Architectural History*, Vol. 34 (1991), p. 63.

8. Howard, *Venice and the East*, p. 109.

9. Wren, *Parentalia*, p. 173.

10. Howard, *Venice and the East*, p. 33.

11. Ibid., p. 40.

12. Ibid.

13. Howard, 'Venice and Islam in the Middle Ages', p. 40.

14. Otto Demus and Ferdinando Forlati, *The Church of San Marco in Venice: History, Architecture and Sculpture*, Washington, DC: Dumbarton Oaks Research Library and Collection, 1960, p. 104.

15. Ibid., p. 147.

16. Lowden, *Early Christian and Byzantine Art*, pp. 70–1.

17. Howard, 'Venice and Islam in the Middle Ages', p. 63.

18. Victoria and Albert Museum, Islamic Middle East Room 42, The Jameel Gallery, Case 5.

19. Howard, *Venice and the East*, p. 162.

20. Ibid., p. 12.

21. Ibid., p. 159.

22. Ibid., p. 65.

23. Ibid., p. 204.

24. Ibid., p. 65.

25. Ruskin, *Stones of Venice: Vol. 1*.

26. Howard, 'Venice and Islam in the Middle Ages', p. 67.

27. Ibid.

28. Howard, *Venice and the East*, p. 194.

29. Ibid., p. 175.

30. Mack, *Bazaar to Piazza*, p. 41.

31. 'Syria clashes destroy ancient Aleppo minaret', BBC News, 24 April 2013, https://www.bbc.co.uk/news/world-middle-east-22283746, last accessed 27 January 2020.

32. Howard, 'Venice and Islam in the Middle Ages', p. 68.

33. Ross Burns, *Aleppo: A History*, Abingdon: Routledge, 2016, p. 178.

34. Deborah Howard, 'Death in Damascus: Venetians in Syria in the Mid-fifteenth Century', *Muqarnas*, Vol. 20 (2003), p. 143.

35. Ibid.

36. Burns, *Aleppo*, p. 195.

37. Howard, 'Venice and Islam in the Middle Ages', p. 68.

38. Ibid.

39. Howard, *Venice and the East*, p. 153.

40. Ibid.

41. Ibid., p. 169.

42. Ruskin, *Stones of Venice: Vol. 1*.

43. John Ruskin, 'The Nature of Gothic', *The Stones of Venice: Volume the Second*, London: Smith, Elder & Co., 1853.

44. Howard, *Venice and the East*, p. 178.

45. Mack, *Bazaar to Piazza*, p. 113.

46. Peña, The Christian Art of Byzantine Syria, p. 232.

47. Stuart Cristo, 'The Art of Ravenna in Late Antiquity', *The Classical Journal*, Vol. 70, No. 3 (February–March 1975), p. 17.

48. Ibid., p. 23.

49. Schoolman, *Rediscovering Sainthood in Italy*, p. 4.

50. Christa Schug-Wille, *Art of the Byzantine World*, New York: Abrams, 1969, p. 102.

51. Flood, Palaces of Crystal, Sanctuaries of Light, pp. 72–3.

52. Arnold, *Islamic Palace Architecture in the Western Mediterranean*, p. 176.

53. Toomer, *Eastern Wisdom and Learning*, p. 7.

54. Diana Darke, *North Cyprus*, Chalfont St Peter: Bradt, 2015, p. 154.

55. Ian Robertson, *Cyprus*, Blue Guides, London: Ernest Benn, 1981, p. 179.

56. Darke, *North Cyprus*, p. 155.

57. Steven Runciman, *A History of the Crusades*, New York: Cambridge University Press, 1951.

58. I am indebted for this observation to Dr Paul Chevedden, an Amercian historian of the Crusades.

59. T.S.R. Boase, *Castles and Churches of the Crusading Kingdom*, London: Oxford University Press, 1967, p. 52.

60. T.E. Lawrence, *Crusader Castles*, London: Michael Haag, 1986, p. 93.

61. Jean Sauvaget, 'La Citadelle de Damas', *Syria: Archéologie, art et histoire*, Vol. 11 (1930), pp. 59–90.

62. Stephen C. Spiteri, 'Naxxar and its Fortifications', *Arx: Online Journal of Military Architecture and Fortification*, Selected Papers: Issues 1–4 (2008), p. 13.

63. David James Cathcart King, *The Castle in England and Wales: An Interpretative History*, London: Croom Helm, 1988, pp. 84–7.

64. R. Allen Brown, *Allen Brown's English Castles*, Woodbridge: Boydell Press, 2004, p. 62.

65. Charles Oman, *A History of the Art of War in the Middle Ages, Vol. 2: 1278–1485*, London: Greenhill Books, 1991, p. 33.

66. Burns, *Monuments of Syria*, p. 146.

67. Boase, *Castles and Churches*, p. 56.

68. Kenneth M. Setton, Norman P. Zacour and Henry W. Hazard, *A History of the Crusades, Vol V: The Impact of the Crusades on the Near East*, Madison, WI: University of Wisconsin Press, 1985, p. 42.

69. Laurence Turner and Roy Gregory, *Windmills of Yorkshire*, Catrine: Stenlake Publishing, 2009, p. 2.

70. Hitti, *History of the Arabs*, p. 664.

71. Ibid., p. 479.

72. L.A. Mayer, *Saracenic Heraldry: A Survey*, Oxford: Clarendon Press, 1933, pp. 23–4.

73. L.A. Mayer, 'Saracenic Arms and Armour', *Ars Islamica*, Vol. 10 (1943), p. 8.

74. H.A.R. Gibb, 'Review of *Saracenic Heraldry: A Survey* by L. A. Mayer', *Bulletin of the School of Oriental Studies, University of London*, Vol. 7, No. 2 (1934), p. 427.

75. Mayer, *Saracenic Heraldry*, p. 4.

76. Archer, *Stained Glass*, p. 26.

77. Hitti, *History of the Arabs*, p. 668.

78. Archer, *Stained Glass*, pp. 7–8.

79. John Talbot, *Brabourne in History*, Brabourne: Brabourne Church Publishing, 2003, p. 13.

80. Ibid., p. 204.

81. Ibid., p. 205.

82. Archer, *Stained Glass*, p. 438.

83. Ibid., p. 669.

8. THE SELJUKS, THE OTTOMANS AND SINAN (1075–1924)

1. Wren, *Parentalia*, p. 137.

2. Necipoğlu, *Age of Sinan*, p. 13.

3. Doğan Kuban, 'The Style of Sinan's Domed Structures', *Muqarnas*, Vol. 4 (1987), pp. 72–97.

4. Godfrey Goodwin, *Sinan: Ottoman Architecture and Its Values Today*, London: Saqi Books, 2003.

5. Le Corbusier, *Une Maison—un Palais*, Paris: Éditions G. Crès et Cie, 1928, pp. 77–8.

6. Le Corbusier, 'Five Points of Architecture', *L'Esprit Nouveau*, 1926.

7. Kuban, 'The Style of Sinan's Domed Structures', p. 79.

8. Ibid., p. 95.

9. Luis Calvo, 'Le Corbusier and the Mezquita', Hotel Viento, 30 November 2017, https://hotelviento10.es/en/art/90-le-corbusier-y-la-mezquita-de-cordoba, last accessed 1 April 2020.

10. Yerasimos, *Constantinople*, p. 45.

11. Ibid., p. 46.

12. Lowden, *Early Christian and Byzantine Art*, p. 64.

13. Ibid., p. 69.

14. Grupico, 'The Dome in Christian and Islamic Sacred Architecture', p. 4.

15. Lowden, *Early Christian and Byzantine Art*, p. 69.

16. Speros Vryonis, *Byzantium and Europe*, New York: Harcourt, Brace and World, 1969, p. 152.

17. Pope Innocent III, Ep 136, *Patrologia Latina* 215, 669–702, trans. James Brundage, *The Crusades: A Documentary History*, Milwaukee, WI: Marquette University Press, 1962, pp. 208–09, accessed via Fordham University Medieval Sourcebook.

18. Ousterhout, *Master Builders of Byzantium*, p. 50.

19. Doğan Kuban, The Miracle of Divriği, An Essay on the Art of Islamic Ornamentation in Seljuk Times, Istanbul, 2001, p.154.

20. Howard, *Venice and the East*, p. 100.

21. R. King, *Brunelleschi's Dome: How a Renaissance Genius Reinvented Architecture*, New York: Penguin Putnam Inc., 2000, p. 170, n. 5.

22. Barry Jones, Andrea Sereni and Massimo Ricci, 'Building Brunelleschi's Dome: A Practical Methodology Verified by Experiment', *Journal of the Society of Architectural Historians*, Vol. 69, No. 1 (March 2010).

23. Grupico, 'The Dome in Christian and Islamic Sacred Architecture', p. 6.

24. Kuban, 'The Style of Sinan's Domed Structures', p. 82.

25. Necipoğlu, *Age of Sinan*, p. 163.

26. Ibid., p. 165.

27. I am indebted to Alan Jones, emeritus professor of classical Arabic, University of Oxford, for providing me with these translations.

28. Also thanks to Alan Jones.

29. Wren, *Parentalia*, p. 237.

30. Ibid., p. 245.

31. Ibid., p. 246.

32. Ibid., p. 247.

33. Jardine, *On a Grander Scale*, p. 422.

34. Ibid., p. 468.

35. Ibid., p. 466.

36. Necipoğlu, *Age of Sinan*, p. 134.

37. Ibid., p. 147.

38. Ibid., p. 135.

39. Ibid., p. 138.

40. Quote from a speech by Paul Waterhouse, president of the Royal Institute of British Architects, on 26 February 1923, the bicentennial of Wren's death, at the Wren Banquet.

9. THE REVIVALS: NEO-GOTHIC, NEO-SARACENIC, NEO-MOORISH (1717–2026)

1. Robert Wood, *The Ruins of Palmyra; Otherwise Tedmor, in the Desart*, London: Robert Wood, 1753; and Robert Wood, *The Ruins of Balbec; Otherwise Heliopolis, in Coelosyria*, London: Robert Wood, 1757.

2. Kenneth Clark, *The Gothic Revival: An Essay in the History of Taste*, New York: Scribners, 1929.

3. Richard Taylor, *Pugin: God's Own Architect*, BBC Four, January 2012.

4. 'Sezincote: India in the Cotswolds', https://www.sezincote.co.uk, last accessed 1 April 2020.

5. A.W.N. Pugin, *Contrasts*, New York: Leicester University Press, 1969.

6. A.W.N. Pugin, *The True Principles of Pointed or Christian Architecture*, London: J. Weale, 1841.

7. M.H. Port (ed.), *The Houses of Parliament*, New Haven: Yale University Press, 1976, p. 161.

8. Rosemary Hill, *God's Architect: Pugin and the Building of Romantic Britain*, New Haven: Yale University Press, 2009, p. 482.

9. Burns, *Monuments of Syria*, p. 35.

10. Ernst Herzfeld, 'Damascus: Studies in Architecture', *Ars Islamica*, Vol. 9 (1942), p. 35.

11. Taylor, *Pugin: God's Own Architect*.

12. W. Montgomery Watt, *The Influence of Islam on Medieval Europe*, Edinburgh: Edinburgh University Press, 1972, p. 29.

13. Daryl Ogden, 'The Architecture of Empire: "Oriental" Gothic and the Problem of British Identity in Ruskin's Venice', *Victorian Literature and Culture*, Vol. 25, No. 1 (1997), p. 111.

14. Ibid., p. 113.

15. Ibid., p. 116, from Ruskin's *Stones of Venice* (11: 41–42).

16. Ibid., p. 117, from Ruskin's *Stones of Venice* (10: 459).

17. Ibid., p. 118.

18. Sally Shuttleworth, 'John Ruskin, environmental campaigner', Oxford Arts Blog, 4 February 2019, http://www.ox.ac.uk/news/arts-blog/john-ruskin-environmental-campaigner, last accessed 27 January 2020.

19. Georges Poisson, *Eugène Viollet-le-Duc: 1814–1879*, Paris: Picard, 2014, p. 96.

20. Ibid., p. 114.

21. Ibid., p. 138.

22. John Ruskin, *The Seven Lamps of Architecture*, London: Smith, Elder & Co., 1849.

23. Poisson, *Eugène Viollet-le-Duc*, p. 307.

24. Eugène Viollet-le-Duc, *Du style gothique au dix-neuvième siècle*, Paris: Didron, 1846.

25. Ibid.

26. Eugène Viollet-le-Duc, *Dictionnaire raisonné de l'architecture française du XIe au XVIe siècle*, Paris: B. Bance, 1858.

27. Arnold, 'Mathematics and the Islamic Architecture of Córdoba'.

28. Judith Rodríguez Vargas, 'Antoni Gaudí, la visión de un genio', Artes e Historia México, https://web.archive.org/web/20110929004526/http://www.arts-history.mx/semanario/especial.php?id_nota=22062007173805, last accessed 29 September 2011.

29. Carlos Flores, *Los Iliçons de Gaudí*, Barcelona, 2002, p. 58.

30. Christina Lau, 'Modernism and Nature: Antoni Gaudi's Inspirations', *HausMag*, 19 September 2016, http://hausmag.hausie.com/modernism-nature-antoni-gaudis-inspiration, last accessed 27 January 2020.

31. Flores, *Los Iliçons de Gaudí*, p. 89.

32. Daniel Giralt-Miracle, 'Gaudí: Nature in Architecture', p. 5, https://www.iemed.org/publicacions/quaderns/4/agiralt.pdf, last accessed 27 January 2020.

33. Ibid., p. 3.

34. Jaume Torreguitart, 'Inside Sagrada Família: Barcelona's Unfinished Masterpiece', 28 June 2019, https://www.youtube.com/watch?v=_di-VI-iKC0, last accessed 27 January 2020.

35. Tristram Carfrae, 'Inside Sagrada Família: Barcelona's Unfinished Masterpiece', 28 June 2019, https://www.youtube.com/watch?v=_di-VI-iKC0, last accessed 27 January 2020.

36. Margot Hornblower, 'Heresy or Homage in Barcelona', *Time*, 28 January 1991.

CONCLUSION

1. Wren, *Parentalia*, p. 137.

2. Teresa Larraz, 'Sephardic Jews leave genetic legacy in Spain', Reuters, 5 December 2008, https://www.reuters.com/article/us-spain-genetics/sephardic-jews-leave-genetic-legacy-in-spain-idUSTRE4B45II20081205, last accessed 27 January 2020.

3. Louise Gray, 'Prince of Wales hits out at modern buildings as "energy-guzzling glass boxes"', *The Telegraph*, 3 February 2012, https://www.telegraph.co.uk/news/earth/earthnews/9056928/Prince-of-Wales-hits-out-at-modern-buildings-as-energy-guzzling-glass-boxes.html, last accessed 27 January 2020.

LIST OF ILLUSTRATIONS
AND FIGURES

LIST OF ILLUSTRATIONS AND FIGURES

LIST OF ILLUSTRATIONS AND FIGURES

BIBLIOGRAPHY

Allen Brown, R., *Allen Brown's English Castles*, Woodbridge: Boydell Press, 2004.

Archer, Michael, *Stained Glass*, Andover: Pitkin Pictorials, 1994.

Arnold, Felix, *Islamic Palace Architecture in the Western Mediterranean: A History*, New York: Oxford University Press, 2017.

———, 'Mathematics and the Islamic Architecture of Córdoba', *Arts*, MDPI (August 2018).

Ball, Warwick, *Rome in the East: The Transformation of an Empire*, London: Routledge, 2000.

Barrucand, Marianne and Achim Bednorz, *Moorish Architecture in Andalusia*, Cologne: Taschen, 1992.

Behrens-Abouseif, Doris, *Beauty in Arabic Culture*, Princeton, NJ: Markus Wiener Publishers, 1999.

———, *Cairo of the Mamluks*, London: I.B. Tauris, 2007.

Bernstein, Susan, *Goethe's Architectonic Bildung and Buildings in Classical Weimar*, Baltimore: John Hopkins University Press, 2000.

Boase, T.S.R., *Castles and Churches of the Crusading Kingdom*, London: Oxford University Press, 1967.

Bon, Ottaviano, John Greaves (ed.), *A description of the grand signour's seraglio, or Turkish emperours court*, trans. Robert Withers, London: Printed for Jo. Martin and Jo. Ridley, at the Castle in Fleet-street by Ram Alley, 1650.

Bony, Jean, *French Gothic Architecture of the Twelfth and Thirteenth Centuries*, Berkeley: University of California Press, 1983.

Born, Wolfgang, 'The Introduction of the Bulbous Dome into Gothic Architecture and Its Subsequent Development', *Speculum*, Vol. 19, No. 2 (April 1944).

Briggs, Martin S., revised by Stephen Platten, *Cathedral Architecture*, London: Pitkin Publishing, 2006.

Brill, Robert H., and Patricia Pongracz, 'Stained Glass from Saint-Jean-des-Vignes (Soissons) and Comparisons with Glass from Other Medieval Sites', *Journal of Glass Studies*, Vol. 46 (2004).

Butler, H.C., *Early Churches in Syria: Fourth to Seventh Centuries*, Princeton, NJ: Princeton University, 1929.

Cathcart King, David James, *The Castle in England and Wales: An Interpretative History*, London: Croom Helm, 1988.

Clark, Kenneth, *The Gothic Revival: An Essay in the History of Taste*, New York: Scribners, 1929.

Cox, G.A., O.S. Heavens, R.G. Newton and A.M. Pollard, 'A Study of the Weathering Behaviour of Medieval Glass from York Minster', *Journal of Glass Studies*, Vol. 21 (1979).

Creswell, K.A.C., *Early Muslim Architecture*, Vol. 1, Part 1, Oxford: Clarendon Press, 1969.

————, J.W. Allan (ed.), *A Short Account of Early Muslim Architecture*, Aldershot: Scolar Press, 1989.

Davies, C.S.L., 'The Youth and Education of Christopher Wren', *The English Historical Review*, Vol. 123, No. 501 (April 2008).

Davies, C.S.L. and Jane Garnett (eds), *Wadham College*, Oxford: Wadham College, 1994.

Dell'Acqua, Francesca, 'Enhancing Luxury through Stained Glass, from Asia Minor to Italy', *Dumbarton Oaks Papers*, Vol. 59 (2005), p. 204.

Demus, Otto and Ferdinando Forlati, *The Church of San Marco in Venice: History, Architecture and Sculpture*, Washington, DC: Dumbarton Oaks Research Library and Collection, 1960.

de Vogüé, Melchior, *Syrie centrale: Architecture civile et religieuse du Iᵉʳ au VIIᵉ siècle*, Paris: J. Baudry, 1865–77.

Draper, Peter, 'Islam and the West: The Early Use of the Pointed Arch Revisited', *Architectural History*, Vol. 48 (2005).

Dussart, Odile, Bruce Velde, Pierre-Marie Blanc and Jean-Pierre Sodini, 'Glass from Qal'at Sem'an (Northern Syria): The Reworking of Glass during the Transition from Roman to Islamic Compositions', *Journal of Glass Studies*, Vol. 46 (2004).

Eastlake, Charles L., J. Mordaunt Crook (ed.), *A History of the Gothic Revival*, Leicester: Leicester University Press, 1970 [1872].

Ecker, Heather, 'The Great Mosque of Córdoba in the Twelfth and Thirteenth Centuries', *Muqarnas*, Vol. 20 (2003).

Ettinghausen, Richard and Oleg Grabar, *The Art and Architecture of Islam, 650–1250*, New Haven: Yale University Press, 1987.

Fairchild Ruggles, D., *Islamic Gardens and Landscapes*, Philadelphia: University of Pennsylvania Press, 2008.

Flood, Finbarr Barry, *Palaces of Crystal, Sanctuaries of Light: Windows, Jewels and Glass in Medieval Islamic Architecture*, PhD thesis, University of Edinburgh (1993).

Frishman, Martin and Hasan Uddin Khan (eds), *The Mosque: History, Architectural Development and Regional Diversity*, New York: Thames and Hudson, 2002.

Frothingham, Arthur Lincoln, *Stephen bar Sudaili, The Syrian Mystic and The Book of Hierotheos*, Eugene, OR: Wipf and Stock, 2010 [Leiden: Brill, 1886].

Fuentes, Paula and Santiago Huerta, 'Geometry, Construction and Structural Analysis of the Crossed-Arch Vault of the Chapel of Villaviciosa, in the Mosque of Córdoba', *International Journal of Architectural Heritage*, Vol. 10, No. 5 (2016).

Gibb, H.A.R. and J.H. Kramers (eds), *Shorter Encyclopaedia of Islam*, Leiden: Brill, 1974.

Gilento, Piero, 'Ancient Architecture in the Village of Umm al-Surab, Northern Jordan', *Syria*, No. 92 (2015).

Goodwin, Godfrey, *Sinan: Ottoman Architecture and Its Values Today*, London: Saqi Books, 2003.

Grabar, André, *Byzantium, from the Death of Theodosius to the Rise of Islam*, London: Thames and Hudson, 1966.

Grabar, Oleg, *The Formation of Islamic Art*, New Haven: Yale University Press, 1973.

———, *The Shape of the Holy: Early Islamic Jerusalem*, Princeton, NJ: Princeton University Press, 1996.

———, *Islamic Visual Culture, 1100–1800: Volume II*, Constructing the Study of Islamic Art, Hampshire: Ashgate Publishing Limited, 2005.

Graf, David F., 'Arabs in Syria: Demography and Epigraphy', *Topoi: Orient-Occident*, Vol. 4 (2003).

Grainger, John D., *Syrian Influences in the Roman Empire to AD 300*, London: Routledge, 2018.

Grupico, Theresa, 'The Dome in Christian and Islamic Sacred Architecture', *Forum on Public Policy: A Journal of the Oxford Round Table*, Vol. 2011, No. 3 (2011).

Hamilton, R.W. and Oleg Grabar, *Khirbat al Mafjar: An Arabian Mansion in the Jordan Valley*, Oxford: Clarendon Press, 1959.

Hart, Vaughan, *St Paul's Cathedral: Sir Christopher Wren*, London: Phaidon, 1995.

Herzfeld, Ernst, 'Damascus: Studies in Architecture', *Ars Islamica*, Vol. 9 (1942).

Hill, Rosemary, *God's Architect: Pugin and the Building of Romantic Britain*, New Haven: Yale University Press, 2009.

Hillenbrand, Robert, *Islamic Architecture: Form, Function and Meaning*, Edinburgh: Edinburgh University Press, 1994.

Hitti, Philip K., *History of the Arabs*, London: Macmillan, 1974.

Hoag, J.D., *Islamic Architecture*, London: Faber & Faber, 1987.

Horn, Walter, 'On the Origins of the Medieval Cloister', *Gesta*, Vol. 12, No. 1/2 (1973).

Howard, Deborah, 'Venice and Islam in the Middle Ages: Some Observations on the Question of Architectural Influence', *Architectural History*, Vol. 34 (1991).

————, *Venice and the East: The Impact of the Islamic World on Venetian Architecture, 1100–1500*, New Haven: Yale University Press, 2000.

————, 'Reflexions of Venice in Scottish Architecture', *Architectural History*, Vol. 44 (2001).

————, 'Death in Damascus: Venetians in Syria in the Mid-fifteenth Century', *Muqarnas*, Vol. 20 (2003).

————, *The Architectural History of Venice*, New Haven: Yale University Press, 2004.

Hull Stookey, Laurence, 'The Gothic Cathedral as the Heavenly Jerusalem: Liturgical and Theological Sources', *Gesta*, Vol. 8 (1969).

Jacob, Margaret C., *Living the Enlightenment: Freemasonry and Politics in Eighteenth-Century Europe*, New York: Oxford University Press, 1991.

Jacoby, David, 'Raw Materials for the Glass Industries of Venice and the Terraferma, about 1370–about 1460', *Journal of Glass Studies*, Vol. 35 (1993).

Jardine, Lisa, *On a Grander Scale: The Outstanding Career of Sir Christopher Wren*, London: Harper Collins, 2003.

Jayyusi, Salma Khadra (ed.), *The Legacy of Muslim Spain*, Leiden: Brill, 1992.

Joffe, Lawrence, *An Illustrated History of the Jewish People*, London: Anness Publishing, 2011.

Johnstone, Michael, *The Freemasons: An Ancient Brotherhood*, London: Arcturus Publishing, 2005.

Jones, Barry, Andrea Sereni and Massimo Ricci, 'Building Brunelleschi's Dome: A Practical Methodology Verified by Experiment', *Journal of the Society of Architectural Historians*, Vol. 69, No. 1 (March 2010).

Jones, Owen, *The Grammar of Ornament: A Visual Reference of Form and Colour in Architecture and the Decorative Arts*, Princeton, NJ: Princeton University Press, 2016 [London: Bernard Quaritch, 1868].

Jovinelly, Joann and Jason Netelkos, *The Crafts and Culture of a Medieval Guild*, New York: Rosen Publishing Group, 2006.

Kennedy, Hugh, *Muslim Spain and Portugal: A Political History of Andalusia*, New York: Longman, 1996.

———, *The Byzantine and Early Islamic Near East*, Farnham: Ashgate, 2006.

King, G.R.D., 'The Origins and Sources of the Umayyad Mosaics in the Great Mosque of Damascus', PhD thesis, School of Oriental and African Studies (1976).

Krautheimer, Richard and Slobodan Ćurčić, *Early Christian and Byzantine Architecture* (Fourth Edition), New Haven: Yale University Press, 1992.

Kuban, Doğan, *The Miracle of Divriği, An Essay on the Art of Islamic Ornamentation in Seljuk Times*, Istanbul, 2001.

Lane-Poole, Stanley, *The Art of the Saracens in Egypt*, London: Chapman and Hall, 1886.

Louth, Andrew, *Denys the Areopagite*, London: Geoffrey Chapman, 1989.

Mack, Rosamond E., *Bazaar to Piazza: Islamic Trade and Italian Art, 1300–1600*, Berkeley: University of California Press, 2002.

Mayer, L.A., *Saracenic Heraldry: A Survey*, Oxford: Clarendon Press, 1933.

Meinecke, Michael, *Patterns of Stylistic Changes in Islamic Architecture: Local Traditions Versus Migrating Artists*, New York: New York University Press, 1996.

Menocal, María Rosa, *The Ornament of the World: How Muslims, Jews, and Christians Created a Culture of Tolerance in Medieval Spain*, Boston: Little, Brown, 2002.

Michell, George, *Architecture of the Islamic World: Its History and Social Meaning*, London: Thames and Hudson, 1984.

Millon, Henry A. and Craig Hugh Smyth, *Michelangelo Architect: The Facade of San Lorenzo and the Drum of the Dome of St Peter's*, Milan: Olivetti, 1988.

Murray, Douglas, *The Strange Death of Europe: Immigration, Identity, Islam*, London: Bloomsbury, 2017.

Necipoğlu, Gülru, 'Geometric Design in Timurid/Turkmen Architectural Practice: Thoughts on a Recently Discovered Scroll and Its Late Gothic Parallels', in Lisa

Golombek and Maria Subtelny (eds), *Timurid Art and Culture: Iran and Central Asia in the Fifteenth Century*, Leiden: Brill, 1992.

———, *The Age of Sinan: Architectural Culture in the Ottoman Empire*, London: Reaktion Books, 2005.

Ogden, Daryl, 'The Architecture of Empire: "Oriental" Gothic and the Problem of British Identity in Ruskin's Venice', *Victorian Literature and Culture*, Vol. 25, No. 1 (1997).

Ogilvie, Sheilagh, *The European Guilds: An Economic Analysis*, Princeton, NJ: Princeton University Press, 2019.

Oman, Charles, *A History of the Art of War in the Middle Ages, Vol. 2: 1278–1485*, London: Greenhill Books, 1991.

Ousterhout, Robert, *Master Builders of Byzantium*, Princeton, NJ: Princeton University Press, 1999.

Ousterhout, Robert and D. Fairchild Ruggles, 'Encounters with Islam: The Medieval Mediterranean Experience Art, Material Culture, and Cultural Interchange', *Gesta*, Vol. 43, No. 2 (2004).

Peña, Ignacio, *The Christian Art of Byzantine Syria*, Reading: Garnet Publishing, 1997.

Phelps, Matt, Ian C. Freestone, Yael Gorin-Rosen and Bernard Gratuze, 'Natron Glass Production and Supply in the Late Antique and Early Medieval Near East: The Effect of the Byzantine-Islamic Transition', *Journal of Archaeological Science*, Vol. 75 (2016).

Poisson, Georges, *Eugène Viollet-le-Duc: 1814–1879*, Paris: Picard, 2014.

Pugin, A.W.N., *Contrasts*, New York, Leicester University Press, 1969.

Roaf, Michael, *Cultural Atlas of Mesopotamia and the Ancient Near East*, Abingdon: Andromeda Oxford Books, 2004.

Ruskin, John, *The Seven Lamps of Architecture*, London: Smith, Elder & Co., 1849.

———, *The Stones of Venice: Volume the First*, London: Smith, Elder & Co., 1851.

———, *The Stones of Venice: Volume the Second*, London: Smith, Elder & Co., 1853.

Ruskin, John, Harold L. Shapiro (ed.), *Ruskin in Italy: Letters to his Parents, 1845*, Oxford: Clarendon Press, 1972.

Schmoranz, Gustav, *Old Oriental gilt and enamelled glass vessels extant in public museums and private collections*, published by the Imperial Handels-Museum of Vienna with the sanction and assistance of the Imperial Austrian Ministry of Education. English version, Vienna, London, 1899.

Schoolman, Edward M., *Rediscovering Sainthood in Italy: Hagiography and the Late Antique Past in Medieval Ravenna*, London: Palgrave Macmillan, 2016.

Schug-Wille, Christa, *Art of the Byzantine World*, New York: Abrams, 1969.

Scott, Leader, *The cathedral builders: the story of a great masonic guild*, New York: C. Scribner's sons, 1899.

Spiteri, Stephen C., 'Naxxar and its Fortifications', *Arx: Online Journal of Military Architecture and Fortification*, Selected Papers: Issues 1–4 (2008).

Stalley, Roger, *Early Medieval Architecture*, Oxford: Oxford University Press, 1999.

Strube, Christine, 'Die Formgebung der Apsisdekoration in Qalbloze unde Qalat Siman', *Jahrbuch für Antike und Christentum*, Vol. 20 (1977).

Swaan, Wim, *The Gothic Cathedral*, Elek, London, 1968.

Talbot Rice, David, *Islamic Art*, London: Thames and Hudson, 1975.

Tonna, Jo, 'The Poetics of Arab-Islamic Architecture', in Oleg Grabar (ed.), *Muqarnas*, Vol. 7 (1990).

Toomer, G.J., *Eastern Wisdom and Learning: The Study of Arabic in Seventeenth-Century England*, Oxford: Clarendon Press, 1996.

Warren, John, 'Creswell's Use of the Theory of Dating by the Acuteness of the Pointed Arches in Early Muslim Architecture', *Muqarnas*, Vol. 8 (1991).

Watson, Katherine, *French Romanesque and Islam: Andalusian Elements in French Architectural Decoration c. 1030–1180*, Series 488, Oxford: BAR, 1989.

Watt, W. Montgomery, *The Influence of Islam on Medieval Europe*, Edinburgh: Edinburgh University Press, 1972.

Wren, Christopher, *Life and Works of Christopher Wren: From the Parentalia or Memoirs by his son Christopher*, London: Edward Arnold, 1903.

Yerasimos, Stéphane, *Constantinople: Istanbul's Historical Heritage*, Königswinter: Tandem Verlag, 2007.

Yoltar-Yildirim, Ayşin, 'Raqqa: The Forgotten Excavation of an Islamic Site in Syria by the Ottoman Imperial Museum in the Early Twentieth Century', *Muqarnas*, Vol. 30 (2013).

INDEX

Note: bold = major entry, *bold italics* = photo/image

INDEX

INDEX

INDEX

INDEX

INDEX